Karl Marx's *Grundrisse*

Written between 1857 and 1858, the *Grundrisse* is the first draft of Marx's critique of political economy and, thus, also the initial preparatory work on *Capital*. Despite its editorial vicissitudes and late publication, *Grundrisse* contains numerous reflections on matters that Marx did not develop elsewhere in his oeuvre and is therefore extremely important for an overall interpretation of his thought.

In this collection, various international experts in the field, analysing the *Grundrisse* on the one-hundred-and-fiftieth anniversary of its composition, present a Marx in many ways radically different from the one who figures in the dominant currents of twentieth-century Marxism. The book demonstrates the relevance of the *Grundrisse* to an understanding of *Capital* and of Marx's theoretical project as a whole, which, as is well known, remained uncompleted. It also highlights the continuing explanatory power of Marxian categories for contemporary society and its present contradictions. Musto's volume is divided into three parts. The first consists of eight chapters on the main themes that emerge from a reading of the *Grundrisse*: method, value, alienation, surplus value, historical materialism, ecological contradictions, socialism, and a comparison between the *Grundrisse* and *Capital*. The second reconstructs the biographical and theoretical context in which Marx wrote these manuscripts; while the third presents a full account of their dissemination and reception throughout the world.

With contributions from such scholars as Eric Hobsbawm and Terrell Carver, and covering subject areas such as political economy, philosophy and Marxism, this book is likely to become required reading for serious scholars of Marx across the world.

Marcello Musto is a Researcher at the University of Naples 'L'Orientale', in Naples, Italy.

Routledge frontiers of political economy

Karl Marx's *Grundrisse*

Foundations of the critique of
political economy 150 years later

Edited by Marcello Musto

With a special foreword by Eric Hobsbawm

Routledge
Taylor & Francis Group

LONDON AND NEW YORK

Transferred to digital printing 2010
First published 2008
by Routledge
2 Park Square, Milton Park, Abingdon, Oxon OX14 4RN

Simultaneously published in the USA and Canada
by Routledge
270 Madison Ave, New York, NY 10016

Routledge is an imprint of the Taylor & Francis Group, an informa business

Typeset in Times by Wearset Ltd, Boldon, Tyne and Wear

British Library Cataloguing in Publication Data
A catalogue record for this book is available from the British Library

Library of Congress Cataloging in Publication Data
Karl Marx's Grundrisse: foundations of the critique of political economy
150 years later / edited by Marcello Musto.
p. cm.
Includes bibliographical references and index.
1. Marx, Karl, 1818–1883. Grundrisse der Kritik der politischen
Ökonomie. 2. Marxian economics. I. Musto, Marcello. II. Title:
Grundrisse.
HB97.5.M3319K37 2008
335.4'12—dc22   2008008096

ISBN10: 0-415-43749-0 (hbk)
ISBN10: 0-415-58871-5 (pbk)
ISBN10: 0-203-89210-0 (ebk)

ISBN13: 978-0-415-43749-3 (hbk)
ISBN13: 978-0-415-58871-3 (pbk)
ISBN13: 978-0-203-89210-7 (ebk)

Contents

Figures

Contributors

Christopher J. Arthur, formerly University of Sussex (UK), author of *Dialectics of Labour*, Blackwell 1986 and *The New Dialectic and Marx's 'Capital'*, Brill 2002 and co-editor of *The Circulation of Capital: Essays on Volume Two of Marx's 'Capital'*, Macmillan Press 1998.

Joachim Bischoff, co-editor of the review *Sozialismus* (Germany) and author of *Gesellschaftliche Arbeit als Systembegriff* [*Work in Society as a Systems Concept*], 1973; *Grundbegriffe der marxistischen Theorie* [*Fundamental Terms of Marxist Theory*], 1978; and *Zukunft des Finanzmarktkapitalismus* [*The Future of Finance-market Capitalism*], 2006 – all VSA.

Terrell Carver, University of Bristol (UK), author of *Marx and Engels: The Intellectual Relationship*, Wheatsheaf Books 1983; and *The Postmodern Marx*, Manchester University Press 1998; and editor of *Karl Marx: Texts on Method*, Basil Blackwell 1975 and *Karl Marx: Later Political Writings*, Cambridge University Press 1996.

Enrique Dussel, University of Mexico City (Mexico), author of *La producción teórica de Marx. Un comentario a los Grundrisse* [*Marx's Theoretical Production. A Commentary on the Grundrisse*], Siglo XXI 1985 and *Towards an Unknown Marx. A Commentary on the Manuscripts of 1861–63*, Routledge 2001.

Iring Fetscher, formerly University of Frankfurt (Germany), author of *Von Marx zur Sowjetideologie* [*From Marx to the Soviet Ideology*], Diesterweg 1956; and *Karl Marx und Marxismus* [*Karl Marx and Marxism*], Piper 1967 and editor of *Karl Marx–Friedrich Engels. Studienausgabe* [*Karl Marx–Friedrich Engels. Study edition*] (5 vols.), Aufbau 2004.

John Bellamy Foster, University of Oregon (USA) and *Monthly Review Foundation* (USA), author of *The Theory of Monopoly Capitalism*, 1986, *The Vulnerable Planet*, 1994, *Marx's Ecology*, 2000, *Ecology against Capitalism*, 2002, *Naked Imperialism*, 2006 – all Monthly Review Press.

Stanislav Hubík, University of Brno (Czech Republic), author of *Sociologie vědění* [*Sociology of Knowledge*], Slon 1999.

Ho-Gyun Kim, University of Myongji (South Korea), translator of *Grundrisse* Korean version and author of *Shinjeongchigyeongjehakgaeron* [*A New Introduction to Political Economy*], Irongwashilcheon Publishing 1993 (Korean) and *Jesameuigilgwa Jisikgibangyeongje* [*The Third Way and the Knowledge-based Economy*], Baikeui Publishing 2001.

Michael R. Krätke, University of Amsterdam (the Netherlands), co-author of *Kritik der Staatsfinanzen* [*Critique of State Finances*], VSA 1984 and author of *Geschichte der Weltwirtschaft* [*History of the World Economy*], VSA 2001. Currently working on publication of MEGA^2 IV/14 *Marx–Engels Exzerpte und Notizen 1857–8* [*Marx–Engels Excerpts and Notes 1857–8*].

Ferenc L. Lendvai, University of Miskolc (Hungary), co-author of *Magyar filozófia a XX. Században, I and II* [*Hungarian Philosophy in the 20th Century, I and II*], Áron 2000–1.

Christoph Lieber, editor of VSA publishing house (Germany) and co-author of *Ausbeutung, Selbstverrätselung, Regulation. Der 3. Band des 'Kapital'* [*Exploitation, Self-mystification, Regulation. The 3rd volume of Capital*], VSA 1993.

Birger Linde, Roskilde University (Denmark), author of *De Store Kriser I. Kriseteori og kriser i 1800-tallet – inspirationen frå Marx* [*The Great Crises, vol. 1, Crisis Theory and Crises in the 19th Century – the Inspiration from Marx*], Roskilde University 2004.

John Milios, University of Athens (Greece), co-author of *Karl Marx and the Classics. An Essay on Value, Crises and the Capitalist Mode of Production*, Ashgate 2002.

Ernst Theodor Mohl, formerly University of Hanover (Germany), author of *Folgen einer Theorie. Essays über Das Kapital von Karl Marx* [*Consequences of a Theory. Essays on Karl Marx's Capital*], Suhrkamp 1967.

Marcello Musto, University of Naples (Italy), editor of *Sulle tracce di un fantasma. L'opera di Karl Marx tra filologia e filosofia* [*On the Track of a Spectre. The Work of Karl Marx between Philology and Philosophy*], Manifestolibri 2005.

Kamran Nayeri, University of California (USA), author of 'Marx va Engeles va Ettehadieh-haye kargari' ['Marx and Engels and Trade Unions'], *Negah*, no. 17, 2005.

José Paulo Netto, Federal University of Rio de Janeiro (Brazil), author of *Crise do socialismo e ofensiva neoliberal* [*The Crisis of Socialism and the Neoliberal Offensive*], Encadernação 1993, and of *Marxismo impenitente* [*Unrepentant Marxism*], Cortez 2004.

Vesa Oittinen, University of Helsinki (Finland), author of *Spinozistische Dialektik* [*Spinozan Dialectics*], Peter Lang 1994 and editor of *Marx ja Venäjä* [*Marx and Russia*], Kikimora 2006.

Rafael Pla León, University Las Villas (Cuba), and author of *Una lógica para pensar la liberación de América* [*A Logic for Thinking about the Liberation of America*], Editorial Ciencias Sociales 1994.

Holger Politt, President of the *Rosa Luxemburg Foundation* in Warsaw (Poland).

Moishe Postone, University of Chicago (USA), author of *Time, Labour and Social Domination: A Reinterpretation of Marx's Critical Theory*, Cambridge University Press 1993 and co-editor of *Catastrophe and Meaning: The Holocaust and the Twentieth Century*, University of Chicago Press 2003.

Pedro Ribas, University of Madrid (Spain), author of *Aproximación a la historia del marxismo español 1869–1939* [*An Approach to the History of Spanish Marxism 1869–1939*], Endymion 1990 and editor of *Escritos de Marx sobre España. Extractos de 1854* [*Marx's Writings on Spain. Extracts from 1854*], Trotta 1998.

Gheorghe Stoica, University of Bucharest (Romania), author of *Machiavelli filosofo della politica* [*Machiavelli, Philosopher of Politics*], La Citta del Sole 2003.

E. Ahmet Tonak, Bilgi University of Istanbul (Turkey), co-author of *Measuring the Wealth of Nations: The Political Economy of National Accounts*, Cambridge University Press 1994.

André Tosel, formerly University of Nice (France), author of *L'esprit de scission. Études sur Marx, Gramsci et Lukacs* [*The Mentality of Splits. Studies of Marx, Gramsci and Lukacs*], Belles Lettres 1995 and *Études sur Marx (et Engels). Vers un communisme de la finitude* [*Studies of Marx (and Engels). Towards a Communism of Finitude*], Kimé 1996.

Mario Tronti, formerly University of Siena (Italy), and author of *Operai.e. capitale* [*Workers and Capital*], Einaudi 1966 and *La politica al tramonto* [*Politics in Decline*], Einaudi 1998.

Hiroshi Uchida, Senshu University (Japan), author of *Keizaigakuhihan'yoko no kenkyu* [*A Study of the Grundrisse*], Shinhyoron 1982; and *Marx's 'Grundrisse' and Hegel's 'Logic'*, Routledge 1988 and editor of *Marx for the 21st Century*, Routledge 2006.

Lyudmila L. Vasina, Russian State Archive of the Social and Political History of Moscow (Russia), co-editor of volumes II/2 Dietz Verlag, 1980, II/12 Akademie Verlag, 2005, IV/3 Akademie Verlag, 1998, and IV/4 Dietz Verlag, 1988 of the MEGA^2.

Lino Veljak, University of Zagreb (Croatia), author of *Marksizam i teorija odraza* [*Marxism and the Theory of Reflection*], Naprijed 1979 and *Od ontologije do filozofije povijesti* [*From Ontology to Philosophy of History*], HFD 2004.

Ellen Meiksins Wood, York University, Toronto (Canada), author of *Peasant-Citizen and Slave*, Verso 1988, *The Pristine Culture of Capitalism*, Verso 1992, *Democracy Against Capitalism*, Cambridge University Press 1995, *The Origin of Capitalism: A Longer View*, Verso 2002, and *Empire of Capital*, Verso 2003.

Zhongpu Zhang, Compilation and Translation Bureau of Beijing (China), co-translator of *Grundrisse* Chinese version, author of *Zi ben lun di yi gao 1857–1858 yan jiu* [*A Research on the First Version of Capital. Economic Manuscripts of 1857–58*], Shandong Renmin Press 1992 and co-author of *Guan yu ma ke si ji hua xie de liu ce jing ji xue zhu zuo* [*Exploring the Continuation of Capital. On the Six Books of Economics Works that Marx Planned to Write*], China Finance Press 1995.

Foreword

The odyssey of the publication of the *Grundrisse*

The place of the *Grundrisse* in Karl Marx's oeuvre and its fortunes are in many respects peculiar. First, they are the only example of a major set of Marx's mature writings which, for practical purposes, were entirely unknown to Marxists for more than half a century after Marx's death; and indeed almost completely unavailable until almost a century after the composition of the manuscripts which have been brought together under this name. Whatever the debates about their significance, the writings of 1857–8, clearly part of the intellectual effort that was to produce *Capital*, represent Marx in his maturity, not least as an economist. This distinguishes the *Grundrisse* from the other earlier posthumous addition to the Marxian corpus, the 1932 *Frühschriften* (early works). The exact place of these writings of the early 1840s in Marx's theoretical development has been much debated, rightly or wrongly, but there can be no such disagreement about the maturity of the writings of 1857–8.

Second, and somewhat surprisingly, the entire publication of the *Grundrisse* took place under what may safely be regarded as the least favourable conditions for any original development of Marx studies and Marxist thinking, namely in the USSR and the German Democratic Republic, at the height of the era of Stalin. The publication of texts by Marx and Engels remained a matter subject to the imprimatur of political authority even later, as editors engaged in foreign editions of their works have had reason to discover. It is still not clear how the obstacles to publication were overcome, including the purging of the Marx–Engels Institute and the elimination and eventual murder of its founder and director David Ryazanov, or how Paul Weller, who was in charge of work on the manuscript from 1925 to 1939, survived the terror of 1936–8 to do so. It may have helped that the authorities did not quite know what to make of this large and difficult text. However, they plainly had their doubts about its precise status, not least because J.V. Stalin's view was that draft manuscripts were of less importance than the three volumes of *Capital* which reflected Marx's mature position and views. The *Grundrisse* were not in fact fully published in a Russian translation until 1968–9, and neither the original German edition of 1939–41 (published in Moscow) nor its 1953 (Berlin) reprint were published as parts of MEGA (but only 'in the format of MEGA') or as part of the Marx–Engels *Werke* [Works] (MEW). However, unlike the *Frühschriften* of 1844, which disappeared from the official Marx corpus after their original appearance in MEGA (1932), they actually were published even at the peak of the Stalin era.

The third peculiarity is the long-lasting uncertainty about the status of the 1857–8 manuscripts which is reflected in the fluctuating name of the papers in the Marx–Engels–Lenin Institute of the 1930s until they acquired their title *Grundrisse* shortly before going into print. Indeed, the exact nature of their relation to the three volumes of *Capital*, as published by Marx and reconstructed by Friedrich Engels and from the notes of 1861–3 by Kautsky as a sort of volume 4 (*Theories on Surplus Value)*, remains a matter of debate. Kautsky, who went through them, does not seem to have known what to do about them. He published two extracts from them in his review *Die Neue Zeit*, but no more. They were the brief *Bastiat and Carey* (1904), which made little impact, and the so-called *Introduction* to the *A Contribution to a Critique of Political Economy* (1903), never completed and therefore not published with the book of the same name in 1859, which was to become an early text for those wishing to extend Marxist interpretation beyond prevailing orthodoxies, notably the Austro-Marxists. To date it is probably the most widely discussed part of the *Grundrisse*, although a few commentators cited in the book question whether they form part of it. The rest of the manuscripts remained unpublished, and indeed unknown to commentators, until Ryazanov and his collaborators in Moscow acquired photocopies of them in 1923, put them in order and planned to publish them in the MEGA. It is interesting to speculate what impact they might have had if they had been published in 1931, as originally planned. The date of their actual publication – at the end of 1939 and a week after Hitler's invasion of the USSR in 1941 – meant that they remained almost totally unknown in the West until the 1953 reprint in East Berlin, although rare copies reached the USA and from 1948 on the work was analysed by the great pioneer explicator of the *Grundrisse*, Roman Rosdolsky, recently arrived in the USA via Auschwitz and various other concentration camps (Rosdolsky 1977). It is difficult to believe that the bulk of the original German edition, 'sent . . . to the war front as material for agitation against German soldiers and later to camps as study materials for prisoners of war' (p. 204) achieved their theoretical or practical objectives.

The full reprint of 1939–41, which became the *editio princeps* for the international reception of the *Grundrisse*, was republished in East Germany in 1953, some years before the publication of the MEW, but deliberately unconnected with these. With one exception, the work did not begin to make a serious mark on Marx studies until the 1960s. That exception is the section on 'Forms which Precede Capitalist Production', which was first published separately in Russian in 1939 (as, somewhat earlier, was the 'Chapter on Money') translated into Japanese in 1947–8, reprinted in German in 1952, and then translated into Hungarian (1953) and Italian (1954), and certainly discussed among Marxist historians in the English-speaking world. The English translation (Marx 1964), with an explicatory introduction, was soon published in Spanish versions in Argentina (1966) and Franco's Spain (1967). Presumably its special interest for Marxist historians and social anthropologists helps to explain the wide distribution of this text, well before the availability of the full *Grundrisse*, and also its specific relevance to the much-disputed Marxist analysis of Third World societies. It threw light on the 'Asiatic mode of production' debate, controversially revived in the West by works like Karl August Wittfogel's *Oriental Despotism: A Comparative Study of Total Power* (Wittfogel 1957).

On the history of the reception of the *Grundrisse*

The history of the reception of the 1857–8 manuscripts really begins with the major effort, following the crisis of 1956, to free Marxism from the straitjacket of Soviet orthodoxy, both within and outside the no longer monolithic Communist parties. Since they did not belong to the canonical corpus of 'the classics' but were unquestionably by Marx, both the 1844 writings and the 1857–8 manuscripts could, as several chapters of the third part of this collection show, be regarded inside Communist parties as the basis for a legitimate opening of hitherto closed positions. The almost simultaneous international discovery of Antonio Gramsci's writings – the first publication of his writings in the USSR was in 1957–9 – had the same function. The belief that the *Grundrisse* had the potential for heterodoxy is shown by the appearance of unofficial freelance translations such as those of the reformists of the French Editions Anthropos (1967–8) and, under the auspices of the *New Left Review*, Martin Nicolaus (Marx 1973). Outside the Communist parties the *Grundrisse* had the function of justifying a non-Communist, but unquestionable Marxism, but this did not become politically significant until the era of student rebellions in the 1960s, although their significance had already been recognized in the 1950s by scholarly Germans close to the Frankfurt tradition, but not in the milieu of political activism, like George Lichtheim and the young Jürgen Habermas. Student radicalization in rapidly expanding universities also provided a larger body of readers than could have been expected in the past for extremely difficult texts such as this. But for this commercial publishers like Penguin Books would surely not have been prepared to publish the *Grundrisse*, even as part of a 'Pelican Marx Library'. In the meantime the text had been, more or less reluctantly, accepted as an integral part of the corpus of Marx's writings in the USSR, being added to the previous edition of the Marx–Engels works in 1968–9, though in a smaller edition than *Capital*. Publication in Hungary and Czechoslovakia soon followed.

It is thus not easy to separate the debates on the *Grundrisse* from the political setting in which they took place, and which stimulated them. In the 1970s, when they were at their most intense, they also suffered from a generational or cultural handicap, namely the loss of most of the (mainly central and east European) pioneer generation of Marxian textual scholars of monumental devotion and learning, of men like Ryazanov and Rosdolsky. Some serious efforts were indeed made by younger Trotskyist intellectuals to build on the earlier analyses of the place of the 1857–8 manuscripts in the development of Marx's thought, and more specifically on their place in the general plan of what became the torso of *Capital*. However, prominent Marxist theoretical polemics might be launched by writers like Louis Althusser in France and Antonio Negri in Italy with a frankly insufficient formation in Marxian literature and received by young men and women who themselves might well as yet lack much knowledge of the texts, or ability to judge the past controversies about them, if only for linguistic reasons. Small wonder that what is said in the chapter on Italy, that the 'reception of the *Grundrisse* had a rather peculiar character' is true of more than one country.

Overview

The present collective volume appears at a time when Marxist parties and movements are only rarely significant actors on the global scene and when debates about their doctrines, strategies, methods and objectives are no longer the inevitable framework of debates about the writings of Marx, Engels and their followers. And yet it also appears at a time when the world appears to demonstrate the perspicacity of Marx's insight into the economic modus operandi of the capitalist system. Perhaps this is the right moment to return to a study of the *Grundrisse* less constricted by the temporary considerations of leftwing politics between Nikita Khrushchev's denunciation of Stalin and the fall of Mikhail Gorbachev. It is an enormously difficult text in every respect, but also an enormously rewarding one, if only because it provides the only guide to the full range of the treatise of which *Capital* is only a fraction, and a unique introduction to the methodology of the mature Marx. It contains analyses and insights, for instance about technology, that take Marx's treatment of capitalism far beyond the nineteenth century, into the era of a society where production no longer requires mass labour, of automation, the potential of leisure, and the transformations of alienation in such circumstances. It is the only text that goes some way beyond Marx's own hints of the communist future in the *German Ideology*. In a few words, it has been rightly described as Marx's thought at its richest.

This collection is divided into three parts. The first is made up of eight chapters which interpret the main themes (method, value, alienation, surplus value, historical materialism, ecological contradictions, socialism, and a comparison between the *Grundrisse* and the *Capital*) coming from reading the *Grundrisse*. The second reconstructs the intellectual biography of its author between 1857 and 1858. The third, finally, presents a complete and rigorous account of the dissemination and the reception of this Marx's work throughout the world.

In short, this volume makes a successful attempt both to display some of the riches of *Grundrisse* and to place its origin fortunes in their international setting.

Eric Hobsbawm

References

Marx, Karl (1964) *Pre-capitalist Economic Formations*, Eric J. Hobsbawm (ed.), London: Lawrence & Wishart.

Marx, Karl (1973) *Grundrisse: Foundations of the Critique of Political Economy (Rough Draft)*, Harmondsworth: Penguin.

Rosdolsky, Roman (1977) *The Making of Marx's 'Capital'*, London: Pluto Press.

Wittfogel, Karl August (1957) *Oriental Despotism: A Comparative Study of Total Power*, New Haven: Yale University Press.

Acknowledgements

This collection of essays came about to mark the one-hundred-and-fiftieth anniversary of the composition of Marx's *Grundrisse*. The volume, containing 32 chapters by 31 authors, is divided into three parts: the first consists of eight chapters on the main themes that emerge from a reading of the *Grundrisse*: method, value, alienation, surplus value, historical materialism, ecological contradictions, socialism, and a comparison between the *Grundrisse* and *Capital*; the second reconstructs the biographical and theoretical context in which Marx wrote these manuscripts; while the third presents a comprehensive account of the dissemination and reception of the *Grundrisse* in all languages into which it has been translated in full.

The greatest complications arose in this third part, where it was necessary to locate all the translated editions of the *Grundrisse*, to find researchers capable of writing the history of its reception in individual countries, and to track down the critical literature on this Marxian text. This specific task, accomplished by the various authors, was supplemented with work of my own at the libraries of the *Stiftung Archiv der Parteien und Massenorganisationen* (SAPMO) in Berlin and the *Internationaal Instituut voor Sociale Geschiedenis* (IISG) in Amsterdam, and correspondence (made possible through the help of Lyudmila Vasina) with the *Rossiiskii Gosudarstvennyi Arkhiv Sotsial'no-Politicheskoi Istorii* (RGASPI) in Moscow. The next stage was then to translate the various texts and to homogenize their content.

Begun in March 2006, the preparation of this volume took place in a Babel of languages, involving more than 1,500 e-mails and – in the case of those who do not use this means of communication – dozens of letters and telephone calls. I received valuable informations from some 200 academics, political militants and librarians, whom it would be impossible to name here. Thanks are due to them both from myself and from all the authors of this book. Given the problematic character of the third section, the reader is kindly requested to send a note of any inaccuracies to the e-mail address: grundrisse.musto@gmail.com.

I would like to thank the *Istituto Italiano per gli Studi Filosofici* (IISF) in Naples (Italy), in the person of Antonio Gargano, for the support it gave to the research underpinning this work; Routledge editor Terry Clague, who appreciated its value in taking the decision to publish it in this collection; the editorial assistant Sarah Hastings for her courteous collaboration; and Patrick Camiller, who translated my own chapters into English and helped me, with great professionalism, to revise certain texts in the book. I would also like to express my special gratitude to Terrell Carver, who gave me suggestions throughout the work and, with a kindness equalled only by his modesty, read the chapters I had written.

Finally, without the help and 'militant support' of my mother Lucia I would certainly not have managed to complete the book in the scheduled time and with the same efficiency. To her alone I dedicate the fruits of my work.

Marcello Musto
Berlin, 2008

Prologue

We are the last to deny that *capital* contains contradictions. Our purpose, rather, is to develop them fully.

Karl Marx, Grundrisse

We are like dwarfs on the shoulders of giants, so that we can see more than they, and things at a greater distance, not by virtue of any sharpness of sight on our part, or any physical distinction, but because we are carried high and raised up by their giant size.

Bernard of Chartres

Part I

Grundrisse

Critical interpretations

1 History, production and method in the 1857 'Introduction'

Marcello Musto

Introduction

In 1857 Marx was convinced that the financial crisis developing at international level had created the conditions for a new revolutionary period throughout Europe. He had been waiting for this moment ever since the popular insurrections of 1848, and now that it finally seemed to have come he did not want events to catch him unprepared. He therefore decided to resume his economic studies and to give them a finished form.

Where to begin? How to embark on the critique of political economy, that ambitious and demanding project which he had begun and interrupted several times before? This was the first question that Marx asked himself as he got down to work again. Two circumstances played a crucial role in determining the answer: he held the view that, despite the validity of certain theories, economic science still lacked a cognitive procedure with which to grasp and elucidate reality correctly;[1] and he felt a need to establish the arguments and the order of exposition before he embarked on the task of composition. These considerations led him to go more deeply into problems of method and to formulate the guiding principles for his research. The upshot was one of the most extensively debated manuscripts in the whole of his oeuvre: the so-called 'Introduction' of 1857.

Marx's intention was certainly not to write a sophisticated methodological treatise but to clarify for himself, before his readers, what orientation he should follow on the long and eventful critical journey that lay ahead. This was also necessary for the task of revising the huge mass of economic studies that he had accumulated since the mid-1840s. Thus, along with observations on the employment and articulation of theoretical categories, these pages contain a number of formulations essential to his thought that he found indispensable to summarize anew – especially those linked to his conception of history – as well as a quite unsystematic list of questions for which the solutions remained problematic.

This mix of requirements and purposes, the short period of composition (scarcely a week) and, above all, the provisional character of these notes make them extremely complex and controversial. Nevertheless, since it contains the most extensive and detailed pronouncement that Marx ever made on epistemological questions, the 'Introduction' is an important reference for the understanding of his thought[2] and a key to the interpretation of the *Grundrisse* as a whole.

History and the social individual

In keeping with his style, Marx alternated in the 'Introduction' between exposition of his own ideas and criticism of his theoretical opponents. The text is divided into four sections:

(1) Production in general
(2) General relation between production, distribution, exchange and consumption
(3) The method of political economy
(4) Means (forces) of production and relations of production, relations of production and relations of circulation, etc.

(Marx 1973: 69)

The first section opens with a declaration of intent, immediately specifying the field of study and pointing to the historical criterion: 'the object before us, to begin with, material production. Individuals producing in society – hence socially determined individual production – is, of course, the point of departure.' Marx's polemical target was 'the eighteenth-century Robinsonades' (Marx 1973: 83), the myth of Robinson Crusoe (see Watt 1951: 112) as the paradigm of *homo oeconomicus*, or the projection of phenomena typical of the bourgeois era onto every other society that has existed since the earliest times. Such conceptions represented the social character of production as a constant in any labour process, not as a peculiarity of capitalist relations. In the same way, civil society [*bürgerliche Gesellschaft*] – whose emergence in the eighteenth century had created the conditions through which 'the individual appears detached from the natural bonds, etc. which in earlier historical periods make him the accessory of a definite and limited human conglomerate' – was portrayed as having always existed (Marx 1973: 83).

In reality, the isolated individual simply did not exist before the capitalist epoch. As Marx put it in another passage in the *Grundrisse*: 'He originally appears as a *species-being, tribal being, herd animal*' (Marx 1973: 496, trans. modified). This collective dimension is the condition for the appropriation of the earth, 'the great workshop, the arsenal which furnishes both means and material of labour, as well as the seat, the *base* of the community [*Basis des Gemeinwesens*]' (Marx 1973: 472). In the presence of these primal relations, the activity of human beings is directly linked to the earth; there is a 'natural unity of labour with its material presuppositions', and the individual lives in symbiosis with others like himself (Marx 1973: 471). Similarly, in all later economic forms based on agriculture where the aim is to create use-values and not yet exchange-values,[3] the relationship of the individual to 'the objective conditions of his labour is mediated through his presence as member of the commune'; he is always only one link in the chain (Marx 1973: 486). In this connection, Marx writes in the 'Introduction':

> The more deeply we go back into history, the more does the individual, and hence also the producing individual, appear as dependent [*unselbstständig*], as belonging to a greater whole: in a still quite natural way in the family and in the family expanded into the clan [*Stamm*]; then later in the various forms of communal society arising out of the antitheses and fusions of the clans.[4]
>
> (Marx 1973: 84)

Similar considerations appear in *Capital*, vol. I. Here, in speaking of 'the European Middle Ages, shrouded in darkness', Marx argues that:

> instead of the independent man, we find everyone dependent, serfs and lords, vassals and suzerains, laymen and clergy. Personal dependence here characterizes the social relations of production just as much as it does the other spheres of life organized on the basis of that production.
>
> (Marx 1996: 88)

And, when he examined the genesis of product exchange, he recalled that it began with contacts among different families, tribes or communities, 'for, in the beginning of civilization, it is not private individuals but families, tribes, etc., that meet on an independent footing' (Marx 1996: 357). Thus, whether the horizon was the primal bond of consanguinity or the medieval nexus of lordship and vassalage, individuals lived amid 'limited relations of production [*bornirter Productionsverhältnisse*]', joined to one another by reciprocal ties (Marx 1973: 162).[5]

The classical economists had inverted this reality, on the basis of what Marx regarded as fantasies with an inspiration in natural law. In particular, Adam Smith had described a primal condition where individuals not only existed but were capable of producing outside society. A division of labour within tribes of hunters and shepherds had supposedly achieved the specialization of trades: one person's greater dexterity in fashioning bows and arrows, for example, or in building wooden huts, had made him a kind of armourer or carpenter, and the assurance of being able to exchange the unconsumed part of one's labour product for the surplus of others 'encourage[d] every man to apply himself to a particular occupation' (Smith 1961: 19). David Ricardo was guilty of a similar anachronism when he conceived of the relationship between hunters and fishermen in the early stages of society as an exchange between owners of commodities on the basis of the labour-time objectified in them (see Ricardo 1973: 15, cf. Marx 1987a: 300).

In this way, Smith and Ricardo depicted a highly developed product of the society in which they lived – the isolated bourgeois individual – as if he were a spontaneous manifestation of nature. What emerged from the pages of their works was a mythological, timeless individual, one 'posited by nature', whose social relations were always the same and whose economic behaviour had a historyless anthropological character (Marx 1973: 83). According to Marx, the interpreters of each new historical epoch have regularly deluded themselves that the most distinctive features of their own age have been present since time immemorial.[6]

Marx argued instead that 'production by an isolated individual outside society ... is as much of an absurdity as is the development of language without individuals living *together* and talking to each other' (Marx 1973: 84).[7] And, against those who portrayed the isolated individual of the eighteenth century as the archetype of human nature, 'not as a historical result but as history's point of departure', he maintained that such an individual emerged only with the most highly developed social relations (Marx 1973: 83). Marx did not entirely disagree that man was a ζῷον πολιτικόν [*zoon politikon*], a social animal, but he insisted that he was 'an animal which can individuate itself only in the midst of society' (Marx 1973: 84). Thus, since civil society had arisen only with the modern world, the free wage-labourer of the capitalist epoch had appeared only after a long historical process. He was, in fact, 'the product on one side of the dissolution of the feudal forms of society, on the other side of the new forces of production developed since the sixteenth century' (Marx 1973: 83). If Marx felt the need to repeat a point he considered all too evident, it was only because works by Henry Charles Carey, Frédéric Bastiat and Pierre-Joseph Proudhon had brought it up for discussion in the previous 20 years.[8] After sketching the genesis of the capitalist individual and demonstrating that modern production conforms only to 'a definitive stage of social development – production by social individuals', Marx points to a second theoretical requirement: namely, to expose the mystification practised by economists with regard to the concept of 'production in general' [*Production im Allgemeinem*]. This is an abstraction, a category that does not exist at any concrete stage of reality. However, since 'all epochs of production have certain common traits, common characteristics' [*gemeinsame Bestimmungen*], Marx recognizes that 'production in general is a rational abstraction in so far as it really brings out and fixes the common element', thereby saving pointless repetition for the scholar who undertakes to reproduce reality through thought (Marx 1973: 85).

So, abstraction acquired a positive function for Marx. It was no longer, as in his early critique of G.W.F. Hegel, synonymous with idealist philosophy and its substitution of itself for reality (see Marx 1975a: 180ff.), or, as he put it in 1847 in *The Poverty of Philosophy*, a metaphysics that transformed everything into logical categories (Marx 1976: 163). Now that his materialist conception of history (as it was later denominated) had been solidly elaborated, and now that his critical reflections were operating in a context profoundly different from that of the early 1840s, Marx was able to reconsider abstraction without the prejudices of his youth. Thus, unlike representatives of the 'Historical School', who in the same period were theorizing the impossibility of abstract laws with universal value,[9] Marx in the *Grundrisse* recognized that abstraction could play a fruitful role in the cognitive process.[10]

This was possible, however, only if theoretical analysis proved capable of distinguishing between definitions valid for all historical stages and those valid only for particular epochs, and of granting due importance to the latter in the understanding of reality. Although abstraction was useful in representing the broadest phenomena of production, it did not correctly represent its specific aspects, which were alone truly historical.[11] If abstraction was not combined with the kind of determinations characteristic of any historical reality, then production changed from being a specific, differentiated phenomenon into a perpetually self-identical process, which concealed the 'essential diversity' [*wesentliche Verschiedenheit*] of the various forms in which it manifested itself. This was the error committed by economists who claimed to show 'the eternity and harmoniousness of the existing social relations' (Marx 1973: 85). In contrast to their procedure, Marx maintained that it was the specific features of each social-economic formation which made it possible to distinguish it from others, gave the impetus for its development and enabled scholars to understand the real historical changes (Korsch 1938: 78f.).

Although the definition of the general elements of production is 'segmented many times over and split into different determinations', some of which 'belong to all epochs, others to only a few', there are certainly, among its universal components, human labour and material provided by nature (Marx 1973: 85). For, without a producing subject and a worked-upon object, there could be no production at all. But the economists introduced a third general prerequisite of production: 'a stock, previously accumulated, of the products of former labour', that is, capital (Mill 1965: 55).[12] The critique of this last element was essential for Marx, in order to reveal what he considered to be a fundamental limitation of the economists. It also seemed evident to him that no production was possible without an instrument of labour, if only the human hand, or without accumulated past labour, if only in the form of primitive man's repetitive exercises. However, while agreeing that capital was past labour and an instrument of production, he did not, like Smith, Ricardo and John Stuart Mill, conclude that it had always existed.

The point is made in greater detail in another section of the *Grundrisse*, where the conception of capital as 'eternal' is seen as a way of treating it only as matter, without regard for its essential 'formal determination' (*Formbestimmung*). According to this,

> capital would have existed in all forms of society, and is something altogether unhistorical.... The arm, and especially the hand, are then capital. Capital would be only a new name for a thing as old as the human race, since every form of labour, including the least developed, hunting, fishing, etc., presupposes that the product of prior labour is used as means for direct, living labour.... If, then, the specific form of capital is abstracted away, and only the content is emphasized ... of course nothing is easier than to demonstrate that capital is a necessary condition for all human production. The proof of this proceeds precisely by abstraction [*Abstraktion*]

from the specific aspects which make it the moment of a specifically developed *historical* stage of human production [*Moment einer besonders entwickelten* historischen *Stufe der menschlichen Production*].

(Marx 1973: 257–8)

In these passages Marx refers to abstraction in the negative sense: to abstract is to leave out the real social conditions, to conceive of capital as a thing rather than a relation, and hence to advance an interpretation that is false. In the 'Introduction' Marx accepts the use of abstract categories, but only if analysis of the general aspect does not obliterate the particular aspect or blur the latter in the indistinctness of the former. If the error is made of 'conceiving capital in its physical attribute only as instrument of production, while entirely ignoring the economic form [*ökonomischen Form*] which makes the instrument of production into capital' (Marx 1973: 591), one falls into the 'crude inability to grasp the real distinctions' and a belief that 'there exists only one single economic relation which takes on different names' (Marx 1973: 249). To ignore the differences expressed in the social relation means to abstract from the *differentia specifica*, that is the nodal point of everything.[13] Thus, in the 'Introduction', Marx writes that 'capital is a general [*allgemeines*], eternal relation of nature', 'that is, if I leave out just the specific quality which alone makes "instrument of production" and "stored-up labour" into capital' (Marx 1973: 86).

In fact, Marx had already criticized the economists' lack of historical sense in *The Poverty of Philosophy*:

Economists have a singular method of procedure. There are only two kinds of institutions for them, artificial and natural. The institutions of feudalism are artificial institutions, those of the bourgeoisie are natural institutions. In this they resemble the theologians, who likewise establish two kinds of religion. Every religion which is not theirs is an invention of men, while their own is an emanation from God. When the economists say that present-day relations – the relations of bourgeois production – are natural, they imply that these are the relations in which wealth is created and productive forces developed in conformity with the laws of nature. These relations therefore are themselves natural laws independent of the influence of time. They are eternal laws which must always govern society. Thus there has been history, but there is no longer any.

(Marx 1976: 174)

For this to be plausible, economists depicted the historical circumstances prior to the birth of the capitalist mode of production as 'results of its presence' with its very own features (Marx 1973: 460). As Marx puts it in the *Grundrisse*:

The bourgeois economists who regard capital as an eternal and *natural* (not historical) form of production then attempt ... to legitimize it again by formulating the conditions of its becoming as the conditions of its contemporary realization; i.e. presenting the moments in which the capitalist still appropriates as not-capitalist – because he is still becoming – as the very conditions in which he appropriates *as capitalist*.

(Marx 1973: 460)

From a historical point of view, the profound difference between Marx and the classical economists is that, in his view, 'capital did not begin the world from the beginning, but rather encountered production and products already present, before it subjugated them beneath its process' (Marx 1973: 675). For

the new productive forces and relations of production do not develop out of nothing, nor drop from the sky, nor from the womb of the self-positing Idea; but from within and in antithesis to the existing development of production and the inherited, traditional relations of property.

(Marx 1973: 278)

Similarly, the circumstance whereby producing subjects are separated from the means of production – which allows the capitalist to find propertyless workers capable of performing abstract labour (the necessary requirement for the exchange between capital and living labour) – is the result of a process that the economists cover with silence, which 'forms the history of the origins of capital and wage labour' (Marx 1973: 489).

A number of passages in the *Grundrisse* criticize the way in which economists portray historical as natural realities. It is self-evident to Marx, for example, that money is a product of history: 'to be money is not a natural attribute of gold and silver,' but only a determination they first acquire at a precise moment of social development (Marx 1973: 239). The same is true of credit. According to Marx, lending and borrowing was a phenomenon common to many civilizations, as was usury, but they 'no more constitute credit than working constitutes industrial labour or free wage labour. And credit as an essential, developed relation of production appears *historically* only in circulation based on capital' (Marx 1973: 535). Prices and exchange also existed in ancient society, 'but the increasing determination of the former by costs of production, as well as the increasing dominance of the latter over all relations of production, only develop fully ... in bourgeois society, the society of free competition'; or 'what Adam Smith, in the true eighteenth-century manner, puts in the prehistoric period, the period preceding history, is rather a product of history' (Marx 1973: 156). Furthermore, just as he criticized the economists for their lack of historical sense, Marx mocked Proudhon and all the socialists who thought that labour productive of exchange value could exist without developing into wage labour, that exchange value could exist without turning into capital, or that there could be capital without capitalists (see Marx 1973: 248).

Marx's chief aim in the opening pages of the 'Introduction' is therefore to assert the historical specificity of the capitalist mode of production: to demonstrate, as he would again affirm in *Capital*, vol. III, that it 'is not an absolute mode of production' but 'merely historical, transitory' (Marx 1998: 240).

This viewpoint implies a different way of seeing many questions, including the labour process and its various characteristics. In the *Grundrisse* Marx wrote that

> the bourgeois economists are so much cooped up within the notions belonging to a specific historic stage of social development that the necessity of the objectification of the powers of social labour appears to them as inseparable from the necessity of their alienation.
>
> (Marx 1973: 832)

Marx repeatedly took issue with this presentation of the specific forms of the capitalist mode of production as if they were constants of the production process as such. To portray wage labour not as a distinctive relation of a particular historical form of production but as a universal reality of man's economic existence was to imply that exploitation and alienation had always existed and would always continue to exist.

Evasion of the specificity of capitalist production therefore had both epistemological and political consequences. On the one hand, it impeded understanding of the concrete historical levels of production; on the other hand, in defining present conditions as unchanged and unchangeable, it presented capitalist production as production in general and bourgeois social relations as natural human relations. Accordingly, Marx's critique of the theories of economists had a twofold value. As well as underlining that a historical characterization was indispensable for an understanding of reality, it had the precise political aim of countering the dogma of the immutability of the capitalist mode of production. A demonstration of the historicity of the capitalist order would also be proof of its transitory character and of the possibility of its elimination.

An echo of the ideas contained in this first part of the 'Introduction' may be found in the closing pages of *Capital*, vol. III, where Marx writes that 'identification of the social production process with the simple labour process' is a 'confusion' (Marx 1998: 870). For,

> to the extent that the labour process is solely a process between man and Nature, its simple elements remain common to all social forms of development. But each specific historical form of this process further develops its material foundations and social forms. Whenever a certain stage of maturity has been reached, the specific historical form is discarded and makes way for a higher one.
>
> (Marx 1998: 870)

Capitalism is not the only stage in human history, nor is it the final one. Marx foresees that it will be succeeded by an organization of society based upon 'communal production' [*gemeinschaftliche Production*], in which the labour product is 'from the beginning *directly* general' (Marx 1973: 172).

Production as a totality

In the succeed pages of the 'Introduction', Marx passes to a deeper consideration of production and begins with the following definition: 'All production is appropriation [*Aneignung*] of nature on the part of an individual within and through a specific form of society [*bestimmten Gesellschaftsform*]' (Marx 1973: 87). There was no 'production in general' – since it was divided into agriculture, cattle-raising, manufacturing and other branches – but nor could it be considered as 'only particular production'. Rather, it was 'always a certain social body [*Gesellschaftskörper*], a social subject [*gesellschaftliches Subject*], active in a greater or sparser totality of branches of production' (Marx 1973: 86).

Here again, Marx developed his arguments through a critical encounter with the main exponents of economic theory. Those who were his contemporaries had acquired the habit of prefacing their work with a section on the general conditions of production and the circumstances which, to a greater or lesser degree, advanced productivity in various societies. For Marx, however, such preliminaries set forth 'flat tautologies' (Marx 1973: 86) and, in the case of John Stuart Mill, were designed to present production 'as encased in eternal natural laws independent of history' and bourgeois relations as 'inviolable natural laws on which society in the abstract is founded' (Marx 1973: 87). According to Mill, 'the laws and conditions of the production of wealth partake of the character of physical truths.... It is not so with the distribution of wealth. That is a matter of human institutions solely' (Mill 1965: 199).[14] Marx considered this a 'crude tearing-apart of production and distribution and of their real relationship' (Marx 1973: 87), since, as he put it else-where in the *Grundrisse*, 'the "laws and conditions" of the production of wealth and the laws of the "distribution of wealth" are the same laws under different forms, and both change, undergo the same historic process; are as such only moments of a historic process' (Marx 1973: 832).[15]

After making these points, Marx proceeds in the second section of the 'Introduc-tion' to examine the general relationship of production to distribution, exchange and consumption. This division of political economy had been made by James Mill, who had used these four categories as the headings for the four chapters comprising his book of 1821, *Elements of Political Economy*, and before him, in 1803, by Jean-Baptiste Say, who had divided his *Traité d'économie politique* into three books on the production, distribution and consumption of wealth.[16]

Marx reconstructed the interconnection among the four rubrics in logical terms, in accordance with Hegel's schema of universality–particularity–individuality (see Hegel 1969: 666f.) 'Production, distribution, exchange and distribution form a regular syllogism; production is the universality, distribution and exchange the particularity, and consumption the individuality in which the whole is joined together'. In other words, production was the starting-point of human activity, distribution and exchange were the twofold intermediary point – the former being the mediation operated by society, the latter by the individual – and consumption became the end point. However, as this was only a 'shallow coherence', Marx wished to analyse more deeply how the four spheres were cor-related with one another (Marx 1973: 89).

His first object of investigation was the relationship between production and consumption, which he explained as one of immediate identity: 'production is consumption' and 'consumption is production'. With the help of Spinoza's principle of *determinatio est negatio*, he showed that production was also consumption, in so far as the productive act used up the powers of the individual as well as raw materials (see Spinoza 1955: 370). Indeed, the economists had already highlighted this aspect with their terms 'productive consumption' and differentiated this from 'consumptive production'. The latter occurred only after the product was distributed, re-entering the sphere of reproduction, and constituting 'consumption proper'. In productive consumption 'the producer objectifies himself', while in consumptive production 'the object he created personifies itself' (Marx 1973: 90–1).

Another characteristic of the identity of production and consumption was discernible in the reciprocal 'mediating movement' that developed between them. Consumption gives the product its 'last finish' and, by stimulating the propensity to produce, 'creates the need for *new* production' (Marx 1973: 91). In the same way, production furnishes not only the object for consumption, but also 'a need for the material'. Once the stage of natural immediacy is left behind, need is generated by the object itself; 'production not only creates an object for the subject, but also a subject for the object' – that is, a consumer (Marx 1973: 92). So,

> production produces consumption (1) by creating the material for it; (2) by determining the manner of consumption; and (3) by creating the products, initially posited by it as objects, in the form of a need felt by the consumer. It thus produces the object of consumption, the manner of consumption and the motive of consumption.
>
> (Marx 1973: 92)

To recapitulate: there is a process of unmediated identity between production and consumption; these also mediate each other in turn, and create each other as they are realized. Nevertheless, Marx thought it a mistake to consider the two as identical – as Say and Proudhon did, for example. For, in the last analysis, 'consumption as urgency, as need, is itself an intrinsic moment of productive activity'.

Marx then turns to analyse the relationship between production and distribution. Distribution, he writes, is the link between production and consumption, and 'in accordance with social laws' it determines what share of the products is due to the producers (Marx 1973: 94). The economists present it as a sphere autonomous from production, so that in their treatises the economic categories are always posed in a dual manner. Land, labour and capital figure in production as the agents of distribution, while in distribution, in the form of ground rent, wages and profit, they appear as sources of income. Marx opposes this split, which he judges illusory and mistaken, since the form of distribution 'is not an arbitrary arrangement, which could be different; it is, rather, posited by the form of production itself' (Marx 1973: 594). In the 'Introduction' he expresses his thinking as follows:

> An individual who participates in production in the form of wage labour shares in the products, in the results of production, in the form of wages. The structure of distribution is completely determined by the structure of

production. Distribution itself a product of production, not only in its object, in that only the results of production can be distributed, but also in its form, in that the specific kind of participation in production determines the specific forms of distribution, i.e. the pattern of participation in distribution. It is altogether an illusion to posit land in production, ground rent in distribution, etc.

(Marx 1973: 95)

Those who saw distribution as autonomous from production conceived of it as mere distribution of products. In reality, it included two important phenomena that were prior to production: distribution of the instruments of production and distribution of the members of society among various kinds of production, or what Marx defined as 'subsumption of the individuals under specific relations of production' (Marx 1973: 96). These two phenomena meant that in some historical cases – for example, when a conquering people subjects the vanquished to slave labour, or when a redivision of landed estates gives rise to a new type of production (see Marx 1973: 96) – 'distribution is not structured and determined by production, but rather the opposite, production by distribution' (Marx 1973: 96). The two were closely linked to each other, since, as Marx puts it elsewhere in the *Grundrisse*, 'these modes of distribution are the relations of production themselves, but *sub specie distributionis*' (Marx 1973: 832). Thus, in the words of the 'Introduction', 'to examine production while disregarding this internal distribution within it is obviously an empty abstraction'.

The link between production and distribution, as conceived by Marx, sheds light not only on his aversion to the way in which John Stuart Mill rigidly separated the two but also on his appreciation of Ricardo for having posed the need 'to grasp the specific social structure of modern production' (Marx 1973: 96). The English economist did indeed hold that 'to determine the laws which regulate this distribution is the principal problem in Political Economy' (Ricardo 1973: 3), and therefore he made distribution one of his main objects of study, since 'he conceived the forms of distribution as the most specific expression into which the agents of production of a given society are cast' (Marx 1973: 96). For Marx, too, distribution was not reducible to the act through which the shares of the aggregate product were distributed among members of society; it was a decisive element of the entire productive cycle. Yet this conviction did not overturn his thesis that production was always the primary factor within the production process as a whole:

The question of the relation between this distribution and the production it determines belongs evidently within production itself.... [P]roduction does indeed have its determinants and preconditions, which form its moments. At the very beginning these may appear as spontaneous, natural. But by the process of production itself they are transformed from natural into historic determinants, and if they appear to one epoch as natural presuppositions of production, they were its historic product for another.

(Marx 1973: 97, trans. modified)

For Marx, then, although the distribution of the instruments of production and the members of society among the various productive branches 'appears as a presupposition of the new period of production, it is ... itself in turn a product of production, not only of historical production generally, but of the specific historic mode of production' (Marx 1973: 98).

When Marx lastly examined the relationship between production and exchange, he also considered the latter to be part of the former. Not only was 'the exchange of activities and abilities' among the workforce, and of the raw materials necessary to prepare the finished product, an integral part of production; the exchange between dealers was also wholly determined by production and constituted a 'producing activity'. Exchange becomes autonomous from production only in the phase where 'the product is exchanged directly for consumption'. Even then, however, its intensity, scale and characteristic features are determined by the development and structure of production, so that 'in all its moments ... exchange appears as either directly comprised in production or determined by it'.

At the end of his analysis of the relationship of production to distribution, exchange and consumption, Marx draws two conclusions:

1   production should be considered as a totality; and
2   production as a particular branch within the totality predominates over the other elements.

On the first point he writes: 'The conclusion we reach is not that production, distribution, exchange and consumption are identical, but that they all form the members of a totality, distinctions within a unity' (Marx 1973: 99). Employing the Hegelian concept of totality,[17] Marx sharpened a theoretical instrument – more effective than the limited processes of abstraction used by the economists – one capable of showing, through the reciprocal action among parts of the totality, that the concrete was a differentiated unity (see Hall 2003: 127) of plural determinations and relations, and that the four separate rubrics of the economists were both arbitrary and unhelpful for an understanding of real economic relations. In Marx's conception, however, the definition of production as an organic totality did not point to a structured, self-regulating whole within which uniformity was always guaranteed among its various branches. On the contrary, as he wrote in a section of the *Grundrisse* dealing with the same argument: the individual moments of production 'may or may not find each other, balance each other, correspond to each other. The inner necessity of moments which belong together, and their indifferent, independent existence towards one another, are already a foundation of contradictions'. Marx argued that it was always necessary to analyse these contradictions in relation to capitalist production (not production in general), which was not at all 'the absolute form for the development of the forces of production', as the economists proclaimed, but had its 'fundamental contradiction' in overproduction (Marx 1973: 415).

Marx's second conclusion made production the 'predominant moment' [*übergreifende Moment*] over the other parts of the 'totality of production' [*Totalität der Production*] (Marx 1973: 86). It was the 'real point of departure' [*Ausgangspunkt*] (Marx 1973: 94), from which 'the process always returns to begin anew', and so 'a definite production determines a definite consumption, distribution and exchange as well as *definite relations between these different moments*' (Marx 1973: 99). But such predominance did not cancel the import-ance of the other moments, nor their influence on production. The dimension of consumption, the transformations of distribution and the size of the sphere of exchange – or of the market – were all factors jointly defining and impacting on production.

Here again Marx's insights had a value both theoretical and political. In opposition to other socialists of his time, who maintained that it was possible to revolutionize the prevailing relations of production by transforming the instru-ment of circulation, he argued that this clearly demonstrated their 'misunder-standing' of 'the inner connections between the relations of production, of distribution and of circulation' (Marx 1973: 122). For not only would a change in the form of money leave unaltered the relations of production and the other social relations determined by them; it would also turn out to be a nonsense, since circulation could change only together with a change in the relations of production. Marx was convinced that 'the evil of bourgeois society is not to be remedied by "transforming" the banks or by founding a rational "money system"', nor through bland palliatives such as the granting of free credit, nor through the chimera of turning workers into capitalists (Marx 1973: 134). The central question remained the overcoming of wage labour, and first and foremost that concerned production.

In search of method

At this point in his analysis, Marx addressed the major methodological issue: how to reproduce reality in thought? How to construct an abstract categorial model capable of comprehending and representing society?

The third and most important section of his 'Introduction' is devoted to 'the relationship between scientific presentation and the real movement' (Marx 1973: 86). It is not a definitive account, however, but offers insufficiently developed ways of theorizing the problem and barely sketches out a number of points. Certain passages contain unclear assertions, which sometimes contradict one another, and more than once the adoption of a language influenced by Hegelian terminology adds ambiguities to the text. Marx was elaborating his method when he wrote these pages, and they display the traces and trajectories of his search.

Like other great thinkers before him, Marx started from the question of where to begin – or, in his case, what political economy should take as its analytic starting-point. The first hypothesis he examined was that of beginning 'with the real and the concrete, with the real precondition', 'the foundation and subject of the entire social act of production': the population (Marx 1973: 100). Marx considered that this path, taken by the founders of political economy, William Petty and Pierre de Boisguillebert, was inadequate and erroneous. To begin with such an indeterminate entity as the population would involve an overly generic image of the whole; it would be incapable of demonstrating the division into classes (bourgeoisie, landowners and proletariat), since these could be differentiated only through knowledge of their respective foundations: capital, land ownership and wage labour. With an empirical approach of that kind, concrete elements like the state would dissolve into abstract determinations such as division of labour, money or value.

Nevertheless, though judging this method inadequate for an interpretation of reality, in another part of the *Grundrisse* Marx recognized that it 'had a historic value in the first tentative steps of political economy, when the forms still had to be laboriously peeled out of the material, and were, at the cost of great effort, fixed upon as a proper object of study' (Marx 1973: 853).

No sooner had the eighteenth-century economists finished defining their abstract categories than 'there began the economic systems, which ascended from simple relations, such as labour, division of labour, need, exchange value, to the level of the state, exchange between nations and the world market'. This procedure, employed by Smith and Ricardo in economics as well as Hegel in philosophy, may be summed up in the thesis that 'the abstract determinations lead towards a reproduction of the concrete by way of thought'; it was this that Marx described as the 'scientifically correct method' [*wissenschaftlich richtige Methode*]. With the right categories, it was possible 'to retrace the journey until one finally arrives at population again, only this time not as the chaotic conception of the whole, but as a rich totality of many determinations and relations' (Marx 1973: 100–1). Hegel, in fact, had written in *The Science of Logic* that the first requisite for a synthetic and systematic science was to begin:

> with the subject matter in the form of a universal.... The *prius* must be ... something simple, something abstracted from the concrete, because in this form alone has the subject-matter the form of the self-related universal.... It is easier for cognition to grasp the abstract simple thought determination than the concrete subject matter, which is a manifold connection of such thought determinations and their relationships.... The universal is in and for itself the first moment of the Notion because it is the simple moment, and the particular is only subsequent to it because it is the mediated moment; and conversely the simple is the more universal, and the concrete ... is that which already presupposes the transition from a first.
>
> (Hegel 1969: 800–1)

Yet, contrary to what certain commentators on the 'Introduction' have argued,[18] Marx's definition of the 'scientifically correct method' does not at all mean that it was the one he subsequently employed himself (Marx 1973: 101). First of all, he did not share the conviction of the economists that their logical reconstruction of the concrete at the level of ideas was a faithful reproduction of reality (see

Dal Pra 1965: 461). The procedure synthetically presented in the 'Introduction' did, it is true, borrow various elements from Hegel's method, but it also displayed radical differences. Like Hegel before him, Marx was convinced that 'the method of rising from the abstract to the concrete is the only way in which thought appropriates the concrete', that the recomposition of reality in thought should start from the simplest and most general determinations. For both, moreover, the concrete was 'the concentration of many determinations, hence unity of the diverse'; it appeared in thought as 'a process of concentration, as a result, not as a point of departure', although for Marx it was always necessary to keep in mind that the concrete was 'the point of departure for observation [*Anschauung*] and conception'.

Beyond this common base, however, there was the difference that 'Hegel fell into the illusion of conceiving the real as the product of thought', whereas for Marx 'this is by no means the process by which the concrete itself comes into being'. In Hegelian idealism, Marx argues, 'the movement of the categories appears as the real act of production ... whose product is the world'; 'conceptual thinking is the real human being' and 'the conceptual world as such is thus the only reality', not only representing the real world in ideas but also operating as its constitutive process. For Marx, by contrast, the economic categories exist as 'abstract relation[s] within an already given, concrete, living whole' (Marx 1973: 101); they 'express the forms of being, the determinations of existence' [*Daseinsformen, Existenzbestimmungen*] (Marx 1973: 106). Exchange value, for instance, presupposes population and the fact that it produces within determinate relations. Marx emphasized several times, in opposition to Hegel, that 'the concrete totality, [as] a totality of thoughts, [qua] concrete in thought, [is] in fact a product of thinking and comprehending', but that it is 'not in any way a product of the concept which thinks and generates itself'. For 'the real subject retains its autonomous existence outside the head just as before.... Hence, in the theoretical method, too, the subject, society, must always be kept in mind as the presupposition' (Marx 1973: 101–2).

In reality, however, Marx's interpretation does not do justice to Hegel's philosophy. A number of passages in the latter's work show that, unlike the transcendental idealism of Johann Gottlieb Fichte and the objective idealism of Friedrich Schelling, his thought did not confuse the movement of knowledge with the order of nature, the subject with the object. Thus, in the second paragraph of the *Encyclopedia of the Philosophical Sciences*, he clearly writes:

> [The] thinking study of things may serve, in a general way, as a description of philosophy ... the strictly human and thought-induced phenomena of consciousness do not originally appear in the form of a thought, but as a feeling, a perception, or mental image – all of which aspects must be distinguished from the form of thought proper.
>
> (Hegel 1892: 4)

In the *Philosophy of Right*, too, in an addition to Paragraph 32 inserted by Eduard Gans in the second edition of 1827,[19] some sentences not only confirm the error of Marx's interpretation of Hegel but actually demonstrate the way in which they influenced his own reflections (see Jánoska *et al.* 1994: 115–19).

> [W]e cannot say that property existed [*dagewesen*] before the family, yet, in spite of that, property must be dealt with first. Consequently you might here raise the question why we do not begin at the highest point, i.e. with the concretely true. The answer is that it is precisely the truth in the form of a result that we are looking for, and for this purpose it is essential to start by grasping the abstract concept itself. What is actual, the shape in which the concept is embodied, is for us therefore the secondary thing and the sequel, even if it were itself first in the actual world. The development we are studying is that whereby the abstract forms reveal themselves not as self-subsistent but as false.
>
> (Hegel 1952: 233)

In the 'Introduction', Marx goes on to ask whether the simple categories could exist before, and independently of, the more concrete ones. In the case of possession or property – the category with which Hegel had begun the *Philosophy of Right* – he maintained that it could not have existed before the emergence of 'more concrete relations' such as the family, and that it would be absurd to analyse 'the individual savage' as a property-owner. But the question was more complicated. For money existed 'historically before capital existed, before banks existed, before wage labour existed' (Marx 1973: 102). It appeared before the development of more complex realities, thereby demonstrating that in some cases the sequence of logical categories follows the historical sequence – the more developed as well as the more recent (see Marx 1973: 247) – and 'the path of abstract thought, rising from the simple to the combined, would correspond to the real historical process' (Marx 1973: 102).[20] In antiquity, however, money performed a dominant function only in trading nations. Hence it 'makes a historic appearance in its full intensity only in the most developed conditions of society'; or, 'although the simpler category may have existed historically before the more concrete, it can achieve its full (intensive and extensive) development precisely in a combined form of society'.

This conclusion applied even more to the category of labour. For, although it appeared with the first civilizing of human beings and seemed to be a very simple process, Marx underlined that, 'when it is economically conceived ... "labour" is as modern a category as are the relations which create this simple abstraction' (Marx 1973: 103). The exponents of bullionism and mercantilism had maintained that the source of wealth was lodged in money, and that it therefore had greater importance than labour. Subsequently, the Physiocrats argued that labour was the ultimate creator of wealth, but only in the form of agricultural labour. Smith's work finally put an end to any 'limiting specification of wealth-creating activity', so that now labour was considered no longer in a particular form but as 'labour as such': 'not only manufacturing, or commercial or agricultural labour, but one as well as the others.' In this way, the 'abstract expression' was discovered 'for the simplest and most ancient relation in which human beings – in whatever form of society – play the role of producers'. As in the case of money, the category of 'labour' could be extracted only where there was 'the richest possible concrete development', in a society where 'one thing appears as common to many, to all'. Thus, 'indifference towards any specific kind of labour presupposes a very developed totality of real kinds of labour, of which no single one is any longer predominant'.

In capitalist society, moreover, 'labour in general' is not only a category but 'corresponds to a form of society in which individuals can with ease transfer from one labour to another, and where the specific kind is a mater of chance for them, hence of indifference'. The worker's labour then loses the corporate, craft character that it had in the past and becomes 'labour in general', 'labour *sans phrase*' – 'not only the category, labour, but labour in reality' (Marx 1973: 104). Wage labour 'is not this or another labour, but labour pure and simple, abstract labour; absolutely indifferent to its particular specificity [*Bestimmtheit*], but capable of all specificities' (Marx 1973: 296). In short, it is a question of 'a purely mechanical activity, hence indifferent to its particular form' (Marx 1973: 297).[21]

At the end of his discussion of the relationship between the simplest and the most concrete categories, Marx concluded that in the most modern forms of bourgeois society – he had in mind the United States – the abstraction of the category 'labour in general' was becoming 'true in practice'. Thus, 'the simplest abstraction, . . . which modern economics places at the head of its discussions, and which expresses an immeasurably ancient relation valid in all forms of society, nevertheless achieves practical truth as an abstraction only as a category of the most modern society' (Marx 1973: 104–5). Or, as he reaffirmed elsewhere in the *Grundrisse*, the category 'becomes real only with the development of a particular material mode of production and of a particular stage in the development of the industrial productive forces' (Marx 1973: 297).[22]

Indifference to the particular kind of labour is, however, a phenomenon common to a number of historical realities. In this case too, therefore, it was necessary to underline the distinctions: 'There is a devil of a difference between barbarians who are fit by nature to be used for anything, and civilized people who apply themselves to everything.' Once again relating the abstraction to real history,[23] Marx found his thesis confirmed:

> This example of labour shows strikingly how even the most abstract categories, despite their validity – precisely because of their abstractness – for all epochs, are nevertheless, in the specific character of this abstraction, themselves likewise a product of historic relations, and possess their full validity only for and within these relations.
>
> (Marx 1973: 105)

Having made this point, Marx turned to another crucial issue. In what order should he set out the categories in the work he was about to write? To the question as to whether the complex should furnish the instruments with which to understand the simple, or the other way round, he decisively opted for the first possibility.

> Bourgeois society is the most complex historic organization of production. The categories which express its relations, the comprehension of its structure, thereby also allow insights into the structure and the relations of production of all the vanquished social formations out of whose ruins and elements it built itself up, whose partly still unconquered remnants are carried along with it.
>
> (Marx 1973: 105)

It is the present, then, which offers the indications for a reconstruction of the past. 'Human anatomy contains a key to the anatomy of the ape ... [and] the intimations of higher development among the subordinate animal species ... can be understood only after the higher development is already known' (Marx 1973: 105). This well-known statement should not, however, be read in evolutionist terms. Indeed, Marx explicitly criticized the conception of 'so-called historical evolution', based on the banality that 'the latest form regards the previous ones as steps leading up to itself' (Marx 1973: 106). Unlike the theorists of evolutionism, who posited a naïvely progressive trajectory from the simplest to the most complex organisms, Marx chose to use an opposite, much more complex logical method and elaborated a conception of history marked by the succession of modes of production (ancient, Asiatic, feudal, capitalist), which was meant to explain the positions and functions that the categories assumed within those various modes (cf. Hall 2003: 133).[24] It was bourgeois society, therefore, which provided the clues for an understanding of the economies of previous historical epochs – although, given the profound differences between societies, the clues should be treated with moderation. Marx emphatically repeated that this could not be done 'in the manner of those economists who smudge over all historical differences and see bourgeois relations in all forms of society' (Marx 1973: 105).

Although this argument is in line with those expressed in previous works, Marx here tackles differently the thorny question of the order to be assigned to the economic categories. He had already addressed it in *The Poverty of Philosophy*, where, in opposition to Proudhon's wish to follow not 'history in accordance with the order of events, but in accordance with the succession of ideas' (Proudhon 1972: 184), he had criticized the idea of 'constructing the world by the movement of thought' (Marx 1976: 175). Thus in 1847, in his polemic with the logical–dialectical method employed by Proudhon and Hegel, Marx had preferred a rigorously historical sequence. But ten years later, in the 'Introduction', his position changed: he rejected the criterion of chronological succession for the scientific categories, in favour of a logical method with historical–empirical checks. Since the present helped one to understand the past, or the structure of man the structure of the ape, it was necessary to begin the analysis from the most mature stage, capitalist society, and more particularly from the element that predominated there over all others: capital. 'Capital is the all-dominating economic power of bourgeois society. It must form the starting-point as well as the finishing-point' (Marx 1973: 107). And Marx concluded:

> It would therefore be unfeasible and wrong to let the economic categories follow one another in the same sequence as that in which they were historically decisive. Their sequence is determined, rather, by their relation to one another in modern bourgeois society, which is precisely the opposite of that which seems to be their natural order or which corresponds to historical development. The point is not the historic position of the economic relations in the succession of different forms of society. Even less is it their sequence 'in the idea' (Proudhon) (a muddy notion of historic movement). Rather, their order within modern bourgeois society.
>
> (Marx 1973: 107–8)

In essence, setting out the categories in a precise logical order and the working of real history do not coincide with each other – and moreover, as Marx wrote in the manuscripts for the third volume of *Capital*, 'all science would be superfluous if the outward appearance and the essence of things directly coincided' (Marx 1998: 804).

Marx, then, arrived at his own synthesis by diverging from the empiricism of the early economists, which yielded a dissolution of concrete elements into abstract definitions; from the method of the classical economists, which reduced thought about reality to reality itself; from philosophical idealism – including, in Marx's view, Hegel's philosophy – which he accused of giving thought the capacity to produce the concrete; from gnoseological conceptions that rigidly counterposed forms of thought and objective reality; from historicism and its dissolution of the logical into the historical; and, finally, from his own conviction in *The Poverty of Philosophy* that he was essentially following 'the march of history' (Marx 1976: 172). His aversion to establishing a one-to-one correspondence between the concrete and thought led him to separate the two by recognizing the specificity of the latter and assigning to the former an existence independent of thought, so that the order of exposition of the categories differed from that which manifested itself in the relations of the real historical process (cf. Althusser and Balibar 1979: 47–8, 87). To avoid limiting the cognitive process to a mere repetition of the stages of what had happened in history, it was necessary to use a process of abstraction, and therefore categories that allowed for the interpretation of society in all its complexity. On the other hand, to be really useful for this purpose, abstraction had to be constantly compared with various historical realities, in such a way that the general logical determinations could be distinguished from the concrete historical relations. Marx's conception of history thereby gained in efficacy and incisiveness: once a symmetry of logical order and actual historical order had been rejected, the historical became decisive for the understanding of reality, while the logical made it possible to conceive history as something other than a flat chronology of events.[25] For Marx, it was not necessary to reconstruct the historical genesis of every economic relationship in order to understand society and then give an adequate description of it. As he put it in one passage of the *Grundrisse*:

> our method indicates the points where historical investigation must enter in, or where bourgeois economy as a merely historical form of the production process points beyond itself to earlier historical modes of production. In order to develop the laws of bourgeois economy, therefore, it is not necessary to write the real history of the relations of production. But the correct observation and deduction of these laws, as having themselves become in history, always leads to primary equations ... which point towards a past lying behind this system. These indications, together with a correct grasp of the present, then also offer the key to the understanding of the past.... This correct view likewise leads at the same time to the points at which there is an indication of the overcoming of the present form of production relations – and hence foreshadowings of the future, a movement of becoming. Just as, on one side, the pre-bourgeois phases appear as *merely historical*, i.e. superseded presuppositions, so do the contemporary conditions of production likewise appear as engaged in *superseding themselves* and hence in positing the *historical presuppositions* for a new society.
>
> (Marx 1973: 460–1, trans. modified)

The method developed by Marx had provided him with tools not only to understand the differences among all the modes in which production had manifested itself in history, but also to discern in the present the tendencies prefiguring a new mode of production and therefore confounding all those who had proclaimed the inalterability of capitalism. His own research, including in epistemology, never had an exclusively theoretical motive; it was always driven by the need to interpret the world in order to engage better in the political struggle.

In fact, Marx broke off the section on method with a sketch of the order in which he intended to write his 'Economics'. It is the first of the many plans for his work that he drafted in the course of his life, one that goes back over his reflections in the preceding pages of the 'Introduction'. Before he actually began to compose the *Grundrisse*, he had intended to deal with:

> (1) the general, abstract determinations which obtain in more or less all forms of society [...; then] (2) the categories which make up the inner structure of bourgeois society and on which the fundamental classes rest [:] capital, wage labour, landed property [;] (3) concentration of bourgeois society in the form of the state. Viewed in relation to itself [;] (4) the international relation of production.... International exchange [; and] (5) The world market and crises.
>
> (Marx 1973: 108)

Such at least was Marx's schema in August 1857, which subsequently underwent so many changes.

The uneven relationship between material and intellectual production

The last section of the 'Introduction' comprises a brief and fragmentary list of eight arguments that Marx intended to deal with in his work, plus a few considerations on the relationship between Greek art and modern society. On the eight points, Marx's main notes concern: his conviction that the characteristics of wage labour manifested themselves in the army even earlier than in bourgeois society; the idea of a dialectic between productive forces and relations of production; and what he calls the 'uneven development' [*ungleiche Entwicklung*] between relations of production and legal relations, particularly the derivation of the law of nascent bourgeois society from Roman private law. All this is by way of a memorandum, however, without any structure, and it provides only a vague idea of Marx's thinking on these matters.

His reflections on art are somewhat more developed, focusing on the 'uneven relationship [*ungleiche Verhältniß*] between material production and artistic development' (Marx 1973: 109, trans. modified). Marx had already tackled the relationship between production and forms of consciousness in two early works. In the *Economic and Philosophical Manuscripts of 1844* he had argued that 'religion, family, state, law, morality, science, art, etc., are only *particular* modes of production, and fall under its general law' (Marx 1975b: 297), and in *The German Ideology* he had declared:

> The production of ideas, of conceptions, of consciousness, is at first directly interwoven with the material activity and the material intercourse of men.... Conceiving, thinking, the mental intercourse of men appear at this stage as the direct efflux [*direkter Ausfluß*] of their material behaviour.
>
> (Marx and Engels 1976: 36)

In the 'Introduction', however, far from affirming the kind of rigid parallelism that many Marxists later postulated, Marx stressed that there was no direct relationship between social–economic development and artistic production. Reworking certain ideas in *The Historical View of the Literature of the South of Europe* by Leonard Simonde de Sismondi, which he had read and excerpted in one of his 1852 notebooks,[26] he now wrote: 'In the case of the arts, it is well known that certain periods of their flowering are out of all proportion to the general development of society, hence also to the material foundation [*materiellen Grundlage*], the skeletal structure ... of its organization'. He also pointed out that certain art forms – the epic, for instance – 'are possible only at an undeveloped stage of artistic development. If this is the case with the relation between different kinds of art within the realm of the arts, it is already less puzzling that it is the case in the relation of the entire realm to the general development of society' (Marx

1973: 110). Greek art presupposed Greek mythology, that is, an 'unconsciously artistic' representation of social forms. But, in an advanced society such as that of the modern age, in which people conceive of nature rationally, not as an external power standing over and against them, mythology loses its *raison d'être* and the epic can no longer be repeated: 'Is Achilles possible with powder and lead? Or the *Iliad* with the printing press...? Do not the song and the saga and the muse necessarily come to an end with the printer's bar, hence do not the necessary conditions of epic poetry vanish' (Marx 1973: 111)?[27]

For Marx, then, art and intellectual production in general must be investigated in their relationship to the material conditions of society, but without drawing a rigid correspondence between the two spheres. Otherwise one would fall into Voltaire's error (recalled by Marx in his economic manuscripts of 1861–3) of thinking that 'because we are further ahead than the ancients in mechanics' we should 'be able to make an epic too' (Marx 1989a: 182–3).

Having considered the artist as a creating subject, Marx turned to artistic production and the public that derives enjoyment from it. This presented the greatest difficulties of interpretation. The difficulty was 'not in understanding that the Greek arts and epic are bound up with certain forms of social development', but 'that they still afford us artistic pleasure and that in a certain respect they count as a norm and as an unattainable model'. The real problem was to understand why the artistic creations of antiquity were still a source of enjoyment for modern men and women. According to Marx, the answer was that the Greek world represents 'the historic childhood of humanity', a period that exercises an 'eternal charm' as 'a stage never to return' (Marx 1973: 111). Hence the conclusion:

> The charm of their art for us is not in contradiction to the undeveloped stage of society on which it grew. [It] is its result, rather, and is inextricably bound up ... with the fact that the unripe social conditions under which it arose, and could alone arise, can never return.
>
> (Marx 1973: 111)

The value of Marx's statements on aesthetics in the 'Introduction' does not, however, lie in the sketchy and sometimes unconvincing solutions they offer, but rather in his anti-dogmatic approach as to how the forms of material production are related to intellectual creations and behaviour. His awareness of their 'uneven development' involved rejection of any schematic procedure that posited a uniform relationship among the various spheres of the social totality (Marx 1973: 109). Even the well-known thesis in the 'Preface' to *A Contribution to the Critique of Political Economy*, published two years after Marx wrote the 'Introduction' – 'the mode of production of material life conditions the general process of social, political and intellectual life' (Marx 1987a: 263) – should not be interpreted in a determinist sense;[28] it should be clearly distinguished from the narrow and predictable reading of 'Marxism-Leninism', in which the superstructural phenomena of society are merely a reflection of the material existence of human beings.[29]

Conclusion

When Marx embarked on the *Grundrisse*, he intended to preface his 'Economics' with a section on his research methodology. The 'Introduction' was not composed simply for the purpose of self-clarification; it was supposed to contain, as in the writings of other economists, the author's preliminary observations on his general subject. In June 1859, however, when Marx sent the first part of his studies for publication as *A Contribution to the Critique of Political Economy*, he decided to omit the section setting forth his motivation:

> A general introduction, which I had drafted, is omitted, since on further consideration it seems to me confusing to anticipate results which still have to be substantiated, and the reader who really wishes to follow me will have to decide to advance from the particular to the general [*von dem Einzelnen zum Allgemeinen aufzusteigen*]
>
> (Marx 1987a: 261)

Hence, the guiding aim of 1857 – 'rising from the abstract to the concrete' (Marx 1973: 101) – changed in the text of 1859 to 'to advance from the particular to the general' (Marx 1987a: 261). The starting-point of the 'Introduction' – the most abstract and universal determinations – was replaced with a concrete and historically determined reality: the commodity, but, since the text of 1857 had remained unpublished, no explanation was given of the change. In fact, already in the last passage of the *Grundrisse*, after hundreds of pages in which he had scrupulously analysed the capitalist mode of production and the concepts of political economy, Marx asserted that 'the first category in which bourgeois wealth presents itself is that of the *commodity*' (Marx 1973: 881). He would devote to its investigation the first chapter both of the *A Contribution to the Critique of Political Economy* and of *Capital*, where the commodity is defined as the 'elementary form' (Marx 1996: 45, trans. modified) of capitalist society, the particular with whose analysis the research had to begin.

Instead of the planned introduction, Marx opened the work of 1859 with a brief 'Preface' in which he succinctly outlined his intellectual biography and the so-called materialist conception of history. Subsequently he no longer engaged in the discourse on method, except on very rare occasions and with a few swift observations. Certainly the most important of these was the 1873 'Postscript' to the first volume of *Capital*, in which, having been roused by the reviews that accompanied its publication, he could not refrain from expressing himself about his method of investigation and revisiting some of the themes present in the 'Introduction'. Another reason for this was the need he felt to assert the difference between method of exposition and method of investigation: whereas the former could start with the general, moving from the universal form to historically determined forms and hence – in a confirmation of the formulation of 1857 – 'rising from the abstract to the concrete', the latter had to start from the immediate reality and, as he put it in 1859, move 'from the particular to the general':

the method of presentation [*Darstellungsweise*] must differ in form from that of inquiry [*Forschungsweise*]. The latter has to appropriate the material in detail, to analyse its different forms of development, to trace out their inner connexion. Only after this work is done, can the actual movement be adequately described.[30]

(Marx 1996: 19)

In his work after the 1857 'Introduction', then, Marx no longer wrote on questions of method in the open and problematizing way that had characterized that text but expressed his finished ideas on them without betraying the complex genesis through which they had been worked out (cf. Carver 1975: 135). For this reason, too, the pages of the 'Introduction' are extraordinarily important. In a close encounter with the ideas of some of the greatest economists and philosophers, Marx there reaffirms profound convictions and arrives at significant theoretical acquisitions. First of all, he insists again on the historical specificity of the capitalist mode of production and its social relations. Second, he considers production, distribution, exchange and consumption as a totality, in which production constitutes the element predominating over the other parts of the whole. Moreover, with regard to the reproduction of reality in thought, Marx does not resort to a merely historical method but makes use of abstraction, having come to recognize its value for the construction of the path of knowledge. Finally, he underlines the uneven relationship that obtains between the development of the relations of production and intellectual relations.

In the 100 years since they were first published, these reflections have made the 'Introduction' an indispensable theoretical text as well as a fascinating one from a literary point of view, for all serious interpreters and readers of Marx. This will surely be the case also for those who come anew to his work in future generations.

[Translated from the Italian by Patrick Camiller]

Notes

1 In a letter to Ferdinand Lassalle on 12 November 1858, Marx wrote that 'economics as a science in the German sense of the word has yet to be tackled' (Marx and Engels 1983: 355).
2 The voluminous critical literature on the 'Introduction' is one token of its importance. Since its first publication in 1903, all the main critical interpretations, intellectual biographies and introductions to Marx's thought have taken account of it, and it has been the object of numerous articles and commentaries. Among the latter, see in particular Carver (1975: 88–158).
3 Marx dealt with these themes in detail in the section of the *Grundrisse* devoted to 'Forms which Precede Capitalist Production' (Marx 1973: 471–513).
4 This conception of an Aristotelian matrix – the family preceding the birth of the village – recurs in *Capital*, vol. I, but Marx was said later to have moved away from it. Friedrich Engels pointed out in a note to the third German edition of 1883:

[s]ubsequent very searching study of the primitive conditions of man led the author [i.e. Marx – MM] to the conclusion that it was not the family that origin-

ally developed into the tribe, but that, on the contrary, the tribe was the primitive and spontaneously developed form of human association, on the basis of blood relationship, that out of the first incipient loosening of the tribal bonds, the many and various forms of the family were afterwards developed.

(Marx 1996: 356)

Engels was referring to the studies of ancient history made by himself at the time and by Marx during the final years of his life. The main texts that he read or summarized in his anthropological notebooks, which are still unpublished, were *Researches into the Early History of Mankind and the Development of Civilization* by Edward Burnett Tylor, *Ancient Society* by Lewis Henry Morgan, *The Aryan Village in India and Ceylon* by John Budd Phear, *Lectures on the Early History of Institutions* by Henry Summer Maine and *The Origin of Civilization and the Primitive Condition of Man* by John Lubbock.

5 This mutual dependence should not be confused with that which establishes itself among individuals in the capitalist mode of production: the former is the product of nature, the latter of history. In capitalism, individual independence is combined with a social dependence expressed in the division of labour (see Marx 1987b: 465). At this stage of production, the social character of activity presents itself not as a simple relationship of individuals to one another,

> but as their subordination to relations which subsist independently of them and which arise out of collisions between mutually indifferent individuals. The general exchange of activities and products, which has become a vital condition for each individual – their mutual interconnection – here appears as something alien to them, autonomous, as a thing.
>
> (Marx 1973: 157)

6 The economist who, in Marx's view, had avoided this naïve assumption was James Steuart. Marx commented on numerous passages from Steuart's main work – *An Inquiry into the Principles of Political Economy* – in a notebook that he filled with extracts from it in the spring of 1851 (see Marx 1986).

7 Elsewhere in the *Grundrisse* Marx stated that 'an isolated individual could no more have property in land and soil than he could speak' (Marx 1973: 485); and that '[l]anguage as the product of an individual is an impossibility. But the same holds for property' (Marx 1973: 490).

8 In his editorial commentary on the 'Introduction', Terrell Carver points out (see Carver 1975: 93–5) that Marx's remarks concerning Bastiat's use of Robinson Crusoe do not correspond to what the author actually says. For, according to Bastiat,

> Daniel Defoe would have deprived his novel of every trace of verisimilitude if ... he had not made necessary social concessions by allowing his hero to save from the shipwreck a few indispensable objects, such as provisions, gunpowder, a rifle, an axe, a knife, rope, boards, iron, etc. – decisive evidence that society is man's necessary milieu, since even a novelist cannot make him live outside it. And note that Robinson Crusoe took with him into solitude another *social* treasure worth a thousand times more ... I mean his ideas, his memories, his experience, and especially his language.
>
> (Bastiat 1964: 64)

Nevertheless, Bastiat displays a lack of historical sense in other parts of his work, where the actions of the individual seem dictated by rational economic calculation and are presented in accordance with the splits peculiar to capitalist society: 'An individual in isolation, provided he could survive for any length of time, would be at once capitalist, entrepreneur, workman, producer and consumer' (p. 174). And so Crusoe once again becomes the economists' prosaic stereotype: 'Our Robinson Crusoe will not, therefore, set about making the tool unless he can foresee, when the work is done, a definite saving of his labour in relation to his satisfaction, or an increase in satisfactions for the same amount of labour' (p. 175). Most probably these were the assertions that attracted Marx's attention.

9   See, in particular, the work of its main representative, Wilhelm Roscher (Roscher 1972). In *Capital*, vol. I, Marx made fun of Roscher's 'anatomico-physiological method' (Marx 1996: 216).

10   Shortly after the publication of Marx's 'Introduction' in 1903, and with various analogies to Marx's formulations, Max Weber stressed the utility of 'abstract economic theory' in synthesizing historical phenomena (see Weber 1949: 48f.). In its 'conceptual purity', he wrote, an

> ideal typical concept is not a description of reality but aims to give unambiguous expression to such a description.... This mental construct cannot be found anywhere in reality. It is a utopia. Historical research faces the task of determining in each individual case the extent to which this ideal-construct approximates to or diverges from reality.
>
> (p. 48)

The abstract ideal type represents

> a conceptual construct which is not the historical reality ... it serves neither more nor less than as a schema in which reality is taken as an example: it has the significance of a purely ideal limiting concept, whose reality has to be measured and compared, for the explication of certain significant parts of its empirical content.
>
> (p. 51, trans. modified)

11   A similar idea had already been expressed by Marx in *The German Ideology*, where he and Engels wrote that:

> [t]hese abstractions in themselves, divorced from real history, have no value whatsoever. They can only serve to facilitate the arrangement of historical material, to indicate the sequence of its separate strata.... On the contrary, the difficulties begin only when one sets about the examination and the arrangement of the material – whether of a past epoch or of the present – and its actual presentation.
>
> (Marx and Engels 1976: 37)

12   The more elaborate exposition of this idea is to be found in John Stuart Mill (Mill 1965: 55f.).

13   See Marx's criticisms of Proudhon on this point (Marx 1973: 265).

14   These statements aroused Marx's interest, and in September 1850 he wrote notes on them in one of his notebooks of extracts (see Marx 1983: 36). A few lines further on, however, Mill partly disavowed his categorical assertion, though not in the sense of a historicization of production. 'Distribution', he wrote, 'depends on the laws and customs of society', and since these are the product of 'the opinions and feelings of mankind' – themselves nothing but 'consequences of the fundamental laws of human nature' – the laws of distribution 'are as little arbitrary, and have as much the character of physical laws, as the laws of production' (Mill 1965: 200). His 'Preliminary Remarks' at the beginning of the book may offer a possible synthesis: '[u]nlike the laws of production, those of distribution are partly of human institution: since the manner in which wealth is distributed in any given society depends on the statutes or usages therein prevalent' (Mill 1965: 21).

15   Hence, those like Mill who consider the relations of production as eternal and only their forms of distribution as historical 'show that [they] understand neither the one nor the other' (Marx 1973: 758).

16 Marx knew both texts very well: they were among the first works of political economy he studied, and he copied many extracts from them into his notebooks (see Marx 1981a and Marx 1981b).

17

> For the truth is concrete; that is, whilst it gives a bond and principle of unity, it also possesses an internal source of development. Truth, then, is only possible as a universe or totality of thought; and the freedom of the whole, as well as the necessity of the several sub-divisions, which it implies, are only possible when these are discriminated and defined.
>
> (Hegel 1892: 24)

18 The interpretations of Althusser, Negri and Della Volpe, for example, fall into the error of equating this with Marx's method (see Althusser and Balibar 1979: 87–8; Negri 1991: 47; Della Volpe 1971: 177).

19 The 'additions' [*Zusätze*] inserted by Gans, whose philological scruple has always been doubted by many commentators, are based on certain of Hegel's manuscripts and on transcriptions of his lectures on the philosophy of right after 1821, the year of publication of the first edition.

20 Reflecting on Peruvian society, however, Marx pointed out the opposite: that 'there are very developed but nevertheless historically less mature forms of society, in which the highest forms of economy, e.g. cooperation, a developed division of labour, etc., are found, even though there is no kind of money' (Marx 1973: 102)

21 In another passage, Marx wrote that 'the developed principle of capital is precisely to make special skill superfluous ... to transfer skill, rather, into the dead forces of nature' (Marx 1973: 587).

22 In the *Grundrisse* Marx showed how 'capital in general' was also no mere abstraction but a category that had 'real existence' in capitalist society. Just as particular capitals belong to individual capitalists, so does capital in its general form – which is accumulated in banks, as the capital of a particular nation that can be loaned and thereby valorized – become 'damn real.... While the general is therefore on the one hand only a mental mark of distinction, it is at the same time a particular real form alongside the form of the particular and the individual' (Marx 1973: 450).

23 In a letter to Engels of 2 April 1858 Marx wrote: '[o]n closer examination, the most abstract definitions invariably point to a broader, definite, concrete, historical basis. (Of course, since to the extent that they are definite they have been abstracted there from)' (Marx and Engels 1983: 302).

24 Hall rightly notes that the theory developed by Marx represented a break with historicism, though not a break with historicity.

25 The complexity of the method synthesized by Marx is apparent in the fact that it was misrepresented not only by many students of his work but also by Friedrich Engels. Not apparently having read the theses in the 1857 'Introduction', Engels wrote in 1859, in a review of *A Contribution to the Critique of Political Economy*, that once Marx had elaborated his method he could have undertaken the critique of political economy 'in two ways – historically or logically'. But, as 'history often moves in leaps and bounds and in zigzags, and as this would have [had] to be followed throughout ... the logical method of approach was the only adequate one'. Engels wrongly concluded, however, that this was,

> indeed nothing but the historical method, only stripped of the historical form and of interfering contingencies. The point where this history begins must also be the starting-point of the train of thought, and its further progress will be simply the reflection, in abstract and theoretically consistent form, of the course of history.
>
> (Engels 1980: 475)

In short, Engels held that there was a parallelism between history and logic, which Marx had decisively rejected in the 'Introduction'. And, having been attributed to Marx by Engels, that position later became still more barren and schematic in the Marxist-Leninist interpretation.

26 Sismondi had noted that the highest moments in the older French, Italian, Spanish and Portuguese literature coincided with periods of decline in the very societies that had expressed them. Marx's extracts from Sismondi's work are due to be published for the first time in volume IV/10 of the MEGA². I am grateful to Klaus Pezold for the information regarding Marx's manuscripts.

27 Friedrich Theodor Vischer, in his *Ästhetik oder Wissenschaft des Schönen*, discussed the power of capitalism to dissolve myths. Marx drew inspiration from this work and summarized parts of it in his notebooks, scarcely three months before he wrote the 'Introduction'. But the approaches of the two authors could not have been more different: Vischer treated capitalism as an unalterable reality and deplored in romantic style the aesthetic impoverishment of culture that it brought about; whereas Marx, though constantly fighting for the overcoming of capitalism, emphasized that both materially and ideologically it represented a more advanced reality than previous modes of production (cf. Lukács 1956: 267–8).

28 Evidence of this is the fact that, when Marx quoted this statement in a note to the 1872–5 French edition of *Capital*, he preferred to use the verb *dominer* for the German *bedingen* (more usually translated as '*déterminer*' or '*conditionner*'): 'Le mode de production de la vie matérielle *domine* [dominates] en général le développement de la vie sociale, politique et intellectuelle' (see Marx 1989b: 62, emphasis added). His aim in doing this was precisely to avoid the risk of positing a mechanical relationship between the two aspects (cf. Rubel 1971: 298).

29 The worst and most widely disseminated interpretation of this kind is Joseph Stalin's in *Dialectical and Historical Materialism*: 'the material world represents objective reality ... [and] the spiritual life of society is a reflection of this objective reality'; and 'whatever is the being of a society, whatever are the conditions of material life of a society, such are the ideas, theories, political views and political institutions of that society' (Stalin 1941: 15).

30 Marx added that when this is completed 'it may appear as if we had before us a mere a priori construction', but in reality the outcome is the representation of the concrete in thought. See the letter of 1 February 1858 to Engels, in which Marx makes the following important assertion with regard to Lassalle: '[h]e will discover to his cost that it is one thing for a critique to take a science to the point at which it admits of a dialectical presentation, and quite another to apply an abstract, ready-made system of logic' (Marx and Engels 1983: 261).

References

Althusser, Louis and Balibar, Étienne (1979 [1968]) *Reading Capital*, London: Verso.

Bastiat, Frédéric (1964 [1850]) *Economic Harmonies*, Princeton, NJ: D. van Nostrand Co. Inc.

Carver, Terrell (1975) *Karl Marx: Texts on Method*, Oxford: Blackwell.

Dal Pra, Mario (1965) *La dialettica in Marx*, Bari: Laterza.

Della Volpe, Galvano (1971 [1956]) *Rousseau e Marx*, Rome: Editori Riuniti.

Engels, Friedrich (1980 [1859]) 'Karl Marx, *A Contribution to the Critique of Political Economy*', in *Marx and Engels Collected Works*, vol. 16: *Marx and Engels 1858–60*, London: Lawrence & Wishart, pp. 465–77.

Hall, Stuart (2003 [1974]) 'Marx's Notes on Method: A "Reading" of the "1857 Introduction"', *Cultural Studies*, vol. 17, No. 2: 113–49.

Hegel, G.F.W. (1892 [1817]) *The Logic of Hegel* [*Encyclopedia of the Philosophical Sciences*], 2nd edn, London: Oxford University Press.

Hegel, G.F.W. (1952 [1821]) *Philosophy of Right*, London: Oxford University Press.

Hegel, G.F.W. (1969 [1812, 1813, 1816]) *Science of Logic*, London: George Allen & Unwin.

Korsch, Karl (1938) *Karl Marx*, London: Chapman & Hall.

Jánoska, Judith, Bondeli, Martin, Kindle, Konrad and Hofer, Marc (1994) *Das «Methodenkapitel» von Karl Marx*, Basel: Schwabe & Co.

Lukács, Geörgy (1956 [1954]) 'Karl Marx und Friedrich Theodor Vischer', in *Beiträge zur Geschichte der Ästhetik*, Berlin: Aufbau Verlag.

Marx, Karl (1973 [1857–8]) *Grundrisse: Foundations of the Critique of Political Economy* (*Rough Draft*), Harmondsworth: Penguin.

Marx, Karl (1975a [1843]) 'Contribution to the Critique of Hegel's Philosophy of Law', in *Marx Engels Collected Works*, vol. 3: *Marx and Engels, 1843–44*, Moscow: Progress Publishers, pp. 3–129.

Marx, Karl (1975b [1844]) 'Economic and Philosophic Manuscripts of 1844', *Marx Engels Collected Works*, vol. 3: *Marx and Engels, 1843–44*, Moscow: Progress Publishers, pp. 229–346.

Marx, Karl (1976 [1847]) 'The Poverty of Philosophy', in *Marx Engels Collected Works*, vol. 6: *Marx and Engels 1845–48*, Moscow: Progress Publishers.

Marx, Karl (1981a [1843–4]) 'Exzerpte aus Jean-Baptiste Say: *Traité d'économie politique*', in *Marx Engels Gesamtausgabe* (MEGA²), vol. IV/2, Berlin: Dietz, pp. 301–27.

Marx, Karl (1981b [1844]) 'Exzerpte aus James Mill: *Élemens d'économie politique*', in *Marx Engels Gesamtausgabe* (MEGA²), vol. IV/2, Berlin: Dietz, pp. 428–70.

Marx, Karl (1983 [1850]) 'Exzerpte aus John Stuart Mill: *Principles of Political Economy*', in *Marx Engels Gesamtausgabe* (MEGA²), vol. IV/7: *Karl Marx Friedrich Engels Exzerpte und Notizen September 1849 bis Februar 1851*, Berlin: Dietz Verlag, pp. 39–41.

Marx, Karl (1986 [1851]), 'Exzerpte aus James Steuart: *An Inquiry into the Principles of Political Economy*', in *Marx Engels Gesamtausgabe* (MEGA²), vol. IV/8: *Karl Marx Exzerpte und Notizen März bis Juni 1851*, Berlin: Dietz Verlag, pp. 304, 312–25, 332–49, 373–80, 400–1, 405–8, 429–45.

Marx, Karl (1987a [1859]) 'A Contribution to the Critique of Political Economy', in *Marx and Engels Collected Works*, vol. 29: *Marx 1857–61*, Moscow: Progress Publishers, pp. 257–417.

Marx, Karl (1987b [1958]) 'Original Text of the Second and the Beginning of the Third Chapter of *A Contribution to the Critique of Political Economy*', in *Marx and Engels Collected Works*, vol. 29: *Marx 1857–61*, Moscow: Progress Publishers, pp. 430–510.

Marx, Karl (1989a [1861–3]) 'Theories of Surplus Value', in *Marx Engels Collected Works*, vol. 31: *Economic Manuscripts of 1861–63*, Moscow: Progress Publishers.

Marx, Karl (1989b [1872–5]) 'Le Capital', in *Marx Engels Gesamtausgabe* (MEGA²), vol. II/7, Berlin: Dietz.

Marx, Karl (1996 [1867]), '*Capital*, vol. I', in *Marx and Engels Collected Works*, vol. 35: *Capital, Vol. I*, New York: International Publishers.

Marx, Karl (1998 [1863–7]) '*Capital*, vol. III', in *Marx Engels Collected Works*, vol. 37: *Capital, Vol. III*, New York: International Publishers.

Marx, Karl and Engels, Friedrich (1976 [1845–6]), 'German Ideology', in *Marx Engels Collected Works*, Vol. 5: *Marx and Engels April 1845–April 1847*, Moscow: Progress Publishers.

Marx, Karl and Engels, Friedrich (1983) *Marx and Engels Collected Works*, vol. 40: *Letters 1856–59*, Moscow: Progress Publishers.

Mill, John Stuart (1965 [1848]) *Principles of Political Economy*, vol. I, London: Routledge & Kegan Paul.

Negri, Antonio (1991 [1979]) *Marx beyond Marx: Lessons on the* Grundrisse, New York: Autonomedia.

Proudhon, Pierre-Joseph (1972 [1846]) 'System of Economical Contradictions or, The Philosophy of Misery', in *Works of P. J. Proudhon*, vol. IV: *The Evolution of Capitalism*, New York: Arno Press.

Ricardo, David (1973 [1817]) *The Principles of Political Economy and Taxation*, London: J.M. Dent & Sons.

Roscher, Wilhelm (1972 [1854]) *Principles of Political Economy*, New York: Arno Press.

Rubel, Maximilien (1971 [1957]) *Karl Marx. Essai de biographie intellectuelle*, Paris: Rivière et Cie.

Smith, Adam (1961 [1776]) *The Wealth of Nations*, vol. 1, London: Methuen.

Spinoza, Baruch (1955) 'Letter to Jarig Jellis, 2 June 1674', in *On the Improvement of the Understanding and Other Works*, New York: Dover.

Stalin, J. (1941 [1938]) *Dialectical and Historical Materialism*, London: Lawrence & Wishart.

Vischer, Friedrich Theodor (1975 [1846–57]) *Ästhetik oder Wissenschaft des Schönen*, Hildesheim: Olms.

Watt, Ian (1951) 'Robinson Crusoe as a Myth', *Essays in Criticism*, vol. I, No. 2: 95–119.

Weber, Max (1949 [1904]) '"Objectivity" in Social Science and Social Policy', in *The Methodology of the Social Sciences*, New York: The Free Press.

2 The concept of value in modern economy

On the relationship between money and capital in *Grundrisse*

Joachim Bischoff and Christoph Lieber

Grasping the interconnectedness of the totality

In his outline of a critique of political economy, Marx states that he is to articulate the 'self-criticism of bourgeois society' (Marx 1973: 106). He claims, that is, to combine an understanding of the historical dynamic of the basic economic structures of the capitalist mode of production with an understanding of the way that they unfold on the surface of society. Thus he effectively claims to account for the total social process, in an analysis encapsulated in the concept of 'modern bourgeois society'. In his rough draft of 1857–8, capitalism is conceived of not as an inalterably crystallized structure, but as an 'organic system' (Marx 1973: 278).

The problematic underlying Marx's mode of enquiry and mode of exposition is directly bound up with the conception of capitalism just evoked. Whence the special relevance of Marx's rough draft to the history of his theory: the *Grundrisse* offers insights into the way he deciphers the historically self-totalizing capitalist mode of production from the standpoint of value theory, and of the way he goes about reconstructing it. In the Marxian texts posterior to the *Grundrisse* in which this critique of political economy is pursued, the various levels of the determination of socio-economic forms are ever more finely differentiated and analysed. The fact that Marx's rough draft is, in contrast, a kind of preliminary sketch makes it easier to grasp the interconnectedness of the whole. Whence our central thesis about the *Grundrisse*: Marx's sketch makes it possible to arrive at a notion of bourgeois society as a totality.

Marx would later say about the critique of political economy that 'the basis, the starting-point for the physiology of the bourgeois system – for the understanding of its internal organic coherence and its life-process – is the determination of *value by labour-time*' (Marx 1989: 391). The physiological metaphor reflects the projected structure of his analysis, which sets out to reconstruct the internal interrelations of the bourgeois–capitalist world system. To understand this particular economic form of society as a self-reproducing, evolving process, it is necessary to grasp the material life-process. Here one must not be led astray by surface appearances; one has to delve beneath the surface to expose the anatomy or physiology of bourgeois society. At the surface level, the existing world of commodities with its autonomous forms of wealth – wage labour, capital, and ground rent – appears, under the conditions of competition, as the multiplicity of market processes. Marx, however, proposes to reconstruct the various phenomenal forms and the movement on the surface of capitalist society as an organic, internal totality by setting out from value and the objective form in which this social labour appears. He contends that a grasp of the anatomy and phenomenal life-process at the surface also holds the key to the anatomy of pre-capitalist social formations. Thus he affirms that 'political economy perceives, discovers the root of the historical struggle and development' (Marx 1989: 392).

Proceeding from the hypothesis that value is determined by labour-time to a reconstruction of the economic categories in a systematic structure thus pre-supposes a lengthy research process, both in society and also individually. His task would have been an easy one if it could be taken for granted that the key category of 'value' constitutes, as it were, a universal starting point. But one of the most important results of the *Grundrisse*, as Marx saw it, was his realization that 'the economic concept of value does not occur in antiquity ... the concept of value is entirely peculiar to the most modern economy' (Marx 1973: 776). This leads on to the conclusion that the fundamental task 'for critique' is 'to take a science to the point at which it admits of a dialectical presentation' (Marx and Engels 1983: 261). Only after repeatedly approaching the question of how to present the categories in the *Grundrisse* does Marx conclude that 'the first cat-egory in which bourgeois wealth presents itself is that of the *commodity*' (Marx 1973: 881), and that it is possible to grasp determinate economic relationships – exchange value, value, the value form – in the material body of the commodity. It then becomes possible to derive, from determinations of the commodity, both money and simple commodity exchange. The problem for the exposition here is that 'the process by which values within the money system are determined by labour time does not belong in the examination of money itself, and falls outside circulation; proceeds behind it as its effective base and presupposition' (Marx 1973: 794).

In the *Grundrisse* Marx works out his point of departure (the commodity as the elementary form of bourgeois wealth) by reducing the many interconnec-tions among the economic categories. Yet he is at pains to keep the social back-ground visible throughout. 'It will be necessary later', he admonishes himself, 'to correct the idealist manner of the presentation, which makes it seem as if it were merely a matter of conceptual determinations and of the dialectic of these concepts' (Marx 1973: 151).

The production of wealth and relations of domination

At the centre of Marx's reduction of the circular movement of the categories stands, above all, the theory of surplus value, the conception of the capitalist production process as a process of labour, valorization and exploitation. Grasp-ing the system of exploitation as a whole calls – like the mode of exposition developed by Marx – for intense conceptual effort. It is a well documented historical fact that, long before capitalism, societies produced surplus products on the basis of surplus labour. The production of this wealth is bound up with prevailing relations of domination. The hierarchical forms and structures required by production (patriarchal relations, slavery, serfdom and so on) determine the forms of labour and the appropriation of surplus product or surplus labour. Capitalism relegates these forms of domination to the margins and, with capital as a set of objective social relations resting on the exchange of commodities and money, engenders a specific relation of domination rooted in the separation of civil society from state–political society. This transformation allows insights into the structures of earlier historical processes. The imperative need to generate surplus labour – on the basis of a thoroughly transformed dynamic of the development of needs and the social division of labour – leads to the creation of an excess product and the freeing up of socially available labour time. The resulting form of interrelation between labour and surplus labour differs from that prevailing in 'the earlier mode of production', but it is a form

> which heightens the continuity and intensity of labour; increase production, is more favourable to the development of *variations in labour capacity* and accordingly to the differentiation of modes of labour and gaining a living, and finally dissolves the relationship between the owner of the conditions of labour and the workers into a pure *relation of purchase and sale*, or a money *relation*, and *eliminates* from the relation of exploitation all patriarchal, political or even religious admixtures.
>
> (Marx 1994: 431)

The argument does not purport to show that traditional forms of domination and subordination were dissolved and then lapsed into insignificance; rather, the objective is to grasp the specific form of the socialization of labour in bourgeois society. This, in turn, grounds a systematic discussion of the historical process and a conceptualization of various relations of domination and oppression. Bourgeois society is based on separation from the political sphere and the state.

> This indeed is a condition very different from that in which the individual or the individual member of a family or clan (later, community) directly and naturally reproduces himself, or in which his production activity and his share in production are bound to a specific form of labour and of product.
>
> (Marx 1973: 157)

The material social life-process appears for itself, while the structures of dependency in the capital–wage labour relation seem to spring from nature or to be an objective expression of the forms of social labour. The capitalist's domination of the wage-labourer appears as an objective constraint, and the nature of objectified labour imposes the subordination of the living capacity for labour; this structure is simultaneously the 'elaboration and emergence of the general *foundation* of the relations of personal dependence'. Capitalist commodity production makes possible an appropriation of pre-capitalist history and is, at the same time, an 'epoch-making mode of exploitation, which in the course of its historical development revolutionizes the entire economic structure of society by its organization of the labour process and its gigantic extension of technique, and towers incomparably above all earlier epochs' (Marx 1997: 43).

The fundamental difficulty when it comes to apprehending or intellectually reconstructing the internal interrelations of the economic categories or the hidden structure of the bourgeois economic system stems from the fact that abstract determinations such as value, labour and so on only become possible with bourgeois society, on the one hand, but, on the other, are expressions of general determinations valid for pre-bourgeois societies as well. One must, after all, steer clear of the mistaken notion that the internal connections between the categories are at all points identical with the real historical process. Marx summarizes this crucial result of his research in the *Grundrisse* in a letter to his friend and political comrade Engels: value is the concept that holds the key to the hidden internal structure of bourgeois society. 'Value "as such"', he writes,

> has no substance other than actual labour. This definition of value … is simply bourgeois wealth in its most abstract form. As such, it already presupposes 1. the transcending of indigenous communism (India, etc.) 2. of all undeveloped, pre-bourgeois modes of production, which are not in every respect governed by exchange. Although an abstraction, it is an historical abstraction and hence feasible only when grounded on a specific economic development of society.
>
> (Marx and Engels 1983: 298)

Regarding labour as a historically specific abstraction paves the way to comprehension of the economic categories, since the various derivative and combined forms of social wealth are here bracketed out, revealing the source of wealth and thus of surplus labour to be 'labour as such' (Marx 1973: 103). 'This economic relation', Marx says of wage labour,

> therefore develops more purely and adequately in proportion as labour loses all the characteristics of art; as its particular skill becomes something more and more abstract and irrelevant.… Here it can be seen once again that the particular specificity of the relation of production, of the category … becomes real only with the development of a particular *material mode of production* and of a particular stage in the development of the industrial *productive forces*
>
> (Marx 1973: 297)

This would seem to mandate the conclusion that an examination of the internal physiology or anatomy of the economic structure of bourgeois society should set out directly from the category of social labour. Marx rejects this fallacy, because social labour, precisely, does not appear as the elementary form of bourgeois wealth. What appears in its place is its objective inversion; in other words, social labour presents itself, so to speak, as a natural attribute of the commodity and other ossified forms of social wealth.

> To develop the concept of capital it is necessary to begin not with labour but with value, and, precisely, with exchange value in an already developed movement of circulation. It is just as impossible to make the transition directly from labour to capital as it is to go from the different human races directly to the banker, or from nature to the steam engine.
>
> (Marx 1973: 259)

The inversion of subject and object, the transformation of subjective interrelations into a web of seemingly natural relations between things, dominates the whole of the bourgeois life-process; if it is to be comprehended and criticized, the starting point has to be the determination of value by labour-time.

This dovetailing of the different levels of the problem, analysed by Marx in the *Grundrisse*, has long engendered debates and misunderstandings ranged under the rubrics 'dialectical and historical materialism'. Marx's fundamental thesis has it that the central categories grounding an understanding of capital and, as well, of the general preconditions of capitalist production – value, money and so on – can be elaborated only on the basis of a determinate level of development of capitalist society. Yet these abstract moments do not, by themselves, make it possible to grasp a real, historical stage of production (see Marx 1973: 88).

Political economy, one of the sciences of bourgeois society, has to do with specific social forms of wealth and the forms of its production. These general determinations, common to all levels of production, were of scientific interest

> in the first beginnings of the science, when the social forms of bourgeois production had still laboriously to be peeled out of the material, and, with great effort, to be established as independent objects of study. In fact, however, the use value of the commodity is a given presupposition – the material basis in which a specific economic relation presents itself. It is only this specific relation which stamps the use value as a commodity.
>
> (Marx 1973: 881)

> The wealth of those societies in which the capitalist mode of production prevails, presents itself as 'an immense accumulation of commodities'; the individual commodity appears as its elementary form. Our investigation therefore begins with the analysis of the commodity.
>
> (Marx 1996: 45, trans. modified)

Because the commodity form of the product of labour or the value form of the commodity is the basis or simplest structure of bourgeois society, the critique of political economy has to begin with a critical analysis of this economic cell or elementary form. In this simplest relation, it is already possible to discern the inversion that makes social relations appear as relations between things which ultimately hold sway over human beings. Without their own active involvement and awareness, people find the forms of the social creation of value in something that exists, ready-made, as an objective totality standing outside them and alongside them:

> Men are … related to each other in their social process in a purely atomistic way. Hence their relations to each other in production assume a material character independent of their control and conscious individual action. These facts manifest themselves at first by products as a general rule taking the form of commodities.
>
> (Marx 1996: 103, trans. modified)

When one sets out from the analysis of this particular social relation (commodity value) and its contradictions, it becomes possible to develop the category of money; from the analysis of money, or, rather, simple circulation as a surface feature of bourgeois society, it becomes possible to develop the determinations of the concept of capital.

> The exact development of the concept of capital [is] necessary, since it is the fundamental concept of modern economics, just as capital itself, whose abstract, reflected image [is] its concept, [is] the foundation of bourgeois society. The sharp formulation of the basic presuppositions of the relation must bring out all the contradictions of bourgeois production, as well as the boundary where it drives beyond itself.
>
> (Marx 1973: 331)

The bourgeois–capitalist law of appropriation

In the 'Chapter on Money', Marx begins with the idea that capital as a relation of production is subordinate to simple circulation:

> In this first section, where exchange values, money, prices are looked at, commodities always appear as already present. The determination of forms is simple. We know that they express aspects of social production, but the latter itself is the precondition. However, they are *not posited* in this character (of being aspects of social production).
>
> (Marx 1973: 227)

At the same time, however, he wonders, as we have seen, whether the elementary forms of value, precisely because of their elementary, general character, are not attributable to all modes of production, rather than being the specific, most abstract expression of capital *alone*. That is why the systematic presentation of the *Grundrisse* does not begin with the elementary form of *bourgeois* wealth *strictu sensu*. Similarly, the 'Manifestation of the law of appropriation in simple circulation' (Marx 1987a: 461) is not as exactly conceived as it will be later. Thus we find the following programmatic formulation in the passage that serves as a transition from the 'Chapter on Money' to the 'Chapter on Capital':

> As we have seen, in simple circulation as such (exchange value in its movement), the action of the individuals on one another is, in its content, only a reciprocal, self-interested satisfaction of their needs; in its form, [it is] exchange value among equals (equivalents). Property, too, is still posited here only as the appropriation of the product of labour by labour, and of the product of alien labour by one's own labour, in so far as the product of one's own labour is bought by alien labour. Property in alien labour is mediated by the equivalent of one's own labour. This form of property – quite like freedom and equality – is posited in this simple relation. In the further development of exchange value this will be transformed, and it will ultimately be shown that private property in the product of one's own labour is identical with the separation of labour and property, so that labour will create alien property and property will command alien labour.
>
> (Marx 1973: 238)

The notion that the first law of appropriation is identical with the second – even if this identity is taken to arise from the immanent development of value or its various forms – does not provide the basis for an adequate conception of the typical 'dialectical reversal' of the laws of appropriation of the bourgeois–capitalist mode of production. Marx has not quite seen through the deceptive appearance of the first law of appropriation, which emerges solely on the basis of the specifically capitalist mode of appropriation and itself reveals, if in mystified fashion, that that *is* its basis. The reason is that his point of departure here is the propertyless individual who is transformed into a property-owner only as the consequence of a process of appropriation. Property grounded in one's own labour is *posited* only when such property is shown to be the phenomenal form of an altogether different process, the capitalist production process, thus revealing that the identity presumed earlier was merely apparent.

This inadequate theorization of the historically specific character of the conditions of simple circulation breeds further misconceptions. Thus, in considering the transition to capital, Marx evokes the return of exchange value to its source, the activity which posits exchange values, as if this activity had already been an object of the foregoing discussion. Similarly, he evokes the positing of labour as wage labour, in consequence of which 'labour has changed its relation to its objectivity' (Marx 1973: 263), quite as if he had earlier assumed the existence of some other, non-alienating type of appropriation.

Marx manages to dispense with this set of problems in the course of writing his 'rough draft', but only after delving further into the interrelation between value and capital. It then emerges that value is a relation posited, in its social average, by capital itself, and that it shapes the whole process of reproduction. Once it has been understood that the concept of value is, in every respect, a historically determinate abstraction of the capitalist mode of production, a preliminary discussion of the general characteristics of production or of exchange value not only seems quite superfluous, but is, indeed, positively ruled out: 'Everything else is empty chatter. Only at the end, and as a result of the whole development, can it become clear which aspects belong in the first section, "Production in General", and which in the first section of the second section, "Exchange Value in General"' (Marx 1973: 320).

The exact definition of the 'dialectical' reversal in the law of capitalist appropriation forms a decisive turning point in the *Grundrisse*, making it easier to work out the historical determinacy of the abstraction of value and, on that basis, to decide how to begin the systematic presentation of the economic categories 'commodity', 'money' and 'capital'. For the 'system of exchange rests on *capital* as its foundation, and, when it is regarded in isolation from capital, as it appears on the surface, as an *independent* system, then it is a mere *illusion*, but a *necessary illusion*' (Marx 1973: 509). The appearance worn by 'simple circulation' must then be analysed as part of capital's surface structure, so that the concept of value may be shown to be the most abstract expression of capital, even in its simplest elementary forms, the commodity and money. Because, at the outset of the *Grundrisse*, this problem has not yet been solved, Marx's way of presenting things in the 'Chapter on Money' is marred by idealist distortions, observable in the order in which the determinations of value are set out and in the transitions between them; the 'limits of the dialectical form of presentation' have not yet been taken into proper account. Thus his description of the historical development of all sciences – 'science, unlike other architects, builds not only castles in the air, but may construct separable habitable storeys of the building before laying the foundation stone' (Marx 1987b: 297) – holds, at this point, for his own mode of enquiry as well. The 'multitude of contradictory moves' in the 'Chapter on Money' afford us glimpses into the Marxian problematic of enquiry and exposition, and the difficulty of finding a workable resolution to the problem of where to begin the critique of political economy.

Value determination and historical periodization

Marx opens the *Grundrisse* with a critique of the socialist alternatives proposed in his day. These undoubtedly arose in reaction to the unhealthy course and the crises of bourgeois society, without really abandoning the terrain of its economic anatomy. In Marx's estimation, it was not possible to surmount bourgeois society at the economic level by reforming money or the circulation of money and credit. He argued that it was necessary, rather, to arrive at a precise understanding of the internal structure of bourgeois society (commodities, value, money, capital and so on):

> in order to avoid setting impossible tasks, and in order to know the limits within which monetary reforms and transformations of circulation are able to give a new shape to the relations of production and to the social relations which rest on the latter.
>
> (Marx 1973: 145–6)

The *Grundrisse* demonstrates that, and in what sense, the 'golden age' conjured up by the bourgeois economists is a pure fiction spawned by the overarching structure constituted by objective economic forms – commodities and money – and an illusory simple commodity circulation. In the 'Chapter on Money', Marx grapples with the fact that the social character of production is not immediately manifest, but only expressed and activated by way of particular, objective mediating forms, namely, commodities and money. Classical political economy had already tried to define, in terms of a theory of value, the system of the production of wealth behind the externalized forms of commodities, money and prices, as well as of revenues in the form of profit, interest, rent and wage labour. But the classical political economists ultimately failed in their attempt to identify a satisfactory substantial mediation between their concept of value and the surface forms of the total reproduction process of capital: the vicissitudes of competition, fluctuations in market prices, and relations between supply and demand. Thus Marx affirms, in the 1850–3 London notebooks containing excerpts from his reading, that:

> Ricardo abstracts from everything that he regards as *accidental*. It is something else entirely to present *the real process*, in which that which he calls accidental motion, when it is solid and real, and its law, the average relation, both appear equally essential
>
> (Marx 1986: 362).

Against this background, it is hard to explain the one-sided historical reception of the *Grundrisse* even after the increased attention that the text has enjoyed since the publication of Roman Rosdolsky's commentary. Although the bulk of the 'rough draft' concerns itself with the circulation of capital and with capital and profit, commentators have focused on the 'Chapter on Money' and Marx's treatment of the concept of value at the beginning of this draft first chapter. This is understandable. Often, however, no attempt is made to arrive at a comprehensive understanding of the text, running from Marx's initial difficulty in finding a starting point for his presentation on through the body of his manuscript to the end result of his research, an explicit rectification of the way he initially presented matters:

> It has become apparent in the course of our presentation that value, which appeared as an abstraction, is possible only as such an abstraction, as soon as money is posited; this circulation of money in turn leads to capital, hence can be fully developed only on the foundation of capital, just as, generally, only on this foundation can circulation seize hold of all moments of production.
>
> (Marx 1973: 776)

Hence 'the concept of value is entirely peculiar to the most modern economy, since it is the most abstract expression of capital itself and of the production resting on it' (Marx 1973: 776). The rough draft accordingly closes with a short section entitled '1) Value. This section to be brought forward' (Marx 1973: 881). The overarching structure of the text reflects Marx's acute awareness, from the outset, that a problematic, very complex evolving relationship links the determination of value in the simple forms of commodities and money, the capitalist mode of production, and the total system of reproduction specific to this particular social formation. Nevertheless, given his presentation of com-modities and money in the 'Chapter on Money', Marx cannot simultaneously thematize the socially specific system for reproducing wage labour and capital.

The actual course of history down to his day, observes Marx, was such that the real development of the sources of wealth occurred, so to speak, behind society's back. Bourgeois society, precisely, is distinguished by the fact that it vigorously develops these sources of social wealth in contrast to those who actu-ally produce it.

> Just as capital on one side creates surplus labour, surplus labour is at the same time equally the presupposition of the existence of capital. The whole development of wealth rests on the creation of disposable time. The relation of *necessary* labour time to the *superfluous* (such it is, initially, from the standpoint of necessary labour) changes with the different stages in the development of the productive forces.
>
> (Marx 1973: 398)

In pre-capitalist social formations, in which human needs were not highly developed and productivity remained low, exchange was conditioned by surplus and surplus labour-time. Only capitalism promotes the development of a system of needs, different types of work, and labour productivity. In this social forma-tion, people not only develop the forces of production and their own needs as well, they also create the preconditions for bringing the sources of wealth under their control and achieving a qualitatively superior way of managing time in the interests of society:

> Just as in the case of an individual, the multiplicity of its development, its enjoyment and its activity depends on economization of time. Economy of time, to this all economy ultimately reduces itself. Society likewise has to distribute its time in a purposeful way, in order to achieve a production ade-quate to its overall needs; just as the individual has to distribute his time correctly in order to achieve knowledge in proper proportions or in order to satisfy the various demands on his activity. Thus, economy of time, along with the planned distribution of labour time among the various branches of production, remains the first economic law on the basis of communal pro-duction. It becomes law, there, to an even higher degree.
>
> (Marx 1973: 172–3)

The determination of value as an altogether historically specific abstraction of capital can be consistently elaborated only with reference to the interrelation between the production of relative surplus value as a form of economic activity peculiar to capital and the competitive cost economy engendered by such production. Capitalism's historical conditions of existence, and, consequently, its specific structures of domination and alienation

> are by no means given with the mere circulation of money and commodities. It can spring into life, only when the owner of the means of production and subsistence meets in the market with the free labourer selling his labour power. And this one historical condition comprises a world history. Capital, therefore, announces from its first appearance a new epoch in the process of social production.
>
> (Marx 1996: 180)

Marxist historical periodization must always set out from 'a correct grasp of the present', which in turn 'offers the key to the understanding of the past' (Marx 1973: 461).

In modern capitalism, wage labour and specific illusions about free, equal owners of commodities go hand-in-hand. 'Insight into this process is = to the statement that capital is not only ... command over alien labour ... but ... the power to appropriate alien labour *without exchange, without equivalent*, yet with the semblance of exchange' (Marx 1973: 551).

Competition and the concept of value

The relationship between the theoretical appropriation of the epoch-making mode of exploitation specific to the capitalist mode of production and the structure and history of the pre-capitalist social formation long shaped the reception of Marx in the workers' and trade-union movement. Franz Mehring, who completed a biography of Marx in 1918, concedes that only a small handful of activists had ever grasped the overall structure of the Marxist critique of political economy.[1] In *Capital*, Marx points out that the abstract presentation of the immediate production and accumulation process in volume I must be put back in the context of the total social life-process. Concretely, 'the new forms that capital assumes while in the sphere of circulation', or the 'concrete conditions of reproduction hidden under these forms' are as crucial to grasping capitalism as are the fragmentation of social surplus value into its surface forms and the mediating movement of those forms in competition (Marx 1996: 565). 'Surplus value, therefore, splits up into various parts. Its fragments fall to various categories of persons, and take on various forms independent forms'; these forms, in turn, obey autonomous laws of motion. Yet only a few specialists were able to seize these interrelations (Marx 1996: 564).

In later periods as well, the reception of the critique of political economy was marked by limited understanding of the capitalist production process. Little light was shed on the way the theoretical reconstruction of the immediate production process grows over into the reproduction of capital at the level of society as a whole – on how 'capital develops to its totality' (Marx 1973: 278) – or even on the fact *that* it does. But Marx's *Grundrisse*, precisely, can sharpen our appreciation of the real difficulties involved in presenting this problem. What Marx must ultimately account for – a task that is also imposed by his later account of the immediate production process – is how the histori- cally novel way of managing the process of production, based on the real socialization of the relations of production, corresponds, at the surface level, to a particular system of regulation, without which it would be impossible to imagine how the capitalist mode of production could become practical truth.

In order to adequately analyse the modern capitalist mode of production, then, one has to accommodate in a logically consistent scheme of development both the simple forms of the commodity and money on the one hand and of capital on the other. Yet, in recent, now popular analyses of (state) monopoly capitalism, this 'methodological imperative' of the Marxist critique of political economy has often been shunted aside in favour of arguments rooted in theories of power, and this precisely in a period when, with the greater interest in the *Grundrisse* stirred up in the late 1960s by Rosdolsky's commentary, it might have found a broader echo.

> However, the conditions under which limited (monopolistic) competition takes place are irreconcilable with the 'law of value'.... The determination of prices by *power*, initially due to individual groups of enterprises in strong market positions and later generalized with strong help from the state, implies a thoroughgoing autonomization of the business world vis-à-vis the *law of value*, formulated by Marx, that holds sway under the conditions of free competition.
>
> (Hofmann 1968: 265)

Since Rosdolsky's day, however, the *Grundrisse* has had an impact on critical analyses of capitalism seeking, precisely, to take the elasticity of the capitalist mode of production into account without directly questioning the general char- acter of the total process of reproduction. The *Grundrisse* positively rules out readings of the kind that would restrict the Marxian concept of value to a phase of free capitalistic competition, however defined. Our interpretation of Marx's method of enquiry as documented by the *Grundrisse* has shown just what prob- lems Marx himself had to overcome in order to conceive and define the simple determinations of value – commodities and money – and their connection to the 'exact development of the concept of capital' in the various historical stages of the production of a social surplus. The result, however, was an insight rich in its implications: that only 'a correct grasp of the present ... also offers the key to the understanding of the past' (Marx 1973: 461). The complex, multi-layered processes of research and presentation at work in Marx's 'rough draft' accord- ingly point ever more clearly to the thesis that 'the concept of value is entirely peculiar to the most modern economy, since it is the most abstract expression of capital itself and of the production resting on it' (Marx 1973: 776). Although Marx, in defining the simple determinations of value, money, commodities, and their circulation, draws a sharp line between them and the surface forms from the very beginning of his enquiry, he is fully aware of the need to integrate such surface forms into his overall schema, so as to provide, unlike Ricardo and other classical economists, a substantial mediation between 'contingent movements' of prices and revenues and the 'average conditions' of the determination of value by labour-time. 'Competition merely *expresses* as real, posits as an external necessity, that which lies within the nature of capital; competition is nothing more than the way in which the many capitals force the inherent determinants of capital upon one another and upon themselves' (Marx 1973: 651). About the significance and development of competition, we may say something that Marx says at the beginning of the 'Chapter on Capital' about theorizations of the market: 'to be seen at what point the abstract category of the market has to be brought in' (Marx 1973: 281).

Marx's pursuit of the process of enquiry and presentation at work in the *Grundrisse* leads him to elaborate more and more mediating terms and intermediate levels in the total social system of the reproduction of the determination of value. The constantly renewed determination of the average conditions of socially necessary labour-time flows from the immediate capitalist production process, with its endless technological and organizational innovations and reshuffling of levels; yet it is in fact inseparable from the forms regulating it at the level of the social process as a whole. Undoubtedly, the secret of the production of surplus value comes down to the utilization of living labour; at the same time, however, the economy of past labour always presents itself to a particular capital as the problem of lowering production costs in order to raise the profit rate. This means 'that the increase in productive power must be paid for by capital itself, is not free of charge' (Marx 1973: 776). Capital's 'advances – production costs' (Marx 1973: 760) are themselves already commodities that have been produced in a capitalistic framework to serve as elements of capitalist production; that is, they are productive forces produced under capitalist conditions. The explanation of this thesis forms, in turn, a mediating link between Marx's presentation of the methods of producing relative surplus value and the laws of the cost economy at the level of cost-price and profit. In the cost-price, there occurs an integration of both economies, of living and dead labour. This lays the basis for Marx's demonstration of the way the law of value asserts itself in the form of a cost economy mediated by competition.

Accordingly, after the internal structure of the social mode of production has been reconstructed from a determinate form of social labour, the challenge is to develop dimensions of the reproduction of society as a whole. They assert themselves invisibly – Adam Smith's 'invisible hand' comes to mind here – behind the backs of the subjects, albeit by way of their actions; and they assert the power of capital as a social relation, in part against the subjects' will. The systematic presentation of these dimensions of global social reproduction can be carried through only with the help of new determinations of economic form. This engenders still other mediating links to the surface conditions of bourgeois society, and thus to mental and comportmental structures that the subjects find ready-made. In the *Grundrisse*, Marx not only has a relatively clear conception of the basic significance of competition in the overall organization of the process of capitalist reproduction; he also differentiates, in this early phase of his economic critique, between the basic structures of competition, a 'fundamental law in competition' (Marx 1973: 657), and other economic relations or determinate forms grounded in these structures and distortedly reflecting them: 'in short, here all determinants appear in a position which is the *inverse* of their position in capital in general' (Marx 1973: 657). This kind of distinction between the fundamental law in competition and the phenomenal appearance of competition provides the economic basis for a far-reaching critique of the ideology of contemporary neo-liberalism as well, which promotes just these forms of competition as 'the absolute form of free individuality' (Marx 1973: 652). Yet,

> it is not individuals who are set free by free competition; it is, rather, capital which is set free. As long as production resting on capital is the necessary, hence the fittest form for the development of the force of social production, the movement of individuals within the pure conditions of capital appears as their freedom; which is then also again dogmatically propounded as such through constant reflection back on the barriers torn down by free competition.
>
> (Marx 1973: 650)

Thanks to just this value-based theoretical analysis of both the rational aspect of competition as well as its illusory phenomenal form, the perspective sketched in Marx's first draft of *Capital*, the *Grundrisse*, is more relevant than ever. 'The analysis of what free competition really is, is the only rational reply to the middle-class prophets who laud it to the skies or to the socialists who damn it to hell' (Marx 1973: 652).

[Translation from the German by G.M. Goshgarian]

Note

1 Before discussing volumes II and III of *Capital*, Mehring turned to the experts for help: '[i]n attempting to produce a lucid account of the second and third volumes of *Capital* within the narrow scope of my discussion, I have called on the assistance of my friend Rosa Luxemburg' (Mehring 1967: 6).

References

Hofmann, Werner (1968) 'Das "Wertgesetz" in der Erwerbsgesellschaft unserer Tage und in der sozialistischen Planwirtschaft', in Walter Euchner and Alfred Schmidt (eds), *Kritik der politischen Ökonomie heute: 100 Jahre 'Kapital'*, Frankfurt am Main: Europäische Verlagsanstalt.

Marx, Karl (1973) *Grundrisse: Foundations of the Critique of Political Economy (Rough Draft)*, Harmondsworth: Penguin.

Marx, Karl (1986) 'Exzerpte aus David Ricardo, On the Principles of Political Economy', in *Marx–Engels–Gesamtausgabe* (MEGA²), vol. IV/8: *Exzerpte und Notizen, März bis Juni 1851*, Berlin: Dietz Verlag.

Marx, Karl (1987a) 'The Original text of the Second and the Beginning of the Third Chapter of a Contribution to a Critique of Political Economy', in *Marx Engels Collected Works*, vol. 29: *Economic Works, 1857–61*, Moscow: Progress Publishers, pp. 430–507.

Marx, Karl (1987b) 'A Contribution to the Critique of Political Economy: Part One', in *Marx Engels Collected Works*, vol. 29: *Economic Works, 1857–61*, Moscow: Progress Publishers, pp. 257–417.

Marx, Karl (1989) 'Theories of Surplus Value', in *Marx Engels Collected Works*, vol. 31: *Economic Manuscripts of 1861–63* (continuation), London: Lawrence and Wishart.

Marx, Karl (1994) 'Chapter Six. Results of the Direct Production Process', in *Marx and Engels Collected Works*, vol. 34: *Economic Works, 1861–64*, New York: International Publishers, pp. 355–474.

Marx, Karl (1996) '*Capital*, vol. I', in *Marx and Engels Collected Works*, vol. 35: *Capital, Vol. I*, New York: International Publishers.

Marx, Karl (1997) '*Capital*, vol. II', in *Marx and Engels Collected Works*, vol. 36: *Capital, Vol. II*, New York: International Publishers.

Marx, Karl and Engels, Friedrich (1983) *Marx Engels Collected Works*, vol. 40: *Letters, 1856–59*, Moscow: Progress Publishers.

Mehring, Franz (1967) *Karl Marx: Geschichte seines Lebens*, Berlin: Dietz Verlag.

3 Marx's conception of alienation in the *Grundrisse*

Terrell Carver

Introduction

'Alienation' or 'estrangement' [*Entfremdung, Entäußerung, Veräußerung*] was not a featured concept in Marxism, or in scholarship on Marx, before 1932 (though arguably in *History and Class Consciousness* (1923), György Lukács anticipated later exegesis by using 'reification' [*Verdinglichung*][1] as an important category of exposition). Gajo Petrović suggests that *Versachlichung* is an equivalent term (1991b: 464), and David Leopold notes the importance of further terms such as *Trennung* ['divorce or separation'] and *Spaltung* ['division or rupture'] in discussions that use these ideas (Leopold 2007: 68). The term alienation thus generally refers to a family of concepts denoting externalisation or objectification, hence separation or loss, typically of someone from some thing or property that was formerly essential. Reification, so it is suggested, is an extreme form of this (Petrović 1991b: 463). The relation between these various terms has been the subject of modern controversy and debate, particularly in relation to a 'Hegelian' Marx or a 'scientific' one, and particularly from the late 1950s through the 1970s (Petrović 1991a: 13–14; 1991b: 463–5; see also Kilminster 2003; Edgar 1994; Cowling 2006: 323–4). McLellan has argued, very influentially, that:

> the concept is obviously *fundamental* to the *Grundrisse* where Marx is concerned to underline 'not the state of objectification [*Vergegenständlichtsein*] but the state of alienation [*Entfremdet-*], estrangement [*Entäußert-*] and abandonment [*Veräussertsein*], the fact that the enormous objectified power [*gegenständlichen Macht*] which social labour has opposed to itself as one of its elements belongs not to the worker but to the conditions of production that are objectified in capital.
>
> (McLellan 1980: 120, emphasis added; Marx 1953: 716; *Grundrisse* quotation from McLellan's own translation in Marx (1977): 384–5)[2]

The thought behind the terms as used by Marx derives from any number of philosophers and traditions, but there is no doubt that it was particularly developed by G.W.F. Hegel, and in turn by his critic Ludwig Feuerbach. For the former, the idealist philosopher of developmental processes, such a 'movement' of alienation/externalisation and return or 'supersession', through which 'contradictions' would be preserved and maintained whilst also transformed and transcended [*Aufhebung*], was necessary and unregrettable. For the latter, his 'transformative' and 'materialist' critic, Hegel had merely traced a process through which human attributes were alienated and externalised as the properties of gods or other supposed agencies, thus giving rise to mystified sources and real social structures of highly regrettable power and domination (see also Cowling 2006: 321–2).

As is well known, and in fact easily demonstrated from the section on 'the fetishism of commodities' in *Capital*, volume 1, Marx made use of these ideas in his critical attack on the economic practices of commodity-producing societies. There he argued that in commodity-producing societies human powers and processes of productive interchange with the material world are projected into a mysterious realm where relations between things (i.e. commodities-in-exchange) come to control human social relationships in ways that produce vast inequalities of power and wealth (Marx 1996a: 81–94). His brief but telling portrayals of a communist society in which these processes would *not* take place make it clear that such structures of domination would disappear, not because objectification as such has ceased, but because human social properties are not treated in practice as powers supposedly inherent in objects such as money and institutions such as markets (Marx 1996a: 89–92; see also Cowling 2006: 328–30).

Making controversies

As with so many other works by Marx, the *Grundrisse* has been read and re-read in the light of the controversies over alienation, which did not figure at all in Marx's lifetime, and have very little to do *as controversies* with the arguments and vocabulary of the text. From the early 1840s Marx developed his thinking in a fairly smooth and steady process, refining his claims and insights to be sure, but making no drastic changes in thought or vocabulary that he himself defined as major. This process culminated in the publication of *Das Kapital*, Erster Band, Buch 1, in 1867 (known in English as *Capital*, vol. 1). At least this is the process as Marx described it (Marx 1987: 261–5; Marx 1996a: 7). For varying reasons some commentators have sought to make this development more dramatic, finding 'scientific' or ideological 'breaks' or 'breakthroughs' along the way, and thus promoting the importance of some works and manuscripts at the expense of others earlier in the chronological sequence, such that no one, Marx included, need look back (Althusser 1969 [1965]). Others have taken a calmer and more nuanced approach, but directed their search for subtleties somewhat in order to suit concerns and controversies generated outside Marx's world and his textual interventions into it (Oishi 2001; see also Cowling 2006 where both approaches are discussed). So as 'newly discovered' manuscripts, the *Grundrisse* has been 'mined' for enlightenment regarding the 'theory of history' ascribed by Marxists (starting with Engels) to Marx (Hobsbawm 1964), and for information concerning the detailed development of his critical encounter with the classics of political economy, the works of lesser authorities and further evidential sources for his views on the class politics of capitalist societies (Rosdolsky 1977 [1968]). Close examination of the text with respect to Marx's use of the terms later identified with 'alienation' is thus a somewhat factitious exercise (cf. McLellan 1980: 120–2), since this language was evidently not problematic for him in this text. The language only became problematic after 1932, and indeed not notably so until the global debates of the 1960s (see McLellan 1980: 132–3; Kilminster 2003: 11–12; Petrović 1991a: 14–16; Cowling 2006: 319–21).

It is not often noted that the year 1932 figures both ways in the most important controversy over alienation, namely whether it is consistent with, or in contradiction to, the orthodoxies through which Marx's classic works have characteristically been interpreted as 'scientific' (see Carver 2003: 38–94). The so-called 'Early' or '1844' or 'Paris' or 'Economic and Philosophic[al] Manuscripts' [*Ökonomisch–philosophische Manuskripte aus dem Jahre 1844*],[3] where the concept and vocabulary of alienation are extensively deployed, were first published in full in 1932 (MEGA I, 3). The same text, edited by Siegfried Landshut and J.P. Mayer, appeared in Leipzig in another more accessible edition of 1932, 'Historical Materialism: Early Writings' [*Der historische Materialismus: Frühschriften*], under the heading 'Political Economy and Philosophy' [*Nationalökonomie und Philosophie*]. The first 'full' text of *The German Ideology* [*Die Deutsche Ideologie*, written 1845–6 but unpublished, and in particular the 'chapter' 'I. Feuerbach'] also appeared in the MEGA scholarly series in the very same year (I, 5).[4] Neither Marx's extensive use of alienation in the *Economic and Philosophical Manuscripts* (1844), nor his throwaway remark in *The German Ideology* manuscripts dismissing it (just a year or so later), attracted much attention in the later 1930s. The dismissive remark alludes to a problem with 'philosophers': 'This "estrangement" [*Entfremdung*] (to use a term which will be comprehensible to the philosophers)' (Marx 1976: 48; Marx's own hand; Marx *et al.* 2004, 2: 227). This comment repeats the sentiments of the *Manifesto of the Communist Party* (1848, repr. 1872, 1883, and numerous further reprints, with numerous translations from 1850), where Marx and Engels[5] wrote:

> The German literati … wrote their philosophical nonsense under the original French [socialist and communist literature]. For example, under the French critique of monetary relations they wrote 'externalisation [*Entäußerung*] of the human essence'…. The literature of French socialism-communism was thus punctiliously emasculated.
>
> (Marx 1996b: 24; cf. Marx 1976: 511)

The very few comments by Marx *on* 'alienation' (rather than his usage *of* 'alienation') that were published authoritatively in his lifetime were explicitly negative. In *Capital*, volume 1, the relevant terms occur merely in passing as the discussion progresses (see, for example, Marx 1996a: 98–9, 123, 126, 184, 583).

McLellan argues that the term 'occurs repeatedly in *Capital*' (McLellan 1980: 121). Others prefer to see at least some of this usage as merely a synonym for 'sale' (the index entry for 'alienation' is divided this way in Marx 1973: 899). Cowling (2006) generally takes this position on the 'legal' character of the later Marx's terminology. However, it is unclear that this meaning as 'sale' is any less 'philosophical' or 'Hegelian' than 'alienation', given the nature of Marx's critique, the precise point of which was not to take supposedly descriptive or 'objective' or even 'scientific' terminology for granted, let alone 'legal' terms![6] In *Capital*, volume 1, Marx himself explicates the very notion of selling one's labour-power by citing a passage from *Hegel* on alienation *with approval* (Marx 1996a: 178, n. 2); this also effectively licences a view of the earlier discussions in the *Economic and Philosophical Manuscripts* as relating to 'real world' phenomena without so much precise attention to the relevant 'real world' (e.g. 'economic') language. Engels never raised the issue either way. So it is perhaps surprising to find that this concept has played such a major role in the critical reception (and re-construction) of Marx's thought during the twentieth century.

In the first instance this was positive and imaginative, with Marcuse (1983 [1932]), Cornu (1934) and Lefebvre (1968 [1939]) writing major studies. The negative side opposed to the whole enterprise was at first the proverbial 'wall of silence' and then the weapon of doctrinal dismissal (i.e. 'not scientific', or even worse 'Hegelian', as the guardians of Marxist orthodoxy would have it). But beginning with better French translations of the *Economic and Philosophical Manuscripts* in 1947, and influential works and lectures by Kojève (1969 [1947]), Hyppolite (1969 [1955]) and Calvez (1956) on 'alienation', the stage was set for philosophical and 'Hegelianising' studies of Marx, such as works by Bloch (1971 [1959]) and Fromm (1961). These issues concerning the 'humanistic Marx' were taken up in English after the first influential translation of the *Economic and Philosophic Manuscripts* appeared in 1959, followed by other selections and translations from these 'early works' in the 1960s. Studies by Mészáros (1970), Schacht (1970), Mandel and Novack (1970), Ollman (1976 [1971]), Gamble and Walton (1976 [1972]), Plamenatz (1975), Axelos (1976) and others followed in a burst of interest and writing from the mid-1960s through the late-1970s, including important discussions in Avineri (1968), Maguire (1972) and McLellan (1973).

The overt backlash arrived on the scene in French in 1965, with Louis Althusser's *For Marx* (1969), where *The German Ideology*, and in particular its dismissiveness regarding alienation, figured large in a dramatic account of Marx's intellectual development. Althusser argued that Marx and Engels' supposed turn to 'science' and 'materialism' in this text hinged on a *rejection* of their previous engagements with 'philosophy', hence with Marx's prior analyses featuring 'alienation', such as the *Economic and Philosophical Manuscripts* composed in the previous year. Althusser's ambitious project is generally thought to have ended in failure, given his successive admissions that the 'epistemological break' [*coupure épistemologique*] could not be clearly located. If there were a 'break', then Marx's vocabulary and thought on one side of the divide would have to be demonstrably different from his vocabulary and thought on the other side, but Althusser was not convincing when he attempted to demonstrate this. His response was to posit such a 'break' further and further along in Marx's career, until the point at which Marx himself no longer seemed to live up to his own 'scientific' and anti-'philosophical' ideal (as Althusser would have it) (Arditti 2006).

Science, philosophy, orthodoxy

These debates about alienation were in fact driven by somewhat larger issues, in particular the supposed distinction between 'science' and 'philosophy' and what this might mean in a number of respects. Over his career Marx was generally hostile to 'mere' philosophy and 'empty' philosophising, particularly when intellectual activity was performed in such a way that it apparently stood in for politics (and especially when it displaced class struggle). Indeed it is arguable that Marx's early polemical engagements, with German writers on socialism and communism above all, were actually about little else. 'Science' is a more complex issue, in that Marx seems to have stuck to an understanding of it as *Wissenschaft* in the standard Germanic sense of 'disciplined study' (of anything), whereas from the later 1850s onwards Engels shows considerable enthusiasm for 'science' in a more British and empirical/empiricist sense (Carver 2002). This was of the 'natural sciences', especially chemistry and physics, based on a matter-in-motion materialism in which Marx had little sustained interest, and of which his lifetime critical project on political economy shows no trace in its fundamentals, and only a few points of comparison (*and* contrast) (Carver 1983).

Orthodox Marxists followed Engels and his supposedly definitive texts, such as *Anti-Dühring* (1878), *Socialism: Utopian and Scientific* (1880), and *Ludwig Feuerbach and the End of Classical German Philosophy* (1886), whereas those who drifted away from Engels' works and his methodological glosses on Marx, and turned back towards Marx's own works as they were actually (and rather more subtly) argued, were perceived politically as having to make their case against the 'evidence' of orthodoxy. This they did, and therefore any previously unpublished text by Marx was necessarily a 'discovery', given that readings of published texts that were already well known swiftly ran into the orthodox defence that Engels had read them and interpreted them correctly already (and in any case was known to have talked to Marx and corresponded with him). However, in the 12 years by which Engels survived Marx, Engels turned his editorial attentions to the drafts of what became volumes 2 and 3 of *Capital*, rather than to earlier works in the Marx *Nachlaß* in his care, such as the manuscript materials of 1844–6, i.e. the *Economic and Philosophical Manuscripts* and *The German Ideology*. Both titles are editorial inventions which post-date Engels' brief cataloguing of the literary legacy and rather negative comments about such materials, excepting the 11 'Theses on Feuerbach', which he published in 1888 in a version edited by himself (Taubert 1997).

Of course, any 'discovery' in the Marx *Nachlaß* might go either way with respect to the importance and correct understanding of science and materialism, but it is significant that it was the revisionists who had to make the running, and therefore had the incentive to dig into unpublished works as they arrived. At the very least this move then forced orthodoxy onto the defensive, having to explain away new texts by Marx. Althusser was thus symptomatic of an already established battle-line, namely the view that the scientific (in some deterministic, 'natural science' sense of the word) would be the important Marx (as Engels had supposedly discerned). Since revisionists were easily wrong-footed when building their case with works that Marx had already published in Engels' lifetime, they were thrilled to find a Marx to their liking in the *Economic and Philosophical Manuscripts*, precisely because that Marx was so apparently unorthodox in his vocabulary. However, this judgement tends to beg the question as to whether the orthodox view of Marx's published vocabulary as 'scientific' and 'materialist' was itself a correct or even defensible exegesis, since he seldom used those words himself, and in any case, their *meaning* when he did use them was of course very debateable.

So how different was this 'early' Marx from the later one? Some 'revisionists' were content with bracketing off 'the early Marx' as 'theirs' and simply giving up on 'the later Marx' by giving him back to Engels, as it were. Others tackled the problem and argued for continuity. The latter position raised two problems:

1   Those who were enthusiastic about the 'philosophical' character and vocabulary of the 'early Marx' felt themselves ill-equipped to tackle *Capital* in any great detail, precisely because it was perceived by them as 'economic' and not as 'philosophical'. While the stated question for them may have been, 'What was Marx's theory of alienation?', the background and often unstated difficulty was, 'What does *Capital* say that is the same as or different from what is said in the 'early' works of 1844?'

2   If the content of *Capital* is substantially *different* from that of the *Economic and Philosophical Manuscripts*, then the change in vocabulary must make some sense, so the original, earlier vocabulary would require a defence (perhaps as a 'philosophy of man' or of 'human nature' or some such framing). But if the content of *Capital* were substantially *the same*, then why are the idiom and vocabulary of *Capital* less obviously a 'philosophy'?[7]

If the answer is not a simple 'turn' from philosophy to science, as so many thought, and if philosophy (as non-science) and science (in a 'natural science' sense) are *not* perhaps the most relevant explanatory categories in the first place, what *subtler*, perhaps even non-dichotomous conceptions of science and philosophy would help us to understand this intriguing textual conjunction?

After all, Marx himself had raised these general issues about *both* philosophy and science in *The German Ideology* manuscripts, and his subsequent comments on either (or both) were studiously collected as evidence for a debate he was assumed to have started, although he never addressed himself explicitly to his work or his subject-matter by framing his comments as *either* 'science-not-philosophy' *or* 'philosophy-incorporating-science' in a way that addressed this question head-on. Thus in assessing Marx's view on what had in fact become a debate about Engels (given that Engels *had* taken a position – of sorts – on science and philosophy), there is always the problem of hermeneutic fidelity to the original context of Marx's comments, framed as these would be (over some 40 years) with views about *both* science *and* philosophy that were changing, and in any case different in different political and intellectual contexts (Germany, France, England, etc.). In circumstances where the object is to score *ideological* points by turning to Marx for 'apt' quotations, there is perhaps some excuse for paying minimal (if any) attention to such contextual matters. However, in *scholarly* re-construction and assessment, by contrast, there is no excuse for ignoring context and simply stitching comments together, as so often happens.

Different questions – different answers

This chapter, however, 'turns the page' on these debates, and asks a different range of questions, ones formulated such that careful attention to the *Grundrisse* might provide some answers. Taking the *Grundrisse* discussions of alienation as a transitional point between the *Economic and Philosophical Manuscripts* and *Capital*, vol. 1, this chapter poses questions as follows: what is the content of Marx's discussions, and why does this seem an appropriate terminology (given his previous dismissiveness in 1845/6 and 1848)? What, if anything, marks a departure from the earlier outlook? An endorsement of the latter? Does his work show any signs of his previous ambivalence about the concept? What contextual factors, in particular the developing state of Marx's knowledge of the (French- and English-language) literatures on political economy, could explain the nature of this transition? Also, what factors concerning Marx's intended audience (whether himself, his associates or the wider public) could explain these differences? Are there any insights in Marx's discussions that are distinctive to the *Grundrisse* that are of particular intellectual and/or political relevance today? If so, what are they? If not, what *other* questions should we be asking of the *Grundrisse*, and indeed should we be asking it (as it were) about alienation at all?[8]

In arguing that alienation is fundamental to the *Grundrisse* McLellan deals with the problem of Marx's dismissiveness about the term: 'He [Marx] tended to use the actual word less, probably because of its exclusively philosophical connotation' (McLellan 1980: 120). However, he does not spell out at that point precisely why a 'philosophical connotation' was such a problem. To make the point about content, McLellan quotes from the *Grundrisse*, the point of which seems to be that Marx was adopting and defending a set of terms distinct from mere objectification (i.e. the labouring activity of simply making a product). These other terms, and additional content, were indicative of 'alienation, estrangement and abandonment' and demonstrated that the enormous powers created by social labour belong 'not to the worker' but rather 'to the conditions of production'. Marx's argument here is an interesting one, not well captured in the short quotation given by McLellan. It is also one that marks an advance in 'economic' thinking over and beyond what is recorded in the *Economic and Philosophical Manuscripts*.

Taking a number of paragraphs together, then, as McLellan does, Marx is exercising some care in the *Grundrisse* to conceptualise his view of a 'bourgeois economy' as a process in developmental motion, progressive as it were (albeit on its own terms, which he argues are ultimately self-negating). '[T]he human being itself in its social relations' is merely an individualised way of looking at the 'process of social production', which Marx considers to be a long-term process creating 'society itself'. Individuals, albeit in relations with one another, are the subjects of this process, and all the 'objectifications' of this process (driven by 'living labour') are 'moments' of it, and not of something else (presumably 'nature' or some 'givens' that are supposedly outside this process) (Marx 1973: 712). The point of this conceptualisation is clearly to capture capital, not as some entity 'other' than human labour, but as a name for the 'objectified labour' that Marx sees as constitutive of the 'objective conditions of labour' (presumably machines, buildings, distribution systems, etc.). Moreover in the 'bourgeois mode of production' Marx sees a progressive and proportional growth of 'objectified labour' relative to 'living labour' such that 'less immediate labour is required to create a greater product', an allusion not just to accumulating resources of 'social wealth' assigned to capital (and not to 'living labour') but to a concomitant acceleration in productivity to produce ever more 'social wealth'. This is the 'ever more powerful body' of 'subjective, living labour' that is assuming – as 'objectified labour' – 'an ever more colossal independence' [*Selbstständigkeit*] from 'living labour'. In conclusion, Marx writes that 'social wealth confronts labour in more powerful portions as an alien [*fremde*] and dominant power' (Marx 1973: 831–2).

A thorough comparison of Marx's thinking in the *Economic and Philosophical Manuscripts* (1844) with the *Grundrisse* (1857–8), and then of those two with *Capital*, volume 1 (1867), would be a major undertaking, certainly a very long volume. All that can be attempted here is a very limited and merely indicative comparison, offering a very few tentative conclusions, based on selected passages. These are from the texts of the earlier and later works that go over much the same ground as the passage from the *Grundrisse* discussed above. However, the *Economic and Philosophical Manuscripts* are themselves very brief (and somewhat defectively preserved); the *Grundrisse* manuscripts are very lengthy but somewhat unstructured; and *Capital*, volume 1, is both lengthy and highly structured. Moreover the intended audience and state of the text are somewhat different in all three cases. Although personal notebooks, the *Economic and Philosophical Manuscripts* and the *Grundrisse* are of somewhat different status in relation to Marx himself as the intended audience; by the time of the *Grundrisse* he had a plan, already developed and revised, for publishing a critique of political economy. The relationship between the *Economic and*

Philosophical Manuscripts and some intended published work is much less clear, as indeed is the genre and content of anything Marx might have had in mind. McLellan (1980: 120–1) is right to note considerable continuity in terms of the arguments and terminology between *Capital*, volume 1, and both earlier works, and the quotations discussed below, support this view.

However, *Capital*, volume 1, is a work in which Marx's theorisations are developed in close contact with quoted material from the political economists, so the critique of their thought, and the exact ways in which Marx's own work explains and supersedes it, are made as transparent as possible to the reader. The earlier works do not show such detailed, lengthy interchange, nor do they show much sign of Marx's highly elaborated logical structure into which his critical engagement is carefully fitted. Indeed the structure of Marx's opening volume in his projected multi-volume work went through notable changes for the French translation (1872–5) and second German edition (1872), both supervised by the author. My broad conclusion about this sequence is that Marx's detailed critical engagement with the political economists, and detailed use of contemporary and historical materials for factual illustration, 'took off' post-*Grundrisse*. Indeed this is much as one would expect, given the biographical evidence (his circumstances had settled down somewhat) and the voluminous manuscript evidence (much of it now published) from the early 1860s.

Perhaps the preparation of his *A Contribution to the Critique of Political Economy* (1859) for the press (and therefore for 'real readers') was a turning point, as in that volume he made overt efforts to integrate historical and contemporary materials into his theoretical discussions, rather than to produce an 'abstract' volume or section of theory (including detailed critical engagement with the political economists), and then to take readers through more 'empirical' illustration and citation. While his last plan does contain a 'fourth volume' of historical materials, this evidently did not preclude the inclusion of such materials where relevant in the earlier sections of the critique (Carver 1975: 29–37). This is to suggest – following Marx's own distinction enunciated in his 'Afterword' dated 1873 to the second edition of *Capital*, volume 1 – that his own method of inquiry was somewhat different from his method of presentation (Marx 1996a: 19), and that engagement with the latter in the draft materials from which *A Contribution to the Critique of Political Economy* (1859) emerged then subsequently produced a kind of text somewhat different from the *Grundrisse* and the *Economic and Philosophical Manuscripts* – not so much in terms of content, but in terms of genre. Put crudely, writing for the press in order to engage a readership was a somewhat different exercise from ruminating critically in a notebook where ideas flow to please oneself (see also Cowling 2006: 333–4).

Returning then to the *Grundrisse* and Marx's theme – the proportional growth of objectified labour relative to living labour, and the domination of the former over the latter that takes place as productivity and wealth increase – it is possible to find much the same content and vocabulary in the *Economic and Philosophical Manuscripts*. His expression there displays a Young Hegelian style in its use of antithesis and chiasmus, almost a litany, together with the notion of 'realisation', i.e. the fulfilment or completion of the potential within a concept, albeit in negative form:

> The product of labour is labour which has been embodied in an object, which has become material: it is the *objectification* [*Vergegenständlichung*] of labour. Labour's realisation is its objectification [*Vergegenständlichung*]. Under these economic conditions this realisation of labour appears as *loss of realisation* [*Entwirklichung*] for the workers; objectification as *loss* [*Verlust*] *of the object and bondage* [*Knechtschaft*] *to it*; appropriation *as estrangement* [*Entfremdung*], *as alienation* [*Entäußerung*].
>
> (Marx 1975: 272)

However, the Young Hegelian analysis is cashed out in empirical terms, albeit very general ones not involving contemporary and historical citation (such as Marx worked very laboriously into his critique from the published work of 1859 onwards):

> So much does labour's realisation appear as loss of realisation [*Entwirklichung*] that the worker loses realisation to the point of starving to death. So much does objectification appear as loss [*Verlust*] of the object that the worker is robbed of the objects most necessary not only for his life but for his work. Indeed, labour itself becomes an object which he can obtain only with the greatest effort and with the most irregular interruptions. So much does the appropriation of the object appear as estrangement [*Entfremdung*] that the more objects the worker produces the less he can possess and the more he falls under the sway [*Herrschaft*] of his product, capital.
>
> (Marx 1975: 272)

Interestingly, as the passage continues, Marx links this discussion again with an increasingly powerful 'world of objects' that are alien to the worker, but then – speaking in Young Hegelian terms, and perhaps potentially to an audience who would understand that intellectual milieu – he alludes to Feuerbach's famous analysis of religion in general: 'It is the same in religion. The more man puts into God, the less he retains in himself' (Marx 1975: 272).

In the *Grundrisse* passages (Marx 1973: 712, 831–2), the turn of thought is instead to an 'economic' referent, namely increasing labour productivity and social wealth. The import of this is not necessarily that Marx rejected anything particular to do with the Young Hegelian perspective, much less the relevance of Hegelian thought and philosophy to his mode of investigation,[9] but rather it seems more likely that by 1857–8 the political/intellectual milieu *of his audience* had moved on significantly. Young Hegelian arguments were no longer fresh, and indeed the politics of making them had pretty much vanished in the aftermath of the 1848 revolutions. However, while Marx's allusions in the *Grundrisse* to overarching claims in political economy are there in his manuscripts, the detailed citations on the subject, and the painstaking efforts to make transparently logical and systematic arguments that would stand up in print, are not, whereas they are a distinctive feature of *A Contribution to the Critique of Political* Economy, and *Capital*, volume 1. This is not a criticism of the *Grundrisse*; Marx's discursive sweep there has a certain style and appeal. My point is that the published works are more overtly structured, no doubt to make the critical points more telling, and to give an untutored audience some 'scaffolding' from which to build their understanding of arguments that Marx himself confessed would be 'difficult' (Marx 1987: 265; Marx 1996a: 7).

While McLellan is right to point out the overall continuities between the alienated labour sections of the *Economic and Philosophical Manuscripts* and the 'Fetishism of Commodities' section of *Capital*, volume 1, it is possible to find a more detailed parallel to the content of the two passages (which is the crux of McLellan's comments) much later on in *Capital*, volume 1, in Part VII 'The Accumulation of Capital', Chapter XXIII, 'Simple Reproduction':

> the labourer ... is ... a source of wealth, but devoid of all means of making that wealth his own. Since ... his own labour has already been alienated from himself by the sale of his labour power [*sic – seine eigne Arbeit ihm selbst entfremdet*], has been appropriated by the capitalist and incorporated with capital, it must, during the process, be realised in a product that does not belong to him [*fremdem Produkt*]. Since the process of production is also the process by which the capitalist consumes labour power, the product of the labourer is incessantly converted, not only into commodities, but into capital, into value that sucks up the value-creating power, into means of subsistence that buy the person of the labourer, into means of production that command the producers. The labourer therefore constantly produces material, objective wealth, but in the form of capital, of an alien [*fremde*] power that dominates and exploits him.
>
> (Marx 1996a: 570–1)

The next step in the *Grundrisse* discussion was the claim that increasing capital and increasing productivity go together, a development that further dominates and dwarfs the labourer, as it were, in comparison with what 'he' has produced, whereas the argument is put more 'technically' in *Capital*, volume 1:

> But hand-in-hand with the increasing productivity of labour, goes, as we have seen, the cheapening of the labourer, therefore a higher rate of surplus value, even when the real wages are rising. The latter never rise proportionally to the productive power of labour.
>
> (Marx 1996a: 600)

> The powerful and ever-increasing assistance given by past labour to the living labour process under the form of means of production is therefore,

attributed to that form of past labour in which it is alienated [*entfremdeten*], as unpaid labour, from the worker himself, i.e., to its capitalistic form.

(Marx 1996a: 604)

The argument in *Capital*, volume 1, is thus more detailed theoretically, as well as in citations (in footnotes) to political economists, and in incorporation of 'real world' reference to the production process, than the argument in the *Grundrisse*. But there is really no great difference in substance, never mind contradiction or reversal or 'rejection' from one text to the next. What then do we make of Marx's (perhaps overly influential) dismissiveness about philosophy and philosophers dating from 1845–8?

In terms of the polemical context of Marx and Engels' engagements with socialist and communist thought, in which they were at pains to stress the increasing importance of class politics deriving from the proletariat–bourgeoisie cleavage of modern industrial society (or at least their 'over the horizon' expectation of this), Marx and Engels evidently wanted to draw a line between their 'outlook' (*Ansicht*, *Auffassung*) and that of others with common origins in Young Hegelian thought, and (according to Marx and Engels) with insufficient knowledge of both French socialist thought and the contemporary 'science' of political economy. Stylistically they inclined towards extremes of contrast and sarcasm, and given their position as journalists (rather than philosophers, or philosophers manqué) they unsurprisingly drew their line in the sand where they did in the 1840s. Notably in *The German Ideology* manuscripts, where the most extreme advocacy of empirical study and of science (versus philosophy) occurs, the discussion as actually pursued by Marx and Engels is firstly that of a conceptual framework, albeit one built up from what they considered to be sound historical generalisation, and indeed a new conceptualisation of what history is all about in the first place (Marx 1976: 35–7). Given the absence of evidential citation and detail at that point, the passages from *The German Ideology* manuscripts would today fall into the genre 'philosophy of history' (generally finessed by Marxist commentary as 'theory of history'). However, once the polemical context (at least with those now largely forgotten, or at least not well known) Young Hegelians had vanished into post-1848 recrimination and conspiracy, the need to 'sound off' about philosophy perforce subsided. Even Engels, who became increasingly enamoured of the natural sciences from the later 1850s onwards, took 'metaphysics' as its 'other', rather than philosophy as such (Marx 1987: 11–15). And, as is widely known, Marx himself endorsed his own recourse to Hegel's philosophy on notable occasions, not least in his 'Afterword' to the second edition of *Capital*, volume 1 (Marx 1996a: 17–20). This was doubtless to annoy overzealous empiricists, rather than to give readers the decisive clue to his work that – in their quite different ways – both Engels and the much later 'Hegelianising' Marxists found in these deliberately provocative comments.

The view argued here is that the vocabulary of alienation suited Marx's overall argument concerning the relation between labour and capital, between labourers and capitalists, engaged in the social process of production, as it developed in manuscript and published form, from the early 1840s onwards. While there are some differences in the exact turns and phrasing of the argument, the *conception* stands as central (though not comprehensive or summarising or 'key') in his critique. None of these texts is really 'more philosophical' or 'more economic' than any of the others in any very strong sense.[10] Rather there are subtle alterations to do with intellectual milieu, audience, structure and most particularly Marx's knowledge of relevant materials in political economy and in historical and contemporary sources. Those factors, rather than any major intellectual changes, are what explain the changes in form and content between these texts, namely the *Economic and Philosophical Manuscripts*, the *Grundrisse*, and the published 'late' works *A Contribution to the Critique of Political Economy* and *Capital*, volume 1.

McLellan was right to argue that 'alienation' is a common term and theme in Marx's critical project all along the line, though perhaps rather misleading in claiming that it was particularly central to the *Grundrisse*. The *Grundrisse* is rather more like the *Economic and Philosophical Manuscripts* than it is like *Capital*, volume 1, in terms of its *comparatively* unstructured and unsupported character (which is not to say that Marx's discussions lack structure, rather that they are not organised as well and with such thorough attention to citation and evidence as they are in the later work) (see also Cowling 2006: 323, 334). This passage below from the *Grundrisse* can serve as an example. Marx is here reprising the *Economic and Philosophical Manuscripts* without adding anything particularly new, other than the more precise 'economic' terms ('exchange values', 'use values') through which he explicates 'commodity circulation':

> The precondition of commodity circulation is that they be produced as *exchange values*, not as *immediate use values*, but as mediated through exchange value. Appropriation through and by means of divestiture [*Entäusserung*] and alienation [*Veräusserung*] is the fundamental condition. Circulation as the realization of exchange values implies: (1) that my product is a product only in so far as it is for others; hence suspended singularity, generality; (2) that it is a product for me only in so far as it has been alienated, become for others; (3) that it is for the other only in so far as he himself alienates his product; which already implies (4) that production is not an end in itself for me, but a means.
>
> (Marx 1973: 196; cf. Marx 1975: 272)

On the other hand, it is this kind of discussion that makes the *Economic and Philosophical Manuscripts* and the *Grundrisse* popular in some quarters – Marx's analysis seems to race along of its own accord, rather than to fill out a formal structure and format that will compel, through logic and citation, the agreement of the reader. Put plainly, Marx's mode in the manuscript works is amiably discursive rather than formidably 'technical' as in the published ones, involving extensive and detailed citation of the literature of political economy as they do. But aligning this difference in style, tone and presentation with any-thing more complicated and fundamental, such as truly major changes in vocab-ulary or substance, particularly in support of tendentious dichotomies between philosophy and science, is overambitious and unnecessary.

Rosdolsky's (1977 [1968]) work supports this view. In his full-length study of the relationship between the *Grundrisse* and the published volumes of *Capital* (still the only detailed work on this subject) he makes a particular point of citing 'Hegelian' passages, occasionally linking them back to the *Economic and Philo-sophical Manuscripts*, but not making any particular feature or issue out of the alienation terminology on which other commentators had principally focused in the works and debates surveyed in this chapter (see Rosdolsky 1977: 126–9, 175–6, 182, 259 n. 12, 367–8, 420–2, 567). Rosdolsky accounts for the relative (though certainly not complete) absence of alienation terminology in *Capital* by invoking Marx's own distinction between his methods of investigation (which Rosdolsky sees as necessarily 'Hegelian-dialectical') and his methods of presentation, where such 'idealist' language might be open to misinterpretation (Rosdolsky 1977: 114–15, 133–4, 192–3, 375, 565). Crucially he identifies this recourse to Hegelian ideas and language as a way into Marx's '*scientific* work-shop', not some reversion to 'philosophy' (Rosdolsky, 210–11; my emphasis). Indeed he argues that Rosa Luxemburg (among others) made serious mistakes when she disregarded this way of reading Marx's published critique, and gave in to readings and interpretations that Rosdolsky considers naïvely empiricist and therefore conservative, or even worse in political terms (e.g. Stalinist) (Rosdolsky 1977: 189–90, 312–13, 491–4). Thus Rosdolsky locates tendentiousness amongst the orthodox, 'scientific' Marxists, who rejected both Hegel and 'philosophy' and did serious violence to Marx's published ideas in the process. This chapter adds to that view by locating a further tendentiousness in the 'philosophical', Hegelianising schools of commentary on Marx for creating suspicion about his published works, and effectively displacing them from view. Rosdolsky's close attention to Marx's ideas and to the investigative qualities of his unpublished texts, *in order to develop the links with his published ones*, is admirable.

Alienation in the *Grundrisse*

Do we learn more about alienation in the *Grundrisse* than in the *Economic and Philosophical Manuscripts*? Undoubtedly, as the passage above shows, because Marx's specification of these terms is more complex and more referential to the theory of political economy, to the history of production processes, and to contemporary social conditions. Consider the following passages in which the alienation terminology is becoming swamped by Marx's interest in, and exper-tise with, the increasingly complex concepts from political economy through which he was pursuing his critique of contemporary 'bourgeois society':

> Property, too, is still posited here only as the appropriation of the product of labour by labour, and of the product of alien labour [*fremder Arbeit*] by

one's own labour, in so far as the product of one's own labour is bought by alien labour. Property in alien labour is mediated by the equivalent of one's own labour. This form of property – quite like freedom and equality – is posited in this simple relation. In the further development of exchange value this will be transformed, and it will ultimately be shown that private property in the product of one's own labour is identical with the separation [*Trennung*] of labour and property, so that labour will create alien property [*fremdes Eigentum*] and property will command alien labour.

(Marx 1973: 238; emphasis in original)

Finally, the result of the process of production and realization is, above all, the reproduction and new production of the *relation of capital and labour itself, of capitalist and worker.* This social relation, production relations, appears in fact as an even more important result of the process than its material results. And more particularly, within this process the worker produces himself as labour capacity, as well as the capital confronting him, while at the same time the capitalist produces himself as capital as well as the living labour capacity confronting him. Each reproduces itself, by reproducing its other, its negation. The capitalist produces labour as alien; labour produces the product as alien.

(Marx 1973: 458; emphasis in original)

There are some discussions in the *Grundrisse* which would be essentially the same as in *Capital*, volume 1, minus the occasional use of the word 'alien':

Hence, by virtue of having acquired labour capacity in exchange as an equivalent, capital has acquired labour time – to the extent that it exceeds the labour time contained in labour capacity – in exchange *without equivalent*; it has appropriated alien labour time *without exc*hange by means of the form of exchange … the worker receives the equivalent of the labour time objectified in him, and gives his value-creating, value-increasing living labour time. He sells himself as an effect. He is absorbed into the body of capital as a cause, as activity. Thus the exchange turns into its opposite, and the laws of private property … turn into the worker's propertylessness, and the dispossession [*Entäusserung*] of his labour, [i.e.] the fact that he relates to it as alien property and vice versa.

(Marx 1973: 674; emphasis in original)

Interestingly in this passage below one can clearly see Marx taking the alienation idea and projecting it forward beyond the labouring individual to encompass labour in simple 'cooperation', an entire chapter of *Capital*, volume 1:

The first [law of bourgeois property – TC] is the identity of labour with property; the second, labour as negated property, or property as negation of the alien quality of alien labour. In fact, in the production process of capital,

as will be seen more closely in its further development, labour is a totality –
a combination of labours – whose individual component parts are alien to
one another, so that the overall process as a totality is not the work of the
individual worker, and is furthermore the work of the different workers
together only to the extent that they are [forcibly] combined, and do not
[voluntarily] enter into combination with one another. The combination of
this labour appears just as subservient to and led by an alien will and an
alien intelligence – having its *animating unity* elsewhere – as its material
unity appears subordinate to the *objective unity* of the *machinery*, of fixed
capital, which, as *animated monster*, objectifies the scientific idea, and is in
fact the coordinator, does not in any way relate to the individual worker as
his instrument; but rather he himself exists as an animated individual
punctuation mark, as its living isolated accessory … Hence, just as the
worker relates to the product of his labour as an alien thing, so does he
relate to the combination of labour as an alien combination, as well as to his
own labour as an expression of his life, which, although it belongs to him, is
alien to him and coerced from him.

(Marx 1973: 470; emphasis in original)

The 'animated monster' reappears in *Capital*, volume 1, as a 'mechanical
monster', in the succeeding chapter on 'Machinery and Modern Industry'. The
summary conceptualisation of the exchange of labour-power in terms alienation
does not (Marx 1996a: 384–5).

But perhaps we also learn less about alienation in the *Grundrisse* than we do
in the *Economic and Philosophical Manuscripts*, in a sense. The extended discussion of 'species being' drops out (Marx 1975: 275–9), possibly for the political and intellectual reasons cited, and possibly because these other more
specific areas, rather more germane to Marx's critique of political economy,
were taking precedence. Something very like the 'species being' section of the
Economic and Philosophical Manuscripts surfaces in *Capital*, volume 1, on the
labour process, for instance (Marx 1996a: 187–8). But it is very much a case of
slotting the content into a tighter, drier formal structure and a stripped-down
logical argument (cf. Cowling 2006: 330). The *Economic and Philosophical
Manuscripts* were substantially enjoyed by many critics precisely because they
followed that particular train of thought in a way that philosophers, who were
the commentators, could recognise and appreciate. For the philosophically
inclined, the brief discussion in *Capital*, volume 1, may not hold much interest,
and the 'philosophical' Marx won't appear there. The *Economic and Philosophical Manuscripts* inspired many to read more of Marx, because they perceived
'philosophy' to be an easier idiom than 'economics', but perhaps relatively few
to read *Capital*, volume 1, which is a continuing shame. The *Grundrisse*,
whether one is interested in alienation (as in the *Economic and Philosophical
Manuscripts*) or in surplus value (as in *Capital*, vol. 1), is an inspirational text
both ways. And indeed the two concepts are connected, as McLellan makes very
clear (McLellan 1973: 128). Those who look in Marx for enlightenment merely

about alienation should raise their sights (Nicolaus 1973: 21–4; see also Cowling 2006: 332).

Notes

1 The term was only fleetingly used by Marx in manuscripts that became *Capital*, vol. 3 (Petrović 1991b: 463–4).
2 Cf. Marx 1973: 831 which reads:

> not on the state of being objectified, but on the state of being alienated, dispossessed, sold; on the condition that the monstrous objective power which social labour itself erected opposite itself as one of its moments belongs not to the worker, but to the personified conditions of production, i.e. capital.

3 Publication in a 'full' German version was *preceded* by a partial Russian translation and a French translation from the Russian (Rubel 1956: 53).
4 Publication in a 'full' German version was *preceded* by a Russian translation of 'I. Feuerbach' and an English translation from the Russian (Rubel 1956: 56; Marx and Engels 1926: 243–303).
5 Manuscript evidence with individual hands does not survive for this text.
6 Cowling (2006) does not explain what 'legal' is supposed to signify in terms of Marx's writing, career, audience, context etc.
7 'Again, Marx says too much for two-Marx interpreters to feel entirely comfortable, but too little to make it explicit that we are still in the same frame of reference as the young Marx' (Cowling 2006: 327).
8 Cowling (2006) poses similar questions.
9 This is contrary to Cowling's conclusion that 'the previous theoretical framework is basically discarded' (Cowling 2006: 330). In my view Cowling follows the tendency of commentators on the *Economic and Philosophical Manuscripts* to find in those discussions a 'full-blown *theory*' or 'theoretical framework' and a 'general explanation' rather than a critical reconceptualisation of 'real world' phenomena (Cowling 2006: 328, 330, 333, 335).
10 The argument, which Cowling favours, that 'mode of production' supplanted 'alienation' as Marx's work progressed, is not as persuasive as the other option he indicates but accepts in only 'a limited sense': textual change via 'abbreviations' or 'enriching' as content is refined (Cowling 2006: 323, 330).

References

Althusser, Louis (1969 [1965]) *For Marx*, London: Allen Lane.
Arditti, Benjamin (2006) 'Louis Althusser', in Terrell Carver and James Martin (eds), *Palgrave Advances in Continental Political Thought*, Basingstoke: Palgrave Macmillan.
Avineri, Shlomo (1968) *The Social and Political Thought of Karl Marx*, Cambridge: Cambridge University Press.
Axelos, Kostas (1976) *Alienation, Praxis and Techne in the Thought of Karl Marx*, London: University of Texas Press.
Bloch, Ernst (1971 [1959]) *On Karl Marx*, New York: Herder & Herder.
Calvez, Jean-Yves (1956) *La Pensée de Karl Marx*, Paris: Éditions de Seuil.
Carver, Terrell (1975) *Karl Marx: Texts on Method*, Oxford: Blackwell.
Carver, Terrell (1983) *Marx and Engels: The Intellectual Relationship*, Brighton: Harvester/Wheatsheaf.

Carver, Terrell (2002) 'Marx and Marxism', in Theodore M. Porter and Dorothy Ross (eds), *Cambridge History of Science*, vol. 7, *The Modern Social Sciences*. Cambridge University Press.

Carver, Terrell (2003) *Engels: A Very Short Introduction*, Oxford: Oxford University Press.

Cornu, Auguste (1934) *Karl Marx: l'homme et l'œuvre*, Paris: Alcan.

Cowling, Mark (2006) 'Alienation in the Older Marx', *Contemporary Political Theory*, 5: 319–39.

Edgar, Andrew (1994) 'Reification', in William Outhwaite (ed.), *The Blackwell Dictionary of Modern Social Thought*, 2nd edn, Oxford: Blackwell.

Fromm, Eric (1961) *Marx's Concept of Man*, New York: Frederick Ungar.

Gamble, Andrew and Walton, Paul (1976 [1972]) *From Alienation to Surplus Value*, London: Sheed & Ward.

Hobsbawm, Eric (1964) 'Introduction', in Karl Marx, *Pre-Capitalist Economic Formations*, London: Lawrence & Wishart.

Hyppolite, Jean (1969 [1955]) *Studies on Marx and Hegel*, London: Heinemann.

Kilminster, Richard (2003) 'Alienation', in William Outhwaite (ed.), *The Blackwell Dictionary of Modern Social Thought*, 2nd edn, Oxford: Blackwell.

Kojève, Alexandre (1969 [1947]) *Introduction to the Reading of Hegel: Lectures on the Phenomenology of Spirit*, New York: Basic Books.

Lefebvre, Henri (1968 [1939]) *Dialectical Materialism*, London: Cape.

Leopold, David (2007) *The Young Karl Marx: German Philosophy, Modern Politics, and Human Flourishing*, Cambridge: Cambridge University Press.

McLellan, David (1973) *Karl Marx: His Life and Thought*, London: Macmillan.

McLellan, David (1980) *The Thought of Karl Marx*, 2nd edn, London: Macmillan.

Maguire, John (1972) *Marx's Paris Writings: An Analysis*, Dublin: Gill & Macmillan.

Mandel, Ernst and Novack, George (1970) *The Marxist Theory of Alienation*, New York: Pathfinder.

Marcuse, Herbert (1983 [1932]) *From Luther to Popper: Studies in Critical Philosophy*, London: Verso.

Marx, Karl (1953) *Grundrisse der Kritik der politischen Ökonomie*, Berlin: Dietz Verlag.

Marx, Karl (1973) *Grundrisse: Foundations of the Critique of Political Economy* (*Rough Draft*), Harmondsworth: Penguin.

Marx, Karl (1975) 'Economic and Philosophic Manuscripts of 1844', in *Marx and Engels Collected Works*, vol. 3: *Works of Marx, March 1843–August 1844, and Works of Engels, May 1843–June 1844*, Moscow: Progress Publishers.

Marx, Karl (1976) 'The German Ideology', in *Marx and Engels Collected Works*, vol. 5: *Works of Marx and Engels, April 1845–April 1847*, Moscow: Progress Publishers.

Marx, Karl (1977) *Selected Writings*, David McLellan (ed.), Oxford: Oxford University Press.

Marx, Karl (1987) 'A Contribution to the Critique of Political Economy', in *Marx and Engels Collected Works*, vol. 29: *Marx 1857–61*, Moscow: Progress Publishers, pp. 257–417.

Marx, Karl (1996a) '*Capital*, vol. 1', in *Marx and Engels Collected Works*, vol. 35: *Capital*, vol. 1, New York: International Publishers.

Marx, Karl (1996b) *Later Political Writings*, in Terrell Carver (ed.), Cambridge: Cambridge University Press.

Marx, Karl and Engels, Fredrich (1926) 'German Ideology (The Materialist Conception of History)', *The Marxist*, 3: 243–303.

Marx, Karl, Engels, Friedrich and Weydemeyer, Joseph (2004) *Die Deutsche Ideologie: Artikel, Druckvorlagen, Entwürfe, Reinschriftenfragmente und Notizen zu I. Feuerbach und II. Sankt Bruno*, 2 vols, *Text* and *Apparat*, 'Marx–Engels–Jahrbuch 2003', ed. Inge Taubert and Hans Pelger, Berlin: Akademie Verlag.

Mészáros, István (1970) *Marx's Theory of Alienation*, London: Merlin.

Nicolaus, Martin (1973) 'Foreword', in Karl Marx, *Grundrisse: Introduction to the Critique of Political Economy*, Harmondsworth: Penguin.

Oishi, Takahisa (2001) *The Unknown Marx: Reconstructing a Unified Perspective*, London: Pluto.

Ollman, Bertel (1976 [1971]) *Alienation: Marx's Conception of Man in Capitalist Society*, 2nd edn, Cambridge: Cambridge University Press.

Petrović, Gajo (1991a) 'Alienation', in Tom Bottomore (ed.), *A Dictionary of Marxist Thought*, 2nd edn, Oxford: Blackwell.

Petrović, Gajo (1991b) 'Reification', in Tom Bottomore (ed.), *A Dictionary of Marxist Thought*, 2nd edn, Oxford: Blackwell.

Plamenatz, John (1975) *Karl Marx's Philosophy of Man*, Oxford: Clarendon Press.

Rosdolsky, Roman (1977 [1968]) *The Making of Marx's 'Capital'*, London: Pluto.

Rubel, Maximilien (1956) *Bibliographie des œuvres de Karl Marx*, Paris: Marcel Rivière.

Schacht, Richard (1970) *Alienation*, Garden City, NY: Doubleday.

Taubert, Inge (1997) 'Die Überlieferungsgeschichte der Manuskripte der "Deutschen Ideologie" und die Erstveröffentlichungen in der Originalsprache', *MEGA-Studien*, 2: 32–48.

4 The discovery of the category of surplus value

Enrique Dussel

Introduction

> *The surplus value [Mehrwert] which capital has at the end of the produc-tion process* – a surplus value which, as a higher price of the product, is realized only in circulation, but, like all prices, is realized in it by already being ideally presupposed to it, determined before they enter into it – signi-fies, expressed in accord with the general concept of exchange value, that the labour time objectified in the product – or amount of labour (expressed passively, the magnitude of labour appears as an amount of space; but expressed in motion, it is measurable only in time) – is greater than that which was present in the original components of capital. This in turn is pos-sible only if the labour objectified in the price of labour is smaller than the living labour purchased with it.
>
> (Marx 1973: 321)

This is how one of the most critical passages of the *Grundrisse* begins. In these lines we can see the difficulty implied by a reflection on the issue that concerns us here, that is, the problem of the order of categories in Marx's research and exposition. Marx's marked tendency is to move from the simplest to the most complex, from the deepest to the most superficial level, from the abstract to the concrete, but the issue of surplus value requires a recourse to both simple and complex categories, to questions relating to the deepest levels of the production processes and to more superficial ones such as the processes of circulation. In the text above Marx mentions the culmination or end of the process of production (at the deep non-visible level), but he then immediately goes on to write about the price of the product (at the superficial level in the context of circulation). It is well known that all prices associated with circulation are previously budgeted (or defined), in the context of production, in labour time, which is greater than that which was there in the original components of capital. The text concludes with a discussion on the sale and purchase of living labour (the deep level of production) and on the price of labour (wages) in the context of circulation.

Perhaps for this reason Marx eventually decides to include his treatise on wages in volume one of *Capital*, despite having originally assigned it an independent place as the third volume of its initial plan (between the volume on landed property and the one on the state). The question of surplus value cannot be grasped without first addressing the issue of wages (understood as the price of labour). Although situated at the level of production, surplus value is only fully realized in the process of circulation, because of its necessary *antecedent* (wages) and its *subsequent* development (the accumulation of greater value through the sale of the product).

Surplus labour lies at the foundation of surplus value

Marx intuitively grasps the problem of surplus value in his *Economic and Philosophical Manuscripts* of 1844, but starts developing the categories of its explicit formulation much later. The issue first appears in Notebook VIII of his notes, dated April 1851, when, commenting on Ricardo's work, he writes:

> In order for the value of profit to increase, there has to be a third whose value diminishes. When it is said that the capitalist spends 30 of those 100 on raw materials, 20 on machinery, 50 on salary, and then sells those 100 for 110, it is not taken into account that that if he had to disburse 60 for salary he would have obtained no profit at all, unless he had garnered another 8.2% in addition to the 110, etc. He thereby exchanges his product for another whose value is determined by the labour time invested in it.... The surplus does not emerge from the process of circulation although it can only be fully realized in that context.... The value of the wages is reduced in a manner directly proportionate to the increase in the productive forces of labour.[1]

(Marx 1953: 829)

This quote evidences the transition from an intuitive understanding of the question of surplus value to a clearer expression of the categories involved. It is not until the *Grundrisse*, however, that we find the *first elaboration* of the category of surplus value in its definitive form, although further improvements to it are made in the following decade.

First, we need to point out that the categorical distinction between absolute and relative surplus value is initially far from clear. This is of particular significance because the concept of surplus value is applied first and foremost to relative surplus value rather than its absolute expression. Similarly, the initial descriptions of all the key concepts of the theory of wages and of the various forms of capital (industrial, commercial and, long before that, fixed and variable) that were being conceptualized along the way do not exhibit the degree of clarity characteristic of his later treatment of them in *Capital*. But let us venture into the river of ideas where Marx slowly constructs his categories with all its ebbs and flows.

Surplus value emerges as the outcome of an unequal exchange between capital and labour, whereby the labour process as such (the process that produces capital) transforms capital into productive capital that reproduces itself in a process of valorization. Classical political economy had confused this with profit. Marx then needs to *ascend* from this point of departure at the level of circulation (profit) to the level of production (surplus labour) in order to create the theoretical conditions necessary to discover the *foundation* of surplus value in its essential context:

> If living labour reproduced only the labour time objectified in the labour price, this also would be merely formal … [But] no matter that for the worker the exchange between capital and labour, whose result is the price of labour, is a simple exchange; as far as the capitalist is concerned, it has to be a not-exchange. He has to obtain more value than he gives. Looked at from the capitalists' side, the exchange must be only *apparent* [*scheinbarer*]; i.e. must belong to an economic category other than exchange.
>
> (Marx 1973: 321–2)

What is at issue is precisely that other kind of formal economic determination that Marx describes as *surplus value*. In ideological terms capitalist economists 'take refuge in this simple process in order to construct a legitimation [*rechtfertigen*], an apology for capital by explaining it with the aid of the very process which makes its existence impossible' (Marx 1973: 322). This is just another example of how scientific disciplines such as economics can be contaminated by ideology; although even the critical sciences that tend to be less ideological when articulated with processes of liberation of the oppressed, at least in structural terms, may still end up being equally ideological in practice. In fact, they claim, the worker receives a fair wage, the price for all of his labour. If this were the case, Marx asks, where does the increased value come from? If classical political economists were right, capital would be impossible; if they were to explain that capital does not pay the worker the equivalent of the totality of her objectified labour, they would be *unveiling* its ethical perversity, thereby giving rise to a critical contradiction between capitalist theory and practice. The capitalist economist is left with no other alternative than becoming an apologist for the system, which requires that he conceals reality. By not articulating his praxis with the interests of capital, Marx displays an intelligence that is both freer and more clearly determined:

> Surplus value in general is value in excess of the equivalent. The equivalent, by definition, is only the identity of value with itself. Hence surplus value can never sprout out of the equivalent; nor can it do so originally out of circulation; it has to arise from the production process of capital itself.
>
> (Marx 1973: 324)

The equivalent (*tó íson* for Aristotle) denotes what is fair, equal, or of identical value in a relationship, with each term in the exchange being held equal. Capital does not give its own equivalent in praxis, although it appears to deliver the same in the face of *consciousness*. In reality, in fact, it gives less, whilst in its phenomenological appearance it is fair and equal. The sheer power of capitalism with respect to other modes of wealth production is evidenced in its characteristic ideological duplicity; this is reflected in its presentation of the relationship between labour and capital at the superficial level of circulation as one of *equal* exchange, whilst in fact at the deep level of production it is a social process that coerces and violently compels the worker to establish an wholly *unequal* exchange. Surplus value is a category explained by other more fundamental ones, whilst explaining more superficial categories such as profit; it thus needs to be explicitly and clearly constructed in order to express, and explain, the apparent equality of an inequality. The first quote of this chapter ought to be understood in this context. There, Marx is exploring the question of surplus value in all its depth and complexity. The category of surplus value is a formal economic determination, which is to say, it is not situated at the first material level of the productive process except in so far as it has been subsumed and determined by capital. Unlike objectified labour, it is not a material determination; it is formal in character and in economic terms, for example when related to prices. Furthermore, it is an extremely complex category because it includes many other simpler, abstract and fundamental categories, such as currency, commodities and labour as determinations of capital, and necessary labour, which is the foundation of the development of the concept of surplus value. But let us return to Marx's texts:

> If the worker needs only half a working day in order to live a whole day, then, in order to keep alive as a worker, he needs to work only half a day. The second half of the labour day is forced labour; surplus-labour [*surplus-Arbeit*]. What appears as surplus value on capital's side appears identically on the worker's side as surplus labour [*Mehrarbeit*] in excess of his requirements as worker, hence in excess of his immediate requirements for keeping himself alive.
>
> (Marx 1973: 324)

For Marx, then, the worker as capital is not the same as the worker as a human being. In the first case her life consists solely in being utilized as a force of production; in the second case additional dimensions such as the fulfilment of cultural and spiritual needs need to be taken into account. Here we already have the seeds of the concept of necessary labour. The more interesting question is how capitalism accomplishes the worker's submission to *forced* labour without the worker being conscious of this coercion. The key is that capital is able to conceal the relationship of domination at its core under the cloak of wage labour.

> As far as they are concerned, capital does not exist as capital, because autonomous wealth as such can exist only either on the basis of *direct* forced labour, slavery, or *indirect* forced labour, *wage labour*. Wealth con-

fronts direct forced labour not as capital, but rather as *relation of domination* [*Herrschaftsverhältnis*].

(Marx 1973: 326)

The surplus value produced by the worker for capital is perceived as a fair contract of equal exchange. Capital conceals unpaid surplus labour in the system of wages. This is where 'the creation [*Entstehung*] of value' takes place in the form of surplus value (Marx 1973: 326). Neither Ricardo nor the Physiocrats nor Adam Smith managed to grasp this.

Only a concept of capital as *process* makes the appearance of capital possible both in the context of circulation and in that of production, with its final realization in circulation, and its inclusion of the process of production within itself: 'Capital itself is mediator between production and circulation.... *Capital* is *direct unity* of product and money or, better, of production and circulation. Thus it itself is again something *immediate*, and its development consists of positing and suspending itself as this unity' (Marx 1973: 332).

Because of this, capital hides its process of self-realization from the worker and produces surplus labour in an unequal exchange as if it were equal. After it is *objectified*, this surplus labour is transformed into surplus value. Subjectively, in the worker, surplus labour is the *creator* of surplus value, as an objective moment of capital as capital. How does capital manage to place this surplus labour at its disposal?

Surplus labour and surplus value as a civilizing process

Marx begins his discussion of this issue in the terms that characterize the fundamental aspects of surplus value, which he would later refer to in *Capital*: relative and absolute surplus value. This is understandable, given the discussion above. The surplus value that is not pocketed by the worker, nor in full by the capitalist himself, is that which results from capital itself (as a mechinery, for example, to that of constant capital) and not simply from the absolute increase of the time invested in labour (absolute surplus value). The latter is better grasped by consciousness as a relation of domination in its purest and simplest form. This is why Marx begins with the most developed manifestation of surplus value, in order to proceed thereafter to an exploration of its most primitive level of development (both as a category and as a historical phenomenon). Capital needs more surplus labour to increase its own value:

> The great historic quality of capital is to *create* this *surplus labour*, superfluous labour from the standpoint of mere use value, mere subsistence; and its historic destiny [*Bestimmung*] is fulfilled ... when the development of the productive powers [*Produktivkräfte*] of labour, which capital incessantly whips onward with its unlimited mania for wealth ... have flourished to the stage where the possession and preservation of general wealth require a lesser labour time of society as a whole.... Capital's ceaseless striving

towards the general form of wealth drives labour beyond the limits of its natural paltriness [*Naturbedürftigkeit*], and thus creates the material elements for the development of the rich individuality which is as all-sided in its production as in its consumption ... in which natural necessity in its direct form has disappeared; because a historically created need has taken the place of the natural one. This why *capital is productive*.... It ceases to exist as such only where the development of these productive forces themselves encounters its barrier in capital itself.... Hence the great civilizing influence of capital.[2]

(Marx 1973: 325, 409)

Progress and civilization in general thus entail the transcendence of established needs, but capital transcends established boundaries not in service of humanity but for the increase of the value of capital itself. Capital's drive is expressed in its 'constant movement to create more of the same [surplus value]. The quantitative boundary of the surplus value appears to it as a mere natural barrier, as a necessity which it constantly tries to violate and beyond which it constantly seeks to go' (Marx 1973: 334–5).

Its obstacles arise out of its own propulsion, when capital finds its barrier in capital itself. To move beyond these limits is to increase production:

The increase in the productive force of living labour increases the *value* of capital (or diminishes the value of the worker) not because it increases the quantity of products or use values created by the same labour ... but rather because it diminishes *necessary* labour [*notwendigen Arbeit*], hence, in the same relation as it diminishes the former, it creates *surplus labour*, or, what amounts to the same thing, surplus value.

(Marx 1973: 339)

Necessary labour is what enables the worker to consume through the mediation of the money received as the price of her living objectified labour (the wages), and to subsist as a worker (as a mere productive force rather than as a human being). Thus everything in the shadow of capital is aimed at diminishing 'the relation of *necessary labour* to *surplus labour*, and only in the proportion in which it diminishes this relation. Surplus value is exactly equal to surplus labour; the increase of the one [is] exactly measured by the diminution of *necessary labour*' (Marx 1973: 339).

However, it is worth noting that 'the less time the society requires to produce wheat, cattle, etc., the more time it wins for other production, material or mental [...] Economy of time: to this all economy ultimately reduces itself' (Marx 1973: 172–3). Whilst this might be true of human beings who produce collectively for their own benefit as a community, so long as the savings of necessary labour time is based on capital, they consist of living labour and are not for the benefit of humanity but rather at the service of a desired increase of the value of capital itself. Marx's attention is drawn towards the fact that the saved *necessary time* and the increase of the value of capital are inversely proportional, and here we glimpse the beginning of a foreseeable crisis in capitalist development: even if productivity is doubled the value of capital increases only by half: 'if necessary labour = 1/4 of the living work day and the productive force doubles, then the value of capital does not double, but grows by 1/8; which is equal to 1/4 or 2/8 [...] – 1/4 divided by 2, or = 2/8 minus 1/8 = 1/8' (Marx 1973: 339).

In this example productivity doubles (an increase of 100 per cent), while surplus value increases from three-quarters of the work-day (75 per cent) to 7/8 of that work-day (87.5 per cent). Surplus value only increases 12.5 per cent versus a 100 per cent increase in productivity. This leads Marx to another conclusion:

> The larger the surplus value of capital *before the increase of productive force*, the larger the amount of presupposed surplus labour or surplus value of capital; or, the smaller the fractional part of the working day which forms the equivalent of the worker, which expresses necessary labour, the smaller is the increase in surplus value which capital obtains from the increase of productive force.
>
> (Marx 1973: 340)

This passage is crucial to understand the questions posed by *dependency theory*, when capitals compete against each other with varying levels of *previously* generated surplus value, because 'the more developed capital already is, the more surplus labour it has created, the more terribly must it develop the productive form in order to realize itself in only smaller proportion' (Marx 1973: 340). The civilizing impulse of capital, its desperate need to increase its own value by overcoming new limits that are constantly set at higher levels and ever more distant and difficult to reach is the product of a tendency that Marx defines as follows: 'The self-realisation of capital becomes more difficult to the extent that it has already been realised' (Marx 1973: 340).

However, this analysis is an abstraction in so far as it is based on the systematic removal of many variables; the inclusion of many other concrete variables would change its conclusion, but this '*actually already belongs in the doctrine of profit*' (Marx 1973: 341), which is situated at the most complex and superficial level of circulation. As we can see, for Marx the question of surplus value is situated, on the contrary, in the transition from labour to product, as abstract determinations of capital.

Increase of the value. Relative and absolute surplus value

As I have previously suggested Marx is mainly interested in the most hidden form of surplus value, relative surplus value, that here takes on the visible form of surplus labour:

> If capital has already raised surplus labour to the point where the entire living work day is consumed in the production process (and we here assume

the working day to be the natural amount of labour time which the worker is able to put at the disposal of capital . . .), then an increase in the productive force cannot increase labour time, nor, therefore, objectified labour time.

(Marx 1973: 342)

If the worker labours for 16 hours he reaches the limits of his endurance and may become ill or die. It is not possible to increase the natural or absolute limits of surplus labour any further; instead, by means of the technical increase of productivity, it is possible to achieve higher levels of production within the same period of time (which makes it possible to reduce necessary labour):

> [In this case] its value increased not because the *absolute* but because the *relative amount of labour* grew, i.e. the total amount of labour did not grow; the working day is as long before as after; hence no absolute increase in surplus time (surplus labour time); rather the *amount of necessary labour decreased*, and that is how relative surplus labour increased.

(Marx 1973: 342)

The decrease of necessary labour time is equal to the decrease of real wages, since the worker is now paid the same amount for a job that produces more. Here lies the secret of profit in the context of the circulation processes (which are addressed in more detail further on). In these passages Marx grasps the whole question with greater clarity than before, as evidenced by his observation that 'according to Ricardo, the element of the accumulation of capitals is posited just as completely with relative surplus labour as with absolute – impossible any other way' (Marx 1973: 345).

Then there is a period of surplus time during which surplus labour is carried out and, once objectified, is then transformed into surplus value. This surplus value is *absolute* when natural labour time is added to it, i.e. if the worker 'had worked ten hours instead of eight in the earlier relation, [and] had increased his absolute labour time' (Marx 1973: 345). It is *relative* when there is a proportionate relationship between the increase of productivity and the decrease of necessary labour time, and therefore an *absolute increase* in surplus value (although it involves a *decrease in the rate* or index of surplus value, as Marx has already begun to discover). Because of this, once there is an increase in value, it becomes increasingly difficult to for it to grow further, because capital must apply itself to the task of increasing surplus value with improvements that are too costly:

> Every increase in the mass of capital employed can increase the *productive force* not only at an arithmetical but at a geometrical rate; although it can increase profit at the same time ... only at a much lower rate. The influence of the increase of capital on the increase of productive force is thus infinitely greater than that of the increase of the productive force on the growth of capital.

(Marx 1973: 346)

Nonetheless, capital manages to find a way to increase its value not only through relative increases achieved by greater productivity, but also through absolute increases derived from greater amounts of labour time. There are also other ways to increase value:

> in motion: [it] can realize itself only in *new* living labour (whether labour which had been dormant is set into motion), or *new workers* are created (population [growth] is accelerated) or again a new circle of exchange values, of exchange values in circulation, is expanded, which can occur on the production side if the liberated exchange value opens up a *new branch of production* … or the same is achieved when objectified labour is put in the sphere of circulation in a new country, by an expansion of trade.
>
> (Marx 1973: 348)

Note how Marx relates the growth of urban populations to the inclusion of populations in colonial possessions as possible modes of capital growth and as elements of the same issue of absolute surplus labour. Ricardo had never referred to population growth as a relevant factor of increases in exchange values. This in turn determines a cycle whereby: 'Capitals accumulate faster than the population; thus wages rise; thus population; thus grain prices; thus the difficulty of production and hence the *exchange values*' (Marx 1973: 351).

In the medium term, population growth causes a fall in wages due to an excess supply of living labour. Ultimately, Marx is searching for a solution: he gets side-tracked along the way in certain digressions, goes around in circles at times, turns back on its track, starts again, and repeats himself. He advances slowly, as we follow in his footsteps.

Permanence of the value of the material and instrument of labour

So far Marx's discourse has relied upon two opposite categories: 'We have always spoken only about the two elements of capital, the two parts of the living work day, of which one represents wages, the other profit; one, necessary labour, the other, surplus labour' (Marx 1973: 354).

As we can see Marx equates profit (situated at the superficial level of circulation) with surplus value, and he analyses this in the following chapter. So far Marx has used concepts such as wages and profits (surplus value), together with necessary labour and surplus labour. What is missing are the means of production: 'But what about the other two parts of capital, which are realized in the material of labour and the instrument of labour?' (Marx 1973: 354)

This is the beginning of his development of the critical concept of constant capital, which appears shortly thereafter for the *first time*; but its meaning is not yet clear. In the 'simple production process' labour always employs instruments and materials necessary for its deployment (Marx 1973: 354). This is the material of labour (raw materials) as material and the instrument (from machines to an entire factory) as instrument, i.e. as use-values; however, the subsumption of the material-instrument is produced as a moment of capital. This autonomous entity is thus ontologically subsumed by capital: 'but are they, as components [als Bestandteile] of capital, values which labour must replace? [...] Such objections [were] heaped on Ricardo; that he regarded profit and wages only as components of production costs, not the machine and the material' (Marx 1973: 354).

Clearly, for Marx the material and the instruments of labour are moments of capital, given that money has been invested or trans-substantiated in them. As essential determinations of capital, raw material or the material and instruments of technology are now moments of capital itself, between labour and the product. As capital both are value, products as products and exchangeable commodities whose ability to be exchanged is their essence, and whose exchange must be produced. The question now is whether this value is destroyed, which would result in the annihilation of value and thus of capital, or whether it can persist in a modified form; whether it not only persists in a constant form as capital whose value has been preserved, but in fact also as value that can be increased. When mere cotton is trans-formed – changes form – into a garment, the value of the cotton not only disappears but is also subsumed under a superior form, thus increasing its value. The creation of new value without the destruction of old value is accomplished by the worker's labour without any cost being incurred by the capitalist:

> The worker has not created the objectified labour contained in yarn and spindle ... for him they were and remain material to which he gave another form and into which he incorporated new labour.... That their old value is preserved happens because a new one is added to them, not that the old is itself reproduced, created.
>
> (Marx 1973: 355–6)

As the worker transforms the object through her labour the material at her disposal increases in value, acquires greater value than before, but this is a value placed at the service of capital with no benefits to the worker:

> Like every other natural or social power of labour unless it is the product of previous labour, or of such previous labour as does not need to be repeated ... this natural animating [belebende] power of labour ... becomes a power of capital, not of labour.
>
> (Marx 1973: 358)

So far, Marx has explored the question of raw material transformed by labour, rather than that of the instrument of labour itself; this is why the concept of constant capital has not emerged.

Money, as money, has an autonomous existence at its origin. It is the presupposition of the first appearance of capital, as money transformed into capital and then invested into wages and means of production. This is the second expression of money, but the first expression of capital. As capital, money also appears at the end of the process of production, which includes surplus value as profit, and in its third form it finds its most adequate expression.

> Just as money at first appeared as the presupposition, the cause of capital, so it now appears as its effect. In the first movement, money arose out of simple circulation; in the second it arises from the production process of capital. In the first, it *makes a transition to* capital; in the second it appears as a presupposition of capital posited by capital itself.
>
> (Marx 1973: 358)

In this conclusion Marx returns to the starting point of his discussion: money. And in fact, in the end, the increase of value is nothing but the increase of money as a result of the processes of both production and circulation: after the product transformed into a commodity has been sold and when the value injected at the beginning of the cycle and the profit obtained along the way are both present (including surplus value). Many more pages of his *Notebooks* are dedicated to this: they are the space of realization of Marx's theoretical work where these concepts are fully developed and expressed with sufficient clarity.

We can see then that in December 1857 the formulation of several key categories of Marx's theory had already taken on a definitive form, while others were still in the ambiguous state of mere intuitions that had not achieved sufficient conceptual force. His critique of the entire system of categories of bourgeois political economy had already taken crucial steps forward, but his overall task had barely been undertaken, when only a month had passed since the moment of clarity when for the first time in his work he discovered the category of surplus value.

Notes

1 These are the notes which correspond to the chapter on profit in Ricardo's *Principles of Political Economy and Taxation.* Marx should have begun with the issue of profit and circulation in order to raise it to its deepest, most hidden, level behind the scenes: to that of the process of production.
2 See the rest of this text:

> Thus, just as production founded on capital creates universal industriousness on one side ... so does it create on the other side a system of general exploitation of the natural and human qualities, a system of general utility, utilising science itself just as much as all the physical and mental qualities [*geistigen*], while there appears nothing higher in itself, nothing legitimate for itself, outside [*ausser*] this circle of social production and exchange. Thus the capital creates the bourgeois society.... It is destructive towards all of this [all traditional, confined, complacent, encrusted satisfaction of present needs], and constantly revolutionizes it, tearing down all the barriers which hem in the development of the forces of production, the expansion of needs ... of natural and spiritual forces [*Geisteskräfte*].
>
> (Marx 1973: 409)

References

Marx, Karl (1953) *Grundrisse der Kritik der politischen Ökonomie (Rohentwurf) 1857–1858. Anhang 1850–1859*, ed. Marx–Engels–Lenin Institute Moskau, Berlin: Dietz Verlag.

Marx, Karl (1973) *Grundrisse: Foundations of the Critique of Political Economy (Rough Draft)*, Harmondsworth: Penguin.

5 Historical materialism in 'Forms which Precede Capitalist Production'

Ellen Meiksins Wood

Introduction

'The general theory of historical materialism', wrote Eric Hobsbawm in his introduction to the first English translation of the 'Forms which Precede Capitalist Production',

> requires only that there should be a succession of modes of production, though not necessarily any particular modes, and perhaps not in any particular predetermined order. Looking at the actual historical record, Marx thought that he could distinguish a certain number of socio-economic formations and a certain succession. But if he had been mistaken in his observations, or if these had been based on partial and therefore misleading information, the general theory of historical materialism would remain unaffected.
>
> (Hobsbawm 1964: 20)[1]

This seems, on the face of it, a very large claim. Can it really be sustainable to say that Marx could have been seriously mistaken in his historical observations and still be right in his general theory? At first glance, this claim suggests a rather casual approach to the relation between empirical specificity and theoretical generalization, or, perhaps, a reduction of historical materialism to an empty methodological abstraction, all form and no substance. Yet, on closer consideration, much can be learned by putting Marx to this test and asking how well his general theory stands up irrespective of historical error. So let us begin with an even larger claim: Marx was indeed seriously wrong in his historical observations, for reasons having less to do with his own shortcomings than with the existing state of historical scholarship at the time of his writing the *Grundrisse*; but the edifice he constructed on the foundation of this faulty knowledge reveals the power, not the weakness, of historical materialism as he conceived it, which pushed him beyond the limitations of existing scholarship.

Marx and pre-capitalist history: oriental and ancient

Marx in 'Forms which Precede Capitalist Production' set out to examine the various ways in which a division of labour disrupted the primitive unity of the tribal community, not only the unity among its members but, more particularly, the unity of workers with the conditions of their labour and subsistence. Capitalism would be the final product of that disruption, the final 'release of the worker from the soil as his natural workshop' (Marx 1973: 471). But it was preceded by forms of property which had moved beyond primitive communalism, though the worker still related 'to the objective conditions of his labour as his property' and there remained a 'natural unity of labour with its material [*sachlich*] presuppositions'. In these pre-capitalist property forms – which included 'small, free landed property as well as ... communal landownership resting on the oriental commune' – the worker had 'an objective existence independent of labour', relating to himself 'as proprietor, as master of the conditions of his reality' and to others either as co-proprietors of communal property or as independent proprietors like himself (Marx 1973: 471).

Marx distinguished essentially three pre-capitalist forms, the oriental or Asiatic, the ancient or classical (Greek and Roman), and the feudal form, derived, in specific conditions, from a 'Germanic' path out of primitive communalism. It is not always clear whether we should regard all or any of these as points in a process of historical succession or as alternative routes out of the most primitive communal property. Perhaps the most likely reading is that the 'Asiatic' form stands more or less by itself as the least dynamic route out of the primitive state, while the ancient alternative is more dynamic. The feudal form that follows it is, of course, the one that leads to capitalism. It may not even matter whether Marx had in mind a historical sequence, if his principal objective was to explain the specificity of capitalism (his discussion of pre-capitalist forms is, after all, part of a discussion of capital), in contrast to other ways in which humanity has related to the conditions of its labour and subsistence. Whatever his intentions, for the moment it suffices to say that his accounts of all three major forms were, in varying ways and degrees, misleading, when not downright wrong.

The oriental form has probably been the most controversial. This form, which according to Marx is the most long-lasting and resistant to development, retains a type of communal property embodied in a higher authority, typically a despotic state. This communal authority stands over and above smaller local communities, where manufacture and agriculture are united, and takes surplus labour in the form of tribute. Among the objections levelled at this model is that it collapses modern forms – particularly modern India – into ancient 'oriental despotisms'. Sometimes Marx is accused of Eurocentrism, especially because of his insistence on the stagnation of the 'oriental' form – although, since he includes in this category certain non-Asiatic societies, the objection may have less to do with a distinction between east and west than with his use of the term 'oriental' or 'Asiatic' to describe the stagnant type. Yet in some respects, his account of the Asiatic mode has more to recommend it than do his descriptions of the other two major forms. There is ample historical and archaeological evidence of ancient states very much like Marx's oriental or 'Asiatic' form, even if they have not been exclusively or even predominantly in Asia. In fact, it is arguable that these states were more the rule than the exception in ancient civilizations – a point to which we shall return. What is most misleading about Marx's account has to do with how he situates it on his historical map and in particular, as we shall see, where he places it in relation to the ancient form.

The ancient form turns out to be the most problematic of all, and the misleading account of this type certainly has profound consequences for Marx's view of historical development. When the archaeological discoveries of the late nineteenth and early twentieth centuries, together with more recent scholarship on slavery and other aspects of ancient Greco-Roman history, revolutionized our understanding of classical antiquity, they threatened apparently important aspects of historical materialism, not just Marx's suggestions about the sequence of modes of production but, more fundamentally, theories about the origins and development of property, class and the state that we associate with Marx and Engels.[2]

In the ancient form, which appears to emerge directly out of primitive communalism, property is still communal, but the commune is now a civic community to which members belong as citizens, in a society already characterized by a division of labour between town and country. The ancient form is an urban civilization founded on agriculture and landed property. 'Membership in the commune remains the presupposition for the appropriation of land and soil, but, as a member of the commune, the individual is a private proprietor' (Marx 1973: 475). The natural presuppositions of labour belong to the proprietor, 'but this belonging [is] mediated by his being a member of the state'. The community of citizens stands over and against those outside it who cannot own property, most particularly slaves, who themselves constitute a major part of the city's communal property. In *The German Ideology*, Marx and Engels had elaborated on this division between the citizen community and the body of slaves, describing it as a class relation, with the state as an association of citizens against a producing class of slaves. In *The Origin of the Family, Private Property and the State*, Engels spells out the sequence of development, which also seems to underlie Marx's analysis in 'Forms which Precede Capitalist Production': the tribal or gentile order, still visible in the 'heroic' age of the Homeric epics, gives way to the state, as primitive communalism is disrupted by a division of labour and the emergence of classes.[3]

Archaeological discoveries, the decipherment of the ancient Mycenaean script, Linear B, and recent scholarship present a rather different picture. They reveal advanced civilizations in Bronze Age Greece, long before the age of Homer and very different from the 'heroic' society he depicts. Minoan and Mycenaean Greece apparently had states that much more closely resembled Marx's Asiatic form, if on a smaller scale than in the ancient empires of Asia: bureaucratic states in which the central monarchical power was the principal appropriating force, extracting surpluses from surrounding villages of peasant producers, where the division between appropriators and producers was a direct relation between state and subjects, and where private property and class were undeveloped. Although Homeric heroes purport to represent these pre-classical Greek civilizations, it is now clear that the society described in the epics, to the extent that it existed at all, was something much closer to Homer's own day, long after the collapse of the Bronze Age states and with a very different type of state, the classical polis, already in prospect. The collapse of the old states remains a mystery, but it seems reasonable to believe that the aristocracy already visible in the Homeric epics does not represent the early dissolution of a primitive community, tribal disintegration and emerging class divisions, but rather a remnant of an earlier, more developed state with a much more structured hierarchy.

At the very least, then, we can draw certain conclusions which challenge the old Marxist picture: the 'purest, classic' form of class division did not 'spring directly and mainly out of class oppositions which develop in gentile society itself'. There are no known examples of an 'ancient' form, as a pristine transition from primitive communalism and an alternative to the 'Asiatic'. If anything, the 'Asiatic' form begins to look more like the 'purest, classic' pathway out of primitive communalism. If this is so, then we must adopt a very different view of the development of class and state. We have to consider the strong possibility that some form of state, as a direct appropriator of surplus labour, preceded private property and class, and that the development of landed aristocracies such as emerged in ancient Greece and Rome may presuppose the prior existence, and the destruction, of such hierarchical state structures.

It also needs to be said that the development of slavery on a significant scale in ancient Greece was a later development and that its growth was the product of an already existing class division within the civic community (see Wood 1988, Chapter II). Nor did slavery preclude the labour of citizens. The polis had developed to deal with internal divisions between landlords and peasants, and the majority of citizens would continue to labour for a livelihood throughout the democracy. The resolution or containment of the struggles between landlords and labouring classes was achieved by offering peasants and craftsmen a civic identity, strengthening the civic community against aristocratic power and privilege; and this gave an impetus to the enslavement of outsiders by giving citizens a certain protection from various forms of 'extra-economic' exploitation and juridical dependence. The juridical and political freedom of citizens, both appropriators and producers, was a condition of the autonomous development of property and class. It also constituted the dynamic and contradictory relation between state and private property which would be a constant theme in western history.

Does the ancient form fare better if we confine it to the Roman case? The problem here is that we are no more able to identify a pristinely primitive Rome than a 'pure and classic' early Greece. By the time the Romans become visible in the historical record, their society is already shaped by Etruscan and Greek social and political forms. If the city is the hallmark of the ancient form, it is even more true that Rome owes its classic identity to the Etruscans and the Greeks. It may be possible to postulate some kind of early peasant society in Rome, but the aristocratic republic that followed the Roman kings and represents the essence of the Roman classical period presupposes class divisions between peasants and landlords, and those, in turn, may presuppose the hierarchy of the Etruscan state and even interaction with the Greeks. As for the division between citizens and slaves, here too the growth of slavery was preceded by the internal divisions between landlords and peasants, together with the civic identity of peasants which, though weaker than in Greek democracy, encouraged the aristocracy to seek alternative means of exploitation.

From feudalism to capitalism

The Germanic type is problematic for somewhat different reasons. Marx does not present it as a *system* in the same sense as the others. But this formation is in some ways more important to him, because without it there would be no feudalism and hence, presumably, no capitalism. The problems here begin with a historical record that is much more patchy than the Greco-Roman. For that matter, it is not at all clear who the 'Germanic' peoples were, since the category has, from the beginning, included a wide variety of social types and ethnic groups, sometimes including Slavs and Celts (if we can even assume that the latter categories themselves have a precise meaning). At the same time, the historical image of the ancient 'Germans' has been shaped from the start by Roman commentaries, with all their ideological baggage, especially in the works of Tacitus and Julius Caesar, to say nothing of Greek and Roman projections of their own tribal histories and mythologies. Not the least significant factor in this distorted picture is the Greco-Roman tendency to measure other societies by their own standard of 'civilized' life, centred on the political life of the city, the culture and politics of the polis or republic. Barbarians outside the polis were more like wild animals than civilized humans. At the same time, this picture could be stood on its head, to produce a romanticized image of German tribes as free and equal communities of hardy warriors, in contrast to the corrupt, degenerate and decadent Romans. It would be this image, filtered through a mythology of Germanic primitive communism and fierce devotion to freedom perpetuated by nineteenth century social scientists, that would inform the ideology of National Socialism and its propaganda of the German nation.[4]

Yet the archaeological record does little to support this imagery, in either its disdainful or romanticized expressions. For instance, even early records show considerable inequalities of wealth and the existence of an aristocracy among the 'Germans'. Marx's account is, to be sure, somewhat different from either of these mythical images, but it has its own problems. He certainly regards the Germanic relation to property as a form of primitive communalism (not communism), as was, for him, the ancient mode, in the sense that communal property of one type or another still exists. But the commune 'does not in fact exist as a *state* or *political body*, as in classical antiquity' (Marx 1973: 483). Among the Germanic tribes, individual families and chiefs live separately and generally far apart, so the community exists only as a periodic gathering, a 'coming together', as he puts it, rather than a 'being together', although there is still some common property, in the form of land for hunting, grazing or timber. The Germanic community, then, consists of individual, more or less self-sufficient households, which come together when necessary, as in military ventures, but which are far more individualistic than the polis community. Even common property, such as pasturage, is utilized in individualistic ways, by individual household units; and there are, in Marx's view, already signs of class divisions within the community.

Marx probably exaggerates the individualism of the German tribes, since the archaeological record suggests a fairly consistent pattern of village settlement. But the real problems in his account have more to do with traditional conventions about barbarian invasions of the Roman Empire, which seem to suggest incursions by more or less pristinely 'Germanic' tribes, emerging more or less untouched from the forests of the north. Yet the interactions between the Romans and the 'Germans' go much further back than the late mass migrations commonly regarded as 'barbarian invasions'. There had, for instance, been long-standing relations of exchange, which served to aggravate social differentiation within the German tribes and to destabilize relations among Germanic communities themselves, provoking constant warfare and increasing militarization. By the time their incursions into Roman territory became a decisive factor in determining the fate of the Empire, the Germans whose practices and institutions are said to have created feudalism as they took over a disintegrating Roman Empire, were already deeply marked by their long interactions with Rome.

To the extent that Marx is concerned with the transition from feudalism to capitalism, what he says about the feudal form is obviously a matter of some consequence. It is true that he does not, in the *Grundrisse*, set out to explain the transition, although he does talk about the 'primitive accumulation' that preceded capitalism. His objective is rather to highlight the specificity of capitalism in contrast to earlier forms of property and labour. But if there is here *any* transition from one social form to another, it is the passage from feudalism to capitalism that matters most to him; and any weaknesses in his account of the feudal type, or the Germanic forms that led to it, are likely to have the most serious consequences for historical materialism.

Marx's account of feudalism in 'Forms which Precede Capitalist Production' is perhaps most interesting for what is absent from it. Although there can be little doubt of his conviction that feudalism led to capitalism, he has very little to say about the internal dynamics of feudalism that produced this effect. As Hobsbawm has pointed out, there is very little here about feudal agriculture, nor do we find anything like the contradictions, emanating from class divisions, that fatally weakened the ancient type. For that matter, it is not entirely clear what it was in the logic of the Germanic type that conveyed itself to feudalism or helped to bring it into being. The argument seems to be something like this: while the oriental form was a unity of town and country, and the ancient form an urban civilization founded on agriculture and landed property, the Germanic was more decidedly rural, based on the vast agricultural territories that emerged from the conquest of Rome. This type of development meant that the medieval city (however it came into being) developed autonomously, not as a unity of town and country, nor as an urban foundation rooted in agriculture, but as a distinctively free urban community permitting the autonomous development of craft production and trade:

> The history of classical antiquity is the history of cities, but of cities founded on landed property; Asiatic history is a kind of unity of town and countryside ... the Middle Ages (Germanic period) beings with the land as the seat of history, whose further development then moves forward in the contradiction between town and country-side; the modern [age] is the urbanization of the countryside, not ruralization of the city as in antiquity.
>
> (Marx 1973: 479)

It is possible to argue that the individualism imparted by the old Germanic culture plays an important part in Marx's account of the transition to capitalism, but more important still is his view of the relation between Germanic ruralism and medieval urbanism. Here are the basic assumptions underlying the view that capitalism grew not out of the social property relations of feudalism itself but rather, to use Marx's own words, in the 'interstices' of feudalism. The German form, in other words, was important in promoting the development of capitalism not so much because of its own internal dynamic but because it left available spaces within which 'bourgeois' culture and economic activity could freely develop.

It is here that the problems in Marx's account become most starkly visible, and it is striking that in *Capital* he begins to offer a rather different account. In 'Forms which Precede Capitalist Production', he has not yet entirely broken with the most common question-begging accounts of how capitalism originated. Classical political economy and Enlightenment theories of progress had tended to assume the existence of 'commercial society' or capitalism in order to explain its coming into being: the urban economy of merchants and craftsmen contained the elements of 'commercial society', more or less by definition, and all that was required to bring about its full maturity was to release the commercial economy from bondage and sweep away the obstacles to its development. The remnants of this view are still visible in Marx's theory of 'interstices' and his account of the role played by Germanic forms in opening the road to capitalism. The origin of capitalism is here largely a matter of allowing its already existing elements to grow. When he developed his ideas in *Capital*, he was already hinting at a very different explanation, which did indeed begin to seek the source of the transition not in the 'interstices' of feudalism but rather in its own internal dynamics, in its own constitutive property relations, which gave rise to an authentic social transformation.

'Forms which Precede Capitalist Production' and historical materialism

Can we, then, find in 'Forms which Precede Capitalist Production' anything that might have compelled him to look for an alternative, or anything that offered him a fruitful avenue to find it? It is clear, to begin with, that it does not offer a usable sequence of modes of production. But is it just a question of replacing one sequence with another, more informed by recent scholarship? Or should we reconsider the very premise that historical materialism needs such a sequence at all? Does the strength of historical materialism, as Marx himself conceived it, lie elsewhere?

The idea of a succession of modes of production does not, by itself, represent a radical break with the conventions of classical political economy. There, too, history is presented as a series of modes of subsistence, driven by the division of labour, each one more technologically advanced than the previous one and more capable of creating surpluses; and Marx's sequence still has much in common with it. Although his analysis of capitalism clearly recognizes its distinctive drive to constantly improve labour productivity, the whole historical process that culminates in capitalism may still be driven by some inevitable, transhistorical tendency to improve the forces of production through the division of labour and technological improvement. There is even a significant element of Smith's 'commercialization' model, or conceptions of progress as the liberation of the bourgeoisie, in Marx's explanation of how the Germanic form helped bring about the rise of capitalism by leaving room for an autonomous urban economy.

Yet Marx introduces a radical innovation into this historical sequence, which will in the end prove decisive: not only the emphasis on class divisions but, more particularly, the idea that historical progress has been a progressive 'separation of free labour from the objective conditions of its realization – from the means of labour and the material for labour' (Marx 1973: 471), which culminates in the complete separation of the wage labourer in capitalism. Before capitalism, workers related to the basic condition of labour – the land   as their property, whether the communal property of one or another form of primitive communalism or the free landed property of the independent small producing household. Capitalism completely disrupts the 'natural unity of labour with its material presuppositions', and the worker no longer has 'an objective existence independent of labour'. Marx cannot, then, be satisfied with the sequences of classical political economy – such as Adam Smith's progression from hunting, to pasturage, to farming to commercial society, propelled by the division of labour and ever-expanding exchange. Nor can he remain uncritically wedded to conceptions of progress as the forward march of the bourgeoisie. While there are certainly parallels between his sequence and those older conventions, the essential criteria of differentiation among the stages of progress are significantly different. His focus on property relations and the separation of labour from its material presuppositions invites us to look elsewhere for the driving force of history.

In 'Forms which Precede Capitalist Production', the remnants of the older view are still visible. The little that Marx has to say on the transition from feudalism to capitalism here seems to fall back on those earlier conventions, without exerting the full power of his own distinctive insights. It is as if the state of contemporary knowledge holds him back from putting those insights to work on the transition to capitalism. So he relies, against the grain, on an albeit nuanced version of the old commercialization model, in which the emergence of capitalism requires no real explanation, because all it needed was the opening of space within which already existing capitalist elements were free to develop.

Yet against the background of his own deeper insights into the internal dynamics of specific social property relations, the weaknesses in his account of feudalism and the transition to capitalism become starkly apparent. Marx's ideas about the relation of labour to the conditions of its realization seem to propel him ever further away from the conventions of political economy and Enlightenment conceptions of progress. In *Capital* he moves further still beyond his original account, applying the general theory of social property relations outlined in the *Grundrisse*: 'The capitalist system,' he writes in volume I,

> pre-supposes the complete separation of the labourers from all property in the means by which they can realise their labour. As soon as capitalist production is once on its own legs, it not only maintains this separation, but reproduces it on a continually extending scale. The process, therefore, that clears the way for the capitalist system, can be none other than the process which takes away from the labourer the possession of his means of production; a process that transforms, on the one hand, the social means of subsistence and of production into capital, on the other, the immediate producers into wage-labourers. The so-called primitive accumulation, therefore, is nothing else than the historical process of divorcing the producer from the means of production.
>
> (Marx 1996: 705)

It is striking that the process of capitalist development is here not based in the city but in the countryside. It occurred in its first and 'classic' form with the expropriation of direct producers in English agriculture, establishing a new system of relations between landlords, tenants and wage-labourers, in which landlords – unlike their counterparts elsewhere – increasingly derived their rents from the profits of capitalist tenants, while many small producers became propertyless wage-labourers. That social transformation – and not, as it was for classical political economy, the mere accumulation of wealth by means of commercial activity – was, for Marx, the *real* 'primitive accumulation'.

It would be left to later Marxist historians to develop these insights into a comprehensive explanation of the transition to capitalism. But the fundamental principles are already present, and these are the essential principles of historical materialism. What, then, does this tell us about the essence of historical materialism and its general theory of history? The first and most important point is that it has nothing to do with a mechanical sequence of modes of production. Nor is it about some transhistorical drive which inevitably leads one social form to be succeeded by a more productive one.[5] By the time of 'Forms which Precede Capitalist Production', Marx is less and less inclined to posit a transhistorical mechanism of historical change. He is increasingly insistent on the specificity of capitalism with its distinctive laws of motion and, in general, more concentrated on the specificities of every social form, each with its own distinctive relation of direct producers to the means of production and its own specific conditions of survival and self-reproduction. He is increasingly conscious of the ways in which the specific laws of capitalism, its historically specific drive to accumulate and increase productivity by technological means, have been mistakenly read back into history as general laws.

In 'Forms which Precede Capitalist Production', it is becoming increasingly clear that, for Marx, each system of social property relations is driven by its own internal principles and not by some impersonal transhistorical law of techno-logical improvement or commercial expansion. In the introduction to the *Grund-risse*, he distinguishes himself from economists who treat production as responding to 'eternal natural laws independent of history, at which opportunity *bourgeois* relations are then quietly smuggled in as the inviolable natural laws on which society in the abstract is founded' (Marx 1973: 87). To be sure, he writes, 'there are characteristics which all stages of production have in common, and which are established as general ones by the mind; but the so-called *general preconditions* of all production are nothing more than these abstract moments with which no real historical stage of production can be grasped' (Marx 1973: 88). His objective in 'Forms which Precede Capitalist Production' is to distin-guish the various social property relations within which production has histori-cally occurred and thereby to highlight the specificity of capitalism.

It is also clear that in each specific historical stage of production, direct pro-ducers and those who appropriate their surplus labour are operating within the existing property relations and trying to meet the existing conditions of self-reproduction, in order to sustain themselves. This, of course, does not preclude revolt, rebellion or revolution. But the fact remains that transitions from one mode to another are driven by the internal logic of the existing mode, in particu-lar historical conditions; and movement beyond the existing conditions, whether gradual or sudden and violent, is driven not by some external historical necessity but by prevailing social property relations. In other words, the laws of motion of specific social forms – or, more precisely, their 'rules for reproduction', a formula better suited to a recognition of human agency – are at the same time the moving force of history in general.[6]

If anything, Marx in the maturity of his critique of political economy, from the *Grundrisse* onwards, becomes less rather than more a 'determinist', if by that is meant a thinker who treats human agents as passive receptacles of exter-nal structures or playthings of eternal laws of motion. It may seem counterintu-itive to say this, since the most common tendency in dividing the 'early' from the 'late' Marx is to stress his early 'humanism' and his later, hard-nosed economism. Yet it is in the earlier works that Marx finds himself forced to rely on transhistorical laws, such as technological determinism. In his mature work on political economy, notably the *Grundrisse* and *Capital*, he much more consistently works out the implications of his materialism's first principle, a principle that remains constant from the earliest days to the end: that the bottom line for historical materialism is not some disembodied economic 'base' or 'structure' but 'practical activity'. The material base is itself constituted by human practice.

At the same time, the relevant practices entail relations – among human agents and between them and nature. These social relations, which will vary in different historical circumstances, constitute certain specific and irreducible conditions of self-reproduction; and human agency must operate within those specific conditions. Now, some might understand this to mean that, because there is always an infinite variety of such conditions, the best we can do is provide a detailed description of the requirements for reproduction at any given historical moment and in any given place, without generalizations about this or that 'mode of production', this or that set of social property relations. But historical materialism suggests that social property relations, as the irreducible conditions of survival and social reproduction, set the terms of survival and social reproduction in a more fundamental way, allowing us to construct certain generalizations about the rules for reproduction they impose, which operate wherever and whenever those property relations exist, whatever their specific political or cultural context.

In volume III of *Capital*, Marx tells us more about the nature of social property relations. He also explains how their general rules can operate in many empirically specific ways. He elaborates his definition of the essence of each social form, and it is more clear than ever precisely how the relation of labour to the means of its realization, as outlined in the *Grundrisse*, affects the whole social structure: 'the specific economic form in which unpaid surplus labour is pumped out of direct producers ... reveals the innermost secret, the hidden basis of the entire social structure' (Marx 1998: 777–8). In all pre-capitalist forms, where direct producers remained in possession of the means of labour, non-producing appropriators could appropriate their surplus labour only by exercising 'extra-economic' force, political, jurisdictional, military. These pre-capitalist forms, then, had rules for reproduction that directly implicated those extra-economic forms. Only in capitalism, where workers are completely separated from the means of production, is a purely 'economic' form of exploitation possible, based on the propertylessness of workers who must sell their labour-power for a wage, while capital is dependent on the market both to acquire labour power and to realize profits from it. This mode of exploitation, of course, carries with it specific rules for reproduction unlike those of any other form, which include the imperatives of competition, improving labour productivity and 'maximizing' strategies. In both capitalist and pre-capitalist cases, the essential rules for reproduction will always impose their specific requirements. At the same time, Marx goes on to say that 'this does not prevent the same economic basis ...

from showing infinite variations and gradations in appearance, which can be ascertained only by analysis of the empirically given circumstances'. This has several implications: it means, first of all, that we cannot simply read off the empirical specificities of any given society from its economic 'base'; but it also means that the logic of the economic basis is discernible throughout those empirical manifestations.

One way of characterizing what Marx has done, already in the *Grundrisse*, is to say that he has replaced teleology with history – not history as mere contingency, nor history as a mechanical succession of predetermined stages or a sequence of static structures, but history as a process with its own causalities, constituted by human agency in a context of social relations and social practices which impose their own demands on those engaged in them.[7] It is more than a little ironic that the *Grundrisse*, where the *history* in historical materialism truly begins to come into its own, is often viewed as an exercise in teleology. In particular, the famous aphorism, 'human anatomy contains a key to the anatomy of the ape' (Marx 1973: 105) is cited in evidence. Yet it is precisely here that Marx detaches himself most completely from the teleologies of classical political economy. His objective is to emphasize the specificity of capitalism, instead of reading capitalist laws of motion into all history in general and treating 'commercial society' as its preordained destination. Indeed, it is the very specificity of capitalism that allows it to shed light on the earlier forms it replaced, not because it is their natural and inevitable outcome but because it represents their historical other. His purpose is to challenge 'those economists who smudge over all historical differences and see bourgeois relations in all forms of society' (Marx 1973: 105). By insisting on the specificity of capitalism, by refusing to read its principles of motion back into history, and by explaining how every mode of production is governed by its own specific rules for reproduction, Marx is offering precisely the antithesis of teleology.

What, then, of grand narratives in Marx's history? Is there anything left of the Enlightenment story of progress? Is the best we can say simply that, while capitalism generates a historically distinctive drive to improve the forces of production, there is, on balance and overall, a general, incremental tendency to technological improvement throughout history, if only because, once discovered, no advance ever completely disappears? Or can we still believe in a grand emancipatory project grounded in real historical conditions? It is certainly true that Marx's main preoccupation in the *Grundrisse* and later was the very specific operations of capitalism; and, given this preoccupation, we cannot be sure what he might have thought in his maturity about philosophical grand narratives, whether in their simplest Enlightenment form or in all their Hegelian complexity. But it would seem perverse to deny that the critical history embodied in his critique of political economy must have had substantial effects. He could surely not have remained wedded to a simple narrative of progress, in which some general laws of history work themselves out to reach an inevitable goal. But does this mean that he was obliged to give up the emancipatory vision of the Enlightenment?

Marx's critique of political economy liberated history and social theory from the dead hand of capitalist ideology, and it departed from Enlightenment conceptions of progress as a unilinear process governed by transhistorical principles of motion. In place of an abstractly universal history Marx proposed a critical analysis of historical processes which emphasized the specificity of every mode of production and of capitalism in particular. Yet this did not, as is sometimes suggested, weaken the promise of socialism or undermine its claims as the historic destination of class struggle and an emancipatory project with a universal reach. If we conceive of socialism not as the *telos* of a universal technological determinism but as a historical product of capitalism and the outcome of a struggle against capitalist exploitation, this does not oblige us to give up the universality of the socialist project. Capitalism confers its own kind of universality on the struggle against exploitation and oppression. This is so not only because, as Marx suggested, capitalism is the highest form of exploitation, the last stage in the separation of producers from the means of production beyond which lies the abolition of all classes, but also because it has for the first time created a truly universal history, embracing the whole world in its uniquely expansionary dynamic.

Marx's analysis, then, is both more historical and less deterministic than Enlightenment conceptions of progress, more attuned to historical specificity and, at the same time, more truly universalistic in its vision of human emancipation, more conscious of capitalism's systemic coercions and yet more open to the possibilities of human agency and struggle.

Notes

1 In Hobsbawn's translation, the title of this section of the *Grundrisse* is 'Precapitalistic Economic Formations'. The translation 'Forms which Precede Capitalist Production' comes from the Penguin edition being used throughout this volume.

2 For a discussion of these developments, with detailed references, see Wood (1988, especially Chapters II and III).

3 In what Engels calls its 'purest, most classical form', in Athens, 'the state derived directly and mainly from the class antagonisms that developed within gentile society'. In the heroic age depicted by the Homeric epics, the gentile order is, according to this argument, still strong but it is in the process of disintegration, and slavery emerges, first in the form of conquered prisoners and then the enslavement of fellow members of the tribe. The result, writes Engels, was the emergence of:

> a third power which, while ostensibly standing above the conflicting classes, suppressed their open conflict and permitted a class struggle at most in the economic field, in a so-called legal form. The gentile constitution had outlived itself. It was burst asunder by the division of labour and by its result, the division of society into classes. Its place was taken by the *state*.
>
> (Engels 1990: 268)

4 For a discussion of the distortions, ancient and modern, which have shaped this historiography, see Geary (1988: 39–43).

5 To say this is very different from saying that there is no general tendency for the forces of production to improve. That there is such a general tendency, in very broad terms, is almost incontrovertible (and almost vacuous), since technological advances can happen

in any form of society, and the effects are likely to be incremental, since once discovered they are unlikely to disappear altogether. The question here is whether there is
any compulsion for any specific mode of production to be followed by a more productive one. Marx's aphoristic formula about the contradictions between forces and relations of production as the driving force of history (most notably in the 1859 *Preface* to
A Contribution to the Critique of Political Economy) must be weighed against the
whole of his life's work, especially his mature historical accounts, in which technological determinism is strikingly absent as a an explanatory principle. A more detailed
discussion of this point can be found in Wood (1995: 129–40).

6 Robert Brenner lays out the concept of 'rules for reproduction' in Brenner (1986).

7 'Certain critical categories and concepts employed by historical materialism', as E.P.
Thompson once wrote, 'can only be understood as historical categories: that is, as categories or concepts appropriate to the investigation of process ... concepts appropriate
to the handling of evidence not capable of static conceptual representation' (Thompson
1978: 237). It can be said that modes of production as Marx characterizes them in the
Grundrisse belong to precisely such historical categories, not 'static conceptual
representations' or abstract 'structures' but specific processes of social interaction,
contradiction and change.

References

Brenner, Robert (1986) 'The Social Basis of Economic Development', in J. Brenner
(ed.), *Analytical Marxism*, Cambridge: Cambridge University Press.

Engels, Friedrich (1990) 'The Origin of the Family, Private Property and the State', in
Marx Engels Collected Works, vol. 26: *Engels 1882–89*, New York: International Publishers.

Geary, Patrick (1988) *Before France and Germany: The Creation and Transformation of
the Merovingian World*, Oxford: Oxford University Press.

Hobsbawm, Eric J. (1964) 'Introduction', in Karl Marx, *Pre-capitalist Economic Formations*, New York: International Publishers, pp. 9–65.

Marx, Karl (1973) *Grundrisse: Introduction to the Critique of Political Economy*, trans.
Martin Nicolaus, Harmondsworth: Penguin.

Marx, Karl (1996) '*Capital*, Vol. I', in *Marx Engels Collected Works*, vol. 35: *Capital,
Vol. 1*, New York: International Publishers.

Marx, Karl (1998) '*Capital*, Vol. III', in *Marx Engels Collected Works*, vol. 37: *Capital,
Vol. 3*, New York: International Publishers.

Thompson, Edward Palmer (1978) *The Poverty of Theory*, London: Merlin Press.

Wood, Ellen Meiksins (1988) *Peasant-Citizen and Slave: The Foundations of Athenian
Democracy*, London and New York: Verso.

Wood, Ellen Meiksins (1995) *Democracy Against Capitalism: Renewing Historical
Materialism*, Cambridge: Cambridge University Press.

6   Marx's *Grundrisse* and the ecological contradictions of capitalism

John Bellamy Foster

Introduction

In *The Eighteenth Brumaire of Louis Bonaparte* Marx famously wrote: 'Men make their own history, but they do not make it just as they please; they do not make it under circumstances chosen by themselves, but under circumstances directly encountered, given and transmitted from the past' (Marx 1979: 103). The material circumstances or conditions that he was referring to here were the product of both natural and social history. For Marx production was a realm of expanding needs and powers. But it was subject at all times to material limits imposed by nature. It was the tragedy of capital that its narrow logic propelled it in an unrelenting assault on both these natural limits and the new social needs that it brought into being. By constantly revolutionizing production capital transformed society, but only by continually alienating natural necessity (conditions of sustainability and reproduction) and human needs.

Recent research has revealed that an ecological–materialist critique was embedded in all of Marx's work from *The Economic and Philosophical Manuscripts* of 1844 to his *Ethnological Notebooks* of the late 1870s to early 1880s (see Burkett 1999; Foster 2000; Dickens 2004). This can be seen in his materialist conception of nature and history, his theory of alienation (which encompassed the alienation of nature), his understanding of the labour and production process as the metabolic relation between humanity and nature, and his co-evolutionary approach to society–nature relations.

Nevertheless, because Marx's overall critique of political economy remained unfinished, these and other aspects of his larger materialist conception of nature and history were incompletely developed – even in those works, such as *Capital*, volume 1, published in his lifetime. Moreover, the relation of his developed political–economic critique in *Capital* to the wider corpus of his work was left unclear. The *Grundrisse* has therefore become an indispensable means of unifying Marx's overall analysis. It not only stands chronologically between his early writings and *Capital*, but also constitutes a conceptual bridge between the two. At the same time it provides a theoretical–philosophical viewpoint that is in some ways wider in scope than any of his other works.

The form of the *Grundrisse* – the fact that Marx composed it as a set of notebooks primarily for his own self-edification in preparation for his critique of political economy – has made it a difficult work to interpret. One way to understand his general theoretical approach is in terms of the relation between 'production in general' – a conceptual category introduced in the opening pages of the *Grundrisse*, originally conceived as the basis of its 'first section' (Marx 1973: 320) – and specific historical modes of production. The latter included pre-capitalist economic formations and capitalism's immediate historical presupposition, i.e. primitive accumulation – together with capitalism proper.

Marx used the concept of production in general as a basis from which to develop his general theory of needs, which encompassed both natural prerequisites and historic developments – the production of new needs manifested in new use values. It was the conflict between production in general (as represented by use value) and specifically capitalist production (as represented by exchange value) that pointed to capitalism's historical limits and necessary transcendence. A crucial part of the argument in the *Grundrisse* was the distinction between this approach to nature–society and that of Malthus.

The nature–society or ecological dialectic embodied in the *Grundrisse* can thus be seen in terms of five interrelated realms:

1   the attempt to construct a materialist critique encompassing both production in general and its specific historical forms;
2   the articulation of a theory of human needs in relation to both society and nature – pointing beyond the capital relation;
3   the analysis of pre-capitalist economic formations and the dissolution of these forms through primitive accumulation, representing changing forms of the appropriation of nature through production;
4   the question of external barriers/boundaries to capital; and
5   the confrontation with Malthus on population and the earth.

Production in general and natural–historical materialism

The starting point for Marx's critical ontology in the *Grundrisse* was that of production in general. Production in the most concrete sense was always historically specific, i.e. production at a definite stage of social development. Nevertheless, an understanding of these specific forms gave rise to a more general, abstract conception, that of the 'production process in general, such as is common to all social conditions, that is, without historic character' (Marx 1973: 320). 'All epochs of production', Marx wrote,

> have certain common traits, common characteristics. *Production in general* is an abstraction, but a rational abstraction in so far as it really brings out and fixes the common element and thus saves us repetition.... For example. No production possible without an instrument of production, even if this instrument is only the hand. No production without stored-up, past labour,

even if it is only the facility gathered together and concentrated in the hand of the savage by repeated practice.

(Marx 1973: 85–6)

Production in general in Marx's analysis was tied to the production of use values. Use value 'presupposed matter,' and constituted the 'natural particularity' associated with a given human product. It existed 'even in simple exchange or barter'. It constituted the 'natural limit of the commodity' within capitalist production – the manifestation of production in general as opposed to specifically capitalist production (Marx 1973: 267–8).

Closely related to production in general, was labour in general. 'Labour,' Marx wrote in *Capital*,

is, first of all, a process ... by which man through his own actions, mediates, regulates and controls the metabolism between himself and nature.... It [the labor process] is the universal condition for the metabolic interaction [*Stoffwechsel*] between man and nature, the everlasting nature-imposed condition of human existence.

(Marx 1996: 187, 194; translation according to Marx 1976: 283, 290)[1]

This approach to nature and production first appeared in the *Grundrisse*, where Marx discussed the metabolic 'change in matter [*Stoffwechsel*]' associated with 'newly created use value' (Marx 1973: 667). Just as this metabolic relation constituted the universal condition defining production, so the alienation of this metabolism was the most general expression of both human alienation and alienation from nature, which had its highest form in bourgeois society. As Marx explained:

It is not the *unity* of living and active humanity with the natural, inorganic conditions of their metabolic exchange with nature, and hence their appropriation of nature, which requires explanation or is the result of a historic process, but rather the *separation* between these inorganic conditions of human existence and this active existence, a separation which is completely posited only in the relation of wage labor and capital.

(Marx 1973: 489)

It was the historical alienation of human beings from nature under capitalist production rather than their unity in production in general that therefore required critical analysis.

Here Marx was building on an earlier materialist–dialectical conception presented in his 1844 *Economic and Philosophical Manuscripts*, where he had written that:

Nature is man's *inorganic body* – that is, insofar as it is not itself human body. Man *lives* on nature – means that nature is his *body*, with which he must remain in continuous interchange if he is not to die. That man's physical and spiritual life is linked to nature means simply that nature is linked to itself, for man is a part of nature.

(Marx 1975: 276)

This dialectic of organic–inorganic relations was derived from Hegel's *Philosophy of Nature* and was rooted ultimately in ancient Greek philosophy. In this context organic meant pertaining to organs; inorganic referred to nature beyond human (or animal) organs; the 'inorganic body of man' to the extension of the human body by means of tools. (The Greek *organon* encompassed both organs and tools; seeing the former as 'grown-on' forms of the latter, whereas tools were the artificial organs of human beings.) 'In its outwardly oriented articulation', Hegel wrote, 'it [the animal] is a production mediated by its inorganic nature' (Hegel 1970: vol. 3, 185; Foster and Burkett 2000).

In the *Economic and Philosophical Manuscripts* Marx gave this a more materialist reading, arguing that:

the life of the species, both in man and in animals, consists physically in the fact that man (like the animal) lives on inorganic nature; and the more universal man (or the animal) is, the more universal is the sphere of inorganic nature on which he lives.

(Marx 1975: 275)

This was carried forward into the *Grundrisse* where he referred to 'the *natural* conditions of labour and of reproduction' as 'the objective, nature-given inorganic body' of human subjectivity. 'The earth', he stipulated, is 'the inorganic nature of the living individual.... Just as the working subject appears naturally as an individual, as natural being – so does the first objective condition of his labour appear as nature, earth, as his inorganic body' (Marx 1973: 474, 488).[2]

The *Grundrisse* is full of acknowledgements of nature's limits, natural necessity, and the co-evolution of nature and society. The planet itself had evolved, taking on new emergent forms, so that the 'processes by means of which the earth made the transition from a liquid sea of fire and vapour to its present form now lie beyond its life as finished earth' (Marx 1973: 460). With the development of industrialized agriculture, Marx argued – foreshadowing his analysis of the metabolic rift in *Capital* – 'agriculture no longer finds the natural conditions of its own production within itself, naturally, arisen, spontaneous, and ready to hand, but these exist as an independent industry separate from it'. It now requires external inputs, such as 'chemical fertilizers acquired through exchange', the importation of Peruvian guano, 'seeds from different countries, etc.' In this sense a rift had been created in the natural metabolism (Marx 1973: 527).[3]

The theory of needs and the transcendence of capital

There was in Marx's view no exclusively natural character to human needs and identity. But there were nevertheless natural prerequisites to human existence, and a natural substratum to production in general. 'Use value', he wrote, is the 'object of … satisfaction of any system whatever of human needs. This is its [wealth's] material side, which the most disparate epochs of production may have in common' (Marx 1973: 881). Hence all commodity production necessarily consisted of use value as well as exchange value. The natural prerequisites of production, embodied in use values, could be transformed but not entirely transcended through human production. Human needs, 'scant in the beginning', were, in their specifically human character, historically changing needs, developing 'only with the forces of production', erected on top of this natural substratum (Marx 1973: 612). New needs were produced through the continual transformation of both the human relation to nature and of human beings to each other – and hence of human species being. The development of production was therefore nothing but the historical development of human needs and powers in interaction with nature.

> Not only do the objective conditions change in the act of reproduction, e.g. the village becomes a town, the wilderness a cleared field etc., but the producers change, too, in that they bring out new qualities in themselves, develop themselves in production, transform themselves, develop new powers and ideas, new modes of intercourse, new needs and new language.
>
> (Marx 1973: 494; see also Lebowitz 2003: 30–2)

Neither natural history nor social history could be conceived as static; each was complex and forever changing, embodying contingent, emergent, and irreversible aspects, and above all interconnectedness (see Foster 2000). The metabolic relation between human beings and nature was thus necessarily a co-evolving one, in which the dependence of human beings on nature was an insurmountable material fact. Moreover, the future depended on the *dynamic sustainability* of this historically changing relation, in forms that provided for 'the chain of successive generations' (Marx 1998: 799).

This outlook was integral to Marx's materialist conception of nature and history as developed in his work in his work as a whole. In the *German Ideology* Marx and Engels observed that:

> the first premise of all human history is, of course, the existence of living human individuals. Thus the first fact to be established is the physical organisation of these individuals and their consequent relation to the rest of nature.… All historical writing must set out from these natural bases and their modification in the course of history through the action of men.

From such natural prerequisites of history, Marx and Engels proceeded to human history proper: production, as the specifically human relation to nature, was not only the mere satisfaction of needs but the creation at the same time of new needs. (Marx and Engels 1976: 31). These might be far removed from their original natural bases. 'Hunger is hunger', Marx observed in the *Grundrisse*, 'but the hunger gratified by cooked meat eaten with a knife and fork is a different hunger from that which bolts down raw meat with the aid of hand, nail and tooth' (Marx 1973: 92).

Under the regime of capital this dialectic of needs production became inverted, so that the production of use values, reflecting the fulfilment of old needs and the positing of new ones on natural foundations, existed only as a means not an end; while the pursuit of exchange value became the sole object of production. Capitalism created open, endless dissatisfaction, since the pursuit of exchange value as opposed to use value had no natural or social point of satisfaction, but led only to a drive/craving for more. Thus a treadmill of production was generated in which production appeared 'as the aim of mankind and wealth as the aim of production'. This contrasted with the 'loftier' if still 'childish world' of the ancients, in which human satisfaction was still the object of production, albeit from 'a limited standpoint' (Marx 1973: 488).

In the alienated, upside-down world of capital, the dominant necessity driving all others was the unquenchable desire for abstract commodity wealth, which was nothing but the limitless desire for more commodity production. This meant that the original conditions of production – land and even human beings – became mere accessories to production. Generalized commodity production disrupted all original human–natural relations, all relations of sustainability and community, in the ceaseless drive for production for production's sake, wealth for wealth's sake. But 'when the limited bourgeois form is stripped away', Marx asked, 'what is wealth other than the universality of individual needs, capacities, pleasures, productive forces, etc., created through universal exchange? The full development of human mastery over the forces of nature, those of so-called [external] nature as well as of humanity's own nature?' (Marx 1973: 488). Such 'human mastery' was of course not about the robbing of nature but the realization of a wealth of human needs and powers through human production, and not for a single generation, but for successive generations.

Pre-capitalist economic–ecological formations and primitive accumulation

Marx's very detailed (to the extent then possible) treatment of pre-capitalist economic formations in the *Grundrisse*, was meant to lead into the analysis of capitalist development itself, as part of a general historical understanding. Hence that section of the *Grundrisse* had the heading: 'Forms which Precede Capitalist Production (Concerning the process which precedes the formation of the capital relation or of original accumulation)' (Marx 1973: 471). It was preceded by a section headed 'Original Accumulation of Capital'.[4] Moreover, the section on pre-capitalist forms ended with the reconsideration of the original, primitive accumulation of capital arising out of these historical precursors, making it clear that the original basis for accumulation and capitalism's simultaneous dissolution of all earlier economic formations was the central issue here.[5]

The discussion of pre-capitalist economic formations focused on the communal nature of these formations (already substantially broken down in the class societies of the ancient and feudal worlds). Marx's analysis of 'original' or 'primitive' accumulation was thus concerned with the *dissolution* of these remaining communal and collective forms and the complete alienation of the land – providing the ground for the emergence of the modern proletariat and the self-propelling process of capital accumulation. As he wrote in *Capital*, 'private landownership, and thereby expropriation of the direct producers from the land – private landownership by the one, which implies lack of ownership by others – is *the basis of the capitalist mode of production*' (Marx 1998: 798, emphasis added). The main presupposition of capitalism was the dissolution of all previous connections to the land on the part of the direct producers. It was 'the historic dissolution of ... naturally arisen communism' as well as 'a whole series of economic systems' separated from 'the modern world, in which exchange value dominates' (Marx 1973: 882).

The *Grundrisse* provided a trenchant analysis of these processes of dissolution. What was primarily at issue was the '*Dissolution* of the relation to the earth – land and soil – as natural conditions of production – to which he [the human being] relates as to his own inorganic being' (Marx 1973: 497). Living labour, which was originally connected to and in community with the land was now defined by the fact that the earth was the worker's 'not property', i.e. his (and her) 'not-landownership ... the negation of the situation in which the working individual relates to land and soil, to the earth as his own'. This prior communal relation to the earth was now 'historically dissolved' in its entirety by capitalist relations of production (Marx 1973: 498–9). The forcible expropriation of the earth:

> 'clears,' as Steuart says, the land of its excess mouths, tears the children of the earth from the breast on which they were raised, and thus transforms labour on the soil itself, which appears by its nature as the direct wellspring of subsistence, into a mediated source of subsistence, a source purely dependent on social relations.... There can therefore be no doubt that *wage labour* in its *classic form*, as something permeating the entire expanse of society, which has replaced the very earth as the ground on which society stands, is initially created only by modern landed property, i.e. by landed property as a value created by capital itself.
>
> (Marx 1973: 276–7)

The result was 'a dialectical inversion' in which property was entirely on the side of capital, establishing the right of property over alienated labour, which existed only for (and through) its exploitation (Marx 1973: 458). In this dissolution of the traditional relation to the land the labour force was 'released' as formally free labour power, without any recourse for survival except to offer itself up for exploitation by capital. 'In bourgeois economics', Marx wrote, 'this appears as a complete emptying-out ... universal objectification *as total alienation*, and the tearing-down of all limited, one-sided aims as sacrifice of the human end-in-itself to an entirely external end' (Marx 1973: 488, emphasis added).[6]

Barriers and boundaries: capital's absolute limits

For Marx capital was self-expanding value, inseparable from accumulation. As he explained in the *Grundrisse*, 'If capital increases from 100 to 1,000, then 1,000 is now the point of departure, from which the increase has to begin; the tenfold multiplication, by 1,000% counts for nothing' (Marx 1973: 335; see also Mészáros 1995: 568). The increase, from whatever starting point, is all, since it is from this increase that profits are obtained.

This meant that capital had constantly to revolutionize its appropriation of both nature and human labour power. 'Capital', the *Grundrisse* stated,

> is the endless and limitless drive to go beyond its limiting barriers. Every boundary is and has to be a barrier for it. Else it would cease to be capital – money as self-reproductive. If ever it perceived a certain boundary not as a barrier, but became comfortable with it as a boundary, it would itself have declined from exchange value to use value, from the general [abstract] form of wealth to a specific, substantial mode of the same.... The quantitative boundary of the surplus value appears to it as a mere natural barrier, as a necessity which it constantly tries to violate and beyond which it constantly seeks to go.
>
> (Marx 1973: 334–5)

Here Marx was relying on the dialectical treatment in Hegel's *Logic* of the nature of limits (barriers) to growth or expansion (Hegel 1969: 131–7; Hegel 1975: 136–7). A seeming absolute boundary that can be completely overcome is in reality a mere barrier. Nevertheless, capital's ability to overcome all spatial and temporal, and all natural, limits, e.g. through the 'annihilation of space by time' – to treat these as mere barriers (rather than boundaries) to its own self-expansion – was more ideal than real, generating constantly expanding contradictions (Marx 1973: 539). In perhaps the most penetrating passage ever written on the dialectic of natural limits under capital, Marx stated in the *Grundrisse*:

> Just as production founded on capital creates universal industriousness on one side ... so does it create on the other side a system of general exploitation of the natural and human qualities, a system of general utility, utilising science itself just as much as all the physical and mental qualities, while there appears nothing *higher in itself*, nothing legitimate for itself, outside this circle of social production and exchange. Thus capital creates the bourgeois society, and the universal appropriation of nature as well as of the

social bond itself by the members of society. Hence the great civilizing influence of capital; its production of a stage of society in comparison to which all earlier ones appear as mere *local developments* of humanity and as *nature-idolatry*. For the first time, nature becomes purely an object for humankind, purely a matter of utility; ceases to be recognized as a power for itself; and the theoretical discovery of its autonomous laws appears merely as a ruse so as to subjugate it under human needs, whether as an object of consumption or as a means of production. In accord with this tendency, capital drives beyond national barriers and prejudices as much as beyond nature worship, as well all traditional, confined, complacent, encrusted satisfactions of present needs, and reproductions of old ways of life. It is destructive towards all of this, and constantly revolutionizes it, tearing down all the barriers which hem in the development of the forces of production, the expansion of needs, the all-sided development of production, and the exploitation and exchange of natural and mental forces. But from the fact that capital posits every such limit as a barrier and hence gets *ideally* beyond it, it does not by any means follow that it has *really* overcome it, and since every such barrier contradicts its character, its production moves in contradictions which are constantly overcome but just as constantly posited.

(Marx 1973: 409–10)

The juggernaut of capital therefore sees all of nature as a mere object, an external barrier to be beaten down, surmounted, or circumvented. Commenting on Bacon's (1993: 29, 43) maxim that 'nature is only overcome by obeying her' – on the basis of which Bacon proposed to 'subjugate' nature – Marx observed that for capitalism the discovery of nature's autonomous laws 'appears merely as a ruse so as to subjugate it under human needs'.[7] He thus decried the one-sided, instrumental, exploitative relation to nature associated with contemporary social relations. Despite its clever 'ruse', capital is never able fully to transcend nature's limits, which continually reassert themselves with the result that 'production moves in contradictions which are constantly overcome but just as constantly posited'. No thinker in Marx's time, and perhaps no thinker up to our present day, has so brilliantly captured the dialectical complexity of the relationship between capitalism and nature.[8]

This argument takes on added significance for us today at a time when, as István Mészáros claims, we are witnessing 'the activation of capital's absolute limits' (see Mészáros 1995: 142). This takes various forms but is most apparent in the ecological realm. The problem, as Mészáros explains, is that 'neither the degradation of nature nor the pain of social devastation carries any meaning for its [capital's] system of social metabolic control when set against the absolute imperative of self-reproduction on an ever-extended scale' (Mészáros 1995: 173). All of this is inherent in the alienating character of capital, which is rooted in the alienation of the human metabolic relation to nature. 'Under the capitalist modality of metabolic exchange with nature', Mészáros writes, 'the *objectification* of human powers necessarily assumes the form of *alienation* – subsuming productive activity itself under the power of a *reified objectivity*, capital' (Mészáros 1995: 759). In the present age of planetary environmental crisis, capital is increasingly giving evidence of its ultimate 'destructive uncontrollability', imperilling civilization – or worse, life itself (Mészáros 2001: 61; Foster 2007: 2).

Sustainability in relation to the earth was a requirement of production in general, but one which capitalism was compelled to violate. As Marx explained in *Capital*, what was required from the standpoint of production in general was 'a conscious and rational treatment of land as permanent communal property, as the inalienable condition for the existence and reproduction of the chain of human generations'. Instead capitalism brought 'the exploitation and the squandering of the powers of the earth'. The problem came down to capitalism's tendency to:

> provoke an irreparable rift in the interdependent process of social metabolism, a metabolism prescribed by the natural laws of life itself. The result of this is a squandering of the vitality of the soil, which is carried by trade far beyond the bounds of a single country (Liebig).
>
> (Marx 1998: 799; translation according to Marx 1981: 949)

Writing in the nineteenth century, Marx focused on the robbing of the soil of its nutrients, particularly nitrogen, phosphorus, and potassium, and the shipment of these often hundreds and thousands of miles, where, instead of being recirculated to the soil, they ended up as wastes polluting the air, water, and land (Marx 1998: 799). A 'restoration' of the nature–society 'metabolism', Marx argued, was therefore a historical requirement of production in general, but one which could only be fulfilled in a society of associated producers (Marx 1996: 505–8; translation according to Marx 1976: 636–9).

The 'total alienation' to which capitalist society pointed tended to pull the rug out from under it, creating ever greater conflicts between production in general and specifically capitalist production. Such a theory of *total alienation* (*Après moi le déluge!*) required as its negation a theory of total liberation: a revolutionary struggle to unleash human potential in ways that did not contradict the wealth of capacities that resided within all human beings and all generations, and that safeguarded the earth.[9] The goal of production, Marx believed, should be 'the cultivation of all the qualities of the social human being, production of the same in a form as rich as possible in needs, because rich in qualities and relations' (Marx 1973: 409). Yet, this was a future that could only be materialized in a society in which the associated producers rationally controlled their metabolic relation to nature.

Malthus and overpopulation

The distinctiveness of Marx's ecological materialism, when contrasted with the much more limited view of bourgeois political economy, was evident in his critique of Malthus, which took its sharpest most developed form in the *Grundrisse*. Marx's foremost objection to Malthus was that he presented his population law as a transhistorical imperative of human existence in general, applying equally to all types of society and taking only one form. In contrast, Marx, who was much more inclined to speak literally of 'overpopulation' than Malthus (whose strictly equilibrium model of population perpetually pressing on food supply, largely excluded any concept of overpopulation as such [see Foster 2000: 92–3]), saw this as related to production under specific historical conditions, and not inherent in production in general as Malthus supposed. As Marx stated in the *Grundrisse*, 'in different modes of social production there are different laws of the increase of population and of overpopulation ... How small do the numbers which meant overpopulation for the Athenians appear to us!' Malthus' theory was guilty of abstracting

> from these specific historic laws of the movement of population, which are indeed the history of the nature of humanity, the *natural* laws, but natural laws of humanity only at a specific historic development.... Malthusian man, abstracted from historically developed man, exists only in his brain; hence also the geometric method of reproduction corresponding to this natural Malthusian man.
>
> (Marx 1973: 604–6)

Malthus' whole argument, Marx contended, rested on a logical sleight of hand. Malthus made the innate tendency toward a geometric rate of increase of human population into an iron law while treating those predominantly social–historical barriers that checked this growth as mere contingent factors. Conversely, the barriers that checked the growth of plants and animals were treated as absolute, overwhelming any natural tendency to geometric increase on their part, so that their rate of increase was at most arithmetic. Yet, Malthus in the end had no real explanation for his claim that plants and animals (the human food supply) could not also increase at a geometric rate, especially when helped along by the scientific techniques in agriculture. Nor was he able to explain why human beings were to be viewed as abstractly natural beings in this respect, rather than also social beings for whom population increase was historically conditioned.[10]

The truth was that conditions of human reproduction under capitalism had more to do with employment/unemployment and thus the question of relative surplus population (the reserve army of labour constantly reproduced by capital), than any inherent, natural law. Although Marx did not deny problems of population and food supply, he saw these, in contrast to Malthus, as socially constituted and went on to investigate the particular crises of agricultural production introduced by capitalist society and how these might be overcome by rational science.

'The physical composition of the soil', Marx noted, 'suddenly drops out of the sky in Ricardo' and the other classical economists, such as Malthus (Marx 1973: 267). The secret, however, was to see its earthy co-evolution in conjunction with human cultivation. Although human beings had an inherent relation to nature through their need to meet their subsistence needs and hence through production, this was an evolving natural and historical relation, and not as Malthus himself claimed a divine, preordained fact resulting from 'the gracious designs of Providence' (Malthus 1970: 201–12).[11]

The laws of production and exchange under capitalism, Marx observed, were 'indifferent' to a worker's 'organic presence'. Rather capitalism promoted a distinctive social and historical relation to population, designed always to produce relative surplus population – the main lever to accumulation. Capitalism's main presupposition was the dissolution of the relation between the population and the land, and hence between the population and food production (Marx 1973: 604–5). The population problem could not therefore be isolated from the absolute domination of private property, which forcibly separated human beings from the earth and the reproduction of the most basic necessities of life, creating an earth that was for them non-property, non-landownership, and non-earth – while also generating through this same process of expropriation a mass of proletarians who had no means of livelihood except through the sale of their labour power.

Socialism (communism) was to be distinguished from capitalism, in Marx's conception, by its return at a higher level to the requirements of production in general, through the promotion of many-sided needs under a society of associated producers. Such free development required that 'socialized man, the associated producers, govern the human metabolism with nature in a rational way, bringing it under their collective control … accomplishing it with the least expenditure of energy and in conditions most worthy and appropriate for their human nature' (Marx 1998: 807; translation according to Marx 1981: 959). The universality of the new society was to be found not just in the development of the wealth of human needs and potentials for all individuals without exception, but also, and just as importantly, in its rational regulation of the human metabolism with nature. Just as the alienation of society under capitalism had its original basis in the alienation of nature, so socialism could only transcend the former by transcending the latter, and creating a genuine community with the earth.

Notes

1 The significance of both labour in general and production in general was recognized by Georg Lukács. In the former, he observed, Marx abstracted 'from all the social moments of the labour process, in order to work out clearly those moments … *common to all processes of labour*' (Lukács 2000: 98).While an identical logic was evident in the concept of production in general.

2 For a systematic analysis of this part of Marx's analysis see Foster and Burkett (2000).

3 For treatments of Marx's theory of metabolic rift see Foster (1999: 366–405); Foster (2000: 155–63); Burkett (2006: 202–7). Paul Burkett discusses how the development of science, e.g. with respect to agriculture, in Marx's conception, gave new insights into production in general, the understanding of which was formed by 'the *natural-scientific study* of human production and its natural conditions across different modes of production, and not just capitalism' (Burkett 2006: 89–90).

4 These and the other subheadings in the *Grundrisse* were added by the 1939–41/1953 editors based on the index he provided to his seven notebooks (see Marx 1973: 66).

5 For a useful discussion of this part of the *Grundrisse* see Hobsbawm (1964).

6 Edward Wakefield's theory of colonialism argued that the only way to create a basis for industrial wage labour in the colonies was to first create monopolies in the land to prevent workers from escaping into small subsistence plots. This view was, according to Marx, of 'infinite importance' in understanding the presuppositions of capitalism (Marx 1973: 278).

7 Bacon's complex notion of the domination and subjugation of nature, while frequently expounded in the form of metaphors drawn from the domination within society, was compatible with notions of sustainability insofar as it demanded that society follow 'nature's laws'. The Baconian ruse was that nature could be mastered through its own laws. But nature's laws *if followed completely* nonetheless put restrictions on production – those necessitated by reproduction and sustainability. For a discussion of the full complexity of the Baconian view in this respect see Leiss (1974).

8 This paragraph borrows from John Bellamy Foster, 'The Communist Manifesto and the Environment', in Panitch and Leys (1998: 169–89). Michael Lebowitz has demonstrated that Marx pointed to two kinds of barriers to capital, leading to accumulation of contradictions and crises: general barriers common to production in general, and thus having to do with natural conditions, and more specific historical barriers immanent to capital itself (see Lebowitz 1982).

9 '*Après moi le déluge!* Is the watchword of every capitalist and of every capitalist nation. Hence Capital is reckless of the health or length of life of the labourer, unless under compulsion from society' (Marx 1996: 275).

10 Although Malthus later attributed the law of arithmetic increase with regard to food production to the classical theory of rent and diminishing returns, he did not employ this argument in any of the numerous editions of his *Essay on Population*, but only in his later *Summary View of the Principle of Population*. Consequently Marx was to rule it out as an argument in the formation of Malthus' population theory (see Marx 1973: 608; Foster 2000: 142–4).

11 Early works on ecological Marxism, particularly the work of Benton (1989), criticized Marx for failing fully to incorporate a concept of natural limits, and compared Marx unfavourably to Malthus in this respect. Benton's interpretation, however, was later overturned by the much more systematic treatment of Marx's analysis by Burkett (1998a and 1998b). What becomes clear is that Marx's analysis was far more theoretically sophisticated and concrete than the Malthusian suprahistorical conception, even with regard to natural limits, and population itself.

References

Bacon, Francis (1993) *Novum Organum*, Chicago: Open Court.

Benton, Ted (1989) 'Marxism and Natural Limits', *New Left Review*, 178: 51–86.

Burkett, Paul (1998a) 'A Critique of Neo-Malthusian Marxism', *Historical Materialism*, 2: 118–42.

Burkett, Paul (1998b) 'Labor, Eco-regulation and Value', *Historical Materialism*, 3: 119–44.

Burkett, Paul (1999) *Marx and Nature: A Red and Green Perspective*, New York: St. Martin's Press.

Burkett, Paul (2006) *Marxism and Ecological Economics*, Boston: Brill.

Dickens, Peter (2004) *Society and Nature*, Malden, MA: Polity.

Foster, John Bellamy (1998) 'The Communist Manifesto and the Environment', in Leo Panitch and Colin Leys (eds), *The Socialist Register*, New York: Monthly Review Press.

Foster, John Bellamy (1999) 'Marx's Theory of Metabolic Rift', *American Journal of Sociology*, 105(2): 366–405.

Foster, John Bellamy (2000) *Marx's Ecology: Materialism and Nature*, New York: Monthly Review Press.

Foster, John Bellamy (2007) 'The Ecology of Destruction', *Monthly Review*, 58(9): 1–14.

Foster, John Bellamy and Burkett, Paul (2000) 'The Dialectic of Organic/Inorganic Relations', *Organization & Environment*, 13(4): 403–25.

Hegel, G.W.F. (1970) *The Philosophy of Nature*, vols 1–3, Atlantic Highlands, New Jersey: Humanities Press.

Hegel, G.W.F. (1969) *The Science of Logic*, London: George Allen and Unwin.

Hegel, G.W.F. (1975) *Hegel's Logic*, Oxford: Oxford University Press.

Hobsbawm, Eric J. (1964) 'Introduction' in Karl Marx, *Pre-Capitalist Economic Formations*, New York: International Publishers.

Lebowitz, Michael (1982) 'The General and Specific in Marx's Theory of Crisis', *Studies in Political Economy*, 7: 5–25.

Lebowitz, Michael (2003) *Beyond Capital: Marx's Political Economy of the Working Class*, New York: Palgrave Macmillan.

Leiss, William (1974) *The Domination of Nature*, Boston: Beacon Press.

Lukács, Georg (2000) *A Defence of History and Class Consciousness: Tailism and the Dialectic*, London: Verso.

Malthus, Thomas (1970) *An Essay on the Principle of Population and A Summary View of the Principle of Population*, Harmondsworth: Penguin.

Marx, Karl (1973) *Grundrisse: Foundations of the Critique of Political Economy*, Harmondsworth: Penguin.

Marx, Karl (1975) 'Economic and Philosophic Manuscripts of 1844', in *Marx and Engels Collected Works*, vol. 3: *Works of Marx, March 1843–August 1844, Works of Engels, May 1843–June 1844*, Moscow: Progress Publishers.

Marx, Karl (1976) *Capital*, vol. I, New York: Vintage.

Marx, Karl (1979) 'The Eighteenth Brumaire of Louis Bonaparte', in *Marx and Engels Collected Works*, vol. 11: *Marx and Engels 1851–1853*, Moscow: Progress Publishers.

Marx, Karl (1981) *Capital*, vol. II, New York: Vintage.

Marx, Karl (1996) '*Capital*, vol. I', in *Marx and Engels Collected Works*, vol. 35: *Capital, Vol. I*, New York: International Publishers.

Marx, Karl, (1998) '*Capital*, vol. III', in *Marx and Engels Collected Works*, vol. 37: *Capital, Vol. III*, New York: International Publishers.

Marx, Karl and Engels, Friedrich (1976) 'German Ideology', in *Marx and Engels Collected Works*, vol. 5: *Marx and Engels April 1845–April 1847*, Moscow: Progress Publishers.

Mészáros, István (1995) *Beyond Capital*, New York: Monthly Review Press.

Mészáros, István (2001) *Socialism or Barbarism*, New York: Monthly Review Press.

7 Emancipated individuals in an emancipated society

Marx's sketch of post-capitalist society in the *Grundrisse*

Iring Fetscher

Introduction

One of the difficulties in understanding Marx, one that Hannah Arendt encountered, stems from the lack of clarity in his concept of labour. In my view, the passages on labour in the *Grundrisse* can help us overcome the difficulty. In his early writings, Marx emphatically declares that 'the self-creation of man' should be understood the way it is in Hegel, 'as a process': 'objectification as loss of object, as alienation and as suppression of this alienation'. This shows, he says, that Hegel has correctly conceived 'the essence of *labour*', and, in consequence, 'objective man – true, because real man – as the outcome of man's *own* labour' (Marx 1975: 332–3).[1] This emphasis on the significance of labour for the essence of 'true, real man' stands in a problematic relationship to an often quoted formulation in *Capital*, which, however, deserves to be read more carefully than it usually is. In *Capital*, volume III, Marx affirms that

> the actual wealth of society, and the possibility of constantly expanding its reproduction process, therefore, do not depend upon the duration of surplus-labour, but upon its productivity ... the realm of freedom actually begins only where labour which is determined by necessity and mundane considerations ceases; thus in the very nature of things it lies beyond the sphere of actual material production.
>
> (Marx 1998: 807)

In all social orders, people have to earn their livelihood by working:

> Freedom in this field can only consist in socialised man, the associated producers, rationally regulating their interchange with Nature, bringing it under their common control, instead of being ruled by it as by the blind forces of Nature; and achieving this with the least expenditure of energy and under conditions most favourable to, and worthy of, their human nature. But it nonetheless still remains a realm of necessity. Beyond it begins that development of human energy which is an end in itself, the true realm of freedom, which, however, can blossom forth only with this realm

of necessity as its basis. The shortening of the working-day is its basic prerequisite.

(Marx 1998: 807)

Labour, we are here told, is '*necessity and external expediency*'; the 'realm of freedom' lies beyond it. In the *Grundrisse*, we find formulations which suggest, at the very least, that there can one day be *a form of productive activity* no longer governed by 'necessity and external expediency'. Marx accordingly identifies the 'abolition of labour' as the true goal of revolution, a goal he says Charles Fourier, despite his many shortcomings, quite rightly saw. Marx's critique of Adam Smith's conception of labour makes the nature of his own hopes clear. For Smith, labour necessarily implies *drudgery*, so that

> 'tranquillity' appears as the adequate state, as identical with 'freedom' and 'happiness'. Smith fails to see 'that the individual in his normal state of health, strength, activity, skill, facility' [these are Smith's terms] also needs a normal portion of work, and of the suspension of tranquillity.[2] Certainly, labour obtains its measure from the outside, through the aim to be attained and the obstacles to be overcome in attaining it. But Smith has no inkling whatever that this overcoming of obstacles is in itself a liberating activity – and that, further, the external aims become stripped of the semblance of merely external natural urgencies, and become posited as aims which the individual himself posits – hence as self-realization, objectification of the subject, hence real freedom, whose action is, precisely, labour. He is right, of course, that, in its historic form as slave-labour, serf-labour, and wage-labour, labour always appears as repulsive, always as *external forced labour*; and not-labour, by contrast, as 'freedom, and happiness'. This hold doubly [for as long as workers have] not yet created the subjective and objective conditions ... in which labour becomes attractive work, the individual's self-realization.
>
> (Marx 1973: 611)

The distinction between the unfree nature of labour in every social order to date and a conceivably free form of productive work conducive to self-fulfilment would be easier to grasp if Marx had chosen a term other than *Arbeit* to describe such productive activity. 'Attractive work', precisely, denotes the kind of activity, bound up with satisfaction and a consciousness of freedom, which has historically been reserved for a privileged minority (artists and scholars, for example), yet can eventually become a reality for all the members of an emancipated society (such, at any rate, is Marx's hope), thanks to the high labour productivity engendered by the historical constraints of the capitalist mode of production.

Capitalism's preparation of the groundwork for the emancipated society

It is the historical merit of the capitalist mode of production to have brought about the productivity that is the prerequisite for an emancipated society through the development of industry and the attendant application of natural science to productive techniques. Only in passing does Marx mention the fact that the proportion of individuals freed from menial labour and made available for science and artistic activity has risen under capitalism. In *Theories of Surplus Value*, he highlights an insight of James Mill's. Mill, he says, grasped the importance of a middle class freed from toil:

> Man's *perfectibilité*, or the power of advancing continually from one degree of knowledge, and of happiness, to another, seem, in a great measure, to depend upon the existence of a class of men which have *their time at their command*; that is, who are rich enough to be freed from all solicitude with respect to the means of living in a certain state of enjoyment. It is by this class of men that knowledge is cultivated and enlarged; it is also by this class that it is diffused; it is this class of men whose children receive the best education, and are prepared for all the higher and more delicate functions of society, as legislators, judges, administrators, teachers, inventors in all the arts, and superintendents in all the more important works, by which the dominion of the human species is extended over the powers of nature.
>
> (Marx 1989b: 287)

Marx expects, however, in contrast to Mill, that scientific education, hitherto reserved for a privileged social minority, will come within reach of virtually everyone in the foreseeable future. Yet, in those of his writings which seek to heighten the political motivation of the working class, he makes no mention of the fact that the social class which enjoys the freedom to engage in science, research, engineering, and the arts has grown in the course of capitalist development.[3]

Making more free time available to everyone is merely the first condition for emancipation from the constraint of labour and the alienation bred by compulsory work. Two further crucial conditions must be met:

1   as many members of society as possible must become familiar with science; and
2   an end must be put to the isolation of individuals from the creative collective subject which alone is capable of coming to dominate the material conditions of human existence, rather than being dominated by them in the form of a totality subsumed by capital.

This emancipation has a technical aspect as well, embodied in the automated factory. With automation, labour no longer appears so much to be included within the production process; rather, the human being comes to relate more as watchman and regulator to the production process itself. (What holds for machinery holds likewise for the combination of human activities and the development of human intercourse.) No longer does the worker insert a modified natural thing as middle link between the object and himself; rather, he inserts the process of nature, transformed into an industrial process, as a means between himself and inorganic nature, mastering it. He steps to the side of the production process instead of being its chief actor. In this trans-formation, it is neither the direct human labour he himself performs, nor the time during which he works, but rather the appropriation of his own general productive power, his understanding of nature and his mastery over it by virtue of his presence as a social body – it is, in a word, the development of the social individual which appears as the great foundation-stone of produc-tion and of wealth.

(Marx 1973: 705)

As early as 1857–8, Marx took it for granted that the conditions for the trans-ition from the capitalist mode of production to a superior (emancipated) produc-tive mode already obtained. Thus he declares in the *Grundrisse* that

the *surplus labour of the mass* has ceased to be the condition for the devel-opment of general wealth, just as the *non-labour of the few*, for the develop-ment of the general powers of the human head. With that, production based on exchange value breaks down, and the direct, material production process is stripped of the form of penury and antithesis. The free development of individualities, and hence not the reduction of necessary labour time so as to posit surplus labour, but rather the general reduction of the necessary labour of society to a minimum, which then corresponds to the artistic, scientific etc. development of the individuals in the time set free, and with the means created, for all of them.

(Marx 1973: 705–6)

With that, the contradiction immanent in the capitalist mode of production is superseded. It resides in the fact that while labour time is reduced by the indus-trial production energetically developed under capitalism, the working class's surplus-labour time must (at least relatively) simultaneously increase so as to maintain the rate of surplus value (and the profit rate). All industrial means of production, including the automated factory, have hitherto been subsumed by capital; yet they are always only 'natural material transformed into organs of the human will over nature, or of human participation in nature. They are *organs of the human brain, created by the human hand*; the power of knowledge, objecti-fied' (Marx 1973: 706).

From a humane point of view, the capitalist mode of production has made a genuine contribution to the wealth of human society. It is traceable to capitalism's constant tendency to shorten labour-time with the help of mechanical and automated productive processes. This remains true even if capitalism constantly strives to increase real labour-time so as to increase surplus value. Thus we find Marx repeatedly emphasizing that

> real economy – saving – consists of the saving of labour time (minimum, and minimization, of productions costs); but this saving identical with development of the productive force. Hence in no way *abstinence from consumption*, but rather the development of power, of capabilities of production, and hence both of the capabilities as well as the means of consumption. The capability to consume is a condition of consumption, hence its primary means, and this capability is the development of an individual potential, a force of production. The saving of labour time [is] equal to an increase of free time, i.e. time for the full development of the individual, which in turn reacts back upon the productive power of labour as itself the greatest productive power.
>
> (Marx 1973: 711)

From the standpoint of the capitalist mode of production, this means 'production of fixed capital'. In the final analysis, however, fixed capital, which consists of machines and the people who use them, is identical with 'man himself'. Decisive here is the further course of Marx's argument, which points to a different kind of connection between labour and free time than the one argued in the third volume of *Capital*: 'it goes without saying, by the way, that direct labour time itself cannot remain in the abstract antithesis to free time in which it appears from the perspective of bourgeois economy' (Marx 1973: 712). Labour is transformed – on the sole condition, to be sure, that the united producers take possession of the means of production and organize their relations to each another and to (automated) machinery themselves. In the passage just quoted, Marx already looks ahead to the transformation that labour will undergo in emancipated conditions. Of course, it

> cannot become play, as Fourier would like, although it remains his great contribution to have expressed the suspension not of distribution, but of the mode of production itself, in a higher form, as the ultimate object. Free time – which is both ideal time and time for higher activity – has naturally transformed its possessor into a different subject, and he then enters into the direct production process as this different subject. This process is then both discipline, as regards the human being in the process of becoming; and, at the same time, practice, experimental science, materially creative and objectifying science, as regards the human being who has become, in whose head exists the accumulated knowledge of society. For both, in so far as labour requires practical use of the hands and free bodily movement, as in agriculture, at the same time exercise.
>
> (Marx 1973: 712)

Free, creative, active, socialized individuals

On condition that newly available free time is, with the end of the domination of capitalist property relations, no longer transformed into surplus-labour time for the making of surplus value and profit, every producer can use such time in realizing the all-round development of his (in the last analysis, intellectual) capabilities. The assumption that the 'accumulated knowledge of society' exists in the 'head' of 'the human being who has become' does not have a merely utopian ring. It can be understood only if it is presumed that each individual producer consciously sees himself or herself as an integral part of the association of all the producers. For as long as individual producers realize their particular labour in the form of individual products, it does not appear that the real producer is individual's 'combined social activity'. In the context of production based on an advanced division of labour, this relationship is invisible for each particular labourer. Citing passages from the anonymous book *The Source and Remedy of the National Difficulties, Deduced from Principles of Political Economy, In a Letter to Lord Russell* (London, 1821), Marx finally sketches the transition to an emancipated relationship of associated producers to the production process. 'In the production process of large-scale industry', he says, there takes place, 'on the one side', 'the conquest of the forces of nature by the social intellect', objectified in 'the productive power of the means of labour as developed into the automatic process'. On the other, '*the labour of the individual in its direct presence* [is] *posited as suspended individual, i.e., as social, labour*'. With that, he goes on, '*the other basis of the mode of production* [that is, the capitalist economy] *falls away*' (Marx 1973: 709).

To give the reader an idea of what 'really free working' (it can no longer properly be called 'labour') might mean, Marx refers to the activity of musical composition, which, he declares, is by no means, as Fourier once said, 'mere fun, mere amusement', but, rather, 'the most damned seriousness, the most intense exertion'. Such 'free working' presupposes, to be sure, that 'the social character' of material production 'is posited'; that is to say, that the mode of cooperation has been established by the associated producers themselves, not imposed on them by the prevailing social system. Under these conditions, activity is to have 'a scientific and at the same time general character'. Human exertion will then by no means appear in the production process 'in a merely natural, spontaneous form', as 'a specifically harnessed natural force, but as subject ... as an activity regulating all the forces of nature' (Marx 1973: 611–12). Beginning with the development of machine production and, later, automation, the capitalist mode of production brings the technical prerequisites for this emancipated activity of the associated producers into being. Here the difference between Marx and Fourier is patent. Fourier thought that the way to overcome drudgery was to distribute tasks to different individuals and groups with different inclinations, in such a way that the work of each would correspond to his or her spontaneous need for activity. Boys, for example, are well suited to working in dirt, and even like it; Fourier accordingly proposes to give them, among other tasks, that of sweeping the streets. Marx, in contrast, sets out from the premise that every human being takes satisfaction in voluntary intellectual activity of the kind in which the division between mental and manual labour has been superseded. The satisfaction here derives both from the activity as such and also from the solidarity among producers. The best concrete illustration of this emancipated mode of production, Marx suggests, is an orchestra in which each individual musician simultaneously sees himself as part of the whole – as co-producer of, say, the symphony being performed. The musician is aware, thanks to his musical comprehension of the score, that the music belongs, as it were, to him, just as the scientific bases of advanced automated production belong to all educated producers. The paradigm of the orchestra has to be taken with a pinch of salt; yet I think that it provides an avenue of approach to Marx's vision in the *Grundrisse*, which might otherwise be dismissed as utopian.

One of the strengths of this vision of the future, in contrast to that elaborated by Marxian state capitalism, is that it is unbeholden to the goal of unlimited growth, which is irreconcilable with the existence of ecological limits. Furthermore, it shifts the accent from overcoming the constraints on growth set by the capitalist mode of production itself to a basic transformation of human activity and the achievement of satisfaction and happiness made possible by this transformation. This is important in view of the by now obvious fact that globalized capitalism has succeeded in counteracting 'the tendential decline in the profit rate' over so long a term that its effects have to all intents and purposes been neutralized, even as the pressure to increase consumption created by advertising has led to a trivialization of existence and the progressive destruction of the natural bases of life.

In the 'Chapter on Money', Marx refers in passing to the development of productive modes from early, ancient forms through feudalism and capitalism to the emancipated society of the future, which can only emerge on the groundwork laid by the capitalist mode of production. In advanced capitalist society, there exists a

> reciprocal dependence ... expressed in the constant necessity for exchange, and in exchange value as the all-sided mediation. The economists express this as follows: Each pursues his private interest and only his private interest; and thereby serves the private interests of all, the general interest, without willing or knowing it. The real point is not that each individual's pursuit of his private interest promotes the totality of private interests, the general interest. One could just as well deduce from this abstract phrase that each individual reciprocally blocks the assertion of the other's interests, so that, instead of a general affirmation, this war of all against all produces a general negation. The point is rather that private interest is itself already a socially determined interest, which can be achieved only within the conditions laid down by society and with the means provided by society; hence it is bound to the reproduction of these conditions and means. It is the interest of private persons; but its content, as well as the form and means of its realization, is given by social conditions independent of all. The reciprocal and all-sided dependence of individuals who are indifferent to one another forms their social connection. This social bond is expressed in *exchange*

value, by means of which alone each individual's own activity or his product becomes an activity and a product for him; he must produce a general product – *exchange value ... money*. The individual carries his social power, as well as his bond with society, in his pocket.

(Marx 1973: 156–7)

In earlier social formations, exchange value (money) did not yet possess this 'social power'. Necessarily, therefore, 'the power of the community which binds the individuals together' was greater: 'the patriarchal relation, the community of antiquity, feudalism and the guild system' (Marx 1973: 157).

Each individual possesses social power in the form of a thing. Rob the thing of this social power and you must give it to persons to exercise over persons. Relations of personal dependence (entirely spontaneous at the outset) are the first social forms, in which human productive capacity develops only to a slight extent and at isolated points. Personal independence founded on *objective* dependence is the second great form, in which a system of general social metabolism, of universal relations, of all-round needs and universal capacities is formed for the first time. Free individuality, based on the universal development of individuals and on their subordination of their communal, social productivity as their social wealth, is the third stage. The second stage creates the conditions for the third.

(Marx 1973: 158–9)

The three main phases of social and individual development are portrayed differently here than in traditional Marxism. In the beginning is not an imaginary primitive communism, but a human community such that individual consciousness could not yet develop. Every individual is a proprietor only insofar as he is a member of his community. Individualistic consciousness develops only with the rise of market relations. The consequence, in a society based on the division of labour, is that individuals are alienated from their fellow human beings. In fully developed capitalist market society, they carry the epitome of productive society and their individual portion of wealth around with them in their pockets in the form of money. At the same time, however, it is only in this social formation, with its unprecedented dynamic drive to increase the productivity of labour, that men and women's creative scientific, and, accordingly, productive capacities can flower. Initially, humanity's potential could unfold in this alienated form alone. Only on this basis – in an as yet unrealized third phase of development – can a conscious relationship be forged between individuals and the productive totality (which will include the whole human race). The prerequisite is the overcoming of the separation between intellectual and manual labour. As soon as this has been accomplished at the level of society as a whole, individuals can establish ties with everyone through their scientific consciousness. This state of affairs would spell the end of social alienation. Until it comes about, however, only a minority of people from the middle stratum of society, who are no longer obliged to perform strenuous manual labour and have free time at their disposal, can cultivate such a scientific consciousness. No revolutionary impulse arises from this stratum, which is comfortable with its privileges and has no stake in losing its privileged position.

Since bourgeois thought is blind to these perspectives, it is characterized – to the extent that it engages in cultural criticism at all – by the nostalgic backward gaze it turns on earlier social conditions:

> In earlier stages of development the single individual seems to be developed more fully, because he has not yet worked out his relationships in their fullness, or erected them as independent social powers and relations opposite himself. It is as ridiculous to yearn for a return to that original fullness as it is to believe that with this complete emptiness history has come to a standstill. The bourgeois viewpoint has never advanced beyond this antithesis between itself and this romantic viewpoint, and therefore the latter will accompany it as legitimate antithesis up to its blessed end. (The relation of the individual to science may be taken as an example here.)
>
> (Marx 1973: 162)

From the automated factory to the overcoming of compulsory labour

The vision of the future that Marx elaborates in the *Grundrisse* all but ignores the concept of the revolution and the revolutionary cause, and there is scarcely any mention of the international proletariat as the subject of revolutionary emancipation. Marx does, however, occasionally take a backward look at the developments that led to capitalistic industrialism and, in the process, created the preconditions for an emancipated society. The three stages of social formations appear here in a somewhat different light than they do in the reception of Marxist theory by traditional Marxism. In the beginning stands a close-knit community – for example, a tribal group – in which each individual has access to the means of production and consumption solely through the strong (unconscious) link binding him to the social whole. This unconscious collective gives way to class societies of the greatest possible variety, of which, however, only the last – capitalist class society based on wage-labour and, thus, on free labourers – develops the dynamic that engenders the prerequisites for an emancipated society. Ancient slave society and feudal society are both still based on a predominantly agricultural form of production. Commercial capital alone manages to challenge this dominance, although it never comes to dominate and shape society as a whole. Only with the rise of manufacture and factory production brought about by capitalism does commercial capital attain the form adequate to a market economy. This mode of production ultimately forces its way beyond the borders of individual states, moving toward the creation of a unified world market. In the automated factory and through the transformation of the natural sciences into the most important motor of productive development, capital, too, attains an adequate concrete form: that is, a satisfactory final state from the standpoint of bourgeois economics. However, the Marxian critique of political economy, which takes aim at both this bourgeois theory and its presumed object, does not accept the alienation which the producing individuals are summoned to undergo (i.e. which is imposed on them). Yet the passage through the total alienation and disempowerment of the individual is necessary in order to 'bring out' the concrete producer over against the totality of both productive society and the means of production (in the form of automated factories). The decisive next step is supposed to consist in appropriation of the scientific knowledge underpinning production, as well as the conscious inclusion of each individual in an association of producers spanning the world – that is, in transcendence of the isolation characterizing individual consciousness.

Of course, Marx was deeply mistaken about the degree of development possible within the limits of the capitalist mode of production. This is evinced both by his claim, in an 8 October 1858 letter to Engels, that the construction of the world market has already been fully achieved, and, above all, by his comments about the development of the transport and communication techniques which were of decisive importance for the acceleration of the turnover time (circulation time) of commodities. To be sure, Marx lived to see the introduction of the telegraph, but not that of the telephone, radio, television, Internet, and so on. Yet it is precisely in this economic sector that all-important developments have taken place in the last ten to 20 years. In the letter to Engels, Marx writes:

> The proper task of bourgeois society is the creation of the world market, at least in outline; and of the production based on that market. Since the world is round, the colonization of California and Australia and the opening up of China and Japan would seem to have completed this process.
>
> (Marx and Engels 1983: 347)

In the *Grundrisse*, Marx repeatedly underscores the import of the rapidity of communications and the transport of goods; yet he could scarcely have imagined just how rapid communications and transport have become today. He concerned himself, at the time, only with the way the costs of road construction, for example, were calculated with respect to surplus value and the profit on capital. Throughout a prolonged period, the means of communication and transport – such as roads and canals – were built by the state:

> For the capitalist to undertake road building as a business, at his expense, various conditions are required, which all amount to this, that the mode of production based on capital is already developed to its highest stage. *Firstly: Large capital* is itself presupposed.... Hence mostly *share-capital*.... *Secondly*: it must bring *interest*, but not necessarily profit.... *Thirdly*: As presupposition, such a volume of traffic – commercial, above all – that the road pays for itself.... *Fourthly*: A portion of idle wealth which can lay out its revenue for these articles of locomotion.
>
> (Marx 1973: 529–30)

The invention of new means of transport goes unmentioned in this context, although railroads and steamships already existed by 1857, as Marx obviously knew.

Of decisive importance to Marx's conception of the emancipated society and the 'universally developed individuals' in it was the overcoming of compulsory labour of the kind that had prevailed in all social formations hitherto. Such labour was, for Marx, historically conditioned, and could not be equated with human activity as such. Plainly, Theodor Adorno approaches the Marxian vision of the future somewhat differently, even if he rightly criticizes most socialists for their one-sided concentration on quantitative increases in productivity and production. In *Minima Moralia* (1951), Adorno writes:

> The concept of dynamism, which is the necessary complement of bourgeois 'a-historicity', is raised to an absolute, whereas it ought, as an anthropological reflex of the laws of production, to be itself critically confronted, in an emancipated society, with need. The conception of unfettered activity, of uninterrupted procreation, of chubby insatiability, of freedom as frantic bustle, feeds on the bourgeois concept of nature that has always served solely to proclaim social violence as unchangeable, as a piece of healthy eternity. It was in this … that the positive blue-prints of socialism, resisted by Marx, were rooted in barbarism. It is not man's lapse into luxurious indolence that is to be feared, but the savage spread of the social under the mask of universal nature, the collective as a blind fury of activity. The naïve supposition of an unambiguous development towards increased production is itself a piece of that bourgeois outlook which permits development in only one direction because, integrated into a totality, dominated by quantification, it is hostile to qualitative difference.
>
> (Adorno 2005: 156)

Astonishingly, despite his own profound creativity and artistic activity, Adorno does not acknowledge the qualitative difference characteristic of the kind of activity which leads, not to the production of more consumer goods, but to the creation of unique works of art or scientific knowledge. Here is his surprising answer to the question of the reality of 'qualitative difference':

> *Rien faire comme une bête*, lying on water and looking peacefully at the sky, 'being, nothing else, without any further definition and fulfilment', might take the place of process, act, satisfaction…. None of the abstract concepts comes closer to fulfilled utopia that that of eternal peace.
>
> (Adorno 2005: 157)

Ultimately, this last, resigned way out is all that Adorno can propose. This would not have been necessary if the thoughts on the emancipated society and universally developed human beings which Marx suggestively sketches in the *Grundrisse* had been taken up and further developed.

[Translation from the German by G.M. Goshgarian]

Notes

1   The following early passage contains an evocative anticipation of the various exposi-
tions of the concept in the *Grundrisse*:

> The *real*, active orientation of man to himself as a species-being, or his manifesta-
> tion as a real species-being (i.e., as a human being), is only possible if he really
> brings out all his *species-powers* – something which in turn is only possible
> through the cooperative action of all of mankind, only as the result of history –
> and treats these powers as objects: and this, to begin with, is again only possible
> in the form of estrangement.
>
> (Marx 1975: 333)

2

> The great historic quality of capital is to *create* this *surplus labour*, superfluous
> labour from the standpoint of mere use value, mere subsistence; and its historic
> destiny is fulfilled as soon as, on one side, there has been such a development of
> needs that surplus labour above and beyond necessity has itself become a general
> need arising out of individual needs themselves – and, on the other side, when the
> severe discipline of capital, acting on succeeding generations, has developed
> *general industriousness* [emphasis added] as *the general property of the new
> species* [emphasis added] – and, finally, when the development of the productive
> powers of labour, which capital incessantly whips onward with its unlimited
> mania for wealth, and of the sole conditions in which this mania can be realized,
> have flourished to the stage where the possession and preservation of general
> wealth require a lesser labour time of society as a whole, and where the labouring
> society relates scientifically to the process of its progressive reproduction, its
> reproduction in a constantly greater abundance; hence where labour in which a
> human being does what a thing could do has ceased.
>
> (Marx 1973: 325)

Marx here takes it for granted that the industriousness acquired thanks to the discipline imposed by the conditions of life under capitalism is passed on hereditarily, a
notion that has been made obsolete by the Darwinian theory of evolution and,
especially, by genetics. When the *Grundrisse* was written, Lamarckism reigned
uncontested.

3   There are further references to this middle class in *Theories of Surplus Value*:

> [Malthus's] supreme hope, which he himself describes as more or less utopian, is
> that the mass of the middle class should grow and that the proletariat (those who
> work) should constitute a constantly declining proportion (even though it
> increases absolutely) of the total population. This in fact is the *course* taken by
> bourgeois society.
>
> (Marx 1989a: 78)

References

Adorno, Theodor (2005) *Minima Moralia: Reflections on a Damaged Life*, London:
Verso.

Marx, Karl (1973) *Grundrisse: Foundations of the Critique of Political Economy (Rough
Draft)*, Harmondsworth: Penguin.

Marx, Karl (1975) 'Economic and Philosophic Manuscripts of 1844', in *Marx and Engels
Collected Works*, vol. 3: *Works of Karl Marx, March 1843–August 1844, and Works of
Frederick Engels, May 1843–June 1844*, Moscow: Progress Publishers.

Marx, Karl (1989a) 'Theories of Surplus Value', in *Marx and Engels Collected Works*, vol. 31: *Economic Manuscripts of 1861–63*, London: Lawrence and Wishart.

Marx, Karl (1989b) 'Theories of Surplus Value', in *Marx and Engels Collected Works*, vol. 32: *Economic Manuscripts of 1861–63* (continuation), London: Lawrence and Wishart.

Marx, Karl (1998) 'Capital, Vol. III', in *Marx and Engels Collected Works*, vol. 37: *Capital*, vol. III, New York: International Publishers.

Marx, Karl and Engels, Friedrich (1983) *Marx and Engels Collected Works*, vol. 40, *Letters, 1856–59*, Moscow: Progress Publishers.

8 Rethinking *Capital* in light of the *Grundrisse*[1]

Moishe Postone

Critical social theory and the contemporary world

Critical social theory has not kept pace with the far-reaching global transformations of the past three decades. The intense and fruitful revival of Marxian thought and scholarship in the 1960s and early 1970s was followed by a very strong turn away from Marxism on the part of many theorists. The intellectual field became dominated by postmodernist and poststructuralist approaches that appeared plausible to many as critiques of Marxism. It has become increasingly evident, however, that such approaches do not adequately grasp the current epoch; they fail to elucidate the basic historical changes that have reconfigured the world in recent decades. Even major thinkers such as Habermas, Foucault and Derrida now appear as theorists of a fading historical configuration – declining Fordism; their critical approaches illuminate less and less of the contemporary social universe.

One obvious weakness of these post-Marxist discourses has been the absence of serious political–economic considerations, an absence that has become glaring in the face of processes of globalization. At the same time, it is clear that, however important integrating political–economic considerations into critical theories of the present might be, there can be no plausible return to traditional Marxism. That traditional critical framework failed to provide the basis for an adequate historical analysis of Communist regimes of accumulation; its political–economic assumptions were challenged on the basis of the growing importance of scientific knowledge and advanced technology in the process of production; and its emancipatory ideals have become increasingly remote from the themes of much current social and cultural dissatisfaction.

Recent historical tendencies, nevertheless, suggest the importance of a more adequate critical theory of capitalism. Although these tendencies include developments that underline the anachronistic character of traditional Marxist theory – for example the rise of new social movements such as mass ecology movements, women's and gay movements, minority emancipation movements, as well as the growing disaffection expressed in various 'fundamentalist' movements – recent decades have also been characterized by the re-emergence of worldwide economic dislocations and intensifying intercapitalist rivalry on a global scale. These developments suggest that a critical analysis adequate to the contemporary world must be able to grasp both its significant new dimensions and its underlying continuity as capitalism.

Marx's *Grundrisse der Kritik der politischen Ökonomie* could provide a point of departure for a reinvigorated critical analysis based on a fundamental rethinking of the nature of capitalism (Marx 1973). Written in 1857–8, this manuscript was first published in 1939 and did not become widely known until the late 1960s and early 1970s. Although Marx did not work out all aspects of his mature critical theory in the *Grundrisse*, the general thrust of his critique of capitalist modernity and the nature and significance of the fundamental categories of that critique emerge very clearly in this manuscript. *Capital* is more difficult to decipher and is readily subject to misunderstandings inasmuch as it is very tightly structured as an immanent critique – one undertaken from a standpoint immanent to its object of investigation. For this reason, its categories can be misunderstood as affirmative rather than critical. Hence, all too frequently, the *object* of Marx's critique became regarded as its *standpoint* – an issue to which we shall return. This is less of a problem reading the *Grundrisse*, which is not structured as rigorously. Because Marx was still working out his categorial[2] analysis in this manuscript, its strategic intent is more accessible than in *Capital*. Hence, the *Grundrisse* can illuminate the nature and thrust of Marx's mature critique of political economy. When read through the lens of the 1857–8 manuscript, that critique could provide the basis for a more adequate critical theory of the contemporary world than is possible within a traditional Marxist framework.[3]

Traditional Marxism

Before elaborating this contention with reference to some crucially important sections of the *Grundrisse*, let me briefly describe what is meant by 'traditional Marxism' in this chapter. It does not refer to a specific historical tendency in Marxism, but, more generally, to any analysis of capitalism in terms essentially of class relations rooted in private property and mediated by the market. Relations of domination are understood primarily in terms of class domination and exploitation. Within this general interpretive framework, capitalism is characterized by a growing structural contradiction between society's basic social relations (interpreted as private property and the market) and the forces of production (interpreted as the industrial mode of producing). Socialism is understood primarily in terms of collective ownership of the means of production and centralized planning in an industrialized context. That is, it is conceptualized as a just and consciously regulated mode of distribution adequate to industrial production (which is understood as a technical process intrinsically independent of capitalism).

This general understanding is tied to a determinate understanding of the basic categories of Marx's critique of political economy. His category of value, for example, has generally been regarded as an attempt to show that direct human labour always and everywhere creates social wealth, which in capitalism is mediated by the market. His theory of surplus value, according to such views, demonstrates the existence of exploitation in capitalism by showing that labour alone creates the surplus product, which is then appropriated by the capitalist class.[4]

This interpretation is based on a transhistorical understanding of labour as an activity mediating humans and nature that transforms matter in a goal-directed manner and is a condition of social life. 'Labour,' so understood, is posited as the source of wealth in all societies and as that which constitutes what is universal and truly social. In capitalism, however, 'labour' is hindered by particularistic and fragmenting relations from becoming fully realized. Emancipation, then, is realized in a social form where transhistorical 'labour', freed from the distortions of the market and private property, has openly emerged as the regulating principle of society. (This notion, of course, is bound to that of socialist revolution as the 'self-realization' of the proletariat.) 'Labour' here provides the *standpoint* of the critique of capitalism.

Within the basic framework of 'traditional Marxism', so conceptualized, there has been a broad range of very different theoretical, methodological and political approaches.[5] Nevertheless, although powerful economic, political, social, historical and cultural analyses have been generated within this framework, its limitations have long been discernible in the face of twentieth-century historical developments. Coming to terms with the inescapable centrality of capitalism in the world today, then, requires a reconceptualization of capital that breaks with the traditional Marxist framework.

It has become evident, considered retrospectively, that the social/political/economic/cultural configuration of capital's hegemony has varied historically – from mercantilism through nineteenth-century liberal capitalism and twentieth-century state-centric Fordist capitalism to contemporary neo-liberal global capitalism. This suggests that capitalism cannot be identified fully with any of its historical configurations, and raises the question of the nature of the fundamental core of capitalism as a form of social life, that is, of the nature of capital.

The *Grundrisse*: capitalism's core

The *Grundrisse* helps clarify Marx's mature conception of capitalism's core and the nature of its historical overcoming in ways that point beyond the limits of the traditional Marxist interpretation. In a crucially important section of the manuscript entitled 'Contradiction between the *foundation* of bourgeois production (*value as measure*) and its development' (Marx 1973: 704; first emphasis added), Marx explicitly indicates what he regards as the essential core of capitalism and the fundamental contradiction that generates the historical possibility of a postcapitalist form of social life. He begins this section by stating that '[t]he exchange of living labour for objectified labour – i.e., the positing of social labour in the form of the contradiction of capital and wage labour – is the ultimate development of the *value relation* and of production resting on value'

(Marx 1973: 704). The title and initial sentence of this section of the *Grundrisse* indicate that, for Marx, the category of value expresses the basic relations of production of capitalism – those social relations that most fundamentally characterize capitalism as a form of social life. At the same time, the category of value expresses a determinate form of wealth. An analysis of value, then, must elucidate both of these aspects. As a form of wealth, value generally has been understood of as a category of the market mediation of the wealth created by labour. Yet when Marx speaks of 'exchange' in the course of considering the 'value relation' in the passages quoted, the exchange to which he refers is not that of circulation, but of production – 'the exchange of living labour for objectified labour'. Marx's characterization of value as 'the foundation of bourgeois production' indicates that it should not be understood simply as a category of the mode of distribution of commodities, that is, as an attempt to ground the so-called self-regulating market. Rather, it should be understood primarily as a category of capitalist production itself.

In the *Grundrisse*, then, Marx's analysis of the contradiction between the 'relations of production' and the 'forces of production' in capitalism differs from that of traditional Marxist theories, which focus critically on the mode of distribution (market, private property) and understand the contradiction as one between the spheres of distribution and production. He explicitly criticizes theoretical approaches that conceptualize historical transformation in terms of the mode of distribution without considering the possibility that the mode of producing could be transformed, taking as an example John Stuart Mill's statement that 'the laws and conditions of the production of wealth partake of the character of physical truths.... It is not so with the distribution of wealth. That is a matter of human institutions solely'.[6] This separation, according to Marx, is illegitimate: 'The "laws and conditions" of the production of wealth and the laws of "the distribution of wealth" are the same laws under different forms, and both change, undergo the same historic process; are as such only moments of a historic process' (Marx 1973: 832).

If the process of production and the fundamental social relations of capitalism are interrelated, however, the former cannot be equated with the forces of production that eventually come into contradiction with the capitalist relations of production. Instead, the process of production itself should be seen as intrinsically related to capitalism. These passages suggest, in other words, that Marx's understanding of capitalism's fundamental contradiction should not be conceived as one between industrial production, on the one hand, and the market and capitalist private property, on the other. This requires further examination.

When Marx discusses production resting on value, he describes it as a mode of production whose 'presupposition is – *and remains* – the mass of direct labour time, the quantity of labour employed, as the determinant factor in the production of wealth' (Marx 1973: 704; emphasis added). What characterizes value as a form of wealth, according to Marx, is that it is constituted by the expenditure of direct human labour in the process of production, measured temporally. Value is a social form that expresses, and is based on, the expenditure of direct labour time. This form, for Marx, is at the very heart of capital. As a cat-egory of the fundamental social relations that constitute capitalism, value expresses that which is, *and remains*, the basic foundation of capitalist produc-tion. Yet production based on value generates a dynamic that gives rise to a growing tension between this foundation of the capitalist mode of production and the results of its own historical development:

> But to the degree that large industry develops, the creation of real wealth comes to depend less on labour time and on the amount of labour employed than on the power of the agencies set in motion during labour time, whose 'powerful effectiveness' is itself ... out of all proportion to the direct labour time spent on their production, but depends rather on the general state of science and on the progress of technology.... Real wealth manifests itself, rather ... in the monstrous disproportion between the labour time applied, and its product, as well as in the qualitative imbalance between labour, reduced to a pure abstraction, and the power of the production process it superintends.
>
> (Marx 1973: 704–5)

The contrast between value and 'real wealth' is one between a form of wealth based on 'labour time and on the amount of labour employed' and one that does not depend on immediate labour time. This contrast is crucial to understanding Marx's theory of value and his notion of the basic contradiction of capitalist society. It clearly indicates that value does not refer to social wealth in general, but is a historically specific, possibly transitory, category that purportedly grasps the foundation of capitalist society. Moreover, value is not merely a category of the market, one that grasps a historically particular mode of the social distribu-tion of wealth. Such a market-centred interpretation – which is related to Mill's position that the mode of distribution is changeable historically but not the mode of producing – implies the existence of a transhistorical form of wealth that is distributed differently in different societies. According to Marx, however, value is a historically specific form of social wealth and is intrinsically related to a his-torically specific mode of production. This suggests that different forms of society are associated with different forms of wealth. (Marx's discussion here suggests that the form of wealth, the form of labour and the very fabric of social relations differ in various social formations.)

Many arguments regarding Marx's analysis of the uniqueness of labour as the source of value – supportive as well as critical – overlook his distinction between 'real wealth' (or 'material wealth') and value. The *Grundrisse* indic-ates, however, that Marx's 'labour theory of value' is not a theory of the unique properties of labour in general, but is an analysis of the historical specificity of value as a form of wealth and, hence, implicitly, of the labour that supposedly constitutes it. Consequently, it is irrelevant to argue for or against Marx's theory of value as if it were intended to be a labour theory of (transhistorical) wealth – that is, as if Marx had written a political economy rather than a *critique* of political economy.[7] This is not to say, of course, that the interpretation of Marx's category of value as a historically specific category proves his analysis of modern society is correct; but it does require that Marx's analysis be considered in its own historically determinate terms and not as if it were a transhistorical theory of political economy of the sort he strongly criticized.

These considerations suggest that value, within the framework of Marx's analysis, is a critical category that reveals the historical specificity of the form of wealth and of production characteristic of capitalism. The paragraph quoted above shows that, according to Marx, the form of production based on value develops in a way that points to the possible historical negation of value itself. In an analysis that seems quite relevant to contemporary conditions, Marx argues that, as capitalist industrial production develops, value becomes less and less adequate as a measure of social wealth. He contrasts value, a form of wealth bound to human labour time expenditure, to the gigantic wealth-producing potential of modern science and technology; value becomes anachronistic in terms of the potential of the system of production to which it gives rise. The realization of that potential would entail the abolition of value.

This historical possibility does not, however, simply mean that ever-greater masses of goods could be turned out on the basis of the existing industrial mode of producing, and distributed more equitably. The logic of the growing contradiction between 'real wealth' and value, which points to the possibility of the former superseding the latter as the determining form of social wealth, also implies the possibility of a different process of production, one based upon a newer, more emancipatory structure of social labour:

> Labour no longer appears so much to be included within the production process; rather, the human being comes to relate more as watchman and regulator to the production process itself.... He steps to the side of the production process instead of being its chief actor. In this transformation, it is neither the direct human labour he himself performs, nor the time during which he works, but rather the appropriation of his own general productive power, his understanding of nature and his mastery over it by virtue of his presence as a social body – it is, in a word, the development of the *social individual* which appears as the great foundation-stone of production and of wealth. The *theft of alien labour time, on which the present wealth is based*, appears a miserable foundation in face of this new one, created by large-scale industry itself.
>
> (Marx 1973: 705; second emphasis added)

This section of the *Grundrisse* makes abundantly clear that, for Marx, overcoming capitalism involves the abolition of value as the social form of wealth, which, in turn, entails overcoming the determinate mode of producing developed under capitalism. Labour time no longer would serve as the measure of wealth, and the production of wealth no longer would be effected primarily by direct human labour in the process of production: 'As soon as labour in the direct form has ceased to be the great well-spring of wealth, labour time ceases and must cease to be its measure, and hence exchange value [must cease to be the measure] of use value' (Marx 1973: 705).

Marx, in other words, analyses the basic social relations of capitalism, its form of wealth, and its material form of production, as interrelated; production resting on value, the mode of production founded on wage labour, and industrial production based on proletarian labour are intrinsically related in his analysis. Hence, the increasingly anachronistic character of value also signifies the increasingly anachronistic character of the industrial process of production developed under capitalism. Overcoming capitalism, according to Marx, entails a fundamental transformation of the material form of production, of the way people work.

Nevertheless, socialist society, according to Marx, does not emerge automatically as the result of a linear, evolutionary historical development. The radical transformation of the process of production outlined above is *not* a quasi-automatic consequence of the rapid increase in scientific and technical knowledge or its application. It is, rather, a *possibility* that arises from a growing intrinsic social contradiction. Although the course of capitalist development generates the possibility of a new, emancipatory, structure of social labour, its general realization is impossible under capitalism.

> Capital itself is the moving contradiction, [in] that it presses to reduce labour time to a minimum, while it posits labour time, on the other side, as sole measure and source of wealth. Hence it diminishes labour time in the necessary form so as to increase it in the superfluous form, hence posits the superfluous in growing measure as a condition – question of life or death – for the necessary.
>
> (Marx 1973: 706)

The question of 'necessary' and 'superfluous' labour time cannot be fully addressed here. It is important to note, however, that, according to Marx, although capitalism tends to develop powerful forces of production whose potential increasingly renders obsolete an organization of production based upon direct labour time expenditure, its structure is such that it cannot allow the full realization of this potential. The only form of wealth that constitutes capital is one based upon direct labour time expenditure. Hence, despite the growing discrepancy between value as measure and material wealth, value is not simply superseded by a new form of wealth.[8] Instead, according to Marx, it remains the necessary structural precondition of capitalist society (although, as he argues throughout *Capital*, this is not overtly the case).

On the basis of his categories of value, commodity and capital, Marx shows that capitalism is characterized by an intrinsic developmental dynamic. That dynamic, however, remains bound to capitalism; it is not self-overcoming. The categories ground both the dynamic as well as its limits; what becomes 'super-fluous' in terms of the production of material wealth remains structurally 'necessary' for capital. Capitalism *does* give rise to the possibility of its own negation, but it *does not* automatically evolve into something else. That the expenditure of direct human labour time remains central and indispensable for capital, despite being rendered anachronistic by developments generated by capital, gives rise to an internal tension. As I have elaborated in *Time, Labour, and Social Domination*, Marx analyses the nature of industrial production and its developmental trajectory with reference to this tension (Postone 1993: 307–66).

These *Grundrisse* passages indicate that Marx's notion of the structural contradiction in capitalism should not be identified immediately with social antagonism, such as class conflict. They also reveal that Marx's understanding of capitalism's contradiction does not refer most fundamentally to a contradiction between private appropriation and socialized production.[9] Hence, it differs fundamentally from that of traditional Marxism. Marx does *not* analyse the contradiction of capitalism, in the *Grundrisse*, as one between the process of production and value, that is, between production in capitalism and capitalist social relations. Rather, he treats the former as moulded by the latter: production in capitalism is the 'mode of production based on value'. It is in this sense that, in his later writings, Marx refers explicitly to the industrial mode of production as a 'specifically capitalist form of production … (technologically, as well)' (Marx 1994: 428). These passages in the *Grundrisse* imply that the material form of production is to be transformed with the overcoming of capitalism. They also belie the notion that Marx's critical theory is a form of evolutionary technological determinism.[10] On the contrary, he treats technology and the process of production as socially constituted; they are shaped by value. They should not, therefore be identified simply with the 'forces of production' that come into contradiction with capitalism's social relations. Yet, although technology and the process of production are moulded by capitalist relations, they embody a contradiction. Marx's analysis distinguishes between the *actuality* of the form of production constituted by value, and its *potential* – a potential that grounds the possibility of a new form of production. This distinction is ultimately rooted in the contradictory nature of capitalist relations, which Marx, in *Capital*, grounds in the double character of the categories of modern, capitalist social life.

It is clear from the passages cited that when, in the *Grundrisse*, Marx describes the overcoming of capitalism's contradiction and states that the 'mass of workers must themselves appropriate their own surplus labour' (Marx 1973: 708), he is referring not only to the expropriation of private property and the use of the surplus product in a more rational, fair and efficient way. The appropriation of which he speaks also involves the reflexive application of the potential embedded in advanced capitalist production to the process of production itself. The system of social production in which wealth is created through the appropriation of direct labour time and workers labour as cogs of a productive apparatus could be abolished. These two aspects of the industrial capitalist mode of production are related, according to Marx. Hence, overcoming capitalism, as presented in the *Grundrisse*, implicitly involves overcoming both the formal and material aspects of the mode of production founded on wage labour. It entails the abolition of a system of distribution based upon the exchange of labour power as a commodity for a wage with which means of consumption are acquired; it also entails the abolition of a system of production based upon proletarian labour, that is, upon the one-sided and fragmented labour characteristic of capitalist industrial production. With regard to the structure of social labour, then, the Marxian contradiction should be understood as a growing contradiction between the sort of labour people perform under capitalism and the sort of labour they could perform if value were abolished and the productive potential developed under capitalism were reflexively used to liberate people from the sway of the alienated structures constituted by their own labour. Far from entailing the *realization* of the proletariat, overcoming capitalism involves the material *abolition* of proletarian labour. The emancipation *of* labour requires the emancipation *from* (alienated) labour.

This interpretation, by providing the basis for a historical critique of the concrete form of production in capitalism (as well, of course, of the abstract mediation and domination expressed by the categories of value and capital) sheds light on Marx's well-known assertion that the capitalist social formation marks the conclusion of the prehistory of human society (Marx 1987: 264). The notion of overcoming proletarian labour implies that 'prehistory' should be understood as referring to those social formations in which ongoing surplus production exists and is based primarily on direct human labour. This characteristic is shared by societies in which the surplus is created by slave, serf, or wage labour. Yet the formation based upon wage labour, according to Marx, is uniquely characterized by a dynamic that gives rise to the historical possibility that surplus production based on human labour as an internal element of the process of production can be overcome. A new social formation can be created in which the '*surplus labour of the mass* has ceased to be the condition for the development of general wealth, just as the *non-labour of the few*, for the development of the general powers of the human head' (Marx 1973: 705).

For Marx, then, the end of prehistory signifies the overcoming of the opposition between manual and intellectual labour. This opposition cannot be overcome, however, merely by melding existing manual and intellectual labour. Marx's treatment of production in the *Grundrisse* implies that not only the separation of these modes of labour, but also the determining characteristics of each, are rooted in the existing form of production. Their separation could be overcome only by transforming existing modes of both manual and intellectual labour, that is, by the historical constitution of a new structure and social organization of labour. Such a new structure becomes possible, according to Marx's analysis, when surplus production is no longer necessarily based primarily on direct human labour.

The section of the *Grundrisse* on capitalism's fundamental contradiction indicates, then, that Marx's critical theory should be understood essentially as a critique *of* labour in capitalism, rather than a critique of capitalism from the *standpoint* of labour (as in traditional Marxism). This has far-reaching implications for comprehending *Capital* and delineates a fundamental distinction between Marx's critique of political economy and its frequent (mis)interpretation as a critical political economy. To fully elaborate such a reading of *Capital* on the basis of the *Grundrisse* is not possible within the framework of this chapter, of course. In order to be able to sketch its bare outlines, however, it is important first to briefly consider another crucial section of the *Grundrisse*, titled '[t]he method of political economy' (Marx 1973: 100–8).

The *Grundrisse*: Marx's categories

In this section, Marx wrestles with the question of an adequate point of departure for his critical analysis. He makes clear that the categories of his analysis should not be understood in narrow economic terms. Rather, they 'express the forms of being [*Daseinsformen*], the determinations of existence [*Existenzbestimmungen*] ... of this specific society' (Marx 1973: 106, trans. modified). As such, they are, at once, forms of subjectivity and objectivity; they express 'what is given, in the head as well as in reality' (Marx 1973: 106). That is, Marx's categories purport to grasp as intrinsically interrelated, economic, social and cultural dimensions of the modern, capitalist form of life that frequently are treated as contingently related, as extrinsic to one another. This categorial approach contravenes understandings of the relations of social objectivity and subjectivity in terms of a base/superstructure model.[11]

Moreover, Marx makes very clear that the categories of his critique are historically specific. Even categories that appear to be transhistorical and that actually do play a role much earlier historically – such as money and labour – are fully developed and come into their own only in capitalist society (Marx 1973: 103).

> This example of labour shows strikingly how even the most abstract categories, despite their validity ... for all epochs, are, nevertheless, in the specific character of this abstraction, themselves likewise a product of historic relations, and possess their full validity only for and within those relations.
>
> (Marx 1973: 105)

As simple, abstract categories, in other words, they are as 'modern ... as are the relations which create this simple abstraction' (Marx 1973: 103).[12]

Because the categories, as fully developed, are historically specific,

> [i]t would ... be unfeasible and wrong to let the economic categories follow one another in the same sequence as that in which they were historically decisive. Their sequence is determined, rather, by their relation to one another in modern bourgeois society, which is precisely the opposite of that ... which corresponds to historical development.
>
> (Marx 1973: 107)

Instead, critical analysis must begin with what is most essential to its object. In bourgeois society, '[c]apital is the all-dominating economic power' and, therefore, 'must form the starting-point as well as the finishing-point' (Marx 1973: 107).

Marx's emphasis on the historical specificity of the object of investigation is intrinsically linked to the issue of the starting point of his critical analysis. As early as *The German Ideology*, Marx insisted on the social and historical constitution of forms of consciousness, a position refined in the *Grundrisse* with reference to the notion of the objective/subjective character of the structuring categories of capitalist society. This implies that no position, including Marx's, has universal, transhistorical significance. The historical relativization of thought does not mean, however, that a valid theory is impossible; a historically specific theory can be rigorously adequate to its object. This requires that theory be self-reflexive: it must be able to account for its own conditions of possibility by means of the same categories with which it grasps its object, that is, its own context.

The historically specific character of the theory, moreover, is not simply a matter of content, but also a matter of form; its form should not contravene the historically specific character of the theory. The theory cannot present itself in a transhistorical form, for example, as a universally valid 'method' that simply can be applied to a variety of objects, to which it is related only contingently. Rather the historical specificity of the theory requires that the concept be the concept of its object. (Ironically, it is when the theory is self-consciously and reflexively historically specific that this apparently transhistorical Hegelian dictum acquires its validity.)

The point of departure of the critical analysis, therefore, cannot be grounded in a Cartesian manner, in a purportedly indubitable, transhistorically valid, truth. Rather, the point of departure must be historically specific, the core of a historically determinate analysis of the historically specific formation that is its context. If Hegel, in *The Science of Logic* was concerned with the problem of the point of departure for the exposition of a logic that doesn't presuppose a logic, that is, a grounding outside of that which it seeks to demonstrate, Marx was concerned with the problem of a historically specific point of departure for a critical social theory that doesn't ground itself outside of its object/context.

Because such a point of departure cannot be grounded in any transhistorically valid propositions, it can only be rendered plausible immanently – by the course of its unfolding, whereby each successive unfolded moment retroactively justifies that which preceded it. And, indeed, this how *Capital* is structured. The categories of the beginning – for example, commodity, value, use value, abstract labour, concrete labour – are only really justified by the subsequent unfolding of the analysis.[13] What appears to be their transhistorical 'grounding' in the first chapter of *Capital* should be understood with reference to the framework of Marx's rigorously immanent mode of presentation, which does not take a standpoint extrinsic to its object. Understood in this way, what appears to be a transhistorical grounding (of value, for example) is the way in which the subjective/objective forms present themselves. It is a metacommentary on thought that remains bound within the limits of the structuring forms of modern, capitalist society.[14]

Capital in light of the *Grundrisse*

At this point we can briefly outline a reading of *Capital* based on the considerations developed thus far. As is well known, *Capital*'s point of departure is the commodity. On the basis of the *Grundrisse*, it now is evident that the category of the commodity here does not refer to commodities as they might exist in many societies. Nor does it express a (fictitious) historical stage of 'simple commodity production' purportedly antecedent to capitalism. Rather, the category of the commodity here is historically specific. It designates the most fundamental social form of capitalist society, the form from which Marx then proceeded to unfold the essential features and dynamic quality of that society.[15] The characteristics of that form – that it simultaneously is a value and a use value, for example – should also be understood as historically specific (Marx 1996: 84, 87).

As a form of social relations, the commodity is peculiar, according to Marx: it is constituted by labour. Consequently, it necessarily exists in objectified form and has a dualistic character as a form of social mediation and as a product, as value and use value. Marx's conception of the historical specificity of labour in capitalism underlies this description. He maintains that labour in capitalism has a 'double character': it is both 'concrete labour' and 'abstract labour' (Marx 1996: 51–6). 'Concrete labour' refers to labouring activities that mediate the interaction of humans with nature. Although it is only in capitalism that all such activities are considered types of an overarching activity – (concrete) labour – and all products are classed as similar, as use-values, this sort of mediating activity is transhistorical; it exists in all societies. The use-value dimension of the commodity is not historically unique to capitalism. This implies, however, that its value dimension and the labour that constitute it *are* historically specific. Hence, 'abstract labour' is not concrete labour in general, but is a different, historically specific, category. As argued in *Time, Labour, and Social Domination*, it signifies that labour in capitalism has a unique social function that is not intrinsic to labouring activity as such (Postone 1993: 123–85). Rather, commodity-determined labour serves as a kind of quasi-objective means by which the products of others are acquired (Marx 1996: 84). It mediates a new form of interdependence, where people's labour or labour products function as quasi-objective means of obtaining the products of others. In serving as such a means, labour and its products pre-empt that function on the part of manifest social relations.

In Marx's mature works, then, the notion of the essential centrality of labour to social life is historically specific. It should not be taken to mean that material production is the most essential dimension of social life in general, or even of capitalism in particular. Rather, it refers to the historically specific constitution by labour in capitalism of a form of mediation that fundamentally characterizes that society. This mediating activity is not, however, a characteristic that is intrinsic to labouring activity. Consequently, it does not – and cannot – appear as such. Instead, when the commodity is analysed, its historically specific dimension, value, appears to be constituted by labour in general, without any further qualifications – the 'expenditure of human brains, nerves, and muscles' (Marx 1996: 54). That is to say, the historically specific, socially mediating function of labour in capitalism appears as transhistorical concrete labour, as 'labour' – that is, as an ontological essence rather than as a historically specific form. This ontological form of appearance of labour's historically unique socially constituting function in capitalism is a fundamental determination of what Marx refers to as the fetish forms of capitalism; it underlies all approaches that transhistoricize the socially constituting role of labour in capitalism, whether affirmatively (as in classical political economy and traditional Marxism) or negatively (as in *Dialectic of Enlightenment*).[16]

Labour in capitalism, then, not only mediates the interaction of humans and nature, but also constitutes a historically specific social mediation, according to Marx. Hence, its objectifications (commodity, capital) are both concrete labour products and objectified forms of social mediation. According to this analysis, the social relations that most fundamentally characterize the capitalist form of social life are very different in kind from the qualitatively specific and overtly social relations, such as kinship relations, which characterize other forms of social life. The fundamental forms of social relations constitutive of capitalism are peculiarly quasi-objective and formal, and are characterized by a dualistic opposition of an abstract, general, homogenous dimension, and a concrete, particular, material dimension (both of which appear to be natural, rather than social).

This historically specific form of mediation is constituted by determinate forms of practice, but becomes quasi-independent of those practices. The result is a new form of social domination that subjects people to increasingly impersonal 'rational' imperatives and constraints that cannot adequately be grasped in terms of the concrete domination of social groupings such as class or institutional agencies of the state and/or the economy. Like power as conceptualized by Foucault, this form of domination has no determinate locus and appears not to be social at all. However, it is not static, but temporally dynamic. In *Capital*, Marx treats the historically dynamic character of capitalism as a historically determinate, specifying characteristic of that form of social life, grounded in the form of impersonal domination intrinsic to the basic structuring forms of that society. In so doing, he historically relativizes the notion of an intrinsic historical dynamic.

What drives this dynamic is the double character of the underlying social forms of capitalism. It is crucially important to note in this regard that the distinction Marx makes in the *Grundrisse* between value and 'real wealth' reappears in the first chapter of *Capital* as that between value and 'material wealth' (Marx 1996: 53–6). Material wealth is measured by the quantity produced, and is a function of a number of factors in addition to labour, such as knowledge, social organization, and natural conditions (Marx 1996: 50). Value, the dominant form of wealth in capitalism, is constituted by (socially necessary) human time–time expenditure alone, according to Marx (Marx 1996: 49–50, 55–6).

Whereas material wealth, as the dominant form of wealth, is mediated by overt social relations, value is a self-mediating form of wealth.

Beginning with his treatment of the magnitude of value in terms of socially necessary labour time, Marx outlines a dialectical interaction of value and use-value which becomes historically significant with the emergence of relative surplus value and gives rise to a very complex, non-linear, historical dynamic underlying modern society. With the unfolding of this dynamic it becomes increasingly clear that the historically specific form of social domination intrinsic to capitalism's most basic forms of social mediation is the domination of people by time. The dynamic outlined by Marx in *Capital* is characterized, on the one hand, by ongoing transformations of production and, more generally of social life; on the other hand, this historical dynamic entails the ongoing reconstitution of its own fundamental condition as an unchanging feature of social life – namely that social mediation ultimately is effected by labour and, hence, that living labour remains integral to the process of production (considered in terms of society as a whole) regardless of the level of productivity. Capitalism ceaselessly generates the new while constantly reconstituting the same.

This understanding of capitalism's complex dynamic allows for a critical, social (rather than technological) analysis of the trajectory of growth and the structure of production in modern society. Although I cannot elaborate here, Marx's key concept of surplus-value not only indicates, as traditional interpretations emphasize, that the surplus is produced by the working class, but that capitalism is characterized by a *determinate, runaway form of growth*. The problem of economic growth in capitalism, within this framework, is not only that it is crisis-ridden, as has been emphasized frequently and correctly by traditional Marxist approaches. Rather, the form of growth itself, which entails the accelerating destruction of the natural environment for smaller and smaller increases in surplus value, is itself problematic. The trajectory of growth would be very different, according to this approach, if the ultimate goal of production were increased quantities of goods rather than increases in surplus-value.

This approach also provides the basis for a critical analysis of the structure of social labour and the nature of production in capitalism. It indicates that the industrial process of production should not be grasped as a technical process that, although increasingly socialized, is used by private capitalists for their own ends. Rather, the approach I am outlining grasps that process itself as intrinsically capitalist. With the real subsumption of labour, in Marx's account, capital becomes less and less the mystified form of powers that 'actually' are those of the workers. Rather, the productive powers of capital increasingly become socially general productive powers that no longer can be grasped adequately as those of the immediate producers alone. This constitution and accumulation of socially general knowledge renders proletarian labour increasingly anachronistic. That is, it renders the production of material wealth essentially independent of direct human labour time expenditure. This, in turn, opens the possibility of large-scale socially general reductions in labour time and fundamental changes in the nature and social organization of labour. Yet these possibilities are not and cannot be realized in capitalism; the dialectic of value and use value reconstitutes the necessity of proletarian labour. The combination of capital's drive for ongoing increases in productivity, and its grounding in the expenditure of direct human labour time, leads to a determinate mode of production, in which the development of technologically sophisticated production that could liberate people from fragmented and repetitive labour, reinforces such labour instead. Similarly, labour-time is not reduced on a socially general level, but is distributed unequally, even increasing for many.

This preliminary exposition of Marx's notion of the contradiction of capitalism indicates that his analysis seeks to grasp the course of capitalist development as a double-sided development of enrichment and impoverishment. It implies that this development cannot be understood adequately in a one-dimensional fashion, either as the progress of knowledge and happiness, or as the 'progress' of domination and destruction. According to his analysis, although the historical possibility emerges that the mode of social labour *could be* enriching for everyone, social labour *actually* has become impoverishing for the many. The rapid increase in scientific and technical knowledge under capitalism does not, therefore, signify linear progress toward emancipation. According to Marx's analysis of the commodity and capital, such increased knowledge – itself socially constituted – has led to the fragmentation and emptying of individual labour and to the increasing control of humanity by the results of its own objectifying activity; yet it has also increased the possibility that labour could be individually enriching and that humanity could exert greater control over its fate. This double-sided development is rooted in the alienated structures of capitalist society and can be overcome, according to Marx's dialectical analysis, which should not, then, in any way, be identified with a faith in linear scientific progress and/or in social progress.

Marx's analysis thus implies a notion of overcoming capitalism that neither uncritically affirms industrial production as the condition of human progress nor romantically rejects technological progress per se. By indicating that the potential of the system of production developed under capitalism could be used to transform that system itself, Marx's analysis overcomes the opposition of these positions and shows that each takes one moment of a more complex historical development to be the whole. This approach grasps the opposition of faith in linear progress and its romantic rejection as expressing a historical antinomy that, in *both* of its terms, is characteristic of the capitalist epoch (Marx 1996: 568–9, 798ff.). More generally, Marx's critical theory argues neither for simply retaining nor for abolishing what was constituted historically in capitalism. Rather, his theory points to the possibility that what was historically constituted in alienated form could be appropriated and, thereby, fundamentally transformed.

According to the interpretation very briefly outlined here, the *Grundrisse* allows us to see that Marx's critique in *Capital* extends far beyond the traditional critique of bourgeois relations of distribution (the market and private property). It not only entails a critique of exploitation and the unequal distribution of wealth and power, although it, of course, includes such a critique. Rather, it grasps modern industrial society itself as capitalist, and critically analyses capitalism primarily in terms of abstract structures of domination, the increasing fragmentation of individual labour and individual existence, and a blind runaway developmental logic. It treats the working class as the basic element of capital, rather than the embodiment of its negation, and implicitly conceptualizes socialism not in terms of the realization of labour and industrial production, but in terms of the possible abolition of the proletariat and the organization of labour based on proletarian labour (as well as of the dynamic system of abstract compulsion constituted by labour as a socially mediating activity). This approach reconceptualizes a postcapitalist society in terms of the overcoming of the proletariat – the self-abolition of the proletariat and the labour it does – that is, in terms of a transformation of the general structure of labour and of time. In that sense it differs both from the traditional Marxist notion of the 'realization' of the proletariat, and from the capitalist mode of abolishing national working classes by creating an underclass within the framework of the unequal distribution of labour and of time, nationally and globally.

Although the logically abstract level of analysis outlined here does not immediately address the issue of the specific factors underlying the structural transformations of the past 30 years, it can provide a framework within which those transformations can be grounded socially and understood historically. At the same time it could provide the basis for a critical theory of 'actually existing socialist' countries as alternative forms of capitalist accumulation, rather than as social modes that represented the historical negation of capital, in however imperfect a form. Inasmuch as it seeks to ground socially, and is critical of, the abstract quasi-objective social relations and the nature of production, work, and the imperatives of growth in capitalism, this approach could also begin to address a range of contemporary concerns, dissatisfactions and aspirations in ways that could tie them to the development of capital, if not necessarily in traditional class terms.

This reading of Marx, then, attempts to contribute to a critical understanding of the overarching transformations of our social universe in ways that get beyond the weaknesses of post-Marxist discourse while avoiding the pitfalls of traditional Marxist approaches.

Notes

1 I would like to thank Robin Bates and Jake Smith for critical feedback.
2 To avoid misunderstandings that could be encouraged by the term 'categorical', I use 'categorial' to refer to Marx's attempt to grasp the forms of modern social life by means of the categories of his mature critique.
3 Some of the arguments presented here were developed in Moishe Postone, *Time, Labour, and Social Domination: A Reinterpretation of Marx's Critical Theory* (Postone 1993).
4 See, for example, G.A. Cohen, *History, Labour and Freedom* (Cohen 1988: 209–38); Maurice Dobb, *Political Economy and Capitalism* (Dobb 1940: 70–8); Jon Elster, *Making Sense of Marx* (Elster 1985: 127); Ronald Meeks, *Studies in the Labour*

Theory of Value (Meeks 1956); John Roemer, *Analytical Foundations of Marxian Economic Theory* (Roemer 1981: 158–9); Ian Steedman, 'Ricardo, Marx, Sraffa' (Steedman 1981: 11–19); Paul Sweezy, *The Theory of Capitalist Development* (Sweezy 1968: 52–3).

5 This would include both dominant strands of more recent critical Marx interpretations – structuralism and Critical Theory. Althusser, for example, formulated an epistemologically sophisticated and trenchant critique of the 'idealism of labour' and the related conception of people as subjects; he introduced the notion of social relations as structures that are irreducible to anthropological intersubjectivity. Nevertheless, his focus on the question of the surplus in terms of exploitation, as well as on the physical 'material' dimension of production, are related to what ultimately is a traditional understanding of capitalism (Althusser and Balibar 1970: 145–54, 165–82). Lukács and members of the Frankfurt School, seeking to respond theoretically to the historical transformation of capitalism from a market-centred form to a bureaucratic, state-centred form, tacitly recognized the inadequacies of a critical theory of modernity that defined capitalism solely in nineteenth-century terms – that is, in terms of the market and private ownership of the means of production. On the other hand, however, they remained bound to some of the assumptions of that very sort of theory (see Postone 1993: 71–120).

6 John Stuart Mill, *Principals of Political Economy* (2nd edn, London 1849), vol. 1, pp. 239–40 (quoted in Marx, 1973: 832).

7 Jon Elster provides an example of such an argument. He argues against Marx's theory of value and surplus value by denying 'that the workers have a mysterious capacity to create ex nihilo'; he maintains, instead, that 'man's ability to tap the environment makes possible a surplus over and above any given consumption level' (Elster 1985: 141). In addressing the issue of the creation of wealth in this manner, Elster's argument implicitly takes value to be a transhistorical category, thereby obscuring the distinction Marx makes between 'value' and 'real wealth'.

8 The idea that value, for Marx, is not a category of wealth in general, but specifies the form of wealth and of social relations at the heart of capitalist modernity has been misunderstood by thinkers as disparate as Jürgen Habermas, Daniel Bell and Antonio Negri. Both Habermas and Bell maintained in the early 1970s, that the labour theory of value had been superseded historically and that contemporary society requires a 'science and technology theory of value'. Both thereby obscured Marx's distinction between value and 'real wealth' and, hence, the dialectical dynamic he developed (Habermas 1973: 222–9); (Bell 1973: xiv). Negri argued that Marx's description of what I have shown is a postcapitalist organization of production in the *Grundrisse* actually describes contemporary capitalism, which no longer is based on the Law of Value, but on the 'Law of Command' (Negri 1989: 144ff.). Such positions implicitly substitute a linear view of history for Marx's dialectical analysis of necessity and superfluity.

9 The argument that the primary contradiction of capitalism is, for Marx, structural and does not refer simply to social antagonism also has been made by Anthony Giddens. However, he locates that contradiction between private appropriation and socialized production, that is, between bourgeois relations of distribution and industrial production (Giddens 1979: 135–41).

10 For such a position, see G.A. Cohen, 'Forces and Relations of Production' (Cohen 1986: 19–22).

11 For all of their differences, Georg Lukács, Theodor Adorno and Alfred Sohn-Rethel recognized the subjective/objective character of Marx's categories, thereby breaking with the base/superstructure schema.

12 One of Marx's many accomplishments in *Capital* was to ground socially the transhistorical projection of categories fully valid only for capitalist society onto all forms of human social life. He does so by grounding such projections in the various fetish

forms of the categories, which are generated by the interplay of the peculiar abstract and concrete dimensions of the forms of social mediation constitutive of capitalist society.

13 This point is elaborated in M. Postone, *Time, Labour, and Social Domination* (Postone 1993: 138–44, 267–72).

14 See John Patrick Murray, 'Enlightenment Roots of Habermas' Critique of Marx', *The Modern Schoolman*, 57, no. 1 (November 1979), pp. 13ff.

15 Roman Rosdolsky pointed out that the existence of developed capital is assumed at the very beginning of Marx's critique (Rosdolsky 1977: 46).

16 See Theodor Adorno and Max Horkheimer, *Dialectic of Enlightenment* (Adorno and Horkheimer 2002).

References

Adorno, Theodor and Horkheimer, Max (2002) *Dialectic of Enlightenment*, Stanford: Stanford University Press.

Althusser, Louis and Balibar, Etienne (1970) *Reading Capital*, London: NLB.

Bell, Daniel (1973) *The Coming of Post-Industrial Society*, New York: Basic Books.

Cohen, G.A. (1986) 'Forces and Relations of Production', in J. Roemer (ed.), *Analytical Marxism*, Cambridge: Cambridge University Press.

Cohen, G.A. (1988) *History, Labour and Freedom*, Oxford: Clarendon Press.

Dobb, Maurice (1940) *Political Economy and Capitalism*, London: G. Routledge & Sons.

Elster, Jon (1985) *Making Sense of Marx*, Cambridge: Cambridge University Press.

Giddens, Anthony (1979) *Central Problems in Social Theory*, Berkeley: University of California Press.

Habermas, Jürgen (1973) 'Between Philosophy and Science: Marxism as Critique', in Jürgen Habermas, *Theory and Practice*, Boston: Beacon Press.

Marx, Karl (1973) *Grundrisse: Foundations of the Critique of Political Economy*, Harmondsworth: Penguin.

Marx, Karl (1987) 'A Contribution to the Critique of Political Economy', in *Marx and Engels Collected Works*, vol. 29: *Marx 1857–61*, New York: International Publishers.

Marx, Karl (1994) 'Results of the Direct Process of Production', in *Marx and Engels Collected Works*, vol. 34: *Marx 1861–64*, New York: International Publishers.

Marx, Karl (1996) '*Capital*, vol. I', in *Marx and Engels Collected Works*, vol. 35: *Capital, Vol. I*, New York: International Publishers.

Meeks, Ronald (1956) *Studies in the Labour Theory of Value*, New York and London: Lawrence and Wishart.

Murray, John Patrick (1979) 'Enlightenment Roots of Habermas' Critique of Marx', *The Modern Schoolman*, 57(1).

Negri, Antonio (1989) *Marx Beyond Marx: Lessons on the Grundrisse*, New York: J.F. Bergin Publishers.

Postone, Moishe (1993) *Time, Labour, and Social Domination: A Reinterpretation of Marx's Critical Theory*, Cambridge and New York: Cambridge University Press.

Roemer, John (1981) *Analytical Foundations of Marxian Economic Theory*, Cambridge: Cambridge University Press.

Rosdolsky, Roman (1977) *The Making of Marx's Capital*, London: Pluto Press.

Steedman, Ian (1981) 'Ricardo, Marx, Sraffa', in Ian Steedman (ed.), *The Value Controversy*, London: NLB.

Sweezy, Paul (1968) *The Theory of Capitalist Development*, New York: Oxford University Press.

Figure 1 Marx's picture of April 1861 (the oldest surviving photo of Marx).

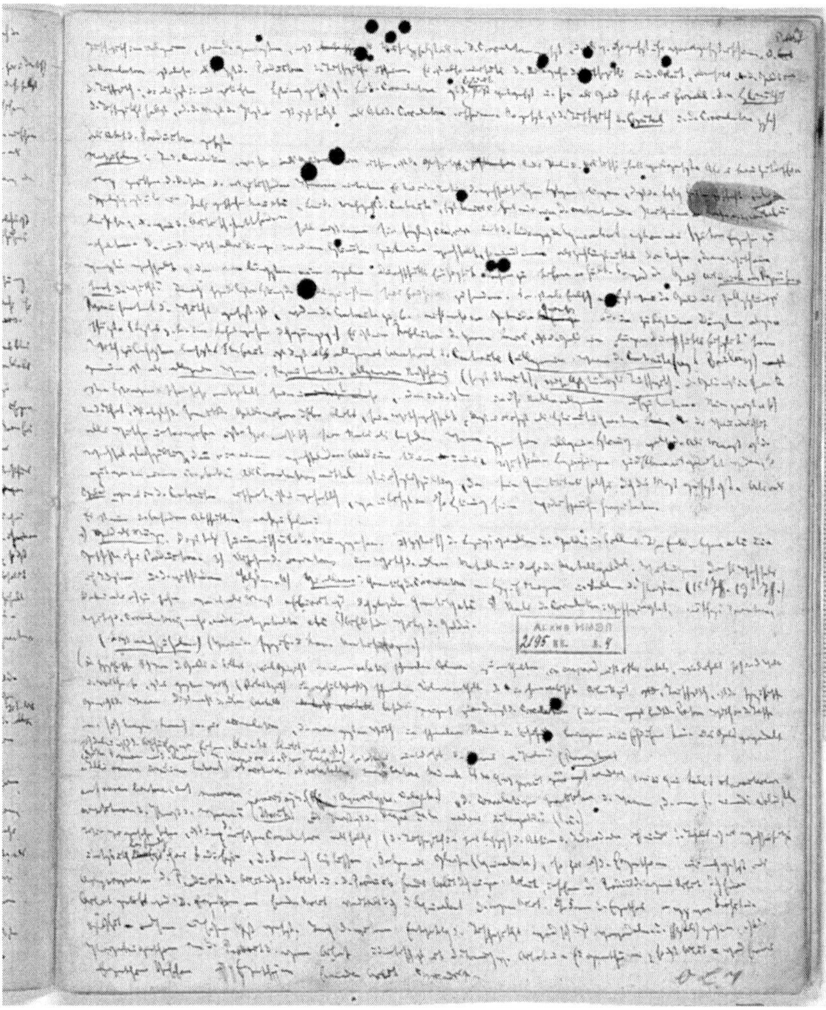

Figure 2 Grundrisse, Notebook II, p. 7.

Figure 3 Grundrisse, Notebook IV, p. 1.

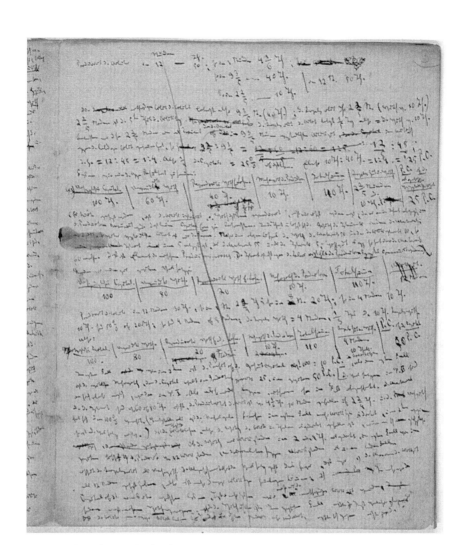

Figure 4 Grundrisse, Notebook IV, p. 3.

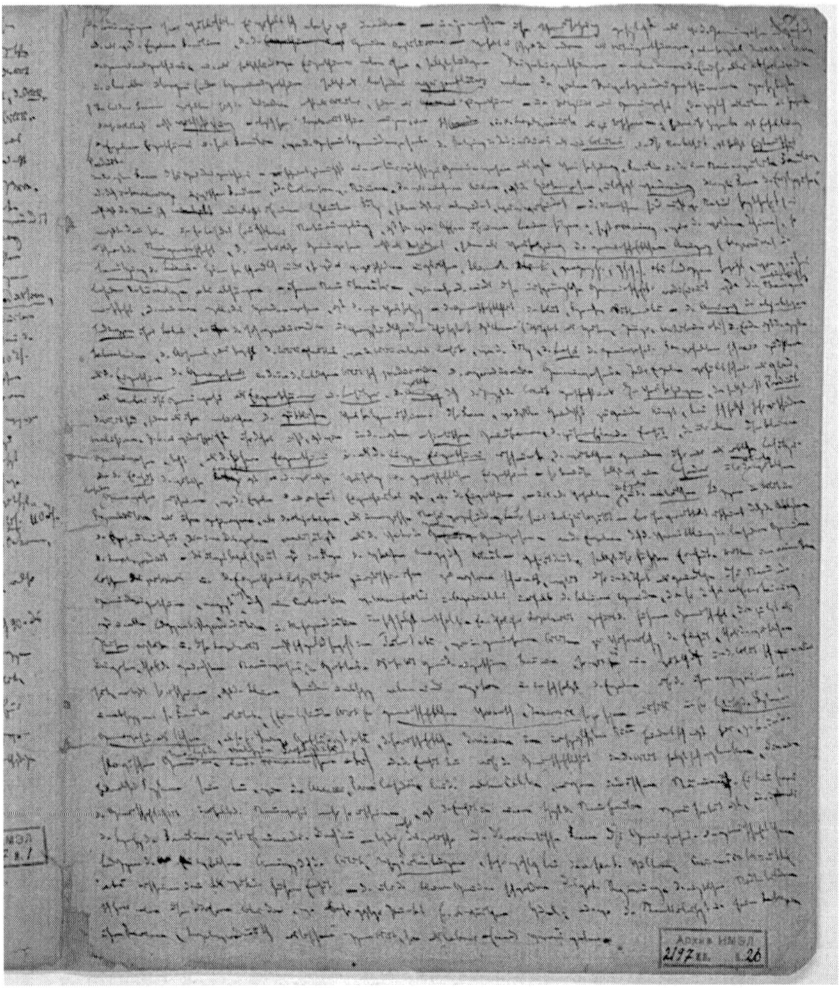

Figure 5 *Grundrisse*, Notebook IV, p. 51.

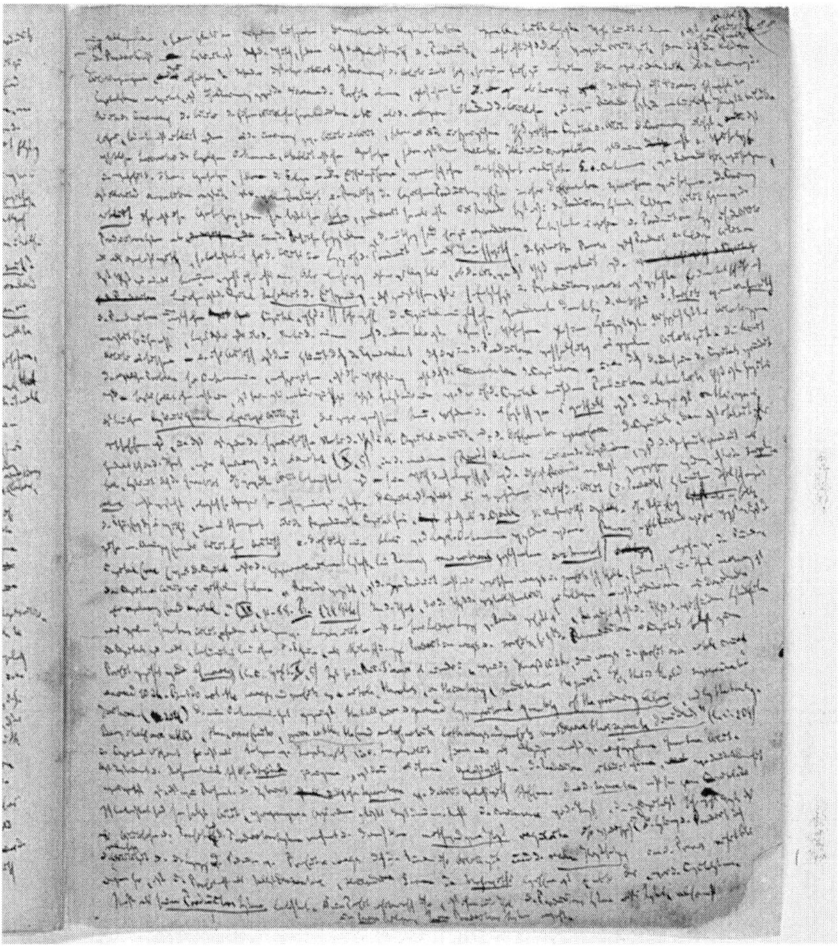

Figure 6 Grundrisse, Notebook V, p. 33.

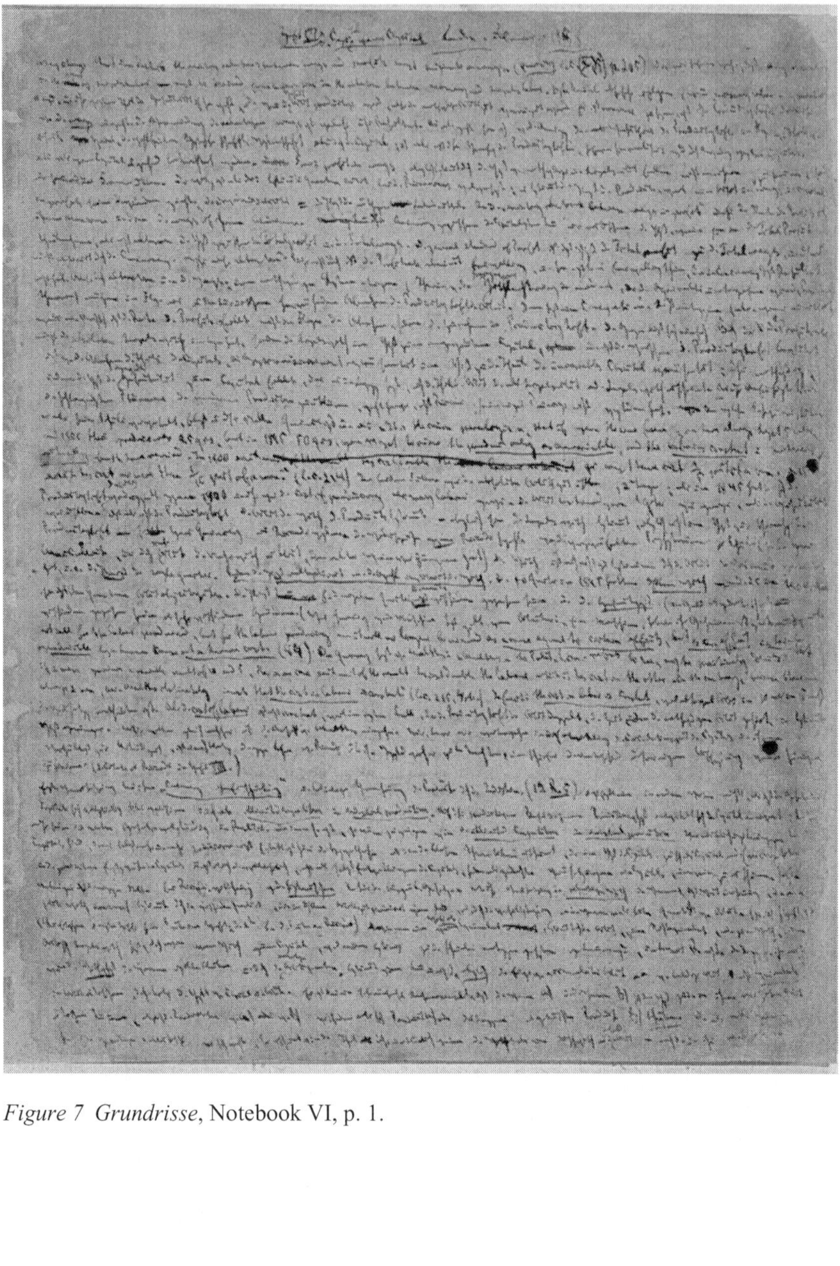

Figure 7 Grundrisse, Notebook VI, p. 1.

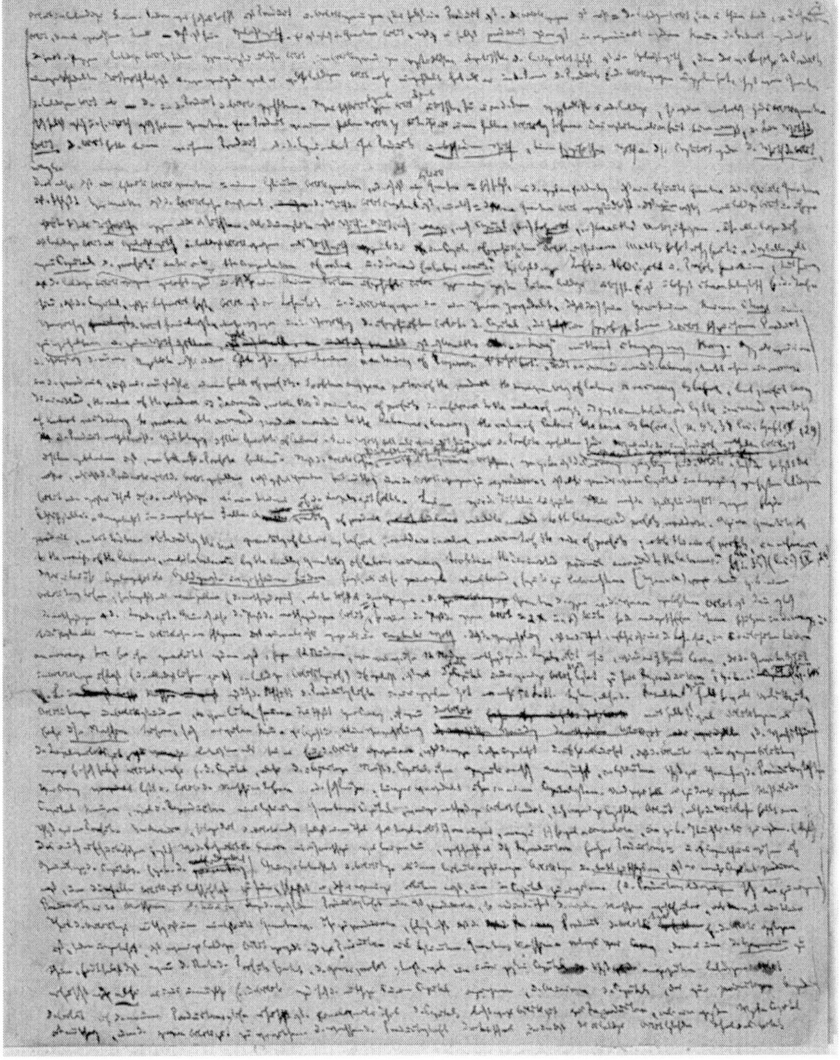

Figure 8 Grundrisse, Notebook VI, p. 7.

Part II

Marx at the time of *Grundrisse*

9 Marx's life at the time of the *Grundrisse*

Biographical notes on 1857–8

Marcello Musto

The date with the revolution

In 1848 Europe was shaken by a succession of numerous popular insurrections inspired by the principles of political freedom and social justice. The weakness of a newly born workers' movement, the bourgeoisie's renunciation of these ideals, which it had initially shared, the violent military repression and the return of economic prosperity generated the defeat of the revolutionary uprisings everywhere, and the powers of reaction firmly regained the reins of state governments.

Marx supported the popular insurrections on the daily *Neue Rheinische Zeitung. Organ der Demokratie*, of which he was founder and chief editor. From the newspaper columns he carried out an intense activity of agitation, supporting the causes of the insurgents and urging the proletariat to promote 'the social and republican revolution' (Marx 1977: 178).[1] In that period he lived between Brussels, Paris and Cologne, and travelled to Berlin, Vienna and Hamburg as well as many other German cities, establishing new connections to strengthen and develop unfolding struggles. Because of this relentless militant activity, he was issued expulsion orders first from Belgium, then from Prussia, and when the new French government under the presidency of Louis Bonaparte demanded that he leave Paris, he decided to move to England. He arrived there in the summer of 1849, at the age of 31, to settle in London. Initially convinced that it would be a short stay, he ended up living there, stateless, for the rest of his life.

The first years of his English exile were characterised by the deepest poverty and ill health that contributed to the tragic loss of three of his children. Although Marx's life was never easy, this period was certainly its worst stage. From December 1850 to September 1856 he lived with his family in a two-bedroom dwelling, at 28 Dean Street in Soho, one of the poorest and shabbiest neighbourhoods of the city. The inheritance gained by his wife Jenny von Westphalen, with the death of her uncle and her mother, unexpectedly gave them a glimmer of hope and enabled him to settle his many debts, retrieve his clothes and personal objects from the pawnshop, and relocate to new premises.

In the autumn of 1856, Marx, his wife and their three daughters Jenny, Laura and Eleanor, with their loyal maid Helene Demuth – who was an integral part of the family – moved to the northern suburbs of London, at 9 Grafton Terrace,

Kentish Town, where the rent was more affordable. The house, where they stayed until 1864, was built in a recently developed area bereft of beaten paths and connections to the centre, and enveloped in darkness at night. But they finally lived in a real house, the minimal requirement for the family to retain 'at least a *semblance* of respectability' (Jenny Marx 1970: 223).[2]

In the course of 1856 Marx completely neglected the study of political economy but the coming of an international financial crisis suddenly changed this situation. In a climate of deep uncertainty, which turned into widespread panic thus contributing to bankruptcies everywhere, Marx felt that the right time for action had come again and foreseeing the future development of the recession, he wrote to Friedrich Engels: 'I don't suppose we'll be able to spend much longer here merely watching' (Marx to Engels, 26 September 1856, Marx and Engels 1983: 70). Engels, already infused with great optimism, predicted a scenario for the future in this way:

> This time there'll be an unprecedented day of wrath; the whole of Europe's industry in ruins … all markets over-stocked, all the upper classes in the soup, complete bankruptcy of the bourgeoisie, war and disorder to the nth degree. I, too, believe that it will all come to pass in 1857.
> (Engels to Marx, 26 September 1856, Marx and Engels 1983: 72)

By the end of a decade that had seen the reflux of the revolutionary movement, and in the course of which Marx and Engels were prevented from actively participating in the European political arena, the two started to exchange messages with renewed confidence in future prospects. The long-awaited date with the revolution now seemed much closer, and for Marx this pointed to one priority above all: resuming his 'Economics' and finishing it as soon as possible.

Fighting misery and diseases

In order to dedicate himself to work in this spirit Marx would have needed some tranquillity, but his personal situation was still extremely precarious and did not allow him any respite. Having employed all the resources at his disposal in the relocation to a new home, he was short of money again to pay the first month's rent. So he reported to Engels, who lived and worked in Manchester at the time, all the troubles of his situation:

> [I am] without prospects and with soaring family liabilities. I have no idea about what to do and in fact my situation is more desperate than it was five years ago. I thought that I had already tasted the quintessence of this shit, but no.
> (Marx to Engels, 20 January 1857, Marx and Engels 1983: 93)

This statement deeply shocked Engels, who had been sure that after the move his friend would finally be more settled, so in January 1857 he spent the money received from his father for Christmas to buy a horse and pursue his great passion: fox-hunting. However, during this period and for his whole life, Engels never denied all of his support to Marx and his family, and, worried about this difficult juncture, he sent Marx £5 a month and urged him to count on him always in difficult times.

Engels' role was certainly not limited to financial support. In the deep isolation Marx experienced during those years, but through the large correspondence exchanged between the two, Engels was the only point of reference with whom he could engage in intellectual debate: 'more than anything I need your opinion' (Marx to Engels, 2 April 1858, Marx and Engels 1983: 303). Engels was the only friend to confide in at difficult times of despondency: 'write soon because your letters are essential now to help me pluck up. The situation is dire' (Marx to Engels, 18 March 1857, Marx and Engels 1983: 106). Engels was also the companion with whom Marx shared the sarcasm solicited by events: 'I envy people who can turn summersaults. It must be a great way of ridding the head of bourgeois anger and ordure' (Marx to Engels, 23 January 1857, Marx and Engels 1983: 99).

In fact uncertainty soon became more pressing. Marx's only income, aside from the help granted by Engels, consisted of payments received from the *New York Tribune*, the most widely circulated English language newspaper at the time. The agreement on his contributions, for which he received £2 per article, changed with the economic crisis that had also had repercussions on the American daily. Aside from the American traveller and writer Bayard Taylor, Marx was the only European correspondent not to be fired, but his participation was scaled down from two articles per week to one, and – 'although in times of prosperity they never gave me an extra penny' (Marx to Weydemeyer, 1 February 1859, Marx and Engels 1983: 374) – his payments were halved. Marx humorously recounted the event: 'There is a certain irony of fate in my being personally embroiled in these damned crises' (Marx to Engels, 31 October 1857, Marx and Engels 1983: 198). However, to be able to witness the financial breakdown was an unparalleled entertainment: 'Nice, too, that the capitalists, who so vociferously opposed the "right to work", are now everywhere demanding "public support" from their governments and … hence advocating the "right to profit" at public expense' (Marx to Engels, 8 December 1857, Marx and Engels 1983: 214). Despite his state of anxiety, he announced to Engels that 'though my own financial distress may be dire indeed, never, since 1849, have I felt so cosy as during this outbreak' (Marx to Engels, 13 November 1857, Marx and Engels 1983: 199).

The beginning of a new editorial project slightly eased the desperation. The editor of the *New York Tribune*, Charles Dana, invited Marx to join the editorial committee for *The New American Cyclopædia*. Lack of money drove him to accept the offer, but he entrusted most of the work to Engels in order to dedicate more time to his research. In their division of labour between July 1857 and November 1860, Engels edited military entries – i.e. the majority of the ones commissioned – whilst Marx compiled several biographical sketches. Although the payment of $2 per page was very low, it was still an addition to his disastrous finances. For this reason Engels urged him to get as many entries from

Dana as possible: 'We can easily supply that amount of "unalloyed" erudition, so long as unalloyed Californian gold is substituted for it' (Engels to Marx, 22 April 1857, Marx and Engels 1983: 122). Marx followed the same principle in writing his articles: 'to be as little concise as possible, so long as it is not insipid' (Marx to Engels, 22 February 1858, Marx and Engels 1983: 272).[3]

Despite efforts, his financial situation did not improve at all. It actually became so unsustainable that, chased by creditors he compared to 'hungry wolves' (Marx to Engels, 8 December 1857, Marx and Engels 1983: 214), and in the absence of coal for heating during the cold winter of that year, in January 1858 he wrote to Engels: 'if these conditions persist, I would sooner be miles under the ground than go on vegetating this way. Always being a nuisance to others whilst, on top of that, being constantly tormented by personal trifles becomes unbearable in the long run' (Marx to Engels, 28 January 1858, Marx and Engels 1983: 255). In such circumstances he also had bitter words for the emotional sphere: 'privately, I think, I lead the most agitated life imaginable.... For people of wide aspiration nothing is more stupid than to get married, thus letting oneself in for the small miseries of domestic and private life' (Marx to Engels, 22 February 1858, Marx and Engels 1983: 273).

Poverty was not the only spectre haunting Marx. As with a major part of his troubled existence, he was also affected at the time by several diseases. In March 1857 the excessive labour done at night gave him an eye infection; in April he was hit by toothache; in May he suffered continuous liver complaints for which he was 'submerged in drugs'. Greatly enfeebled, he was incapacitated and unable to work for three weeks. He then reported to Engels: 'in order that my time should not be entirely wasted I have, in the absence of better things, been mastering the Danish language'; however, 'if the doctor's promises are anything to go by, I have prospects of becoming a human being again by next week. Meanwhile I'm still as yellow as a quince and vastly more irritated' (Marx to Engels, 22 May 1857, Marx and Engels 1983: 132).

Shortly afterwards a much graver occurrence befell the Marx family. In early July Jenny gave birth to their last child, but the baby, born too weak, died immediately after. Bereaved once more, Marx confessed to Engels: 'in itself, this is not a tragedy. But ... the circumstances that caused it to happen were such to bring back heartrending memories [probably the death of Edgar (1847–55), the last child he lost]. It is impossible to discuss this issue in a letter' (Marx to Engels, 8 July 1857, Marx and Engels 1983: 143). Engels was highly affected by this statement and replied: 'things must be really hard for you to write like this. You can accept the death of the little one stoically, but your wife will hardly be able to' (Engels to Marx, 11 July 1857, Marx and Engels 1983: 143).

The situation was further complicated by the fact that Engels fell ill and was seriously hit by a glandular fever, so he could not work for the whole summer. At that point, Marx was in real difficulties. Without his friend's entries for the encyclopaedia, he needed to buy time, so he pretended to have sent a pile of manuscripts to New York, and that they had been lost in the post. Nonetheless, the pressure did not decrease. When the events surrounding the Indian Sepoy rebellion became more striking, the *New York Tribune* expected an analysis from their expert, without knowing that the articles concerning military matters were in fact the work of Engels. Marx, forced by the circumstances to be temporarily in charge of the 'military department' (Marx to Engels, 14 January 1858, Marx and Engels 1983: 249)[4], ventured to claim that the English needed to make a retreat by the beginning of the rainy season. He informed Engels of his choice in these words: 'it is possible that I'll look really bad but in any case with a little dialectics I will be able to get out of it. I have, of course, so formulated my words as to be right either way' (Marx to Engels, 15 August 1857, Marx and Engels 1983: 152). However, Marx did not underestimate this conflict and reflecting on its possible effects, he said: 'in view of the drain of men and bullion which she will cost the English, India is now our best ally' (Marx to Engels, 14 January 1858, Marx and Engels 1983: 249).

Writing the *Grundrisse*

Poverty, health problems and all kind of privations – the *Grundrisse* was written in this tragic context. It was not the product of research by a well-to-do thinker protected by bourgeois tranquillity; on the contrary, it was the labour of an author who experienced hardship and found the energy to carry on only sustained by the belief that, given the advancing economic crisis, his work had become necessary for his times: 'I am working like mad all through the nights at putting my economic studies together so that I may at least get the outlines (*Grundrisse*) clear before the deluge' (Marx to Engels, 8 December 1857, Marx and Engels 1983: 217).

In the autumn of 1857, Engels was still evaluating events with optimism: 'the American crash is superb and will last for a long time.... Commerce will again be going downhill for the next three or four years. Now we have a chance' (Engels to Marx, 29 October 1857, Marx and Engels 1983: 195). Thus he was encouraging Marx: 'in 1848 we were saying: now our moment is coming, and in a certain sense it was, but this time it is coming completely and it is a case of life or death' (Engels to Marx, 15 November 1857, Marx and Engels 1983: 200). On the other hand, without harbouring any doubts about the imminence of the revolution, they both hoped that it would not erupt before the whole of Europe had been invested by the crisis, and so the auspices for the 'year of strife' were postponed to 1858 (Engels to Marx, 31 December 1857, Marx and Engels 1983: 236).

As reported in a letter from Jenny von Westphalen to Conrad Schramm, a family friend, the general crisis had its positive effects on Marx: 'you can imagine how high up the Moor is. He has recovered all his wonted facility and capacity for work, as well as the liveliness and buoyancy of spirit' (Jenny Marx to Schramm, 8 December 1857, Marx and Engels 1983: 566). In fact Marx began a period of intense intellectual activity, dividing his labours between the articles for the *New York Tribune*, the work for *The New American Cyclopædia*, the unfinished project to write a pamphlet on the current crisis and, obviously, the *Grundrisse*. However, despite his renewed energies, all these undertakings proved excessive and Engels's aid became once more indispensable. By the beginning of 1858, following his full recovery from the disease he had suffered, Marx asked him to return to work on the encyclopaedia entries:

> sometimes it seems to me that if you could manage to do a few sections every couple of days, it could perhaps act as a check on your drunkenness that, from what I know of Manchester and at the present excited times, seem to me inevitable and far from good for you ... because I really need to finish off my other works, that are taking up all my time, even if the house should come falling on my head!
>
> (Marx to Engels, 5 January 1858, Marx and Engels 1983: 238)

Engels accepted Marx's energetic exhortation and reassured him that, after the holidays, he 'experienced the need of a quieter and more active life' (Engels to Marx, 6 January 1858, Marx and Engels 1983: 239). Nonetheless, Marx's greatest problem was still lack of time, and he repeatedly complained to his friend that 'whenever I'm at the [British] Museum, there are so many things I need to look up that it's closing time (now 4 o'clock) before I have so much as looked round. Then there's the journey there. So much time lost' (Marx to Engels, 1 February 1858, Marx and Engels 1983: 258). Moreover, in addition to practical difficulties, there were theoretical ones:

> I have been ... so damnably held up by errors in calculation that, in despair, I have applied myself to a revision of algebra. Arithmetic has always been my enemy, but by making a detour via algebra, I shall quickly get back into the way of things.
>
> (Marx to Engels, 11 January 1858, Marx and Engels 1983: 244)

Finally, his scrupulousness contributed to slowing the writing of the *Grundrisse*, as he demanded of himself that he keep on searching for new confirmations to test the validity of his theses. In February he explained the state of his research to Ferdinand Lassalle thus:

> Now I want to tell you how my Economics is getting on. The work is written. I have in fact had the final text in hand for some months. But the thing is proceeding very slowly, because no sooner does one set about finally disposing of subjects that have been the main object of years of study, than they start revealing new aspects and demand to be thought out further.

In the same letter, Marx regretted once again the condition to which he was doomed. Being forced to spend a large part of the day on newspaper articles, he wrote: 'I am not master of my time but rather its slave. Only the nights are left for my own work, which in turn is often disrupted by bilious attacks or recurrences of liver trouble' (Marx to Lassalle, 22 February 1858, Marx and Engels 1983: 268).

In fact, illness had violently befallen him again. In January 1858 he communicated to Engels that he had been in cure for three weeks: 'I had exaggerated working at night – only keeping myself going with lemonades and a large quantity of tobacco' (Marx to Engels, 14 January 1858, Marx and Engels 1983: 247). In March, he was 'very sickly again' with his liver: 'the prolonged work by night and, by day, the numerous petty discomforts resulting from the economical conditions of my domesticity have recently been cause of frequent relapses' (Marx to Engels, 29 March 1858, Marx and Engels 1983: 295). In April, he claimed again:

> I've felt so ill with my bilious complaint this week, that I am incapable of thinking, reading, writing or, indeed, doing anything save the articles for the *Tribune*. These, of course, cannot be allowed to lapse since I must draw on the curs *as soon as possible* to avoid bankruptcy.
> (Marx to Engels, 2 April 1858, Marx and Engels 1983: 296)

At this stage of his life Marx had completely given up political organised and private relations: in letters to his few remaining friend he disclosed that 'I live like a hermit' (Marx to Lassalle, 21 December 1857, Marx and Engels 1983: 225), and 'I seldom see my few acquaintances nor, on the whole, is this any great loss' (Marx to Schramm, 8 December 1857, Marx and Engels 1983: 217). Aside from Engels' continuous encouragement, the recession and its expansion worldwide also fed his hopes and goaded him into carrying on working: 'take[n] all in all, the crisis has been burrowing away like a good old mole' (Marx to Engels, 22 February 1858, Marx and Engels 1983: 274). The correspondence with Engels documents the enthusiasm sparked in him by the progression of events. In January, having read the news from Paris in the *Manchester Guardian*, he exclaimed: 'everything seems to be going better than expected' (Marx to Engels, 23 January 1858, Marx and Engels 1983: 252), and at the end of March, commenting on recent developments, he added: 'in France the bedlam continues most satisfactorily. It is unlikely that conditions will be peaceful beyond the summer' (Marx to Engels, 29 March 1858, Marx and Engels 1983: 296). And whilst a few months earlier he had pessimistically stated that:

> After what has happened over the last ten years, any thinking being's contempt for the masses as for individuals must have increased to such a degree that '*odi profanum vulgus et arceo*'[5] has almost become an imposed maxim. Nonetheless, all these are themselves philistine states of mind, that will be swept away by the first storm.
> (Marx to Lassalle, 22 February 1858, Marx and Engels 1983: 268)

In May he claimed with some satisfaction that 'on the whole the present moment of time is a pleasing one. History is apparently about to take again a new start, and the signs of dissolution everywhere are delightful for every mind not bent upon the conservation of things as they are' (Marx to Lassalle, 31 May 1858, Marx and Engels 1983: 323).

Similarly, Engels reported to Marx with great fervour that on the day of the execution of Felice Orsini, the Italian democrat who had tried to assassinate Napoleon III, a major working-class protest took place in Paris: 'at a time of great turmoil it is good to see such a roll-call take place and hear 100,000 men reply "present!"' (Engels to Marx, 17 March 1858, Marx and Engels 1983: 289–90). In view of possible revolutionary developments, he also studied the sizeable number of French troops and warned Marx that to win it would have been necessary to form secret societies in the army, or, as in 1848, for the bourgeoisie to stand against Bonaparte. Finally, he predicted that the secession of Hungary and Italy and the Slavic insurrections would have violently hit Austria, the old reactionary bastion, and that, in addition to this, a generalised counter-attack would have spread the crisis to every large city and industrial district. In other words, he was certain that 'after all, it's going to be a hard struggle' (Engels to Marx, 17 March 1858, Marx and Engels 1983: 289). Led by his optimism Engels resumed his horse-riding, this time with a further aim; as he wrote to Marx:

> Yesterday, I took my horse over a bank and hedge five feet and several inches high: the highest I have ever jumped … when we go back to Germany we will certainly have a thing or two to show the Prussian cavalry. Those gentlemen will find it difficult to keep up with me.
>
> (Engels to Marx, 11 February 1858, Marx and Engels 1983: 265)

The reply was of smug satisfaction:

> I congratulate you upon your equestrian performances. But don't take too many breakneck jumps, as there will be soon more important occasion for risking one's neck. I don't believe that cavalry is the speciality in which you will be of the greatest service to Germany.
>
> (Marx to Engels, 14 February 1858, Marx and Engels 1983: 266)

On the contrary, Marx's life met with further complications. In March, Lassalle informed him that the editor Franz Duncker from Berlin had agreed to publish his work in instalments, but the good news paradoxically turned into another destabilising factor. A new cause of concern added to the others – anxiety – as recounted in the umpteenth medical bulletin addressed to Engels, this time written by Jenny von Westphalen:

> His bile and liver are again in a state of rebellion…. The worsening of his condition is largely attributable to mental unrest and agitation which now, after the conclusion of the contract with the publishers are greater than ever and increasing daily, since he finds it utterly impossible to bring the work to a close.
>
> (Jenny Marx to Engels, 9 April 1858, Marx and Engels 1983: 569)

For the whole of April, Marx was hit by the most virulent bile pain he had ever suffered and could not work at all. He concentrated exclusively on the few articles for the *New York Tribune*; these were indispensable for his survival, and he had to dictate them to his wife, who was fulfilling 'the function of secretary' (Marx to Engels, 23 April 1857, Marx and Engels 1983: 125). As soon as he was able to hold a pen again, he informed Engels that his silence was only due to his 'inability to write'. This was manifest 'not only in the literary, but in the literal sense of the word'. He also claimed that 'the persistent urge to get down to work coupled with the inability to do so contributed to aggravate the disease'. His condition was still very bad:

> I am not capable of working. If I write for a couple of hours, I have to lie down in pain for a couple of days. I expect, damn it, that this state of affairs will come to an end next week. It couldn't have come at a worst time. Obviously during the winter I overdid my nocturnal labours. *Hinc illae lacrimae.*[6]
>
> (Marx to Engels, 29 April 1858, Marx and Engels 1983: 309)

Marx tried to fight his illness, but, after taking large amounts of medicines without drawing any benefit from them, he resigned himself to follow the doctor's advice to change scene for a week and 'refrain from all intellectual labour for a while' (Marx to Lassalle, 31 May 1858, Marx and Engels 1983: 321). So he decided to visit Engels, to whom he announced: 'I've let my duty go hang' (Marx to Engels, 1 May 1858, Marx and Engels 1983: 312).

Naturally, during his 20 days in Manchester, he carried on working: he wrote the 'Chapter on Capital' and the last pages of the *Grundrisse*.

Struggling against bourgeois society

Once back in London Marx should have edited the text in order to send it to the publishers, but, although he was already late, he still delayed its draft. His critical nature won over his practical needs again. As he informed Engels:

> During my absence a book by Maclaren covering the entire history of currency came out in London, which, to judge by the excerpts in *The Economist*, is first-rate. The book isn't in the library yet.... Obviously I must read it before writing mine. So I sent my wife to the publisher in the City, but to our dismay we discovered that it costs 9/6d, more than the whole of our fighting funds. Hence I would be most grateful if you could send me a mail order for that amount. There probably won't be anything that's new to me in the book, but after all the fuss *The Economist* has made about it, and the excerpts I myself have read, my theoretical conscience won't allow me to proceed without having looked at it.
>
> (Marx to Engels, 31 May 1858, Marx and Engels 1983: 317)

This vignette is very telling. The 'dangerousness' of the reviews in *The Economist* for family peace; sending his wife Jenny to the City on a mission to deal with theoretical doubts; the fact that his savings was not enough even to buy a book; the usual pleas to his friend in Manchester that required immediate attention: what can better describe the life of Marx in those years and particularly what his 'theoretical conscience' was capable of?

In addition to his complex temperament, ill health and poverty, his usual 'enemies' contributed to delay the completion of his work even further. His physical condition worsened again, as reported to Engels: 'the disease from which I was suffering before leaving Manchester again became chronic, persisting throughout the summer, so that any kind of writing costs me a tremendous effort' (Marx to Engels, 21 September 1858, Marx and Engels 1983: 341). Moreover, those months were marked by unbearable economic concerns that forced him constantly to live with the 'spectre of an inevitable final catastrophe' (Marx to Engels, 15 July 1858, Marx and Engels 1983: 328). Seized by desperation again, in July Marx sent a letter to Engels that really testifies to the extreme situation he was living in:

> It behoves us to put our heads together to see if some way cannot be found out of the present situation, for it has become absolutely untenable. It has already resulted in my being completely disabled from doing any work, partly because I have to waste most of my best time running round in fruitless attempts to raise money, and partly because the strength of my abstraction – due rather, perhaps, to my being physically run down – is no longer a match for domestic miseries. My wife is a nervous wreck because of this misery.... Thus the whole business turns on the fact that what little comes in is never earmarked for the coming month, nor is it ever more than just sufficient to reduce debts ... so that this misery is only postponed by four weeks which have to be got through in one way or another ... not even the auction of my household goods would suffice to satisfy the creditors in the vicinity and ensure an unhampered removal to some hidey-hole. The show of respectability which has so far been kept up has been the only means of avoiding a collapse. I for my part wouldn't care a damn about living in Whitechapel [the neighbourhood in London where most of the working class lived at the time], provided I could again at last secure an hour's peace in which to attend to my work. But in view of my wife's condition just now such a metamorphosis might entail dangerous consequences, and it could hardly be suitable for growing girls.... I would not with my worst enemy to have to wade through the quagmire in which I've been trapped for the past eight weeks, fuming the while over the innumerable vexations that are ruining my intellect and destroying my capacity for work'.
>
> (Marx to Engels, 15 July 1858, Marx and Engels 1983: 328–31)

Yet despite his extremely destitute state, Marx did not let the precariousness of his situation triumph over him and, concerning his intention to complete his work, he commented to his friend Joseph Weydemeyer: 'I must pursue my goal at all costs and not allow bourgeois society to turn me into a money-making machine' (Marx to Weydemeyer, 1 February 1859, Marx and Engels 1983: 374).

Meanwhile, the economic crisis waned, and soon enough the market resumed its normal functioning. In fact, in August a disheartened Marx turned to Engels: 'over the past few weeks the world has grown damned optimistic again' (Marx to Engels, 13 August 1858, Marx and Engels 1983: 338); and Engels, reflecting on the way the overproduction of commodities had been absorbed, asserted: 'never before has such heavy flooding drained away so rapidly' (Engels to Marx, 7 October 1858, Marx and Engels 1983: 343). The certainty that the revolution was around the corner, which inspired them throughout the autumn of 1856 and encouraged Marx to write the *Grundrisse*, was now giving way to the most bitter disillusionment: 'there is no war. Everything is bourgeois' (Marx to Engels, 11 December 1858, Marx and Engels 1983: 360). And whilst Engels raged against the 'increasing embourgeoisement of the English proletariat', a phenomenon that, in his opinion, was to lead the most exploitative country in the world to have a 'bourgeois proletariat alongside the bourgeoisie' (Engels to Marx, 7 October 1858, Marx and Engels 1983: 343), Marx held onto every even slightly significant event, until the end: 'despite the optimistic turn taken by world trade [...] it is some consolation at least that the revolution has begun in Russia, for I regard the convocation of "notables" to Petersburg as such a beginning'. His hopes were also set on Germany: 'in Prussia things are worse than they were in 1847', as well as on the Czech bourgeoisie's struggle for national independence: 'exceptional movements are on foot amongst the Slavs, especially in Bohemia, which, though counter-revolutionary, yet provide ferment for the movement'. Finally, as if betrayed, he scathingly asserted: 'It will do the French no harm to see that, even without them, the world moved' (Marx to Engels, 8 October 1858, Marx and Engels 1983: 345).

However, Marx had to resign himself to the evidence: the crisis had not provoked the social and political effects that he and Engels had forecast with so much certainty. Nonetheless, he was still firmly convinced that it was only a matter of time before the revolution in Europe erupted and that the issue, if any, was what world scenarios the economic change would have provoked. Thus he wrote to Engels, giving a sort of political evaluation of the most recent events and a reflection on future prospects:

> We can't deny that bourgeois society has for the second time experienced its sixteenth century, a sixteenth century which, I hope, will sound its death knell just as the first flattered it in its lifetime. The real task of bourgeois society is the creation of the world market, or at least of its general framework, and of the production based on the market. Since the world is round, it seems to me that the colonisation of California and Australia and the opening up of China and Japan would seem to have completed this process. The difficult question for us is this: on the continent the revolution is imminent and will immediately assume a socialist character. Will it not necessarily be crushed in this little corner of the earth, since the movement of bourgeois society is still in the ascendant over a far greater area?'
>
> (Marx to Engels, 8 October 1858, Marx and Engels 1983: 347)

These thoughts include two of the most significant of Marx's predictions: a right one that led him to intuit, better than any of his contemporaries, the world scale of the development of capitalism; and a wrong one, linked to the belief in the inevitability of the proletarian revolution in Europe.

The letters to Engels contain Marx's sharp criticism of all those who were his political adversaries in the progressive camp. Many were targeted alongside one of his favourites, Pierre Joseph Proudhon, the main figure of the dominant form of socialism in France, whom Marx regarded as the 'false brother' communism needed to rid itself of (Marx to Weydemeyer, 1 February 1859, Marx and Engels 1983: 374). Marx often entertained a relationship of rivalry with Lassalle, for instance, and when he received Lassalle's latest book *Heraclitus, the Dark Philosopher*, he termed it as a 'very silly concoction' (Marx to Engels, 1 February 1858, Marx and Engels 1983: 258). In September 1858, Giuseppe Mazzini published his new manifesto in the journal *Pensiero ed Azione* [*Thought and Action*], but Marx, who had no doubts about him, asserted: 'still the same old jackass' (Marx to Engels, 8 October 1858, Marx and Engels 1983: 346). Instead of analysing the reasons for the defeat of 1848–9, Mazzini 'busies himself with advertising nostrums for the cure of ... the political palsy' of the revolutionary migration (Marx 1980: 37). He railed against Julius Fröbel, a member of the Frankfurt council in 1848–9 and typical representative of the German democrats, who had fled abroad and later distanced himself from political life: 'once they have found their bread and cheese, all these scoundrels require is some blasé pretext to bid farewell to the struggle' (Marx to Engels, 24 November 1858, Marx and Engels 1983: 356). Finally, as ironic as ever, he derided the 'revolutionary activity' of Karl Blind, one of the leaders of the German émigrés in London:

> He gets a couple of acquaintances in Hamburg to send letters (written by himself) to English newspapers in which mention is made of the stir created by his anonymous pamphlets. Then his friends report on German newspapers what a fuss was made by the English ones. That, you see, is what being a man of action means.
>
> (Marx to Engels, 2 November 1858, Marx and Engels 1983: 351)

Marx's political engagement was of a different nature. Whilst never desisting from fighting against bourgeois society, he also kept his awareness of his main role in this struggle, which was that of developing a critique of the capitalist mode of production through a rigorous study of political economy and ongoing analysis of economic events. For this reason during the 'lows' of the class struggle, he decided to use his powers in the best possible way by keeping at a distance from the useless conspiracies and personal intrigues to which political competition was reduced at the time: 'since the Cologne trial [the one against the communists of 1853], I have withdrawn completely into my study. My time was too precious to be wasted in fruitless endeavour and petty squabbles' (Marx to Weydemeyer, 1 February 1859, Marx and Engels 1983: 374). As a matter of fact, despite the flood of troubles, Marx continued to work, and he published his *A Contribution to the Critique of Political Economy: Part One* in 1859, for which the *Grundrisse* had been the initial testing ground.

Marx ended the year 1858 similarly to previous ones, as his wife Jenny recounts: '1858 was neither a good nor a bad year for us; it was one where days went by, one completely like the next. Eating and drinking, writing articles, reading newspapers and going for walks: this was our whole life' (Jenny Marx 1970: 224). Day after day, month after month, year after year, Marx kept working on his oeuvre for the rest of his life. He was guided in the burdensome labour of drafting the *Grundrisse* and many other voluminous manuscripts in preparation for *Capital* by his great determination and strength of personality, and also by the unshakeable certainty that his existence belonged to socialism, the movement for the emancipation of millions of women and men.

Notes

1 Translations quoted in the article are the work of the author.
2 According to Marx's wife, this change had become absolutely necessary: 'as everyone was becoming a philistine, we could not keep living like *bohémiens*' (Jenny Marx 1970: 223).
3 Although they included some interesting remarks, the articles for the encyclopaedia were defined by Engels as 'purely commercial work … that can safely remain buried' (Friedrich Engels to Hermann Schlüter, 29 January 1891, Engels 2002: 113).
4 In the MECW edition, this letter is mistakenly dated 16 January 1858.
5 Tr.: 'I hate and shun the vulgar crowd' (Horace 1994: 127).
6 Tr.: 'Hence, those tears' (Terence 2002: 99).

References

Engels, Friedrich (2002) *Marx and Engels Collected Works*, vol. 49: *Letters 1890–92*, London: Lawrence and Wishart.
Horace (1994) *Odes and Epodes*, Ann Arbor: University of Michigan Press.
Marx, Jenny (1970) 'Umrisse eines bewegten Lebens' in *Mohr und General. Erinnerungen an Marx und Engels*, Berlin: Dietz Verlag.
Marx, Karl (1977 [1848]) 'The Bourgeoisie and the Counter-Revolution' in *Marx and Engels Collected Works*, vol. 8: *Articles from 'Neue Rheinische Zeitung'*, London: Lawrence and Wishart.
Marx, Karl (1980 [1858]) 'Mazzini's New Manifesto' in *Marx and Engels Collected Works*, vol. 16: *Letters 1858–60*, London: Lawrence and Wishart.
Marx, Karl and Engels, Friedrich (1983) *Marx and Engels Collected Works*, vol. 40: *Letters 1856–59*, London: Lawrence and Wishart.
Terence (2002) *Andria*, Bristol: Bristol Classical Press.

10 The first world economic crisis
Marx as an economic journalist

Michael R. Krätke

Marx, one of the leading political and economic journalists of his time

In the Prussia of the 1840s, an academic career was no real option for the young Marx. So he started working as a journalist. As early as 1842, he wrote his first articles on economic matters – like the situation of the wine-growers of the Mosel region and the debates on one of the last remnants of the commons Germany, the right to gather wood in the forests. That was the beginning of his life-long affair with political economy. During the 1840s and in particular during the revolution of 1848–9 he became famous as the leading journalist and newspaper editor of the democratic left in Germany, writing and editing hundreds of articles for the *Neue Rheinische Zeitung* [*New Rhine Gazette*]. Marx's first lectures on political economy were published in this newspaper in April 1849. In 1850, just arriving as political refugees in London, Marx and Engels immediately started the project of a new journal. Using the title *Neue Rheinische Zeitung* again, they announced the new journal as a political economic review. In this journal, they declared, they would be able to discuss extensively, following a new scientific approach, the economic relations that serve as the basis for the whole political movement. Three longer political economic reviews were actually published in this journal, the first covering the period January–February 1850, the second the period March–April 1850, the last and longest review covering the period of May–October 1850. In those three reviews, Marx and Engels described the course of events of the crisis of 1847–8 – at large and in three countries – Britain, France and Prussia – in particular. The specific and different course of the crisis in those countries provided the explanation why Britain remained relatively unaffected by the wave of political revolts and revolutions on the continent and returned to a new prosperity while the other European countries still suffered from the crisis. The crisis had initiated a further expansion and restructuring of the world market which would change the course of the crisis cycles in the future. So, the second and the third review ended with a prognosis: the next crisis would come soon and it would be much worse than the preceding one. In its wake, one should expect another revolution. The journal soon went bankrupt, but Marx and Engels continued to support the radical Chartist press in England. Quite a lot of the economic articles in the *Notes to the People* and the *People's Paper* had been written with Marx's direct collaboration.

In 1851, Charles Dana, the editor of the *New York Tribune* (NYT), invited Marx to become one of his European correspondents. Marx accepted, and from August 1851 until February 1862 he and Engels regularly wrote several articles for the NYT a week. Actually, the first series of articles (on 'Revolution and Counterrevolution in Germany') for that journal was provided by Engels and published under Marx's name. In about ten years time, Marx and Engels wrote several hundred articles, the *Tribune* published more than 490 of them, many (about 45 per cent) unsigned, as leading articles. Engels contributed a lot, more than one-quarter of these articles, mostly dealing with military affairs and war events. A large part, about one-third of Marx's articles were devoted to the analysis of actual economic and financial matters, mostly in Britain but also in other European countries and on the level of the world economy at large. As the NYT was rapidly growing, selling eventually nearly 300,000 copies altogether, and became the largest newspaper in the English-speaking world, Marx was actually one of the leading and most widely read economic journalists of his time, a renowned expert on all economic and financial matters whose judgement on monetary and financial crises in Europe was highly respected. Marx also earned himself a reputation as a leading expert of international politics – he wrote on all the major international conflicts and wars of his time.

In 1859, in his 'Foreword' to *A Contribution to the Critique of Political Economy*, Marx referred to his work for the NYT, stressing the fact that he had to acquaint himself with a lot of practical details of economic life that went far beyond the range of the science of political economy proper. While Marx wrote the *Grundrisse* manuscript, his journalistic work, although reduced under the pressure of the crisis, continued as he described and analysed the major events of the great crisis of 1857–8. Actually, a lot of his journalistic work in the preceding year of 1856 had been devoted to monetary crises in Europe which he saw as harbingers of the greater crisis he had been waiting for since 1850. In November 1857, Marx saw to his delight one of his many predictions come true: this time, the British government, pressed hard by the spokesmen of the City, had suspended the Bank Act of 1844 again – exactly as Marx had predicted in an article published a few days before in the NYT. Until the spring and summer of 1858, Marx continued to comment upon the crisis events in Europe and tried to explain the rapid turn to an unexpected recovery as it occurred in Britain and other European countries. His regular work as a journalist ending in 1862, Marx did not comment upon the events of the following crises of 1866 and 1873.[1]

For Marx's political theory as well as for the critique of political economy, his journalistic work is of the utmost importance. In his articles Marx has dealt extensively with topics that he hardly ever broached in his larger manuscripts. Again and again, he has used material from his journalistic work for his larger, unfinished economic manuscripts. Some of the topics that figured prominently in his plan for the comprehensive critique of political economy – like, for instance, money and modern banking, the financial markets and their crises, the world market, the international trade structures by which some (capitalist) nations exploited others, colonies, colonialism and their importance for the development of capitalism, and the different forms of public finance and public economy – have only been treated by Marx in journal articles (cf. Krätke 2006). Some of the most sophisticated reflections on the modern state, its historical development within the context of the European state system, and the development of the main and salient forms of politics in modern bourgeois societies are only to be found in a series of journal articles which Marx wrote on various occasions. Those articles, dealing with political events in different countries like Britain, France, Spain and Prussia, are an indispensable, first-rate source for anybody who wants to study Marx's political theory seriously.

The Indian revolt: Marx' articles on India in 1857–8

While he was beginning his work on the *Grundrisse* Marx was continuing a series of articles for the NYT on the Indian revolt. In early 1857, a local mutiny of some Sepoy regiments had triggered off what had later been called the first Indian war of independence. The revolt and its violent suppression by British intervention forces preoccupied the European as well as the American public. India was crucial for the British Empire, after all, and Britain had a hard time regaining control of its Indian colony. Since his first series of articles dealing with the British rule in India, written and published in 1853, Marx was regarded as an expert on India. He and Engels continued to write on the Indian revolt and its suppression until 1859. Engels, in particular, provided several articles dealing with the military operations that eventually led to the re-conquest of Delhi by British troops. Marx wrote on the political events following the initial revolt in the Indian colonial army which he covered in his first article, published as a leading article in the NYT of 15 July 1857; in the many articles on the Indian revolt that followed he switched between the events in India and the British government and parliament involved in endless debates on how to deal with the 'Indian question'.[2] In September 1857, when it was far from clear whether the British army would be able to regain control on India, he wrote an article dealing with the cost and benefits of the British rule in India: who was actually profiting from the colonial effort, what did it cost and what, if any, benefits did the British people reap from it. In earlier years, he had already written on the tax system and the finances of India. Now he demonstrated the real cost of the Indian dominion for Britain and the British taxpayers. He came to the conclusion that only a few thousand individuals actually profited from the British presence in India while for the majority of the British people, India was just a costly burden (cf. Marx and Engels 1986: 349–52).

Marx on the Great Crisis of 1857–8

From August 1857 onwards, the events of the world crisis of 1857–8 preoccupied both Marx and Engels who regularly exchanged news and views on the crisis in their personal correspondence. As Marx was writing his articles for the NYT in a hurry, as usual, he did regularly report to Engels what he had already written in his articles. Sometimes, he used Engels' reports on crisis events.[3] In his first article on the present monetary crisis in England (published as a leading article on 21 November 1857), Marx launched an all-out attack on the famous Bank Act of 1844: in common times, it does not act at all, in times of crisis it 'adds … a monetary panic created by law to the monetary panic resulting from the commercial crisis' (Marx and Engels 1986: 381). Hence, to overcome the monetary panic it has to be suspended as it had already been during the last crisis of 1847. In his second article (published unsigned on 30 November 1857), Marx proudly remarked that he had rightly anticipated the coming suspension of the Bank Act.[4] In the following articles, he highlighted the peculiarities of the present crisis – in comparison with the earlier crises of 1839 and 1847. This time, the crisis was no longer a local affair but was bound to affect the whole world market; this time, the crisis was to become an industrial crisis exceeding all preceding crises in scale and scope.[5] The monetary crisis was spreading quickly from New York to London and then to the commercial and financial centres of the European continent like Hamburg and Paris. While the monetary crisis in London was easing off the commercial and industrial crisis was gaining momentum and led to an 'industrial breakdown in the manufacturing districts' without precedence (Marx and Engels 1986: 385). All the export markets for the British industry were now heavily overstocked, the commercial crisis, the ever growing number of failures and bankruptcies among the merchants and bankers began to hit back upon the industrial producers and the financial and monetary crisis was spreading from one of the financial centres of the capitalist world to the other (cf. Marx and Engels 1986: 390, 401–2, 411–12). In particular, Marx described and analysed the monetary panic in Hamburg which occurred when the monetary panic in London had already ebbed away (cf. Marx and Engels 1986: 404f., 411). In two articles (published as leading articles on 12 January and 12 March 1858), Marx dealt with the peculiar course of the crisis in France (cf. Marx and Engels 1986: 413f., 459f.).

Altogether, he wrote more than a dozen articles on the crisis events in Europe and sent them to the *Tribune* editors, ten were published from November 1857 until March 1858, eight as leading articles, two more unsigned. Another article, titled 'The Commercial and Industrial State of England' and published as a leading article on 26 December 1857, could be ascribed to Marx as author beyond doubt (cf. Baumgart and Ratajczak 1984). In these articles Marx made frequently use of the material that he was busy collecting in his 'books on crisis'. Two examples: in the article of 26 December 1857, he reproduced the details on failures and bankruptcies in London occurring during the first weeks of December that he had been collecting in his books on crisis at the very same time (cf. Baumgart and Ratajczak 1984: 61). In his article on 'British commerce' (published unsigned in the NYT on 3 February 1858), Marx made extensive use of the statistics on international trade of Great Britain with various other countries and parts of the world that he had collected in his books on crisis in the days and weeks before.

In the aftermath of the Great Crisis

Although Marx and Engels had been largely right in their analysis of the character of the crisis as an industrial crisis on a world scale, the course of the crisis events surprised and puzzled them. As the Great Crisis passed and faded, two riddles or puzzles had to be explained. First why this worldwide crisis, although heavier than any crisis before, had been overcome so rapidly, leaving out the period of lasting depression – at least as far as the British factory industry was concerned – which anyone familiar with the history of crises would have expected. Second the crisis in France – which was quite different from the crisis in other parts of the capitalist world. Marx sought and found the explanation for both phenomena in the structure of British and French world trade, respectively. Britain had been able to shift the bulk of its export from the European continent to its colonies; France was only hit by the crisis once it had attained its major export markets.

In his articles on the crisis, Marx had of course taken to task the popular wisdom of the day. Free trade had obviously not ended the era of business cycles and crises, crises had recurred in regular intervals, hence could not be regarded as mere accidents or mistakes; nor could (over)speculation on the financial markets, itself a result and not more than the 'immediate forerunner of the crash', be regarded as final cause of commercial and industrial crises (cf. Marx and Engels 1986: 400–1). In the aftermath of the Great Crisis, Marx wrote two larger articles, trying to spell out its lessons for political economy. After the suspension of the Bank Act, the British government had appointed a parliamentary commission which should find out what the real causes of the crisis had been. In his first article ('British Trade and Finance', written September 1858 and published on 4 October 1857), Marx commented on the findings of this commission: reproducing the conventional economic wisdom of the day, the commission and its experts had taken the crisis as a singular event, a mere accident. It had failed to disclose the 'laws which rule the crises of the world market' and had ignored its periodical and cyclical character. Hence, the commission had been unable to explain exactly why and how the crisis had recurred in the autumn of 1857. Allowing its peculiar features of this new crisis to overshadow those elements that all crises of the capitalist world economy have in common, they have failed to grasp both. In his second article ('Industry and Trade', written and published a year later, in September 1859), Marx confirmed his view that there were 'laws of the crisis', even laws of the crisis cycle which could be discovered taking the longer view and comparing several successive cycles – like the cycles of 1825–37, 1837–47, 1847–57. Such an exercise provided a regularity, even a law that could be proven with mathematical exactitude as Marx proudly remarked: the maximum level of (industrial) production attained during each period of prosperity served as starting point for the development of production during the following industrial cycle – in the longer run, the path of industrial growth followed an upward line from one cycle to the next.

The crisis of 1857–8 in the *Grundrisse* manuscript

According to Marx's plan of 1857–8, his critique of political economy should culminate in two treatises (or books): on the world market and its crises. Throughout the manuscript of 1857–8 we find remarks, sometimes digressions on the theory and history of modern crisis. In Marx's view a theory of crisis had to be systematically built from the most elementary possibilities of crises inherent to the forms of exchange to the predispositions and tendencies to general overproduction and over-accumulation inherent to the capitalist mode of production. Obviously, Marx was writing under the fresh impression of the events of the Great Crisis on which he was commenting during his daily work as an economic journalist – allusions to crisis events in the present and the recent past abound and the actual crisis of 1857–8 is directly mentioned several times. Already in the first unfinished 'Chapter on Money', Marx describes and analyses the moment of a monetary crisis proper, recurring during all modern crises. In the context of his theory of money – a theory intended to embrace money in general, as well as the fully developed monetary system of modern capitalism in its most advanced forms – monetary crises are important because they show the relevance, even the reality of one specific category, that is money as money (the third basic feature of money in Marx's systematic exposition of the forms and functions of money in general). During the periods of 'general crisis', money in its real or commodity form, as gold and silver, is the only form of money that is generally accepted, in particular in the international circulation where only gold and silver are accepted as immediate and final means of payment and general representative of wealth. The very fact that only real (or commodity) money is accepted as valid means of payment in any (international) monetary crisis demonstrates that money as money is a real economic category even in the most highly developed credit economies of the capitalist world. It is only thanks to the regular succession of monetary crises in 1825, 1839, 1847 and 1857 that the political economists have realized the importance of money as money. The sudden relapse into the monetary system as it occurs in any monetary crisis creates the false appearance as if lack of money (or abundance of credit) were its real causes.

Much later in the manuscript, Marx refers to an article published in *The Economist* of 6 February 1858. In its reflections on the recent crisis, curious ideas about the difference and the relationship between fixed and circulating capital are brought to the fore. Finally, Marx adds a reflection upon the general impact of great crises like the crisis of 1857–8 upon the valorization of capital. Such crises can both be regarded as symptoms of the obsolescence of capitalism and as moments that delay and slow its downfall. Marx's explanation of the latter clearly bears witness to his ongoing reflections upon the causes of the relatively rapid recovery which took place during the first months of 1858: during such crises, capital is depreciated on a large scale. Crises are the moments in the life-cycle of capital whereby 'annihilation of a great portion of capital the latter is violently reduced to the point, where it can go on fully employing its productive powers without committing suicide'. Depreciation, annihilation of capital on a large scale – together with a violent shift in the structure of exports from Europe towards the colonies – that is the main explanation provided by Marx for the rapid recovery in British industry in his journal articles of 1858. Nonetheless, the next crisis will come – 'these regularly recurring catastrophes lead to their repetition on a higher scale, and finally to its overthrow' (Marx 1973: 750). That is the thrust of Marx's intended theory of crisis – any crisis can be overcome but any recovery will inevitably just prepare the ground for the next crisis that will become worse than the previous one.

Notes

1 Actually, Marx continued writing articles for German and Austrian newspapers, notably *Die Presse*, on the course of events and the background of the American Civil War until the end of the year 1862.
2 Until now, the most complete edition of the articles by Marx and Engels dealing with the Indian revolt is to be found in volume 15 of the *Collected Works*. In total, Marx sent 36 articles (11 of which written by Engels) to the NYT from July 1857 to September 1858.
3 Marx kept a notebook (still unpublished) where he noted all the articles he sent to the *Tribune*.
4 Actually, it had been suspended for the second time on 12 November 1857, just as Marx had predicted a few days before (cf. Krätke 2006: 92–3).
5 In particular, Marx tried to explain the effects of the long delay ot the crisis which was, in his view, already overdue in early 1855 (cf. Krätke 2006: 83–4).

References

Baumgart, Klaus and Ratajczak, Gertrude (1984) 'Ein bislang unbekannter Artikel von Karl Marx über die Weltwirtschaftskrise von 1857', *Marx–Engels-Forschungsberichte*, no. 2: 57–63.
Krätke, Michael (2006) 'Marx als Wirtschaftsjournalist', *Beiträge zur Marx–Engels-Forschung. Neue Folge*: 29–97.
Marx, Karl (1973) *Grundrisse: Foundations of the Critique of Political Economy* (*Rough Draft*), Harmondsworth: Penguin.
Marx, Karl and Engels, Friedrich (1986 [1857–8]) *Marx and Engels Collected Works*, vol. 15: *Marx and Engels, 1856–58*, Moscow: Progress Publishers.

11 Marx's 'books of crisis' of 1857–8

Michael R. Krätke

The great crisis of 1857–8

Without the world crisis of 1857–8, Marx probably would not have written the *Grundrisse*. The outbreak of the great crisis in August 1857 spurred Marx to put his thoughts on the critique of political economy, his greatest project, to paper. In a few month's time, from August 1857 to May 1858, he produced a first rough draft of the foundations of his *Economics* in seven notebooks plus an introduction. At the same time, he wrote an impressive number of newspaper articles on various topics, including the events of the crisis. Last, but not least, he filled three voluminous notebooks with copious material on the course of the great crisis of 1857–8.[1]

Marx and Engels had long expected the next crisis, and actually waited for it from 1852 onwards. During the summer of 1850, Marx had studied the economic history of the past decade in much detail and the history of economic crises in Europe since 1815 in particular. He came to the conclusion that the crisis of 1847–8 was behind the outbreak of the revolutionary wave in Europe as well as the returning prosperity had made the victory of reaction possible. Thanks to the renewed prosperity that had already kept Britain apart from the European revolutions, the counter-revolution had prevailed. There could be no revolutionary movement without another economic crisis. But another crisis was bound to come in due time – and hence another revolutionary upsurge. That is why Marx and Engels kept looking for the signs of the next crisis from 1852 onwards.

The crisis finally came, in August 1857, with the downfall of the Ohio Life Insurance Company in New York which triggered off a bank crisis, first in New York and then rapidly spreading throughout the United States. Within a few weeks, the bank crisis affected all the larger financial markets of the capitalist world. Marx was delighted and thrilled by the prospects for another revolutionary upsurge on the continent. What is more, the crisis started exactly as Marx had predicted already in 1850 – with a financial crisis in New York.

Late in August 1857 he switched his work efforts to the critique of political economy. In early October, when he had started writing his first 'Chapter on Money', he began his parallel work on the books of crisis. That was actually another project – the study of the course of the world economic crisis in all details. His work as an empirical researcher, collecting and arranging material on the crisis events in different parts of the world, drawing up statistical tables from various sources, looking for more evidence, kept him busy until the end of January, probably early February of 1858 – while he was writing the 'Chapter on Capital'. Hence, the conventional imagination of Marx, studying first and foremost Hegel's *Science of Logic* while writing the *Grundrisse* manuscripts is misguided. At the same time, he was experimenting with the dialectical form of presentation of the basics of political economy and pursuing a full scale empirical research on the ongoing economic crisis. The books of crisis were not only meant as aid for his work as a journalist. They were also important for the theory, the rational explanation of the phenomenon of modern, cyclical crises which Marx regarded as an indispensable part of his systematic critique of political economy.

Another project: a pamphlet on the crisis, together with Engels

In a letter to Engels, dated 18 December 1857, Marx explained the double work in progress that had completely occupied him ever since late August 1857. On the one hand, he was busy drawing up the essentials of his political economy. It was necessary to get to the bottom of this matter – the capitalist world economy which was now obviously shaken by a great crisis – for the general public, and, for himself 'individually, to get rid of this nightmare'. On the other hand, he had to deal with the present crisis and to follow its course in the different parts of the capitalist world with utmost care. As he told Engels, he was only keeping the records of the crisis events. Nonetheless, this book-keeping took away a lot of his working time. He suggested to his friend that they should write another book together – a book on the present crisis. They should write what he actually called a pamphlet in the spring of 1858 and publish it quickly in German – making their reappearance before the German public and telling it 'that we are around still and again, always the same' (Marx and Engels 1983: 224). As Marx reported to Engels, he had three big notebooks on the present crisis prepared, one on England, one on Germany, and one on France. The material on the crisis in America was to be found in the *New York Tribune* (NYT), the material on most of the other countries was to be found in British newspapers. This plan was confirmed in a letter by Marx to Ferdinand Lassalle, dated 21 December 1857. Here, Marx told Lassalle about his double project: the present crisis had spurned him to write down the principles or fundamentals of his critique of political economy – and to prepare a something (the pamphlet he had proposed to Engels) about the present crisis (see Marx and Engels 1983: 225).

There were several good reasons for this project. After 1847–8 a lot of pamphlets and popular books on the crisis had been published. Marx had studied this literature carefully and he expected another wave of books on the crisis to come. Second, Marx was sure that he and Engels could do a much better job than any of the political economists around explaining not only the inevitability of the modern, cyclical crisis as an inherent feature of modern capitalism but also explaining the peculiarities of the present crisis – why it came so late, why it did leave France relatively unaffected, why its initial phase, the monetary crisis, was quickly passing.

Marx's self-confidence had been boosted because he had predicted the suspension of the Bank Act of 1844 by the British government in November 1857. This time, Marx had been right, the bourgeois experts were wrong. Since the 1840s, he and Engels had attacked the false critique of political economy of the left and in particular their ignorance or lack of mastery of economic facts. Their pamphlet on the crisis should show the public, how to master the facts and how to criticize bourgeois political economy which could never make head nor tail of the cyclical crises inherent to modern capitalism.

The three 'books of crisis' of 1857–8

The books on crisis are different from the other notebooks written by Marx (more than 200 have survived). In these notebooks we find hardly any excerpts from books by political economists nor remarks or reflections by Marx himself. Marx has filled these notebooks with reports on crisis events instead – from day to day, and week to week. Some are excerpts or summaries of articles from various newspapers (*The Economist, The Times, Manchester Guardian, Daily News, Daily Telegraph, Moniteur* and others); a large part of the material on the crisis collected in these notebooks consists of clippings from these newspapers. Sometimes, Marx resumes informal reports (for instance by Friedrich Engels himself) about crisis events. As the many statistical tables in the notebooks clearly show, Marx had not just collected and ordered material on the crisis – both chronologically and in terms of subjects – but has already started working on them. In the books on crisis we find a large variety of statistical tables drawn up by Marx himself in order to arrange and present the salient statistical data on the crisis; in several cases, these tables are only partly filled in. These notebooks are both documents and devices of empirical research on the crisis by Marx.

Marx expected the Bonapartist regime to fall under the impact of the crisis. In August–September 1857, he had written a series of articles on Bonapartist finance for the NYT, none of which was published. His first book on crisis, 31 pages in the original,[2] the smallest of the three, deals with the crisis events in France from October to December. The last entries of this notebook are resuming official reports from London (on bank rates on the continent) and Paris (on tax receipts), dated 22 and 21 January 1858, respectively.

The notebook is organized thematically – the different subject matters are presented in chronological order, sometimes in a table.[3] It starts with a series of stock market quotations from Paris, focussing upon railway shares, the shares of the Bank of France and of the infamous *Crédit mobilier* from October to the end of December 1857. Marx continues with a lengthy report on the state of French state finances, followed by several reports on how the Bank of France tried to support the shares of the railway companies during the first months of the crisis. Next, Marx has compiled a series of reports on the state of French trade and commerce in Paris and other cities, including data and reports on the French corn and wine trade and on the changes in French export and import until December 1857. Obviously, as the reports show in detail, French commerce was much less affected by the crisis than the commerce of other countries, bankrupt-cies, numerous and formidable in London, Hamburg, Vienna, Berlin and so on, were less grave in Paris and other French cities. In between, Marx notes the monthly accounts of the Bank of France from October to December 1857, later supplemented by the accounts of the Bank for December 1857 and January 1858. There is a collection of data on the in and outflow of specie (gold and silver) based on monthly customs reports. Likewise, Marx has drawn up tables for the volume of French export and import for different categories of commodi-ties from 1855 to 1857.

With scornful care, he registered the crisis measures taken by the French government. Napoleon III (Lucifer Boustrapa as Marx called him in this note-book) had decreed no crisis, yet nonetheless had taken a lot of government measures against it. The crisis did not hit France as hard as other European countries and the Bonapartist government immediately claimed the credit for that. Accordingly, Marx has collected a lot of reports on Bonaparte's plans and decrees (dealing with taxes, bank rates, customs), including rumours about imminent financial schemes, during the first months of the crisis.

About ten pages of the original notebooks are devoted to reports on the crisis events in Italy and Spain, mostly dealing with government measures, and Germany (Cologne, Hamburg), mostly dealing with trade and traffic. Next, Marx has collected reports on how the traffic on the Rhine and the railway traffic in several European countries were affected by the crisis. The notebook is concluded by another series of data on the French (Paris) stock market and on French government finances, including the changes of French public debt – Marx left space for data on the changes of French state papers, to be filled later.

The second book on crisis is much longer, 66 pages in the original.[4] On the cover Marx has noted: 'Lond. 12 Dec. 1857 (commenced)'. According to the material collected in this notebook, Marx has worked on it from November 1857 until January 1858. It ends with a report, dated January 1858, about a meeting of unemployed weavers in Spitalsfield which concludes a series of reports on part-time work, wage cuts, redundancies, strikes and protest movements of the unem-ployed and even the paupers in several industrial districts of Britain.

This notebook is organized in a similar way as the first – short headings indi-cating sections dealing with different subjects, sometimes using numbers to indi-cate the order of headings and sub-headings. It starts with a long section on failures, mainly in London, listing the names of the firms going bankrupt, the dates of the declaration of bankruptcies and the capitals lost. Likewise, Marx has noted the origin of the firm (British, German, Greek, American) and their main area of trading (or banking) activities. The next section, titled 'B.[ank] o.[f]

England. (Nov. 14–Dec. 9.)', deals with the course of the monetary crisis in London which reached its climax in mid-November. From week to week, Marx has collected various accounts of the Bank of England which indicate the rapid changes of the state of London as the central financial market of the capitalist world. With care, he notes the events that lead to the suspension of the Bank Act of 1844, as well as the effects that the suspension has.

In the next section, titled 'London Moneymarket v. Week ending 14 Nov.–12 Dec.', he repeats the same exercise for the different financial markets in London, starting with the bullion market and continuing with the foreign exchange market. With particular care, Marx has noted and documented the measures taken both in London and in Hamburg to get the monetary panic under control.

In the following sections, Marx has collected material (newspaper clips, summaries of reports, statistical data) on the course of the crisis in America and in Europe (Hamburg as the financial and commercial hub of Northern Europe, then Scandinavia, Austria, Prussia and the rest of the German states, Holland and even Poland). For Hamburg, in particular, he has collected a vast array of data and reports on the changes in international trade and finance – referring to the monetary crisis in its most classical form that shook the city in November 1857. The next sections are filled with data and reports on the state of the produce market, dealing with a vast array of commodities, from raw materials (in particular for the textile industry) to corn and colonial products, and the industrial market, dealing with the textile industry and its various branches as well as with the heavy industries (coal, iron, steel) in the different industrial districts of Britain for which data were available. In the last section of the notebook, titled 'Labourmarket', Marx has collected reports on the situation of wage labourers, both employed and unemployed, in the British industry, including reports on strikes and other working-class actions.

Marx's third notebook was probably finished in late January or early February 1858. It is 62 pages long in the original.[5] This notebook is the best organized of the three with chapters and sections, indicated by numbers and separate headings. The first chapter deals with the events on the money market and is subdivided into five sections, starting with section one on the Bank of England, followed by a section on the bullion market (import and export of gold and silver), a section on the loan market, a fourth section on failures and ends with section five on the security market. Chapter 2 deals with the 'Producemarket' and is again subdivided into five sections:

1   raw materials for textile fabrics;
2   metals;
3   hides and leather;
4   Mincing-Lane (that is, again, colonial products); and
5   corn market.

In Chapter 3 on the 'Industrial Market', Marx has compiled in loose order reports and data on various industries – from raw materials like iron, coal, coke and wood to manufactured goods like linen, wool or silk. Regarding the dominant position of the British factory industry on the world market, most data reported refer to both exports and imports (volumes and prices). The material on the labour market is now arranged in a separate Chapter 4. The concluding Chapter 5 bears the title 'Miscellaneous' and contains again a vast array of data on international trade and finance (between different parts of the world market and referring to various industries and commodities).

This third book is also remarkable because it contains some material on the effects of the great crisis in Asia, in particular in India and China, and in the Middle East, in particular in Egypt, dealing with the international trade in tea, in cotton and other colonial products. Here, Marx has even collected reports on the money market in the larger trading cities in the overseas countries (for instance in Alexandria and Bombay). With particular care, he collected reports on the finances of the East India Company. Again, we find a lot of reports and data on the course of the crisis in America, in particular in New York and Chicago. Last, but not least, in this notebook Marx has collected some reports on the effects of the crisis in Australia. The crisis of 1857–8 was the first world economic crisis, affecting all regions of the world that were in one way or the other already integrated in or at least connected to the world market. So Marx had to extend the scope and scale of his study of the crisis into all parts of the world market.

Theory and history: how to study and explain a crisis?

Working on the books on crisis, Marx was in regular discussion with Engels. Engels contributed newspapers, statistics, reports and his own astute remarks on the course of events. Comparing the events of 1857–8 to the crisis of 1847–8, Marx and Engels agreed on most matters: the crisis was larger and much more severe than any crisis before, the monetary crisis, although it had presented itself in a classical form (in London and in Hamburg), was only the foreplay to the real crisis, the industrial crisis that would affect the very basis of British prosperity and supremacy. In a letter to Engels, dated 25 December 1857, Marx gave a detailed outline of what might have become the chapter on the crisis in France in the planned book, explaining the relative lateness of the French crisis by the specific structure of French international trade. As the commercial and industrial crisis faded away in the summer of 1858, Marx and Engels continued to discuss its course and trying to understand why it had not turned out as they had expected.

Some of the material Marx compiled in the books on crisis was immediately used by him for a series of newspaper articles. From September 1857 to March 1858, he wrote numerous articles on the crisis, ten of which were published in the NYT. The first and the last one dealt with the crisis in France, five with the crisis in Britain, the rest with the monetary crisis elsewhere in Europe. In these articles, Marx explained both the course of the monetary crisis in Europe and the importance of the industrial crisis which he demonstrated with data referring to the British textile industry and the changes of prices and volumes in the international trade with raw materials and manufactured goods.

In the *Grundrisse* Marx dealt with the theory of crisis at various occasions and the crisis of 1857–8 show up here too. The 'Chapter on Money' starts with an all-out attack against political economists who, like Alfred Darimon, ignore the facts which contradict their theory of crisis and who play with the facts – asserting that crises could easily be avoided by a different organization of credit and money. The crisis of 1857–8 is mentioned twice: as example for a period of general monetary crisis when money as money, money in its elementary commodity form as gold and silver becomes crucial – in particular as the one and only means of international payments. Criticizing Ricardo and his followers who had never understood the real modern crisis, Marx states that one has to go behind the phenomena of the monetary or financial crisis – to the core or the essence of the matter where the inevitable predisposition, the inherent tendency towards overproduction in general is to be found. That is the very nature of the capital relationship which his concept of capital was meant to pinpoint once and for all.

Notes

1 Altogether these three 'books on crisis' will provide a volume of more than 500 pages in print: the volume IV/14 of the MEGA^2, that is currently being edited.
2 They will be about 100 pages in the MEGA^2 edition.
3 There are no charts, although Marx clearly had thought on the possibility to transform his collected data on prices, interest rates, exchange rates, trade balances and so on into curves. As a political economist, he was very much mathematically minded, after all.
4 They will be about 200 pages in the MEGA^2 edition.
5 They will be about 200 pages in the MEGA^2 edition.

Reference

Marx, Karl and Engels, Friedrich (1983) *Marx and Engels Collected Works*, vol. 40: *Letters 1856–59*, London: Lawrence and Wishart.

Part III

Dissemination and reception of *Grundrisse* in the world

12 Dissemination and reception of the *Grundrisse* in the world
Introduction

Marcello Musto

1858–1953: 100 years of solitude

Having abandoned the *Grundrisse* in May 1858 to make room for work on *A Contribution to the Critique of Political Economy*, Marx used parts of it in composing this latter text but then almost never drew on it again. In fact, although it was his habit to invoke his own previous studies, even to transcribe whole passages from them, none of the preparatory manuscripts for *Capital*, with the exception of those of 1861–3, contains any reference to the *Grundrisse*. It lay among all the other drafts that he had no intention of bringing into service as he became absorbed in solving more specific problems than they had addressed.

There can be no certainty about the matter, but it is likely that not even Friedrich Engels read the *Grundrisse*. As is well known, Marx managed to complete only the first volume of *Capital* by the time of his death, and the unfinished manuscripts for the second and third volumes were selected and put together for publication by Engels. In the course of this activity, he must have examined dozens of notebooks containing preliminary drafts of *Capital*, and it is plausible to assume that, when he was putting some order into the mountain of papers, he leafed through the *Grundrisse* and concluded that it was a premature version of his friend's work – prior even to *A Contribution to the Critique of Political Economy* of 1859 – and that it could therefore not be used for his purposes. Besides, Engels never mentioned the *Grundrisse*, either in his prefaces to the two volumes of *Capital* that he saw into print or in any of his own vast collection of letters.

After Engels' death, a large part of Marx's original texts were deposited in the archive of the Social Democratic Party of Germany (SPD) in Berlin, where they were treated with the utmost neglect. Political conflicts within the Party hindered publication of the numerous important materials that Marx had left behind; indeed, they led to dispersal of the manuscripts and for a long time made it impossible to bring out a complete edition of his works. Nor did anyone take responsibility for an inventory of Marx's intellectual bequest, with the result that the *Grundrisse* remained buried alongside his other papers.

The only part of it that came to light during this period was the 'Introduction', which Karl Kautsky published in 1903 in *Die Neue Zeit* [*The New Times*], together with a brief note that presented it as a 'fragmentary draft' dated 23 August 1857. Arguing that it was the introduction to Marx's magnum opus, Kautsky gave it the title *Einleitung zu einer Kritik der politischen Ökonomie* [*Introduction to a Critique of Political Economy*] and maintained that 'despite its fragmentary character' it 'offered a large number of new viewpoints' (Marx 1903: 710 n. 1). Considerable interest was indeed shown in the text: the first versions in other languages were in French (1903) and in English (1904), and it soon became more widely noticed after Kautsky published it in 1907 as an appendix to the *A Contribution to the Critique of Political Economy*. More and more translations followed – including into Russian (1922), Japanese (1926), Greek (1927), and Chinese (1930) – until it became one of the works most commented upon in the whole of Marx's theoretical production.

While fortune smiled on the 'Introduction', however, the *Grundrisse* remained unknown for a long time. It is difficult to believe that Kautsky did not discover the whole manuscript along with the 'Introduction', but he never made any mention of it. And a little later, when he decided to publish some previously unknown writings of Marx between 1905 and 1910, he concentrated on a collection of material from 1861–3, to which he gave the title *Theories of Surplus-Value*.

The discovery of the *Grundrisse* came in 1923, thanks to David Ryazanov, director of the Marx–Engels Institute (MEI) in Moscow and organizer of the *Marx Engels Gesamtausgabe* (MEGA), the complete works of Marx and Engels. After examining the *Nachlass* in Berlin, he revealed the existence of the *Grundrisse* in a report to the Socialist Academy in Moscow on the literary estate of Marx and Engels:

> I found among Marx's papers another eight notebooks of economic studies. … The manuscript can be dated to the middle of the 1850s and contains the first draft of Marx's work [*Capital*], whose title he had not yet fixed at the time; it [also] represents the first version of his *A Contribution to the Critique of Political Economy*.[1]
>
> (Ryazanov 1925: 393–4)

'In one of these notebooks', Ryazanov continues, 'Kautsky found the 'Introduction' to *A Contribution to the Critique of Political Economy*' – and he considers the preparatory manuscripts for *Capital* to be of 'extraordinary interest for what they tell us about the history of Marx's intellectual development and his characteristic method of work and research' (Ryazanov 1925: 394).

Under an agreement for publication of the MEGA among the MEI, the Institute for Social Research in Frankfurt and the SPD (which still had custody of the Marx and Engels *Nachlass*), the *Grundrisse* was photographed together with many other unpublished writings and began to be studied by specialists in Moscow. Between 1925 and 1927 Pavel Veller from the MEI catalogued all the preparatory materials for *Capital*, the first of which was the *Grundrisse* itself. By 1931 it had been completely deciphered and typed out, and in 1933 one part was published in Russian as the 'Chapter on Money', followed two years later by an edition in German. Finally, in 1936, the Marx–Engels–Lenin Institute (MELI, successor to the MEI) acquired six of the eight notebooks of the *Grundrisse*, which made it possible to solve the remaining editorial problems.

In 1939, then, Marx's last important manuscript – an extensive work from one of the most fertile periods of his life – appeared in Moscow under the title given it by Veller: *Grundrisse der Kritik der politischen Ökonomie (Rohentwurf) 1857–1858*. Two years later there followed an appendix (*Anhang*) comprising Marx's comments of 1850–1 on Ricardo's *Principles of Political Economy and Taxation*, his notes on Bastiat and Carey, his own table of contents for the *Grundrisse*, and the preparatory material (*Urtext*) for the 1859 *A Contribution to the Critique of Political Economy*. The MELI's preface to the edition of 1939 highlighted its exceptional value: 'the manuscript of 1857–1858, published in full for the first time in this volume, marked a decisive stage in Marx's economic work' (Marx–Engels–Lenin Institute 1939: VII).

Although the editorial guidelines and the form of publication were similar, the *Grundrisse* was not included in the volumes of the MEGA but appeared in a separate edition. Furthermore, the proximity of the Second World War meant that the work remained virtually unknown: the 3,000 copies soon became very rare, and only a few managed to cross the Soviet frontiers. The *Grundrisse* did not feature in the *Sochineniya* of 1928–47, the first Russian edition of the works of Marx and Engels, and its first republication in German had to wait until 1953. While it is astonishing that a text such as the *Grundrisse* was published at all during the Stalin period, heretical as it surely was with regard to the then indisputable canons of *diamat*, Soviet-style 'dialectical materialism', we should also bear in mind that it was then the most important of Marx's writings not to be circulating in Germany. Its eventual publication in East Berlin in 30,000 copies was part of the celebrations marking *Karl Marx Jahr*, the seventieth anniversary of its author's death and the 150th of his birth.

Written in 1857–8, the *Grundrisse* was only available to be read throughout the world from 1953, after 100 years of solitude.

500,000 copies circulating in the world

Despite the resonance of this major new manuscript prior to *Capital*, and despite the theoretical value attributed to it, editions in other languages were slow to appear.

Another extract, after the 'Introduction', was the first to generate interest: the 'Forms which Precede Capitalist Production'. It was translated into Russian in 1939, and then from Russian into Japanese in 1947–8. Subsequently, the separate German edition of this section and a translation into English helped to ensure a wide readership: the former, which appeared in 1952 as part of the *Kleine Bücherei des Marxismus–Leninismus* [*Small Library of Marxism–Leninism*], was the basis for Hungarian and Italian versions (1953 and 1954 respectively); while the latter, published in 1964, helped to spread it in Anglophone countries and, via translations in Argentina (1966) and Spain (1967), into the Spanish-speaking world. The editor of this English edition, Eric Hobsbawm, added a preface that helped to underline its importance: *Pre-Capitalist Economic Formations*, he wrote, was Marx's 'most systematic attempt to grapple with the problem of historical evolution', and 'it can be said without hesitation that any Marxist historical discussion which does not take [it] into account ... must be reconsidered in its light' (Hobsbawm 1964: 10). More and more scholars around the world did indeed begin to concern themselves with this text, which appeared in many other countries and everywhere prompted major historical and theoretical discussions.

Translations of the *Grundrisse* as a whole began in the late 1950s; its dissemination was a slow yet inexorable process, which eventually permitted a more thorough, and in some respects different, appreciation of Marx's oeuvre. The best interpreters of the *Grundrisse* tackled it in the original, but its wider study – both among scholars unable to read German and, above all, among political militants and university students – occurred only after its publication in various national languages.

The first to appear were in the East: in Japan (1958–65) and China (1962–78). A Russian edition came out in the Soviet Union only in 1968–9, as a supplement to the second, enlarged edition of the *Sochineniya* (1955–66). Its previous exclusion from this was all the more serious because it had resulted in a similar absence from the *Marx–Engels Werke* (MEW) of 1956–68, which reproduced the Soviet selection of texts. The MEW – the most widely used edition of the works of Marx and Engels, as well as the source for translations into most other languages – was thus deprived of the *Grundrisse* until its eventual publication as a supplement in 1983.

The *Grundrisse* also began to circulate in Western Europe in the late 1960s. The first translation appeared in France (1967–8), but it was of inferior quality and had to be replaced by a more faithful one in 1980. An Italian version followed between 1968 and 1970, the initiative significantly coming, as in France, from a publishing house independent of the Communist Party.

The text was published in Spanish in the 1970s. If one excludes the version of 1970–1 published in Cuba, which was of little value as it was done from the French version, and whose circulation remained confined within the limits of that country, the first proper Spanish translation was accomplished in Argentina between 1971 and 1976. There followed another three done conjointly in Spain, Argentina and Mexico, making Spanish the language with the largest number of translations of the *Grundrisse*.

The English translation was preceded in 1971 by a selection of extracts, whose editor, David McLellan, raised readers' expectations of the text: 'The *Grundrisse* is much more than a rough draft of *Capital*' (McLellan 1971: 2); indeed, more than any other work, it 'contains a synthesis of the various strands of Marx's thought.... In a sense, none of Marx's works is complete, but the completest of them is the *Grundrisse*' (McLellan 1971: 14–15). The complete translation finally arrived in 1973, a full 20 years after the original edition in German. Its translator, Martin Nicolaus, wrote in a foreword:

> Besides their great biographical and historical value, they [the *Grundrisse*] add much new material, and stand as the only outline of Marx's full political–economic project.... The *Grundrisse* challenges and puts to the test every serious interpretation of Marx yet conceived.
>
> (Nicolaus 1973: 7)

The 1970s were also the crucial decade for translations in Eastern Europe. For, once the green light had been given in the Soviet Union, there was no longer any obstacle to its appearance in the 'satellite' countries: Hungary (1972), Czechoslova-kia (1971–7 in Czech, 1974–5 in Slovak) and Romania (1972–4), as well as in Yugoslavia (1979). During the same period, two contrasting Danish editions were put on sale more or less simultaneously: one by the publishing house linked to the Communist Party (1974–8), the other by a publisher close to the New Left (1975–7).

In the 1980s the *Grundrisse* was also translated in Iran (1985–7), where it constituted the first rigorous edition in Farsi of any lengthy works of Marx, and in a number of further European countries. The Slovenian edition dates from 1985, and the Polish and Finnish from 1986 (the latter with Soviet support).

With the dissolution of the Soviet Union and the end of what was known as 'actually existing socialism', which in reality had been a blatant negation of Marx's thought, there was a lull in the publication of Marx's writings. Neverthe-less, even in the years when the silence surrounding its author was broken only by people consigning it with absolute certainty to oblivion, the *Grundrisse* continued to be translated into other languages. Editions in Greece (1989–92), Turkey (1999–2003), South Korea (2000) and Brazil (scheduled for 2008) make it Marx's work with the largest number of new translations in the last two decades.

All in all, the *Grundrisse* has been translated in its entirety into 22 languages,[2] in a total of 32 different versions. Not including partial editions, it has been printed in more than 500,000 copies[3] – a figure that would greatly sur-prise the man who wrote it only to summarize, with the greatest of haste, the economic studies he had undertaken up to that point.

Readers and interpreters

The history of the reception of the *Grundrisse*, as well as of its dissemination, is marked by quite a late start. The decisive reason for this, apart from the twists and turns associated with its rediscovery, is certainly the complexity of the frag-mentary and roughly sketched manuscript itself, so difficult to interpret and to render in other languages. In this connection, the authoritative scholar Roman Rosdolsky has noted:

> In 1948, when I first had the good fortune to see one of the then very rare copies ... it was clear from the outset that this was a work which was of

fundamental importance for Marxist theory. However, its unusual form and to some extent obscure manner of expression made it far from suitable for reaching a wide circle of readers.

(Rosdolsky 1977: xi)

These considerations led Rosdolsky to attempt a clear exposition and critical examination of the text: the result, his *Zur Entstehungsgeschichte des Marxschen 'Kapital'. Der Rohentwurf des 'Kapital' 1857–58* [*The Making of Marx's 'Capital'*], which appeared in German in 1968, is the first and still the principal monograph devoted to the *Grundrisse*. Translated into many languages, it encouraged the publication and circulation of Marx's work and has had a considerable influence on all its subsequent interpreters.

The year 1968 was significant for the *Grundrisse*. In addition to Rosdolsky's book, the first essay on it in English appeared in the March–April issue of *New Left Review*: Martin Nicolaus' 'The Unknown Marx', which had the merit of making the *Grundrisse* more widely known and underlining the need for a full translation. Meanwhile, in Germany and Italy, the *Grundrisse* won over some of the leading actors in the student revolt, who were excited by the radical and explosive content as they worked their way through its pages. The fascination was irresistible especially among those in the New Left who were committed to overturn the interpretation of Marx provided by Marxism–Leninism.

On the other hand, the times were changing in the East too. After an initial period in which the *Grundrisse* was almost completely ignored, or regarded with diffidence, Vitali Vygodski's introductory study – *Istoriya odnogo velikogo otkrytiya Karla Marksa* [*The Story of a Great Discovery: How Marx Wrote 'Capital'*], published in Russia in 1965 and the German Democratic Republic in 1967 – took a sharply different tack. He defined it as a 'work of genius', which 'takes us into Marx's "creative laboratory" and enables us to follow step by step the process in which Marx worked out his economic theory', and to which it was therefore necessary to give due heed (Vygodski 1974: 44).

In the space of just a few years the *Grundrisse* became a key text for many influential Marxists. Apart from those already mentioned, the scholars who especially concerned themselves with it were: Walter Tuchscheerer in the German Democratic Republic, Alfred Schmidt in the Federal Republic of Germany, members of the Budapest School in Hungary, Lucien Sève in France, Kiyoaki Hirata in Japan, Gajo Petrović in Yugoslavia, Antonio Negri in Italy, Adam Schaff in Poland and Allen Oakley in Australia. In general, it became a work with which any serious student of Marx had to come to grips. With various nuances, the interpreters of the *Grundrisse* divided between those who considered it an autonomous work conceptually complete in itself and those who saw it as an early manuscript that merely paved the way for *Capital*. The ideological background to discussions of the *Grundrisse* – the core of the dispute was the legitimacy or illegitimacy of approaches to Marx, with their huge political repercussions – favoured the development of inadequate and what seem today ludicrous interpretations. For some of the most zealous commentators on the *Grundrisse* even argued that it was theoretically superior to *Capital*, despite the additional ten years of intense research that went into the composition of the latter. Similarly, among the main detractors of the *Grundrisse*, there were some who claimed that, despite the important sections for our understanding of Marx's relationship with Hegel and despite the significant passages on aliena-tion, it did not add anything to what was already known about Marx.

Not only were there opposing readings of the *Grundrisse*, there were also non-readings of it – the most striking and representative example being that of Louis Althusser. Even as he attempted to make Marx's supposed silences speak and to read *Capital* in such a way as to 'make visible whatever invisible sur-vivals there are in it' (Althusser and Balibar 1979: 32), he permitted himself to overlook the conspicuous mass of hundreds of written pages of the *Grundrisse* and to effect a (later hotly debated) division of Marx's thought into the works of his youth and the works of his maturity, without taking cognizance of the content and significance of the manuscripts of 1857–8.[4]

From the mid-1970s on, however, the *Grundrisse* won an ever larger number of readers and interpreters. Two extensive commentaries appeared, one in Japan-ese in 1974 (Morita and Yamada 1974), the other in German in 1978 (Projekt-gruppe Entwicklung des Marxschen Systems 1978), but many other authors also wrote about it. A number of scholars saw it as a text of special importance for one of the most widely debated issues concerning Marx's thought: his intellec-tual debt to Hegel. Others were fascinated by the almost prophetic statements in the fragments on machinery and automation, and in Japan too the *Grundrisse* was read as a highly topical text for our understanding of modernity. In the 1980s the first detailed studies began to appear in China, where the work was used to throw light on the genesis of *Capital*, while in the Soviet Union a collective volume was published entirely on the *Grundrisse* (Vv. Aa. 1987).

In recent years, the enduring capacity of Marx's works to explain (while also criticizing) the capitalist mode of production has prompted a revival of interest on the part of many international scholars (see Musto 2007). If this revival lasts and if it is accompanied by a new demand for Marx in the field of politics, the *Grundrisse* will certainly once more prove to be one of his writings capable of attracting major attention.

Meanwhile, in the hope that 'Marx's theory will be a living source of know-ledge and the political practice which this knowledge directs' (Rosdolsky 1977: xiv), the story presented here of the global dissemination and reception of the *Grundrisse* is intended as a modest recognition of its author and as an attempt to reconstruct a still unwritten chapter in the history of Marxism.

Appendix 1: chronological table of translations of the *Grundrisse*

1939–41	First German edition
1953	Second German edition
1958–65	Japanese translation

1962–78	Chinese translation
1967–8	French translation
1968–9	Russian translation
1968–70	Italian translation
1970–1	Spanish translation
1971–7	Czech translation
1972	Hungarian translation
1972–4	Romanian translation
1973	English translation
1974–5	Slovak translation
1974–8	Danish translation
1979	Serbian/Serbo-Croatian translation
1985	Slovenian translation
1985–7	Farsi translation
1986	Polish translation
1986	Finnish translation
1989–92	Greek translation
1999–2003	Turkish translation
2000	Korean translation
2008	Portuguese translation

Appendix 2: a few points on the content and structure of Part III

The research on the *Grundrisse* collected in the following pages was undertaken in all the countries where the work has been translated in full. Countries sharing a common language (Germany, Austria and Switzerland for German; Cuba, Argentina, Spain and Mexico for Spanish; the USA, Britain, Australia and Canada for English; Brazil and Portugal for Portuguese), where the dissemination of the *Grundrisse* took place more or less in parallel, have been dealt with in as many common chapters. Similarly, chapters referring to countries where the *Grundrisse* was translated into more than one language (Czechoslovakia and Yugoslavia) include the dissemination history for all the languages concerned. Moreover, since those two countries no longer exist as such, the chapter headings bear the names that they had at the time when the *Grundrisse* was published there.

The sequence of chapters follows the chronological order of publication of the *Grundrisse*. The only exception is the chapter on 'Russia and the Soviet Union', which is placed immediately after 'Germany, Austria and Switzerland' because of the close links between the two, and because the first publication of the *Grundrisse* in German happened in the Soviet Union.

Each chapter contains a detailed bibliography, which is subdivided in such a way as to highlight:

1   the complete editions of the *Grundrisse*;
2   the main partial editions of the *Grundrisse*;

3   the critical literature on the *Grundrisse*; and
4   where necessary, other bibliographical references.

In the first of these divisions, editorial information has sometimes been added on the translation and dissemination of the various texts. When they have been added by the authors inside the text, for the sake of brevity they were not repeated in the Bibliography. The same criteria was adopted for the names of the translators of the *Grundrisse* or of its partial editions (the names of the translators of the books included in 'Critical literature on the *Grundrisse*' and 'Other references' were not added at all) and for the names of the many reviews mentioned.

Since the research uncovered several hundred books or articles dealing with the *Grundrisse*, considerations of space meant that it was possible to include in the bibliography only: (1) the partial editions of the *Grundrisse* preceding the complete edition and, in rare cases, some editions of particular interest which followed it; (2) the critical literature mentioned in the text by each author.

All the titles of non-English books and articles appear first in the original language (transliterated in the cases of Japanese, Chinese, Farsi, Greek and Korean) and then in an English translation. In general, the translation of titles has been given in the text, but, if the chapter in question cites a book or article in accordance with the Harvard reference system (that is, with only the name of the author and the year of publication), the translation may be found in the bibliography. Finally, in the case of books and articles already translated into English, they have always been cited under the title of that translation, even if it differs from a literal one.

[Translated from the Italian by Patrick Camiller]

Notes

1   The Russian version of this report was published in 1923.
2   See the chronological table of translations in Appendix 1. To the full translations mentioned above should be added the selections in Swedish (Karl Marx, *Grunddragen i kritiken av den politiska ekonomin*, Stockholm: Zenit/R&S, 1971) and Macedonian (Karl Marx, *Osnovi na kritikata na politickata ekonomija (grub nafrlok): 1857–1858*, Skopje: Komunist, 1989), as well as the translations of the *Introduction* and *The Forms which Precede Capitalist Production* into a large number of languages, from Vietnamese to Norwegian, as well as in Arabic, Dutch and Bulgarian.
3   The total has been calculated by adding together the print-runs ascertained during research in the countries in question.
4   See Sève (2004), who recalls how 'with the exception of texts such as the *Introduction* [...] Althusser never read the *Grundrisse*, in the real sense of the word reading' (p. 29). Adapting Gaston Bachelard's term 'epistemological break' (*coupure épistémologique*), which Althusser had himself borrowed and used, Sève speaks of an 'artificial bibliographical break (*coupure bibliographique*) that led to the most mistaken views of its genesis and thus of its consistency with Marx's mature thought' (p. 30).

References

Althusser, Louis and Balibar, Étienne (1979) *Reading Capital*, London: Verso.

Hobsbawm, Eric J. (1964) 'Introduction', in Karl Marx, *Pre-Capitalist Economic Formations*, London: Lawrence & Wishart, pp. 9–65.

McLellan, David (1971) *Marx's Grundrisse*, London: Macmillan.

Marx, Karl (1903) 'Einleitung zu einer Kritik der politischen Ökonomie', *Die Neue Zeit*, 21, vol. 1: 710–18, 741–5 and 772–81.

Marx–Engels–Lenin Institute (1939) 'Vorwort' ['Foreword'], in Karl Marx, *Grundrisse der Kritik der politischen Ökonomie (Rohentwurf) 1857–1858*, Moscow: Verlag für Fremdsprachige Literatur, pp. vii–xvi.

Morita, Kiriro and Yamada, Toshio (1974) *Komentaru keizaigakuhihan'yoko* [Commentaries on the *Grundrisse*], Tokyo: Nihonhyoronsha.

Musto, Marcello (2007) 'The Rediscovery of Karl Marx', *International Review of Social History*, 52/3: 477–98.

Nicolaus, Martin (1973) 'Foreword', in Karl Marx, *Grundrisse: Foundations of the Critique of Political Economy (Rough Draft)*, Harmondsworth: Penguin, pp. 7–63.

Projektgruppe Entwicklung des Marxschen Systems (1978) *Grundrisse der Kritik der politischen Ökonomie (Rohentwurf). Kommentar* [*Outlines of the Critique of Political Economy. Rough Draft. Commentary*], Hamburg: VSA.

Rosdolsky, Roman (1977) *The Making of Marx's 'Capital'*, vol. 1, London: Pluto Press.

Ryazanov, David (1925) 'Neueste Mitteilungen über den literarischen Nachlaß von Karl Marx und Friedrich Engels' ['Latest reports on the literary bequest of Karl Marx and Friedrich Engels'], *Archiv für die Geschichte des Sozialismus und der Arbeiterbewegung*, 11: 385–400.

Sève, Lucien (2004) *Penser avec Marx aujourd'hui*, Paris: La Dispute.

Vv. Aa. (1987) *Pervonachal'ny variant 'Kapitala'. Ekonomicheskie rukopisi K. Marksa 1857–1858 godov* [*The first version of Capital, K. Marx's Economic Manuscripts of 1857–1858*], Moscow: Politizdat.

Vygodski, Vitali S. (1974) *The Story of a Great Discovery: How Marx Wrote 'Capital'*, Tunbridge Wells: Abacus Press.

13 Germany, Austria and Switzerland

Ernst Theodor Mohl

Asked, a few years before his death, what he thought of the idea of publishing an edition of his collected works, Marx is supposed to have replied that they had yet to be written (Kautsky 1955: 32). Posterity has rendered a different verdict. The MEGA^2 collected edition of Marx's writings and *Nachlass* will eventually comprise, counting the writings of Engels included in it, 114 volumes. The fact that the *Grundrisse*, as the earliest draft of Marx's magnum opus, stands at the head of the section of MEGA^2 given over to *Capital* and the preliminary studies for it reflects its significance in the overall development of his work.

Marx's *Nachlass* was initially entrusted to Engels. After the latter's death in 1895, it passed, by way of August Bebel, into the archives of the German Social Democratic Party. Although it accompanied the Party's leadership into exile in 1933, it was soon sold, because of 'financial difficulties', to the Amsterdam International Institute of Social History (IISH). Why the bundle of papers making up the 1857–8 'rough draft' and the 1861–3 text known as the 'second draft' of *Capital* did not find its way into the IISH's safes along with the rest of the *Nachlass* remained a mystery until the Moscow archives were opened in the 1990s. Now we know that the Pole Marek Kriger purloined both texts from the SPD's poorly guarded Berlin archives in 1932 and sold them in Vienna three years later to representatives of the Moscow Marx–Engels Institute (MEI). In Moscow, good came of Kriger's evil deed: the manuscript of the 'rough draft' was used as the basis for the laborious transcription of Marx's text, replacing the copies from which the MEI had, until then, been transcribing the text. This labour bore fruit in the 1939–41 first edition of the *Grundrisse*.

The publication history of Marx's 1857–8 manuscripts began in Germany, on the pages of *Die Neue Zeit* [*The New Times*], with two partial publications by Karl Kautsky: the 'Introduction' (Marx 1903) and 'Carey and Bastiat' (Marx 1904). These texts contain a relatively large number of misreadings and often depart from the wording of the manuscripts (Marx 1976, 1981, apparatus: 764). The publication of Marx's fragment on Bastiat and Carey went unnoticed. But the publication of his 'Introduction' did not. For, from 1904 on, both in their books and also in the periodical *Marx-Studien* (1904–23), the 'Austro-Marxists' Otto Bauer, Max Adler and Rudolf Hilferding, among others, made a priority of 'bringing the results of [Marx's] thinking and methodology to bear [...] on modern intellectual life as a whole' (*Marx-Studien* 1904: viif.). In subsequent years, the 'Introduction' often saw separate publication; more importantly, the section of the text on method was frequently paraphrased by Marx's commentators. Opinions vary as to where to situate the 'Introduction' in Marx's work of the period. Kautsky considered it part of the 1859 *A Contribution to a Critique of Political Economy*, publishing it from 1907 on as an appendix to Marx's *Contribution*. The editors of the version of the 1859 *Contribution* first released in East Berlin in 1947 and often reissued thereafter (Marx 1947) followed his lead. The editors of the East Berlin MEW identified it as the draft of a general introduction to a 'major economic work projected' by Marx (Marx 1961: 707 n. 402). Boris Goldenberg published the 'Introduction' as an extract from the *Grundrisse* (Marx 1962: 1272 n. 5). Hans Lieber, for his part, contended that the 'Introduction' made up 'a text in its own right'; that is, he did not classify it as part of any other work (Marx 1964: 1110). In view of these divergent judgements, one might well ask whether the editors of the first, 1939–41 edition of the *Grundrisse*, like those of the MEGA[2] edition (II/1.1), were right to treat the 'Introduction' as an integral part of Marx's 'rough draft' (Marx 1976: 17–45; apparatus: 764f.). Ulrike Galander answers that they were not, on the grounds that Marx originally intended his draft 'Introduction' for a comprehensive economic critique that he later set aside in order to expand his analysis of the capital relation (Galander 1991: 62–7).

The *Grundrisse* was scheduled to be issued for the first time in the 'historical and critical collected edition' of the published works, other writings and letters of Marx and Engels undertaken by the Moscow MEI (Ryazanov 1928: 462). This projected collected edition, the MEGA, remained fragmentary, in part because its general editor David Ryazanov fell victim to what is improperly known as Stalin's 'purges'. Ryazanov's successor Victor Adoratskiĭ was able to pursue the project for only a few more years, concessions to Stalinist orthodoxy notwithstanding. In all, of a projected 42 volumes, a mere 12 saw the light, all in the period 1927–35. The edition of the *Grundrisse* that appeared in Moscow in 1939–41, in two volumes and printed in 3,100 copies, was a late delivery in which one finds no mention of MEGA.

Only a few copies of the Moscow first edition ever reached Marx scholars in the West (Rosdolsky 1968: 7). Not this edition as such, but the 1953 photomechanical reproduction of it, issued by East Berlin's Dietz-Verlag, in a printrun of 30,000 served as the primary source for subsequent collected editions. The reception of the *Grundrisse* that began in 1960 in both East and West Germany was also based on the 1953 reissue.

We shall never know why this reprint was issued three years in advance of the first volumes of the MEW (which began to appear in 1956). Was it because the East German Socialist Unity Party had proclaimed 1953 Marx Memorial Year (it was the one-hundred-and-thirty-fifth anniversary of Marx's birth and the seventieth anniversary of his death) and consequently felt obliged to bring out a new reference work in short order? The handsomely produced book did indeed boast a red band identifying it as 'a new release to mark Karl Marx Year, 1953'.

The idea of publishing the title, moreover, originated with émigrés who had returned to Germany from Moscow and were working for the Dietz Verlag or the Marx–Engels–Lenin Institute in Berlin the year that it appeared. As if to pave the way for it, the important section of the *Grundrisse* entitled 'Forms which Precede Capitalist Production' had been released the year before (Marx 1952) in the series *Kleine Bücherei des Marxismus–Leninismus* (small library of Marxism–Leninism).

Between 1967 and 1974, several re-editions and licensed editions of the 1953 Berlin reprint saw the light in both East and West Germany. After the text of the *Grundrisse* had been checked again and emended by staff workers of the Moscow MEI for publication in MEGA², it was republished in a run of 5,000 under the new title *Karl Marx: Ökonomische Manuskripte 1857/58* [*Karl Marx: Economic Works 1857/58*] (Marx 1976, 1981). This volume does not contain the full text of the first edition, which had provided the basis for versions included in subsequent collected editions. Marx's index to the seven notebooks and the original text of *A Contribution to the Critique of Political Economy* were now placed at the head of the following volume of MEGA² (Marx 1980). The second MEGA² edition of the *Grundrisse*, identical to the first (Marx 1976, 1981), appeared in a single volume in a print run of several hundred copies.

Following publication of the MEGA² edition, the *Grundrisse* appeared, under the same title, as a 'supplementary volume' to the MEW. But this supplementary volume did not see the light until 1983. Why so late? After all, the *Economic and Philosophical Manuscripts* of 1844 had been published as a supplementary volume to the MEW as early as 1968, although this text had long stood outside the approved canon. The explanation offered was that the MEW was intended to be, not a historical–critical edition, but one tailored to the needs of students and other non-specialist readers, so that drafts and preliminary sketches generally had no place in it. However, when the editors of the 39-volume Moscow edition of Marx's works rounded their edition out with supplementary volumes, the MEW's editors followed suit. The *Grundrisse* was not included in the MEW until 1983, it was then said, because the MEW's editors had been waiting to see the revised, MEGA² version of the text.

From the publication of the 1953 photomechanical reprint to the present, the *Grundrisse* has been uninterruptedly available in diverse editions in the language in which it was originally written. Taken together, the East and West German publishers who have issued it have printed and sold an estimated 150,000 copies; documented sales come to 100,000 copies (for purposes of comparison, the three volumes of *Capital* published by Dietz Verlag in East Berlin sold a total of over 2,000,000 copies between 1945 and 1987 [Jahn 1987: 5]). Yet this skeletal account of the diffusion of the *Grundrisse* tells us nothing about who read the text when, where and how, about how it has been understood and misunderstood, or about failed and abandoned attempts to read it. Only reading experiences that have themselves given rise to printed texts can supplement the primary source in ways allowing us to complete our examination of 'author and work' with observation of the third party to the act of communication, the 'reader and critic'.

The obstacles blocking appropriate reception of the *Grundrisse* in the East Germany of the 1950s were also systemic. For the radical political trans-formation that got underway there in 1945 prompted an exodus of the country's 'bourgeois' intelligentsia. One consequence was that Marx's difficult text, which he wrote for the sole purpose of 'self-clarification', failed to find competent readers.

In West Germany, there was no lack of competency. Interest, however, was in short supply, since people were determined not to let 'ideology' stand in the way of the nascent reconstruction of capitalist productive relations and social conditions. In 1957, Helmut Gollwitzer and Gerhard Lehmbruch indicated just how far this wilful ignorance went: Marx and Marxism were repressed to the point that 'even most professors [were] absolutely ignorant of the categories with which Marxism offered to explain the world, society, and history' (Goll-witzer and Lehmbruch 1957: 3). Marxism was in fact the remit of a handful of philosophically and theologically trained specialists in 'defensive action'. The material basis for their work was, exclusively, the major writings of the classic Marxist authors canonized in the East (Wetter 1952; Hommes 1955; *Marxis-musstudien* 1954f.).

Not until the 1960s did conditions for the reception of Marx's work begin to improve in the east, and a willingness to give serious consideration to his theory begin to emerge in the west. Leading the way, Lehmbruch cited the new edition of the *Grundrisse* in his 1958 bibliography for 'the study of Soviet ideology'; he reviewed the volume's contents and lauded 'the first-rate explanatory notes, which can be utilized as a concordance for the study of parallel passages' (Lehmbruch 1959: 33). Lehmbruch's recommendation was endorsed by Jürgen Habermas, who, in a 1960 inventory of 'critical Marxism', cited the *Grundrisse* as an important reference work (Habermas 1967: 192ff.). His suggestion was taken up by a pair of studies, each of which focused on a particular concept. Alfred Schmidt's *Der Begriff der Natur in der Lehre von Marx* [*The Concept of Nature in Marx*] (Schmidt 1962), written under Horkheimer and Adorno's direc-tion, names the *Grundrisse* as the source text 'that undoubtedly contains Marx's philosophically most significant formulations' (Schmidt 1972: 68 n. 43). Helmut Klages' *Technischer Humanismus. Philosophie und Soziologie der Arbeit bei Karl Marx* [*Technical Humanism: the Philosophy and Sociology of Labour in Karl Marx*] (Klages 1964) also treats the *Grundrisse* as on a par with Marx's early writings, while also rejecting the division of his thought into distinct periods, already common by the mid-1960s. Focusing on Marx's concept of labour, Klage shows that it evolves in continuous fashion from the preliminary works to *Capital* itself.

Interest in the *Grundrisse* was further heightened and sustained for years by Roman Rosdolsky's *Zur Entstehungsgeschichte des Marxschen 'Kapital'. Der Rohentwurf des 'Kapital' 1857–58* [*The Making of Marx's Capital*] (Rosdolsky 1968). Marx scholars had already discussed the changes in Marx's plans for his magnum opus (Grossmann 1929; Morf 1951: 75f.; Behrens 1952: 31f.), but Ros-dolsky was able to focus this discussion, thanks to his extensive knowledge of the *Grundrisse* (Rosdolsky 1968: 24–78). His introductory treatment of this subject prefaces another 28 chapters of lucid interpretation. They comprise a seamless general commentary on the *Grundrisse* that offers readers an enlightening entry into Marx's hermetic text. No subsequent study of the 'rough draft' can afford to ignore 'the Rosdolsky', as the book soon came to be called, for its precise, detailed exposition relativizes the hermeneutic circle by keeping the whole in view at all times. Rosdolsky's book thus marks a quantum leap in the interpretation of Marx. A few chapters of it had seen advance publication in the journal *Kyklos* (Basel–Switzerland) from 1952 on, but had been ignored.

One of the reasons for this neglect was doubtless that no one knew Rosdolsky or could put a tag on him. Born in 1898 in Lemberg/Lvov, he joined the socialist movement while still in secondary school. After the First World War, he worked for the MEI in archives in Vienna. The outbreak of the Second World War saw him in Krakow, where he was arrested by the Gestapo in 1942. He survived the concentration camps in Auschwitz, Ravensbrück and Oranienburg, emigrating to the United State in 1947. There, 'by a fluke' (Rosdolsky, Emily 1973: 8), he came across a copy of the first edition of the *Grundrisse* in a library. He spent more than a decade working out his interpretation of it. He did not live to see the publication or even the page proofs of his book, which netted his publisher a bestseller; Roman Rosdolsky died on 20 October 1965 in Detroit.

As early as 1964, Helmut Klages (Klages 1964) stressed the central place that the concept of alienation occupied not only in Marx's early work, but in the *Grundrisse* as well. Friedrich Tomberg sharpened Klages' thesis in his essay 'Der Begriff der Entfremdung in den *Grundrissen*' ['The Concept of Alienation in the *Grundrisse*'] (Tomberg 1969), which shows that although Marx uses the word 'alienation' less in the *Grundrisse* than before, he produces more concrete analysis of what it designates. The fact that this applies even more clearly to *Capital* goes unmentioned. Yet Marx here systematizes the theme of alienation in the form, first, of commodity fetishism and money fetishism, and second – as attention to the matter rather than the manner of his argument reveals – in wage fetishism and capital fetishism. Tomberg is nevertheless right to maintain that one would be mistaken to read Marx's major work, much less his work as a whole, as a theory of alienation (Tomberg 1969: 188).

The 13 August 1961 construction of the Berlin Wall checked the massive emigration of East Germans to the West and established the conditions for a reform of socialist economic planning. It also led, no doubt, to a consolidation of the superstructure. One consequence was enhancement of the capacity to read demanding source texts, undoubtedly strengthened by assimilation of the findings of Soviet Marxology, notably Vitaliĭ Solomonovich Vygodski's *Geschichte einer großen Entdeckung. Über die Entstehung des Werkes 'Das Kapital' von Karl Marx* [*Story of a Great Discovery: How Marx Wrote Capital*] (Vygodski 1967). This short book popularized an approach attentive to the historical development of Marx's work, while the two chapters on the *Grundrisse* provided a competent summary of its contents. In the same period, discussion of Marx's method was stimulated by an import from Czechoslovakia, Jindřich Zelený's

Die Wissenschaftslogik bei Marx und 'Das Kapital' [*The Logic of Marx*](Zelený 1968).

Two authors from the GDR, Rolf Sieber and Horst Richter, responded to the stimulus with a book entitled *Die Herausbildung der marxistischen politischen Ökonomie* [*The Formation of Marxist Political Economy*] (Sieber and Richter 1969). They justified their conspicuously circumspect handling of the *Grundrisse* with the claim that the contents of Marx's rough draft had yet to be fully explored (Sieber and Richter 1969: 152). Fred Oelßner made a similar assessment. 'Scholarly research on Marx, especially his economic work, [was] still just in its beginnings' in his country, Oelßner declared, as revealed by the fact that the *Grundrisse* was often quoted but little studied. These remarks are cited in the preface to Walter Tuchscheerer's investigation, *Bevor 'Das Kapital' entstand. Die Herausbildung und Entwicklung der ökonomischen Theorie von Karl Marx in der Zeit von 1843 bis 1858* [*Before Capital: the Formation and Development of Karl Marx's Economy Theory, 1843–58*] (Tuchscheerer 1968: 9).

Like Vygodski before him, Tuchscheerer also sees that it is possible to reconstruct the history of Marx's criticism of the economy and economics by taking his shifting perceptions of Ricardo's doctrine of labour-value as one's Ariadne's thread. Thus Tuchscheerer focuses on this theme, laying bare the essential features of Marx's reception of Ricardo from his early work (1844–5) to his 1850–1 excerpts from Ricardo (Marx 1953: 765–830) precisely and in detail. Tuchscheerer then takes this discussion as a basis for examining Marx's own theory of value as initially outlined in the *Grundrisse*. Crucially, he avoids the economistic foreshortening characteristic of previous discussion in the East, highlighting, instead, in an admirable chapter entitled 'Aufdeckung des Fetischcharakters' ['The Discovery of Fetishism'], the qualitative, socially critical aspects of Marx's doctrine of value (Tuchscheerer 1968: 369–81). Tuchscheerer's achievement was not, needless to say, a bolt from the blue. From 1951 to 1957, he had studied economics at Moscow's Lomonsov University, amassing stupendous knowledge of Soviet Marx scholarship. The undergraduate thesis he wrote in Moscow also treats the emergence of the labour theory of value in the *Grundrisse*. Tuchscheerer died in 1965 at the age of 38, leaving his analysis of the *Grundrisse* unfinished.

Marxism as a worldview enjoyed a de facto monopoly behind the Iron Curtain, and this in turn grounded a claim to exclusive rights to the interpretation of the Marxist classics. Reactions to the burgeoning interest in Marx observable in West Germany and West Berlin in the wake of the 1967–8 student rebellions were correspondingly jittery and, as a rule, ham-fisted. Witness the assertion that the *Grundrisse* had 'become the preferred object of Marx-interpretation' in the West because Westerners believed that appeals to this esoteric rough draft could justify sidestepping subjects such as the labour theory of value, the theory of class struggle or the theory of revolution (Höfer 1968: 189).

Little attention was wasted on such attacks in West Germany. As in East Germany, too, however, the *Grundrisse* was brought into the discussion of Marx, which is to say that, in West Germany as well, Vygodski, Tuchscheerer and Zelený had a place on the syllabuses of teachers and students who took an interest in his thought. West German reading lists also took in Alfred Schmidt's *Geschichte und Struktur* [*History and Structure*] (Schmidt 1971), which, in treating 'problems of a Marxist theory of history', the subtitle of the original German version of the book, dealt at length with the 'Introduction' and the *Grundrisse*. Schmidt here stresses that Marx does not mobilize speculative logic in order to 'deduce' capitalist relations of production, but 'derives them [...] most impressively from concrete history' (Schmidt 1971: 39).

In *Zur logischen Struktur des Kapitalbegriffs bei Karl Marx* [*On the Logical Structure of the Concept of Capital in Karl Marx*] (Reichelt 1970), Helmut Reichelt shows that Marx's use of Hegelian language in the *Grundrisse* is not owing to the fact that he happened to have leafed through Hegel's *Logic* again shortly before sitting down to write. Rather, the *Logic* holds the key, Reichelt says, to understanding the problems of Marx's method, which Rosdolsky ignores. Yet because Reichelt's study slights all the other literature on Marx, it is narrowly focused in its turn, confining itself to the logic of Marx's mode of presentation.

Backed up by a working group of 28 independent scholars in West Berlin, Joachim Bischoff made a very ambitious entry into the ongoing discussion with a book which, outwardly as well, was in conformity with its subject. The authors of *Grundrisse der Kritik der politischen Ökonomie (Rohentwurf). Kommentar* [*Outlines of a Critique of political Economy* (rough draft). *A Commentary*] (Projektgruppe Entwicklung des Marxschen Systems 1978) sought to outbid 'the Rosdolsky' with a 'systematic commentary on the *Grundrisse*'. However, because the authors interpret the *Grundrisse* in strictly immanent fashion, never venturing beyond textual analysis to criticize or expatiate on Marx's thought, they leave questions of the contemporary validity of Marxian theory and its applicability to contemporary problems unmentioned and unresolved.

In *Die Struktur des Marxschen Hauptwerks. Vom Rohentwurf zum 'Kapital'* [*The Structure of Marx's Major Work. From the 'Rough Draft' to Capital*] (Schwarz 1978), Winfried Schwarz also seeks to deepen prevailing perceptions of the *Grundrisse*. His thesis is that Marx cannot reasonably be said to have had several different, yet equally valid schemes for structuring his work, and that analysing the analysis of the value-form appended to the first volume of *Capital* will yield the criteria needed to choose amongst them. His study contains excellent analyses of individual texts (such as 'Results of the Direct Production Process', a seldom interpreted fragment from the 1861–3 second draft of *Capital*). But it also goes to show that comparatively static analysis of Marx's mode of exposition does not by itself authorize conclusions about the logical status of his theory, the core theme of which is 'capital in motion'.

Without joining one or another of the established cartels of professional Marx-quoters (such as the one that thrives in the climate of Frankfurt), Fred E. Schrader dedicated himself to the study of Marx. His remarkable contribution to Marx scholarship bears the title *Restauration und Revolution. Die Vorarbeiten zum 'Kapital' von Karl Marx in seinen Studienheften 1850–1858* [*Restoration and Revolution: the Preparatory Works on Capital by Karl Marx in his Note-books of 1850–1858]* (Schrader 1980). Under the guidance of Götz Langkau, Schrader bent himself to the task of deciphering and evaluating the drafts and notes – published only in 1983 and thereafter, they appear in volumes seven to nine of the fourth section of MEGA^2 – which Marx began to amass in the 1850s with an eye to a future critique of political economy. By means of carefully doc-umented and ordered investigations, Schrader shows, amongst other things, how the process of reception materialized here finds its continuation in the central theorems of the *Grundrisse*, and also how Marx's rough draft integrates ele-ments of widely disparate provenance.

Unless one makes West German economic indicators as sole standard of measure, it is impossible not to conclude that the GDR's economy scored important successes in the 1970s. It was then, at any rate, that the GDR achieved the highest pro capita income in the Soviet bloc. Marx scholarship in the country flourished as well. All the relevant human and material resources were now mobilized to bring out MEGA^2 (two-thirds of the volumes released in rapid suc-cession from 1979 on had East German editors and editorial staff). Probably because the *Grundrisse* was not part of the (East) Germans's publication pro-gramme, only a handful of works taking that text as their explicit subject appeared in the 1980s.

Worth mentioning is a publication edited by Franz Bolck, *Grundrisse der Kritik der politischen Ökonomie 1857/1858 von Karl Marx* [*Karl Marx's Out-lines of a Critique of Political Economy, 1857/1858*] (Bolck 1974), if only because it indicates that Marx's rough draft had by the 1970s made its debut in East German university life as well. The authors of this work, which originated in a seminar of the University of Jena, manifestly hold no brief for philological 'finesse'. They utilize a single procedure: taking the basic categories of the Marxist-Leninist manuals as their guide, they seize on all the corresponding pas-sages in the *Grundrisse* in order to bring those passages to bear, often quite incongruously, on contemporary philosophical debates.

Manfred Müller's investigation *Auf dem Wege zum 'Kapital'. Zur Entwick-lung des Kapitalbegriffs von Marx in den Jahren 1857–1863* [*On the Way to Capital. The Evolution of Marx's Concept of Capital, 1857–1863*] (Müller 1978) stands in sharp contrast. His bibliography sums up all the relevant titles pub-lished in East or West; more generally, his compact study provides a general introduction to the results of the most recent research on the subject. Also useful is the large-format concordance included in Müller's book: it charts the evolu-tion of various themes from the *Grundrisse* through the 1861–3 second draft of *Capital* to the three volumes of *Capital* itself. The author of this concordance is aware that it offers insight into the interrelations among, and breaks between, Marx's different schemes and his realizations of them, but not a means of grasp-ing conceptual or methodological changes.

That not all scholarship attained the level of Müller's is shown by Horst Richter's lecture on the occasion of the one hundred and twentieth anniversary of the *Grundrisse. Hundertzwanzig Jahre Grundrisse der Kritik der politischen*

Ökonomie [*The Grundrisse. One Hundred and Twenty Years of the Outline of a Critique of Political Economy*] (Richter 1979). Richter's text is purely celebratory: everything about the *Grundrisse* is of 'fundamental importance' and prepares the ground for 'fundamental insights' (Richter 1979: 8, 17). Marx was painfully aware of the weaknesses of his draft, which he hastily dashed off in an eight-month period in which he was plunged in a personal crisis. Richter writes the resulting problems off as merely formal defects in Marx's mode of exposition.

Many of the short texts found in 'Karl Marx, *Grundrisse der Kritik der politischen Ökonomie* – historischer Platz und aktuelle Bedeutung' [*Karl Marx, Outline of a Critique of Political Economy – its Place in History and Contemporary Significance*], by Erhard Lange and 22 of his co-authors, outdo even Richter's hymns of praise. Thus we are here told that 'the *Grundrisse* as a whole has not yet been systematically studied from a philosophical standpoint or from that of the history of philosophy', and, further, that Marx here sketches 'stimulating ideas for the creation of a communist logic'. Indeed, with this text, '*Capital*'s *Ur-Faust*', Marx is said to have forged a 'general conception of science' and even 'a general Marxist research method' (Lange 1982: 639, 624, 643).

Shortly before the spectacular implosion of the East German social formation, Wolfgang Schneider published *Einführung in Marx' 'Grundrisse der Kritik der politischen Ökonomie'* [*Introduction to Marx's Outline of a Critique of Political Economy*]. Whereas Schneider's comrades concentrate on celebrating Marx's Great Discoveries, we read here that much in his 'rough draft' has been left in suspense and that he often does no more than 'pose problems'. Yet, Schneider goes on to say, it is precisely the lack of fully elaborated discussions which lends this text its charm and makes reading it so stimulating. Schneider goes still further: Marx is here warning his readers, Schneider claims, of the pitfalls of 'too mechanical an interpretation of the materialist conception of history' (Schneider 1988: 14, 21).

The wave of commentary on the *Grundrisse* that surged up in the 1960s and 1970s had long since ebbed by the time that a group of Swiss authors began producing a sweeping 'systematic commentary' (so the subtitle of their book) on Marx's chapter on method in 1994 (Jánoska *et al.* 1994). The result is a very respectable study. Unembarrassed by undue reverence for the syntactical and rhetorical monumentality of the text they are studying, the authors take it apart in order to put it back together in such a way as to reveal new strands of meaning in it. However, they fail to compare their findings with Marx's 'method in action'. This is unfortunate, because such comparison would have shown that Marx's statements about 'the right method' prove quite inadequate when measured against the wide variety of methods observable in the excerpts and notes that furnished him his raw material, or the drafts in which he analyses it. The fact that Marx lacked the time adequately to theorize his own methodological practice, as well as the consequences this omission had on his work, are the themes of Alfred Schmidt's and Oskar Negt's contribution to a Frankfurt symposium entitled *Kritik der politischen Ökonomie heute. 100 Jahre 'Kapital'* [*The Critique of Political Economy Today. One Hundred Years of Capital*] (Schmidt and Negt 1968: 30–57).

While no books were burned in public in the course of the East Germans' 'peaceful revolution', ordinary citizens of the GDR (and also 'people's book stores') did unceremoniously dispose of the writings of the Marxist classics ('the brains behind the crime') by the tonne. Then, in the wake of ('re')unification, the West sent its liquidators eastwards to 'deal with' organized Marx scholarship, which had been conducted mainly in university departments of Marxism–Leninism or institutes attached to the SED. They did their work with a vengeance. For quite some time, it was even doubtful whether work on MEGA² would continue.

In West Germany, interest in reading and interpreting Marx was already on the wane by the late 1970s. In the 1980s, it nearly disappeared altogether. One reason was the voluntary dissolution of the opposition critical of the GDR's social system and its ensuing fragmentation in the women's, peace and ecological movements, which soon turned their backs on 'Grand Theories' and, before long, theory as such. Meanwhile, the globalization of capitalist social relations has proceeded unhindered, so that it is now only a matter of time before the baffled turn again to theory in search of answers to the questions thrown up by this centuries-old process. When writings by Marx (and Engels) reappear on syllabuses and in university curricula, the *Grundrisse* and the 1861–3 second draft of *Capital* will surely be amongst them, since commentators have by no means exhausted the potential of either. A still unresolved problem will then, no doubt, find its way back onto the agenda: the research methods of the man who declared in 'Comments on the Latest Prussian Censorship Instruction', his first article written in 1842, that 'the investigation of truth must itself be true' and also that 'truth includes not only the result but also the path to it' (Marx 1975: 113).

[Translated from the German by G.M. Goshgarian]

Bibliography

Complete editions

Marx, Karl (1939, 1941) *Grundrisse der Kritik der politischen Ökonomie (Rohentwurf) 1857–1858. Anhang 1850–1859*, 2 vols, Marx–Engels–Lenin Institute Moskau (ed.), Moskau: Verlag für fremdsprachige Literatur.
Marx, Karl (1953) *Grundrisse der Kritik der politischen Ökonomie (Rohentwurf) 1857–1858. Anhang 1850–1859*, Marx–Engels–Lenin Institute Moskau (ed.), Berlin: Dietz Verlag.
Marx, Karl (1967) *Grundrisse der Kritik der politischen Ökonomie (Rohentwurf) 1857–1858. Anhang 1850–1859*, Frankfurt am Main: Europäische Verlagsanstalt (EVA).
Marx, Karl (1970) *Grundrisse der Kritik der politischen Ökonomie (Rohentwurf) 1857–1858. Anhang 1850–1859*, Frankfurt am Main/Wien: EVA/Europa Verlag. Several thousand copies were published.

Marx, Karl (1974) *Grundrisse der Kritik der politischen Ökonomie (Rohentwurf) 1857–1858. Anhang 1850–1859*, Berlin: Dietz Verlag. Reissued in 1974 and 1975, 40,000 copies were published.

Marx, Karl (1976, 1981) 'Ökonomische Manuskripte 1857/58', in Karl Marx/Friedrich Engels *Gesamtausgabe* (MEGA²), 2 vols (II/1.1 and II/1.2), Institut für Marxismus-Leninismus beim ZK der KPdSU und vom Institut für Marxismus-Leninismus beim ZK der SED (ed.), Berlin: Dietz Verlag. Reissued in 2006 in one volume, ed. Internationalen Marx–Engels-Stiftung, Berlin: Akademie Verlag. 5,000 copies were published.

Marx, Karl (1983) 'Ökonomische Manuskripte 1857/1858', in Karl Marx and Friedrich Engels *Werke* (MEW) vol. 42, Institut für Marxismus-Leninismus beim ZK der SED (ed.), Berlin: Dietz Verlag. This edition is based on the Russian 1968–9 version and on MEGA² of 1976–81.

Partial editions

Marx, Karl (1903) 'Einleitung zu einer Kritik der politischen Ökonomie' ['Introduction to a Critique of Political Economy'], *Die Neue Zeit*, Year 21, vol. 1: 710–18, 741–5, and 772–81.

Marx, Karl (1904) 'Carey und Bastiat. Ein Fragment aus dem Nachlass' ['Carey and Bastiat. A Fragment from the Literary Bequest'], in *Die Neue Zeit*, Year 22, no. 2, 5–16.

Marx, Karl (1907) 'Einleitung' [Introduction] in Karl Marx, *Zur Kritik der politischen Ökonomie* [*A Contribution to a Critique of Political Economy*], Berlin: Dietz Verlag (2nd edn 1907), pp. xi–l.

Marx, Karl (1947) 'Einleitung', in Karl Marx, *Zur Kritik der politischen Ökonomie*, Berlin: Dietz Verlag, pp. 227–60.

Marx, Karl (1952) *Formen die der kapitalistischen Produktion vorhergehen* [*Forms Which Precede Capitalist Production*], Berlin: Dietz Verlag.

Marx, Karl (1961) 'Einleitung' [Zur Kritik der politischen Ökonomie], in Karl Marx and Friedrich Engels *Werke* (MEW) vol. 13, Berlin: Dietz Verlag, pp. 615–42.

Marx, Karl (1962) 'Einleitung zum Rohentwurf des *Kapitals*' ['Introduction to the Rough Draft of *Capital*'], in Karl Marx, *Ausgewählte Schriffen* [*Selected Writings*] ed. Boris Goldenberg, München: Kindler-Verlag, pp. 390–423.

Marx, Karl (1964) 'Einleitung zu einer Kritik der politischen Ökonomie' ['Introduction to a Critique of Political Economy'], in Karl Marx, *Ökonomische Schriften* [Economic Writings], vol. III, ed. Hans-Jouchim Lieber and Benedikt Kautsky, Stuttgart: Cotla-Verlag, pp. 793–833.

Critical literature on the Grundrisse

Bolck, Franz (ed.) (1974) *Grundrisse der Kritik der politischen Ökonomie 1857/1858 von Karl Marx*, Jena: Friedrich Schiller-Universität.

Habermas, Jürgen (1967) 'Zwischen Philosophie und Wissenschaft: Marxismus als Kritik', in *Theorie und Praxis. Sozialphilosophische Studien*, Neuwied am Rhein (2nd edn Berlin: Luchterhand), pp. 162–214.

Jánoska, Judith, Bondeli, Martin, Kindle, Konrad and Hofer, Marc (1994) *Das 'Methodenkapitel' von Karl Marx. Ein historischer und systematischer Kommentar*, Basel: Schwabe & Co. AG Verlag.

Klages, Helmut (1964) *Technischer Humanismus. Philosophie und Soziologie der Arbeit bei Karl Marx*, Stuttgart: Enke.

Lange, Erhard (1982) 'Karl Marx "Grundrisse der Kritik der politischen Ökonomie" – historischer Platz und aktuelle Bedeutung', in *Wissenschaftliche Zeitschrift. Gesellschafts und Sprachwissenschaftliche Reihe*, Year 31, no. 6, pp. 625–766, Jena: Friedrich–Schiller-Universität.

Müller, Manfred (1978) *Auf dem Wege zum 'Kapital'. Zur Entwicklung des Kapitalbegriffs von Marx in den Jahren 1857–1863*, Berlin: Akademie Verlag.

Projektgruppe Entwicklung des Marxschen Systems (1978) *Grundrisse der Kritik der politischen Ökonomie (Rohentwurf) Kommentar*, Hamburg: VSA.

Reichelt, Helmut (1970) *Zur logischen Struktur des Kapitalbegriffs bei Karl Marx*, Frankfurt am Main: EVA.

Richter, Horst (1979) *120 Jahre 'Grundrisse der Kritik der politischen Ökonomie'*, Leipzig: Karl-Marx-Universität.

Rosdolsky, Roman (1968) *Zur Entstehung des Marxschen 'Kapital'. Der 'Rohentwurf' des 'Kapital' 1857–58*, Frankfurt am Main/Wien: EVA/Europa Verlag.

Schmidt, Alfred (1962) *Der Begriff der Natur in der Lehre von Marx*, Frankfurt am Main: EVA.

Schmidt, Alfred (1972) *De Begriff der Natur in der Lehre von Marx* (revised edn), Frankfurt am Main: EVA.

Schmidt, Alfred (1971) *Geschichte und Struktur*, Munich: Carl Hanser Verlag.

Schmidt, Alfred and Negt, Oskar (1968) 'Zum Erkenntnisbegriff der Kritik der politischen Ökonomie' and 'Korreferat', in Walter Euchner and Alfred Schmidt (eds), *Kritik der politischen Ökonomie heute. 100 Jahre Kapitel*, Frankfurt am Main/Wien: EVA/Europa Verlag, pp. 30–57.

Schneider, Wolfgang (1988) *Einführung in Marx 'Grundrisse der Kritik der politischen Ökonomie'*, Berlin: Dietz Verlag.

Schrader, Fred E. (1980) *Restauration und Revolution. Die Vorarbeiten zum 'Kapital' von Karl Marx in seinen Studienheften 1850–1858*, Hildesheim: Gerstenberg Verlag.

Schwarz, Winfried (1978) *Die Strukturgeschichte des Marxschen Hauptwerks. Vom 'Rohentwurf' zum 'Kapital'*, Berlin: deb Verlag das europäische Buch.

Sieber, Rolf and Richter, Horst (1969) *Die Herausbildung der marxistischen politischen Ökonomie*, Berlin: Dietz Verlag.

Tomberg, Friedrich (1969) 'Der Begriff der Entfremdung in den "Grundrissen"', in *Das Argument*, Year 11, no. 3: 187–223.

Tuchscheerer, Walter (1968) *Bevor 'Das Kapital' entstand. Die Herausbildung und Entwicklung der ökonomischen Theorie von Karl Marx in der Zeit von 1843 bis 1858*, Berlin: Akademie Verlag.

Vygodski, Vitali S. (1967) *Die Geschichte einer großen Entdeckung. Über die Entstehung des Werkes 'Das Kapital' von Karl Marx*, Berlin: Verlag die Wirtschaft.

Vygodski, Vitali S. (1978) 'Die "Grundrisse der Kritik der politischen Ökonomie" und ihr Platz im Kampf um die ökonomische Lehre der Arbeiterklasse', in *Marx–Engels–Jahrbuch*, 1: 175–203, Berlin: Dietz Verlag.

Zelený, Jindřich (1968) *Die Wissenschaftslogik bei Marx und 'Das Kapital'*, Berlin: Akademie Verlag and Frankfurt am Main/Wien: EVA/Europa Verlag.

Other references

Behrens, Friedrich (1952) *Zur Methode der politischen Ökonomie*, Berlin: Akademie Verlag.

Bochénski, Joseph M. (1950) *Der sowjetrussische dialektische Materialismus (Diamat)*, Munich: Francke and Bern: Lizenzausgabe Lehnen.

Galander, Ulrike (1991) 'Zu Marx' Untersuchung des ökonomischen Bewegungsgesetzes der kapitalistischen Gesellschaft und deren Bedeutung für eine umfassende Gesellschaftsanalyse' in *Marx–Engels–Jahrbuch*, 13: 55–75.

Gollwitzer, H. and Lehmbruch, G. (1957) *Kleiner Wegweise zum Studium des Marxismus-Leninismus*, Bonn: Bundesministerium für gesamtdeutsche Fragen.

Grossmann, Henryk (1929) 'Die Änderung des Aufbauplanes des Marxschen "Kapitals" und ihre Ursachen', in *Archiv für die Geschichte des Sozialismus und der Arbeiterbewegung*, 14: 305–38.

Höfer, Manfred (1968) 'Zu tedenzen der westdeutschen bürgerlichen Marxkritik' ['On the Tendencies of the Bourgeois Critique of Marx in West Germany'] in Georg Mende and Erhard Lange (eds), *Die aktuelle philosophische Bedeutung des ,Kapital' von Karl Marx* [*The Current Philosophic Meaning of Marx's 'Capital'*], Berling: Deutscher Verlag der Wissenschaften, pp. 187–215.

Hommes, Jakob (1955) *Der technische Eros. Das Wesen der materialistischen Geschichtsauffassung*, Freiburg: Herder.

Jahn, Wolfgang (1987) 'Die Dokumentation der Entstehungsgeschichte des "Kapitals" in der MEGA-Edition und ihre Bedeutung für die gesellschaftswissenschaftliche Forschung', in *Wissenschaftliche Beiträge der Martin-Luther-Universität Halle-Wittenberg*, 43: 5–19.

Kautsky, Karl (1955) 'Mein erster Aufenthalt in London', in Benedikt Kautsky (ed.), *Friedrich Engels Briefwechsel mit Karl Kautsky*, Wien: Danubia Verlag, pp. 17–34.

Lehmbruch, Gerhard (1959) *Kleiner Wegweiser zum Studium der Sowjetideologie*, Bonn: Bundesministerium für gesamtdeutsche Fragen.

Marx, Karl (1975) 'Comments on the Latest Prussian Censorship Instruction', in *Marx and Engels Collected Works*, vol. 1: *Marx August 1835–March 1843*, Moscow: Lawrence & Wishart, pp. 109–31.

Marx, Karl (1980) 'Index zu den 7 Heften' ['Index to the 7 Notebooks'], in *Marx Engels Gesamtausgabe* (MEGA²), vol. II/2, Berlin: Dietz.

Marx, Karl (1994) 'Results of the Direct Process of Production', in *Marx and Engels Collected Works*, vol. 34: *Marx 1861–64*, New York: International Publishers, pp. 355–474.

Marxismusstudien (1954–72) eds Erwin Metzke, Iring Fetscher *et al.*, Tübingen: J.C.B. Mohr.

Marx-Studien (1904) eds Max Adler and Rudolf Hilferding, Wien: Verlag der Wiener Volksbuchhandlung.

Morf, Otto (1951) *Das Verhältnis von Wirtschaftstheorie und Wirtschaftsgeschichte bei Karl Marx*, Bern: Francke.

Rosdolsky, Emily (1973) 'Über den Autor', in Roman Rosdolsky *Studien über revolutionäre Taktik. Zwei unveröffentlichte Arbeiten über die II. Internationale und die österreichische Sozialdemokratie*, Berlin: VSA.

Ryazanov, David (1928) 'Die Marx–Engels-Gesamtausgabe', in *Marx–Engels-Archiv*, Bd. 1, pp. 461–6.

Wetter, Gustav A. (1952) *Der dialektische Materialismus. Seine Geschichte und sein System in der Sowjetunion*, Freiburg: Herder.

14 Russia and the Soviet Union

Lyudmila L. Vasina

The publication of the whole of the *Grundrisse* in the USSR in 1939–41 was preceded by partial publications of Marx's 1857–8 manuscripts. The essay on 'Carey and Bastiat' and the 'Introduction' had already been published in Russian in journals and collections, the former in 1904–5 (Marx 1904 and 1905) and the latter in 1922 (Marx 1922), on the basis of Karl Kautsky's editions in *Die Neue Zeit*. The Russian edition of the 'Introduction' was used by V. Khulu-flu for its translation into Azerbaijanian, issued in Baku in 1930 and 2,000 copies were printed (Marx 1930). The subsequent publications of extracts from the *Grundrisse* were directly based on the work of deciphering and interpretation done on Marx's economic manuscripts, as part of the rest of his works. Around 7,000 pages of these manuscripts were photographed in 1923 at the Archive of the German Social Democratic Party and later reached the Marx–Engels Institute (MEI) in Moscow in the form of photocopies. The first attempt to order and catalogue Marx's draft economic manuscripts was made by Christoph Wurm, who worked at the MEI until January 1925. Pavel Lazarevich Veller took over the project in the 1925–7 and systematised and detailed Marx's economic legacy in the so-called 'Pasporta ekonomicheskikh rukopisei' ['Passports of Economic Manuscripts'], archival catalogues still in use today. Veller named the seven notebooks containing the *Grundrisse* 'Short series', to distinguish them from the 'Long series', i.e. 23 notebooks of the manuscript from 1861–3.

The editorial work on the *Grundrisse* began in 1927. According to a report of the economic section of the Marx–Engels department of the MEI dated 4 October, 1927, all but the last two notebooks (VI and VII) had been deciphered and typewritten (RGASPI 1). Veller could not dedicate himself exclusively to the *Grundrisse* due to his involvement in the preparation of the publication of the *German Ideology* in the MEGA; however, by 1931 the *Grundrisse* had been fully typewritten. Veller's close study of the manuscript enabled him to identify the order in which Marx had written it and to date the *Grundrisse* in the period between October 1857 and May 1858. He wrote the results of his work in 'Marx's Economic Manuscripts of 1857–58, 3 August 1934' (Veller 2001).

The main work of preparation for the publication of the *Grundrisse* was based on the photocopies and took place in the MEI and later in the

Marx–Engels–Lenin Institute (MELI). In 1936 the MELI acquired nearly the entire set of Marx's notebooks of the manuscript from Marek Kriger (Miskievich 2008). From then on, the editors of the *Grundrisse* were able to access the original notebooks in order to resolve difficult editorial problems, including the deciphering, dating and structuring of the manuscripts. Only a notebook with the text of the 'Introduction' and notebook VII, which contains the last part of the manuscript, were kept at the International Institute of Social History in Amsterdam.

In the 1930s the MELI published important parts of the manuscripts of 1857–8 in Russian and German. First, fragments of a preliminary plan of the 'Chapter on Capital' were published in 1932 (Marx 1932). In 1933 the 'Chapter on Money' was published in part, and two years later in full, in Russian and German (Marx 1933 and 1935a). The German version was edited by Veller and the Russian translator was Lev A. Leont'ev. Shortly before the publication of the 'Chapter on Money' Leont'ev published the essay 'K rukopisi Marksa' ['According to Marx's Manuscript'] (Leont'ev 1932). In 1936 Mstislav Bronsky wrote a paper entitled 'Neopublikovannaya rukopis' Marksa o den'gax' ['Marx's Unpublished Manuscript on Money'] (Bronsky 1936).

In 1933, 1935 and 1939 the MELI published extracts from notebooks II and IV in Russian and in part in German (Marx 1933, 1935b and 1939a). The fragment on 'Forms which Precede Capitalist Production' was first published in 1939 and 1940 in the journals *Proletarskaya revolyutsiya* [*Proletarian Revolution*] and *Vestnik drevnej istorii* [*Herald of Ancient History*] (Marx 1939b and 1940a). Two separate editions of it were issued for publication in 1940 with print-runs of 50,000 and 51,200 copies (Marx 1940b). This section was discussed in papers by Sergej Bratus' (1940) and Iosif Lapidus (1941). On the basis of the Russian edition it was then translated into Armenian and 5,000 copies were printed in 1941. In 1952 it was translated into Georgian and 10,000 copies were published in Tbilisi (Marx 1941 and 1952).

In the meantime, throughout the 1930s the MELI continued to work on a publication of the whole of the *Grundrisse* in the original language and in Russian. Initially, in 1931, the *Grundrisse* was planned for publication as volume six of the second section of the first MEGA. Later, in 1936, the manuscript was planned for publication as volume eight and nine of the MEGA, and Veller was made responsible for the editing.

The title *Grundrisse* was not chosen until much later. In the working papers of the MELI from the 1930s, the manuscript was known as: 'A Short Series of Economic Manuscripts', 'A Rough Draft of the *A Contribution to the Critique of Political Economy* (short series)', 'Draft Manuscripts by Marx', 'A Contribution to the Critique of Political Economy, 1857–58 (short series)', 'Drafts of *Capital*', 'The 1857–58 Manuscripts', 'Marx's Economic Manuscript of 1857–58', 'A Contribution to the Critique of Political Economy', 'A Rough Draft on Economic Theory', 'From the Work Preceding *Capital* (Manuscripts of 1857–58)', 'Works Preceding the *A Contribution to the Critique of Political Economy*' (short series)', 'Rough Draft of the *A Contribution to the Critique of*

Political Economy'. The title *Grundrisse* was probably chosen by Veller at the last stage of the editorial work on the manuscript.

According to the 1935 plan of the Marx–Engels Department of MELI, Veller was to elaborate a detailed plan of publication for the *Grundrisse*, beginning in November of the same year (RGASPI 2). However, due to his engagements on other works, the manuscript was assembled for publication in German by Vladislav Rudas, with the help of Paul Scherber, in two volumes entitled 'From the Works Preceding *Capital* (Manuscripts of 1857–58)'. The volumes were edited by the director of the MELI, Vladimir Viktorovich Adoratsky, and the Head of the Marx–Engels Section of MELI, Maksimilian Alekseevich Savel'ev.

In May of 1937, both volumes had been sent to the typesetters and by the end of the year the first volume was finished (RGASPI 3). However, in 1937, at the time of Stalin's great purge, Rudas and Scherber were arrested and the publication postponed first to 1938 and then to 1939. Meanwhile, Veller had returned to his work on the *Grundrisse* in 1938. He was appointed as 'main editor' of the first volume, entitled 'A Draft Essay on Economic Theory'. The 1939 plan of the Marx–Engels Section of the MELI finally features the well-known title *Grundrisse der Kritik der Politischen Ökonomie* (RGASPI 4).

The first volume of the *Grundrisse* was printed at the end of 1939 in 3,140 copies (RGASPI 5). Until March 1941, Veller worked on the second volume, *Anhang [Appendix]*. This included not only comments on the main text of the manuscript, an index of names and a bibliography, but also the first publication of Marx's excerpts from David Ricardo's work *On the Principles of Political Economy*, taken from his 1850–1 notebooks IV and VIII, the manuscript 'Bastiat and Carey', the rough draft (*Urtext*) of Marx's *A Contribution to the Critique of Political Economy* (1859), 'References to My Own Notebooks' and a 'Draft Plan of 1859' of the chapter on capital. Both volumes of the *Grundrisse* followed the guidelines of the first MEGA and were made parts of it. For this reason, they later became known as an edition in the 'format of the MEGA'.

Volume two was scheduled for publication on 21 June 1941 (Marx 1939, 1941). On the following day Hitler attacked the Soviet Union. It eventually came out, in 3,100 copies, on 28 June 1941. The former fellows of the MELI recounted that some of them were sent, together with copies of the first volume from 1939, to the war front as material for agitation against German soldiers and later to camps as study material for prisoners of war. This probably explains why this edition of the *Grundrisse* became so rare. Indeed, as Jack Cohen wrote in 1973, 'it was overwhelmed and forgotten in the cataclysm of World War II' (Cohen 1973: 4).

Alongside the edition of the *Grundrisse* in the original language, the MELI also continued to work on the Russian edition of the manuscript, for which Rostislav Ivanovich Novitsky and Leont'ev were responsible in 1939–40. Initially, the *Grundrisse* was to be issued in Russian as part of 'Marx's and Engels's literary heritage', a 50-volume collection planned for 1940–2 (Novitsky 1939). This was to be divided into two parts: the first would contain Marx's economic manuscripts and the second his excerpts, but the project was never realised. Novitsky suggested a new title for a Russian edition of the *Grundrisse*, 'Critical Investigation on Political Economy. Book I. On Capital (Notes to Himself)' (RGASPI 6). The book, to be published as a volume of the 'Marx–Engels Archive' in March 1941, was never produced. Moreover, in 1940–1 Veller published two articles with a brief characterisation of the *Grundrisse* and information about his work on manuscript (Veller 1940 and 1941).

Due to the complexity of its preparation for publication and the lack of qualified scholars, the *Grundrisse* was not included in the first Russian edition of Marx and Engels' *Sočinenija* [*Collected Works*] issued in 1928–47, in 28 volumes. The most important reason for this decision was Stalin's position. Stalin believed that three volumes of *Capital* were sufficient for the masses to understand Marx's ideas. Former fellows of the MELI and the IML recounted that according to Stalin Marx's draft manuscripts were of less importance because they did not reflect his mature position and views.

Soon after the Second World War, Leont'ev published a monograph *O predvaritel'nom variante 'Kapitala' Marksa* [*On the Previous Version of Marx's Capital*] (1946), which aroused much interest in the *Grundrisse* amongst a new generation of scholars. In celebration of the 100th anniversary of the *Grundrisse*, articles by A.G. Achundov (1957) and Igor' A. Bolduirev (1958) were published. At the same time Albert Kogan emerged as one of the most enthusiastic researchers of the *Grundrisse* in the Soviet Union, but his first papers on the manuscript could not be published until the middle of the 1960s, when Stalin's opinion of the *Grundrisse* appeared to have changed (Kogan 1966 and 1967).

In 1965–8 a partial version of *Grundrisse* (extracts from the 'Chapter on Capital'), edited by Vitali Vygodski under the supervision of Vladimir Brushlinsky, appeared in the journal *Voprosy filosofii* (Marx 1965–8). The *Grundrisse* was not included in the second Russian edition of *Sočinenija*, which was published between 1955 and 1966 in 39 books and 42 volumes. Only once the edition was enlarged to span over 50 books was the *Grundrisse* finally published, in 1968–9, in two books, as volume 46. This new edition, edited by Vygodsky and Izora Kazmina under the supervision of Brushlinsky (Marx 1968, 1969), was given the title *Kritika politicheskoj ekonomii (Chernovoj nabrosok 1857–58 godov)* [*Critique of Political Economy, Rough Draft of 1857–58*], based on Marx's note 'Polit. Econ. Criticism of' in notebook VII (Marx 1976, 1981, apparatus: 777) and his characterisation of his work in a letter to Ferdinand Lassalle dated 22 February 1858. In comparison to the first edition of the *Grundrisse* of 1939–41, the text of the manuscript has a better commentary and includes a new index of names and bibliography, a new index of journal publications, and one of Russian translations of referenced books. The second part includes a subject index for both books. Each of it was issued in 45,000 copies, which is not much for the Soviet Union: in the second Russian edition of *Sočinenija*, for example, *Capital* was printed in 135,000 copies (volume one), 119,000 copies (volume two), and 120,000 and 115,000 copies (volume three in two parts).

Using the experience and materials of the Russian edition of the *Grundrisse*, the IML in Moscow compiled a new edition of the manuscript in German as volume one of the second section of MEGA^2 in two parts (Marx 1976, 1981). This edition was edited by Brushlinsky, Vygodski, Larisa Miskievich, Aleksandr Syrov and Irina Antonova, and Nina Nepomnyashchaya checked the transcription of the manuscript. The work was sponsored by Artur Schnickman of the IML in Berlin.

The work done on the *Grundrisse* at the IML in Moscow and its publications in the 1960s and 1970s inaugurated a new stage in the reception of the *Grundrisse* in the USSR, stimulated by the work of Alexander Ivanovich Maluish (Maluish 1963 and 1966) and Vygodski (Vygodski 1965, 1970, 1974, and Vygodski and Bagaturiya 1976). Vygodski's *Istoriya odnogo velikogo otkruitiya Karla Marksa* [*The Story of a Great Discovery of Karl Marx*] (1965) had enjoyed great popularity and was soon translated into German (1967) and then, from Russian and German, into many other languages. Vygodski's work played an essential role in the dissemination and reception of the *Grundrisse* outside the USSR. Various aspects of the *Grundrisse* are discussed in many of his other papers too.

Since the mid-1960s, the significance and place of the *Grundrisse* in the history of Marx's economic theory has been analysed in all the main textbooks on the history of economic thought, as well as the biographical works and publications on Marx and his theory. The history of the publication of the *Grundrisse* in Russia and the USSR was briefly recounted in a monograph entitled *Literaturnoe nasledstvo K. Marksa i F. Engel'sa. Istoriya publikatsii I izucheniya v SSSR* [*The Literary Bequest of K. Marx and F. Engels: A History of its Publication and Study in the USSR*] (Vv. Aa. 1969).

In the 1970s papers by E. Rezhibek (1974), Konstantin Tronev (1970), Sergei Mareev (1973) and T. Chaika (1976) on various questions relating to the study of the *Grundrisse* attested to its popularity in the USSR. In addition to Vygodsky's work, Kogan's *V tvorcheskoj laboratorii Karla Marksa: (Plan ekonomicheskikh issledovanij 1857–1859 gg. i 'Kapital')* [*In Karl Marx's Creative Laboratory. A Plan of the Economic Investigations of 1857–1859 and 'Capital'*] – first published in Japanese in 1979 –, also met with high appraisal abroad (Kogan 1983).

In the 1980s interest for the *Grundrisse* in the USSR was still growing. Given the rarity of volume 46 of *Sočinenija*, in 1980 the Moscow Publishing house Politizdat issued a new separate edition of it, compiled by the IML in two volumes and published in 45,000 copies (Marx 1980). This new edition took into account the results of the work on the first three volumes of MEGA^2. Some corrections to the transcription were made, the dates of Marx's manuscripts entitled 'Index to My Own Notebooks' and 'Draft Plan of the Chapter on Capital' were changed to the summer of 1861 instead of February 1859 and February–March 1859. There were also clear improvements to the structure of the volume.

Throughout the 1980s interesting papers were written on different theoretical questions raised by the *Grundrisse* by Anno Marx, Kogan (1983), Antonova (1983), Elena Melikyan (1983), Bolduirev (1984), Aleksandr Chepurenko (1985) and Mikhail Ternovsky (Vv. Aa. 1987). The summary characteristic of the main problems of the *Grundrisse* contained a special monograph written by an international group of authors who specialised on the analysis of Marx's economic theory (Vv. Aa. 1987). This monograph attempted to provide a complete analysis of the *Grundrisse* and is still regarded as the best publication on this subject. In 14 chapters it surveys the history, context, theoretical significance and reception of the *Grundrisse*, as well as the discussions it stimulated around the world.

Chapter 3 is of particular interest today as it provides evidence for a new dating of the manuscript (between January 1857 and May 1858). Vygodski, who authored the chapter, claims that this date marks the beginning of Marx's work on the manuscript, in agreement with Leont'ev, who first suggested it in 1933, in his preface to volume two (VII) of the 'Marx–Engels Archive', where the draft Chapter VI of the first volume of *Capital* on the 'Results of the Direct Production Process' was first published in Russian and German (Leont'ev 1933: VI–VII). The same date is proposed in *Karl Marx. Chronik seines Lebens* [*Karl Marx. Chronicle of his Life*] (Vv. Aa. 1934: 162), but then changed to 'between October 1857 and May 1858' in the 1935 publication of the 'Chapter on Money', volume six of 'Marx–Engels Archive'. This dating (between October 1857 and May 1858) has been cited in all the subsequent editions of the *Grundrisse* and Veller agrees on it in all of the working papers on the *Grundrisse* as well as in the edition of 1939–41.

The reason for going back to the initial dating is argued and defended by Inna P. Osobova, who came to this conclusion during her work on volume III/8 of the MEGA[2] in 1990, in her paper 'Über einige Probleme der ökonomischen Studien von Marx im Jahre 1857 vom Standpunkt des Historikers' ['On some Problems of Marx's Economic Studies in 1857 from the Point of View of the Historian'] (Osobova 1990). According to her, Marx begun working on the *Grundrisse* in January 1857, with his analysis of Darimon's *De la réforme des banques*, and kept working on it until the middle of February; he then interrupted his work on the manuscript and did not recover it until October 1857. Vygodski agreed on this new date for the *Grundrisse* (Vygodski 1987), which was also supported by the best expert on the editorial questions of the *Grundrisse*: Brushlinsky. He explains the reasons in *O nekotoruikh netochnostyach v nauchnom apparate pervuikh pyati tomov II otdela MEGA* [*On some Inaccuracies in the Scientific Apparatus of the First Five Volumes of the Second Section of the MEGA Vv. Aa. 1987*] (see Brushlinsky 1987: 189–90).

Moreover, on the basis of the experience matured by Soviet scholars during their work on various Russian editions and the MEGA[2] over time, Progress Publishers (Moscow), together with Lawrence and Wishart (London) and International Publishers (New York), produced an English translation of the *Grundrisse* and, autonomously, a Finnish translation.

All of the editions of the *Grundrisse* issued in the USSR, whether in the original, Russian or other foreign languages, have made an important contribution to the dissemination and reception of the *Grundrisse* all over the world. 90,000 copies of both Russian editions of the *Grundrisse* had already become rare items before 1991. In post-Soviet Russia both the *Grundrisse* and Marx himself had almost disappeared from scientific literature. A handful of scholars from the MEGA team at the RGASPI are now working under the supervision of the International Marx–Engels Foundation on the publication of Marx's works. However, even the advocates of Russian liberalism cannot afford to ignore some of the ideas of the *Grundrisse*, such as the questions it raises on the humanity, freedom, and role of science in society. In fact, Marx's ideas are crucial to our understanding of globalisation and capitalist development in Russia. The recent rise of interest in Marx's theory in its original sense by university students gives one hope that the *Grundrisse* will be appreciated by a new generation of Russians.

Bibliography

Complete editions

Marx, Karl (1939, 1941) *Grundrisse der Kritik der politischen Ökonomie (Rohentwurf) 1857–1858*, 2 vols, Marx–Engels–Lenin Institute Moskau (ed.), Moscow: Verlag für fremdsprachige Literatur.

Marx, Karl (1968, 1969) *Kritika politicheskoj ekonomii (Chernovoj nabrosok 1857–58 godov)*, in K. Marx and F. Engels, *Sočinenija*. 2nd edn, vol. 46: *Ekonomicheskie rukopisi 1857–1859 gg.* [*Economic Manuscripts of 1857–1859*], parts 1–2, Moscow: Izdatel'stvo politicheskoj literaturui.

Marx, Karl (1976, 1981) 'Ökonomische Manuskripte 1857/58', in Karl Marx and Friedrich Engels *Gesamtausgabe* (MEGA²), 2 vols (II/1.1 and II/1.2), Institut für Marxismus–Leninismus beim ZK der KPdSU and Institut für Marxismus–Leninismus beim ZK der SED (ed.), Berlin: Dietz Verlag.

Marx, Karl (1980) *Ekonomicheskie pukopisi 1857 1859 gg. (Pervonachal'nij variant 'Kapitala')* [*Economic Manuscripts of 1857–1859. First Version of Capita*] 2 vols, Moskva: Politizdat.

Partial editions

Marx, Karl (1904) 'Keri i Bastia, Iyul' 1857' ['Carey and Bastiat. July 1857'], *Pravda:* 190–201.

Marx, Karl (1905) *Keri i Bastia* [*Carey and Bastiat*], Saint-Petersburg: Malikh.

Marx, Karl (1922) 'Vvedenie *k kritike politicheskoj ekonomii*' ['*Introduction to the Critique of Political Economy*'], in Karl Marx, *K kritike politicheskoj ekonomii, 3-e izd.* [*A Critique of Political Economy*, 3rd edn], Petrograd: Kommunisticheskij universitet, pp. 8–28.

Marx, Karl (1930) 'Vvedenie k kritike politicheskoj ekonomii' ['Introduction to the Critique of Political Economy'], Baku: Azgiz (in Azerbaijanian).

Marx, Karl (1932) 'Glava o kapitale: Odin iz variantov plana "Kapitala"' ['A Chapter on Capital: One of the Variants of the Plan of "*Capital*"'], *Pravda*, no. 98, April 8: 1.

Marx, Karl (1933) 'Iz podgotovitel'nuikh rabot *k Kritike politicheskoj ekonomii* (Iz neopublikovannuich ekonomicheskikh rukopisei)' ['From the Preliminary Work for *A Contribution to the Critique of Political Economy*. From Unpublished Economic Manuscripts'], in Karl Marx, *K pyatidesyatiletiyu smerti K. Marksa. 1883–1933, sbornik, Institut mirovogo chozyajstva i mirovoj politiki pri Komakademii*, Moscow: Partijnoe izdatel'stvo, pp. 10–111.

Marx, Karl (1935a) 'Glava o den'gach' ['Chapter on Money'], *Archiv Marksa i Engel'sa*, vol. IV, by V. Adoratsky (ed.), Moscow: Partizdat ZK VKP(b).

Marx, Karl (1935b) 'Iz podgotovitel'nuikh tetradej Marksa *k Kritike politicheskoj ekonomii* (tetrad' II, 1858 g.)' ['From Marx's Notebooks *A Contribution to the Critique of Political Economy*. Notebook II, 1858'], in Karl Marx, *K kritike politicheskoj ekonomii*, [Moscow:] Partizdat, pp. 195–201.

Marx, Karl (1939a) 'Iz tetradi IV' ['From Notebook IV'], *Bol'shevik*, no. 11–12: 61–9.

Marx, Karl (1939b) 'Formui, predshestvuyushchie kapitalisticheskomu proizvodstvu' (Forms which precede capitalist production), *Proletarskaya revolyutsiya*, no. 3: 149–86.

Marx, Karl (1940a) 'Formui, predshestvuyushchie kapitalisticheskomu proizvodstvu', ['Forms which Precede Capitalist Production'], *Vestnik drevnej istorii*, no. 1 (10): 8–26.

Marx, Karl (1940b) 'Formui, predshestvuyushchie kapitalisticheskomu proizvodstvu' ['Forms which Precede Capitalist Production'], Marx–Engels–Lenin Institute bei CC VKP(b) (ed.), Moskva: Gosudarstvennoe izdatel'stvo politicheskoj literatury. Published in 50,000 copies, and reissued in 51,200 copies.

Marx, Karl (1941) 'Formui, predshestvuyushchie kapitalisticheskomu proizvodstvu' ['Forms which Precede Capitalist Production'], Erevan: Gospolitizdat Arm. SSR (in Armenian).

Marx, Karl (1952) 'Formui, predshestvuyushchie kapitalisticheskomu proizvodstvu' ['Forms which Precede Capitalist Production'], Tbilisi: Gospolitizdat Grus. SSR (in Georgian).

Marx, Karl (1965–8) 'Iz rukopisi Karla Marksa *Kritika politicheskoj ekonomii* (Chernovoj nabrosok 1857–1858 gg.)' ['From Karl Marx's Manuscript *A Critique of Political Economy* (Rough Draft of 1857–1858'], *Voprosy filosofii*, 1965, no. 8: 126–43; 1966, no. 1: 129–33; no. 5: 131–42; no. 6: 143–56; no. 9: 86–101; no. 10: 114–24; 1967, no. 6: 93–108; no. 7: 106–25; 1968, no. 5: 106–10.

Critical literature on the **Grundrisse**

Achundov, A.G. (1957) 'Kritika Marksom melkoburzhuaznoj teorii "rabochikh deneg"' ['Marx's Critique of the Theory of "Labour Money"'], *Uchenuie zapiski Azerbajdzhanskogo pedagogicheskogo instituta russkogo yazuika i literaturui*: 81–94.

Antonova, Irina K. (1983) 'Rarzrabotka Marksom strukturui I toma *Kapitala* (1857–1867 gg.)' ['Marx's Work in Progress on the First Volume of *Capital*. 1857–1867'], in Vv. Aa., *Ocherki po istorii "Kapitala" K. Marksa*, Moscow: Politizdat, pp. 172–205.

Bolduirev, Igor' A. (1958) 'K voprosu ob analize "kapitala voobzhe" v ekonomicheskoj rukopisi Marksa (1857–1858 gg.)' ['On the Analysis of "Capital as a Whole" in Marx's Economic Manuscript of 1857–1858'], in Vv. Aa., *Nauchnuie zapiski. Odessky pedagogicheskij institut im. K.D. Ushinsky*, vol. 21: 147–68.

Bolduirev, Igor' A. (1984) 'Itak, etot tom gorov … (K istorii sozdaniya okonchatel'nogo varianta I toma "Kapitala" K. Marksa)' ['"So, this volume is ready…". On the History

of the Creation of the Final Version of the First Volume of *Capital* by K. Marx'],
Muisl': 16–30.

Bratus', Sergej N. (1940) 'Voprosui sobstvennosti v rukopisi Marksa *Formui, predshestvuyushchie kapitalisticheskomu proizvodstvu*' ['Questions of Property in Marx's
Manuscript *Forms Which Precede Capitalist Production*'], *Sovetskoe pravo*, no. 11:
28–39.

Bronsky, Mstislav G. (1936) 'Neopublikovannaya rukopis' Marksa o den'gax' ['Marx's
Unpublished Manuscript on Money'], *Problemi ekonomiki*, no. 2: 26–39.

Brushlinsky, Vladimir K. (1987) 'O nekotoruikh netochnostyakh v nauchnom apparate
pervuich pyati tomov II otdela MEGA', *Novye materialui o K. Markse i F. Engel'se i
ob izdanii ikh proizvedeny. Sbornik*, no. 3: 187–94.

Chaika, T.O. (1976) 'K. Marks ob istoricheskikh putyakh i perspektivakh formirivaniya
tselostnoj lichnosti (Na materialakh 'Ekonomicheskikh rukopisej 1857–1858 godov')'
['K. Marx on the Historical Paths and Perspectives of the Formation of Individuality.
On the Materials of the "Economic Manuscripts of 1857–1858"'], *Problemi filosofii:
Mizhvid. nauk. zb.*, no. 37: 16–23 (in Ukrainian).

Chepurenko, Alexander Iu. (1985) 'Nabroski nekotoruikh polozheny vtorogo toma "Kapitala" v economicheskoj rukopisi K. Marksa 1857–1858 godov' ['Sketches of some
Statements in the Second Volume of *Capital* in the Economic Manuscript of
1857–1858 by K. Marx'], *Novye materialui o K. Markse i F. Engel'se i ob izdanii ikh
proizvedeny. Sbornik*, no. 40): 187–98.

Kogan, Albert M. (1966) 'O metodologii plana shesti knig K. Marksa' ['On the Methodology of the Plan of Six Books by K. Marx'], *Obshchestvennuie nauki. Nauchnuie
trudy Moskovskogo ekonomiko-statisticheskogo instituta*, vol. 1: 248–64.

Kogan, Albert M. (1967) 'O neizuchennom plane issledovanij Marksa' ['On the Unstud-
ied Plan of Marx's Research'], *Voprosy filosofii*, no. 9: 77–87.

Kogan, Albert M. (1983) *V tvorcheskoj laboratorii Karla Marksa: (Plan ekonomicheskikh issledovanij 1857–1859 gg. i 'Kapital')*, Moscow: 'Muisl'.

Lapidus, Iosif A. (1941) 'Dokapitalisticheskie formui proizvodstva v svete novoj rukopisi
Marksa' ['Pre-capitalist Forms of Production in the Light of Marx's New Manuscript'], *Problemui ekonomiki*, no. 1: 132–49.

Leont'ev, Lev A. [under pseudonym Alexander Leont'ev] (1932) 'K rukopisi Marksa'
['On Marx's Manuscript'], *Pod znamenem marksizma*, no. 11–12: 41–62.

Leont'ev, Lev A. [under pseudonym Alexander Leont'ev] (1933) 'Predislovie'
['Preface'], *Archiv Marksa i Engel'sa*, vol. II (VII): III–XXIII.

Leont'ev, Lev A. (1946) *O predvaritel'nom variante 'Kapitala' Marksa*, Moscow–
Leningrad: USSR Academy of Sciences Publications.

Maluish, Alexander I. (1963) 'Ekonomicheskie rukopisi Marksa 1857–1858 godov kak
vazhnejshy etap v razvitii marksistskoj politicheskoj ekonomii' ['Marx's Economic
Manuscripts of 1857–1858 as an Important Stage in the Development of Marxist Political Economy'], in Vv. Aa., *Iz istorii marksizma i mezhdunarodnogo rabochego
dvizheniya*, Moscow: Gosudarstvennoe izdatel'stvo politicheskoj literatury, pp.
64–106.

Maluish, Alexander I. (1966) *Formirovanie marksistskoj politicheskoj ekonomii* [*The
Formation of Marxist Political Economy*], Moscow: Politizdat.

Mareev, Sergej N. (1973) 'Edinstvo logicheskogo i istoricheskogo v ekonomicheskikh
rukopisyakh K. Marksa 1857–1858 gg.' ['The Unity of Logical and Historical in K.
Marx's Economic Manuscripts of 1857–185'] in Vv. Aa., *Iz istorii marksizma i mezhdunarodnogo rabochego dvizheniya*, Moscow: Politizdat, pp. 112–34.

Melikyan, Elena A. (1983) 'Razrabotka Marksom teorii deneg v ekonomicheskoj rukopisi 1857–1858 gg.' ['Marx's Work in Progress on the Theory of Money in the Economic Manuscript of 1857–1858'], in Vv. Aa., *Ocherki po istorii "Kapitala" K. Marksa*, Moscow: Politizdat, pp. 34–62.

Osobova (Ossobowa), Inna (1990) 'Über einige Probleme der ökonomischen Studien von Marx im Jahre 1857 vom Standpunkt des Historikers' ['On some Problems of Marx's Economic Studies in 1857 from a Historian's Point of View'], *Beiträge zur Marx–Engels-Forschung* (Berlin), no. 29: 147–61.

Rezhibek, E. Ya. (1974) 'Razrabotka K. Marksom metoda kritiki v protsesse sozdaniya teorii pribavochnoj stoimosti' ['K. Marx's Work in Progress on Critical Method in the Creation of the Theory of Surplus Value'], *Izvestiya Sev.-Kavk. nauchnogo tsentra vuisshej shkolui*, no. 3: 3–16.

Tronev, Konstantin P. (1970) 'Voprosui tovarnogo proizvodstva pri kapitalizme i pri sotsialisme v svete *Ekonomicheskikh rukopisej 1857–1858 godov*' ['Questions of Commodity Production in Capitalism and Socialism in the Light of the *Economic manuscripts of 1857–1858*'], *Vestnik MGU. Seriya 6. Ekonomika*, no. 4: 34–46.

Veller, Pavel L. (1940) 'Ekonomicheskajya rukopis' Marksa 1857–1858 gg.' ['Marx's Economic Manuscript of 1857–1858'], *Proletarskaya revolyutsiya*, no. 1: 197–200.

Veller, Pavel L. (1941) 'Iz opuita rabotui nad literaturnuim nasledstvom Karla Marksa' ['The Experience of Work on Karl Marx's Literary Bequest'], *Sovetskaya nauka*, no. 2: 148–53.

Veller, Pavel (2001) 'Marx' ökonomische Manuskripte von 1857–1858, 3 August 1934', ['Marx's Economical Manuscripts of 1857–1858, 3 August 1934'], *Beiträge zur Marx–Engels-Forschung. Neue Folge. Sonderband 3 (Stalinismus und das Ende der ersten Marx–Engels-Gesamtausgabe. 1931–1941)*: 277–91.

Vygodski, Vitali S. (1965) *Istoriya odnogo velikogo otkruitiya Karla Marksa*, Moscow: Izdatel'stvo Muisl'.

Vygodski, Vitali S. (1970) *K istorii sozdaniya 'Kapitala'* [*Concerning the History of the Creation of Capital*], Moscow: Izdatel'stvo Muisl'.

Vygodski, Vitali S. (1974) *Ekonomicheskoe obosnovanie teorii nauchnogo kommunizma* [*Economic Basis of the Theory of Scientific Communism*], Moscow: Izdatel'stvo politicheskoj literaturui.

Vygodski Vitali S. (1987) 'Zur Frage des Beginns der Marxschen Arbeit am Manuskript 1857/58' ['On the Beginning of Marx's Work on the Manuscript of 1857/58'], *Der hallesche Beitrag zur Marx–Engels-Forschung*, no. 42: 32–9.

Vygodski, Vitali S. and Bagaturiya, Georgij A. (1976) *Ekonomicheskoe nasledie Karla Marksa (istoriya, soderzhanie, metodologiya)* [*The Economic Heritage of Karl Marx. History, Contents, Method*], Moscow: Izdatel'stvo Muisl'.

Vv. Aa. (1987) *Pervonachal'nuy variant 'Kapitala'* (Ekonomicheskie rukopisi K. Marksa 1857–1858 godov) (The first version of '*Capital*'. K. Marx's economic manuscripts of 1857–1858), (Autors: Irina Antonova, Wolfgang Baumgart, Alexander Chepurenko, Rolf Hecker, Wolfgang Jahn, Albert Kogan, Thomas Marxhausen, Larisa Miskievich, Rustem Nureev, Dina Plachotnaya, Mikhail Ternovsky, Vladimir Shkredov, Valentina Smirnova, Nely Numyanzeva, Lyudmila Vasina and Vitali Vygodski), Moscow: Politizdat.

Other references

Cohen, Jack (1973) 'Getting to the Bedrock of Marx', *The Morning Star*, 28 June: 4.

Miskievich, Larisa (2008) 'Wie kamen ökonomische Manuskripte nach Moskau?' ['How did the Economic Manuscripts get to Moscow?'], *MEGA-Studien* 2000/2: 3–18.

Novitsky, Rostislav (1939) 'Predlozheniya k perspektivnomu planu publikatsii rukopisnogo nasledstva Marksa, 10 dekabrya 1939 g.' ['Suggestions for a Prospective Plan of Publication of Marx's Handwritten Bequest, December 10, 1939'], RGASPI. F. 71. Op. 11. D. 12.

RGASPI 1: 'Stand der Arbeiten in der ökonomischen Abteilung' ['State of Work in the Economic Department']. F. 374. Op. 1. D. 12. L. 31.

RGASPI 2: 'Proizvodstvennoe zadanie sortudnikam Sektora Marksa i Engel'sa na IV kvartal 1935 g.' ['Production Task for Colleagues at the Marx–Engels Department for the IVth quarter of 1935']. F. 71. Op. 1. D. 77. L. 88.

RGASPI 3: F. 71. Op. 1. D. 77. L. 106, 107; D. 78. L. 6, 7.

RGASPI 4: F. 71. Op. 1. D. 77. L. 138.

RGASPI 5: 'Produkziya IMEL za 1 kvartal 1939 po III kvartal 1940 g.' ['Publications of the Marx–Engels–Lenin Institute from the First Quarter of 1939 to the Third Quarter of 1940']. Fond 71. Opis 1. Delo 13. L. 11 and 39.

RGASPI 6: Novitsky, Rostislav 'Spravka o rukopisyach Marksa i Engelsa, ne opubliko-vannikh na 1 iyunya 1940 g.' ['Information about Manuscripts by Marx and Engels Unpublished as of July 1, 1940']. F. 71. Op. 1. D. 81. L. 7–37.

Vv. Aa. (1934) *Karl Marx. Chronik seines Lebens in Einzelndaten* [*Karl Marx. A Chronicle of his Life in Dates*], Marx–Engels–Lenin Institute (ed.), Moscow: Marx–Engels-Verlag.

Vv. Aa. (1969) *Literaturnoe nasledstvo K. Marksa i F. Engel'sa: Istoriya publikatsii i izucheniya v SSSR* [*The Literary Bequest of K. Marx and F. Engels: A History of its Publication and Study in the USSR*], Moscow: Politizdat.

15 Japan

Hiroshi Uchida

The translation of the *Grundrisse* was of great significance in Japan because it changed the way of looking at Marx's critique of political economy: it overcame determinist misconceptions of his theory and opened up diverse possibilities for its further development. The study of the *Grundrisse* in Japan may be divided into three historical periods. The first began in 1953, when the complete German text became available in Japan, and ended in 1965, when the Japanese translation was finished. The second started in 1966 and ended in 1974, when *Grundrisse* studies in Japan were summarized by non-orthodox Japanese Marxists in two works (Vv. Aa. 1974; Morita and Yamada 1974). The third and final one stretches from 1975 to the present. Let us look more closely at this history.

The first period (1953–65) saw the publication from 1958 to 1965 of the five-volume *Keizaigakuhihan'yoko* [*Foundations of the Critique of Political Economy*], which included the full content of the 1953 German edition of the *Grundrisse*. Volume one contained the 'Introduction' and the 'Chapter on Money', volumes two and three most of the 'Chapter on Capital', volume four the conclusion of the 'Chapter on Capital' and the extracts from David Ricardo dated 1850–1, and volume five the fragment on 'Bastiat and Carey', the preparatory materials for *A Contribution to the Critique of Political Economy* (*Urtext*) and all the indices of Marx's notebooks drawn up either by himself or by the German editors. Japan thus became the first country where the *Grundrisse* was translated, and in spite of its complexity the printing of more than 57,000 copies ensured a wide circulation. The good quality of the translation also contributed to the spread of Marxian terminology.

In fact, some partial translations of the *Grundrisse* had been published since the 1920s. In 1926 the 'Introduction' appeared in two different versions: one as an appendix to the *Contribution to the Critique of Political Economy* (Marx 1926a), the other (Marx 1926b) in the *Marukusu–Engerusu Chosakushu* edition [*Marx–Engels Selected Works*], published between 1928 and 1935 in 27 volumes (32 books). Three years later, the short text on 'Bastiat and Carey' came out in the same edition (Marx 1929). And in 1936 a third portion of the *Grundrisse* appeared, comprising two fragments from the chapters on money and capital that were thought to help explain the economic crisis of the 1930s (Marx 1936). The last extract, 'Forms which Precede Capitalist Production', appeared in 1947 (Marx 1947). However, it was translated from a Russian edition of 1940, and it was necessary to wait until 1954 for the first translation from German (Marx 1954).

The second period (1966–74) witnessed epoch-making studies of the *Grundrisse*. Kiyoaki Hirata's *Keizaigaku to rekishininshiki* [*Political Economy and Recognition of History*] (Hirata 1971) liberated readings of the text from the viewpoint of 'Marxism–Leninism'. The author inquired why 'Original Accumulation of Capital' and 'Forms which Precede Capitalist Production' (Marx 1973: 459–514) followed 'Inversion of the Law of Appropriation' (Marx 1973: 458). In the very first circuit of capital, he argued, the capital with which the capitalist appropriates labour power is non-surplus capital, that is, accumulation of his own labour ((a) 'law of the appropriation of one's own labour') and his exchange with the wage-labourer for the appropriation of his labour power is based on equivalence ((b) 'law of exchange of equivalents'). However, at the beginning of the second circuit, in a non-equivalent exchange, the capitalist appropriates labour power by means of the wage-labourer's surplus labour that has resulted from the first circuit (conversion of law (b)), so that at the end of the second circuit the capitalist appropriates the other's surplus labour by means of the other's surplus labour itself, not his own labour (conversion of law (a)). It is clear, therefore, that capital is accumulation of another's (the wage-labourer's) surplus labour and that both laws undergo conversion. This twofold conversion is based on labour power that produces another's surplus labour for the capitalist. But how is labour power as a commodity originally given? It is a historical result of primitive accumulation. In 'Forms which Precede Capitalist Production' Marx shows the identity of labour and property, and in 'Original Accumulation of Capital' he demonstrates that their separation brings about the modern proletarian who is destined to subsist as a wage-labourer. Capitalist accumulation and primitive accumulation simultaneously proceed and interconnect worldwide. In Marx's nineteenth-century world, western capitalism combined with pre-capitalist community (*Gemeinwesen*) in India or China (Asiatic despotism), in the New World (Roman slavery) and eastern Europe (Russian serfdom). In Hirata's view, moreover, Marx represented the economically converted relationship of domination–subordination as total slavery. The state was a trader of tributes (surplus product). The capital of advanced nations found an opportunity to initiate commodity exchange with Asian despotic states, thereby turning Asian communities into commodity-producing societies and furthering their shift towards capitalism.

Seiji Mochizuki's work of 1974, *Marukusurekishiriron no kenkyu* [*A Study of Marx's Theory of History*], developed Hirata's study of the *Grundrisse*. Mochizuki defines Marx's theory of history as one that places capitalism within world history, in such a way as to obtain a number of general criteria. These criteria specify past modes of production, such as Asiatic despotism, American slavery, Russian serfdom and west European parcellized agrarian property [*Parzelleneigentum*], from the viewpoint of the identity of labour and property or on the principle that those who labour are entitled to the due product of their labour. According to Mochizuki, Marx's view of the contemporary world corresponds to this conception. His theory analyses world history into geologically progressive strata piled vertically on top of one another, while at the same time it regards contemporary modes of production as world history fallen sideways on to a horizontal plane.

The year 1974 was an especially fruitful year, as two other important works also appeared on Marx's manuscripts of 1857–8. The first, published by the journal *Gendainoriron* [*Present-day Theory*], was the proceedings of a symposium of synthesis and debate *Keizaigakuhihan'yoko kenkyu no shomondai* [*Problems of Grundrisse Studies*], in which Kazumitu Okiura, Suguru Hosomi, Mochizuki, Yamada and Morita had taken part (Vv. Aa. 1974). The main topics of discussion included: the civilizing influence of capital, the Marxian conception of history outlined in 'Forms which Precede Capitalist Production', the labour process in the automatic system of machinery, and the whole issue of free time.

The second work, *Komentaru keizaigakuhihan'yoko* [*Commentaries on the Grundrisse*] (Morita and Yamada 1974), consisted of two volumes of essays by Yamada, Shigenobu Kishimoto, Morita, Hiroshi Uchida, Seiji Kikka, Kimitoshi Mukai, Kazumitsu Okiura, Yoshiko Kuba and the already mentioned Mochizuki. In addition to a chapter-by-chapter commentary on the main sections of the *Grundrisse*, it dealt with the position of *Grundrisse* in Marx's thought, the transformation of money into capital, the circulation and reproduction of capital, humanity and nature in the *Grundrisse* and the theory of alienation.

The third period, since 1975, has seen a new Japanese translation of the *Grundrisse*, which appeared in two volumes in 1981 and 1993, in over 7,000 copies and entitled *1857–58nen no keizaigakusoko* [*Economic Manuscripts 1857–58*]. These were parts 1 and 2 of the nine-volume *Marukusu Shihonronsokoshu* (Marx's manuscripts of *Capital*), published from 1981 to 1994 in the second section of MEGA². The translation is generally improved.

The *Grundrisse* continued to arouse great interest, and three new monographs were devoted to it in the 1980s. In his *Keizaigakuhihan'yoko no kenkyu* [*A Study of the Grundrisse*] (Uchida 1982), Uchida argues that for Marx capital is a civilizing movement that unconsciously creates the potential to emancipate the producers in the form of surplus labour time (which the capitalist actually monopolizes and realizes as profit). As wage-labourers acquire the 'general intellect' needed to create, manage and develop the forces of production, this becomes a capacity to observe capitalist society critically and to recognize that capitalist surplus labour-time is nothing but their own achievement. They will then necessarily claim it as their own free time, to be utilized for social activity, 'artistic, scientific etc development of individuals' (Marx 1973: 706).

Crucially important is the fact that living labour is the basic condition of existence for capital (i.e. the capitalist). As the technology-based capitalist mode of production develops, the ratio of living labour to objectified labour in the form of capital diminishes, and the law of value based on living labour ceases to operate as the basis of the capitalist mode of production. At the same time, wage-labourers with a developed general intellect come to realize that capitalist surplus labour time is in fact their own achievement, to which they are entitled as a fund for their own emancipation. This tendency opens up a non-violent path to post-capitalist society.

Yamada's *Keizaigakuhihan no kindaizo* [*Marx's Vision of Modernity in the Critique of Political Economy*] (Yamada 1985) investigates economic theory in the *Grundrisse* with special reference to contemporary world capitalism. Yamada summarizes his study of the *Grundrisse* under three aspects of modernity: civil society, capitalist society and industrial society, each of which is contradictory. Thus, civil society contains a potential for free individuality, but this remains only a formal potential. Capitalist society develops a potential for wage-labourers to associate to establish a post-capitalist society, but it also blocks any purposive orientation through the labour contract and the degradation or deskilling of wage labour. Industrial society is born at first as a society of subjective industry on the part of self-employed workers, but then this is reified into the industrial power of capitalist production. In the long term, however, Yamada argues, this power of industry increases the objective possibility of free time and hence the potential for the emancipation of wage workers.

In 1985 Uchida published another study of the *Grundrisse*: *Chukimarukusu no keizaigakuhihan* [*The Critique of Political Economy in Marx's Middle Period*]. In Chapter 3, 'The *Grundrisse* and Hegel's *Logic*', he focuses on the letter to Engels of 14 January 1858 in which Marx remarked that Hegel's *Logic* had been very suggestive for his arrangement of the material in the *Grundrisse*, and demonstrates the correspondence between the 'Introduction' and the 'Doctrine of the Notion [*Begriff*]'; the 'Chapter on Money' and the 'Doctrine of Being [*Sein*]', the 'Chapter on Capital' and the 'Doctrine of Essence [*Wesen*]'. An improved and expanded version of this chapter was later published in English under the title *Marx's Grundrisse and Hegel's Logic* (Uchida 1988).

Lastly, mention should be made of two works that have appeared in the course of the last decade. In 1997 a facsimile of Marx's original text of the *Grundrisse* (Marx 1997) was printed in 150 copies with an introduction by Teinosuke Otani – the only such edition available anywhere in the world. And in 2001 another collective work, *Keizaigakuhihan'yoko niokeru rekishi to riron* [*Logic and History in Marx's Grundrisse*] (Nakamura 2001) by Satoru Nakamura, Shuichi Kakuta, Michio Akama, Hiroyoshi Makino and Kimio Noda, received special attention. Placing the *Grundrisse* in a twenty-first-century context, they showed how it opens a broader perspective for systematic analysis of the problems of contemporary world capitalism, especially economic inequality and ecological crisis.

Bibliography

Complete editions

Marx, Karl (1958, 1959, 1961, 1962, 1965) *Keizaigakuhihan'yoko*, Tokyo: Otsukishoten. Vol. 1 trans. by Ikuya Fukamachi, Kojiro Takagi and Shuichi Takemura, and published in 15,050 copies; vol. 2 trans. by Chuhei Sugiyama, Takuji Toyokawa, Hitoshi Sugiyama and Teruetsu Nakamine, and published in 12,092 copies; vol. 3 trans. by Teruetsu Nakamine, Masaki Tejima, Isao Hashimoto and Kinzaburo Sato, and published in 11,564 copies; vol. 4 trans. by Ken Kurita, Ikuya Fukamachi and Kiyotomo Ishido, and published in 9,558 copies; vol. 5 trans. by Ujikata Nakamura and Shuichi Takemura, and published in 9,062 copies.

Marx, Karl (1981, 1993) *1857–58nen no keizaigakusoko*, Tokyo: Otsukishoten. Vol. 1 trans. by Kojiro Takagi (translation supervisor), Nobuo Iimori, Tomonaga Tairako, Ujikata Nakamura and Chikara Rachi, and published in 4,479 copies; vol. 2 trans. by Teinosuke Otani (translation supervisor), Katsuhiko Asami, Masahito Kameda, Susumu Takenaga, Mari Nomura, Nao Hagiwara, Hideki Masutani, Jun Matsuo, Toshiro Miyazawa, Hiromi Morishita and Norimasa Watanabe, and published in 2,773 copies.

Marx, Karl (1997) *Marukusu jihitsugenko fakushimiriban keizaigakuhihan'yoko* [*Foundations of the Critique of Political Economy: Facsimile Reproduction of Marx's Original Manuscripts*], Tokyo: Otsukishoten.

Partial editions

Marx, Karl (1926a), 'Keizaigakuhihan eno josetsu' ['Introduction to the Critique of Political Economy'], trans. by Minoru Miyagawa, in Karl Marx, *Keizaigakuhihan* [*Contribution to the Critique of Political Economy*], Tokyo: Sobunsha, pp. 283–325.

Marx, Karl (1926b) 'Keizaigakuhihan no joron' ['Introduction to the Critique of Political Economy'], trans. by Tsunao Inomata, in *Marukusu–Engerusu Chosakushu*, vol. 7, Tokyo: Shinchosha, pp. 1–52.

Marx, Karl (1929) 'Basutea to keari' ['Bastiat and Carey'], trans. by Kenji Mizushima, in *Marukusu–Engerusu Zenshu*, vol. 7, Tokyo: Kaizosha, pp. 7–21.

Marx, Karl (1936) 'Keizaigakuhihan eno junbitekirosaku kara' ['From Marx's Preparatory Works for *Contribution to the Critique of Political Economy*'], trans. by The Pacific Research Society, in Karl Marx, *Kahei no hatten to kyoko: marukusu kinen ronbunshu* [*Development of Money and Crisis: Essays for the Half-Centennial Anniversary of Karl Marx's Death*], Tokyo: Sobunkaku, pp. 1–70.

Marx, Karl (1947) 'Shihonseiseisan ni senkosuru shokeitai' ['Forms which Precede Capitalist Production'], trans. by Kan'ichi Iida, *Rekishigakukenkyu* [*Studies of History*], No. 129: 89–238.

Marx, Karl (1954) 'Shihonshugitekiseisan ni senkousuru shokeitai' ['Forms which Precede Capitalist Production']), trans. by Susumu Sato, in Karl Marx, *Sekaidaishiso. Marx* [*The Great Thoughts of the World. Marx*], vol. 12, Tokyo: Kawadeshobo, pp. 259–302.

Critical literature on the Grundrisse

Hirata, Kiyoaki (1971) *Keizaigaku to rekishininshiki*, Tokyo: Iwanamishoten.

Mochizuki, Seiji (1974) *Marukusurekishiriron no kenkyu*, Tokyo: Iwanamishoten.

Morita, Kiriro and Yamada, Toshio (1974) *Komentaru keizaigakuhihan'yoko*, Tokyo: Nihonhyoronsha.

Nakamura, Satoru (ed.) (2001) *Keizaigakuhihan'yoko niokeru rekishi to riron*, Tokyo: Aokishoten.

Uchida, Hiroshi (1982) *Keizaigakuhihan'yoko no kenkyu*, Tokyo: Shinhyoron.

Uchida, Hiroshi (1985) *Grundrisse: Chukimarukusu no keizaigakuhihan*, Tokyo: Yuhikaku.

Uchida, Hiroshi (1988) *Marx's Grundrisse and Hegel's Logic*, London: Routledge.

Vv. Aa. (1974) 'Keizaigakuhihan'yoko' kenkyu no shomondai', *Gendainoriron*' [*Present-day Theory*], June.

Yamada, Toshio (1985) *Keizaigakuhihan no kindaizo*, Tokyo: Yuhikaku.

Other reference

Marx, Karl (1973) *Grundrisse: Foundations of the Critique of Political Economy (Rough Draft)*, Harmondsworth: Penguin.

16 China

Zhongpu Zhang

Marx's *Grundrisse* has circulated for a long time and had a significant impact in China. Initially, only some important fragments of the *Grundrisse* were introduced into China. As early as 1930, Li Yimang, a theorist and revolutionary of the Chinese Communist Party, translated and edited selected articles by Marx, where the full text of the translation of the 'Introduction' appeared for the first time (Marx 1930). Later the 'Introduction' was included in the Chinese translations of Marx's *A Contribution to the Critique of Political Economy*. In 1938 the first publication of the Chinese translation of all of the three volumes of *Capital* in China was received with much enthusiasm among theorists and numerous readers.

After the founding of the People's Republic of China in 1949, the translation, publication and research of Marxist works developed rapidly. In 1956 another important part of the *Grundrisse*, 'Forms which Precede Capitalist Production', was translated into Chinese by Ri Zhi and published in a separate edition by the People's Publishing House, arousing a vigorous debate in the academic world (Marx 1956). Prior to the publication of the full translation of the *Grundrisse* in 1963, this pamphlet was reprinted twice.

In the early 1960s, Liu Xiaoran of the Institute of Economics of the Chinese Academy of Sciences began to translate the *Grundrisse* into Chinese from the German edition of 1953. The translation was published in five installments by the People's Publishing House between 1962 and 1978 (No. 2–4 were printed twice) with the title *Zheng zhi jing ji xue pi pan da gang* [*Outlines of the Critique of Political Economy Rough Draft*]. This was the first Chinese translation of the whole text, and although it was only distributed in selected circles and in a limited number of copies, it largely contributed to satisfying theorists and readers' wishes whilst promoting the study and research of Marxist theory.

In 1953 the Central Committee of the Communist Party of China (CCCPC) founded the Central Compilation and Translation Bureau (CCTB) with the aim to compile, translate and study the classical works of Marxism. One of its tasks is to translate and publish a Chinese edition of the Collected Works of Marx and Engels (CWME) in a collective effort. The first Chinese edition of CWME comprises of 50 volumes in total and was published between 1955 and 1985. The *Grundrisse* was included in volume 46 (I–II) of this edition and printed by the

People's Publishing House between 1979 and 1980 in 37,000 and 33,000 copies respectively with the title *Jing ji xue shou gao 1857–1858* [*Economic Manuscripts of 1857–1858*]. This new and improved translation was based on the original German text of the *Grundrisse* published in Moscow in 1939–41, and made use of volume 46 (I and II) of the second Russian edition of 1968–9, reproducing the headings provided by the Russian editors. It includes a preface by the Chinese editors and translators, where the conditions of the manuscripts, its main content and scientific value are introduced, and an appendix of indexes at the end that former Chinese versions lacked.

Once the first Chinese edition of CWME was completed, in 1985 the CCTB began to edit and translate the second Chinese edition of CWME in more volumes, due to a decision of the CCCPC. This edition is divided into four parts, the second of which is '*Capital* and its Manuscripts', comprising of 15 volumes. The *Grundrisse* constitutes the first two volumes of the second part and was printed in 10,000 copies with the same title of the first CWME edition. It is based on the original text of MEGA^2 II/1.1 and II/1.2 (1976–81) and makes use of volume 42 of the German edition of Marx and Engels *Werke* (MEW), published by the former GDR. This edition differs from the first two Chinese editions, and only has a small number of headings inserted where necessary by the editors according to the content, while it retains all of Marx's original headings. Its structure is closer to the original text, the translation is more precise, and the notes and indexes are accurate and complete. It is the most popular and authoritative version in China. After its introduction in China, research on the *Grundrisse* became more and more extensive and thorough.

Moreover, in 1981, the Chinese Research Society on *Capital* was founded. This non-governmental academic organization was created to perform further research in the Marx's main work. One of its units, the group working on the history of the writing of *Capital*, systematically discussed each of the preliminary versions of *Capital* in its annual meetings. Several Chinese academic works have dedicated chapters to the *Grundrisse*, for instance: *Zi ben lun chuang zuo shi* [*A History of Writing Capital*] by Ma Jianxing and Guo Jiyan (1983), *Zi ben lun chuang zuo shi jian bian* [*A Short History of the Writing of Capital*] by Tian Guang and Lu Lijun (1992), and *Ma ke si jing ji xue shou gao yan jiu* [*A Research on Marx's Economic Manuscripts*] by Tang Zaixin (1993). In the last decade of the twentieth century, important monographs on the *Grundrisse* were published in China, such as *Zi ben lun di yi gao (1857–1858 yan jiu)* [*Research on the First Rough Draft of Capital. Manuscripts of 1857–1858*], a collection edited by Zhao Hong (1992), which reflects the outcomes of the study of the *Grundrisse* in Chinese academic circles. Two other books by young Chinese scholars, *Ma ke si huang jin shi dai de li lun jie jing* [*Marx's Theoretical Fruit in His Golden Age – Research on the First Rough Draft of Capital*] by Wang Shuibo (1991) and *Ma ke si bu huo zhi nian de si kao* [*Reflections of Marx in his Forties*] by Gu Hailiang (1993) are praised by educational authorities. Furthermore, a research group composed of a dozen scholars carried out extensive studies on Marx's plan to write six books on economics, formulated in the *Grundrisse*; their work resulted in a long treatise: *Guan yu ma ke si ji hua xie de liu ce jing ji xue zhu zuo* [*Exploring the Continuation of Capital. On the Six Books of Economics Works that Marx Planned to Write*], edited by Tang Zaixin (1995).

Moreover, since the 1960s many politics, social sciences, philosophy, political economy and university journals have published several articles by Chinese authors on the *Grundrisse* and on the matters discussed in them.

Through the Marxist Theoretical Research and Development Project launched at the beginning of the twenty-first century the CCTB aims to compile, translate and publish ten volumes *of Selected Works of Marx and Engels* to meet the needs of a large number of readers. Some important parts of the *Grundrisse* will be soon included in volume nine.

In short, the history of *Grundrisse's* circulation of its far-reaching impact presents one side of the great influence of Marxist theory in China.

Bibliography

Complete editions

Marx, Karl (1962, 1963, 1964, 1975, 1978) *Zheng zhi jing ji xue pi pan da gang*, Beijing: People's Publishing House. Vol. 1: 1975, vol. 2 1962 and 1978, vol. 3 1963 and 1977, vol. 4 1964 and 1978, vol. 5 1978.

Marx, Karl (1979, 1980) *Jing ji xue shou gao 1857–1858*, in *Ma ke si en ge si quan ji* [*Collected Works of Marx and Engels*], vol. 46 (I and II), Beijing: People's Publishing House.

Marx, Karl (1995, 1998) *Jing ji xue shou gao 1857–1858*, in *Ma ke si en ge si quan ji zhong wen di er ban* [*Second Chinese Edition of the Collected Works of Marx and Engels*], vols 30 and 31, Beijing: People's Publishing House.

Partial editions

Marx, Karl (1930) 'Dao yan' ['Introduction']), in Karl Marx, *Ma ke si lun wen xuan yi* [*Selected Articles by Marx*], Shanghai: Shanghai Social Science Research Society.

Marx, Karl (1956) 'Zi ben zhu yi sheng chan yi qian de ge zhong xing shi' ['Forms which Precede Capitalist Production'], Beijing: People's Publishing House.

Critical literature on the Grundrisse

Gu, Hailiang (1993) *Ma ke si bu huo zhi nian de si kao*, Beijing: Renmin University of China Press.

Ma, Jianxing and Guo Jiyan (1983) *Zi ben lun chuang zuo shi*, Shangdong: People's Publishing House.

Tang, Zaixin (1993) *Ma ke si jing ji xue shou gao yan jiu*, Wuhan: Wuhan University Press.

Tang, Zaixin (ed.) (1995) *Guan yu ma ke si ji hua xie de liu ce jing ji xue zhu zuo*, Beijing: China Finance Press.

Tian, Guang and Lu, Lijun (1992) *Zi ben lun chuang zuo shi jian bian*, Zhejiang: Zhejiang People's Publishing House.

Wang, Shuibo (1991) *Ma ke si huang jin shi dai de li lun jie jing*, Beijing: CCCPC Party School Press.

Zhao, Hong (ed.) (1992) *Zi ben lun di yi gao (1857–1858 yan jiu)*, Jinan: Shangdong People's Publishing House.

17 France

André Tosel

The first unabridged translation of the *Grundrisse* into French was published in two volumes in 1967–8. This translation, by Roland Dangeville, was based on the German version of 1953 and printed by Anthropos publishers with the title *Fondements de la critique de l'économie politique* [*Foundations of the Critique of Political Economy*], but later received negative appraisals from specialists. In fact, it contained little philological information on Marx's manuscripts, and did not respect the semantics of the text, characterised by many references to the conceptual apparatus of its Hegelian roots.

However, despite its limitations, this translation enabled intellectuals and political militants to approach this Marxian work for the first time, and this was all the more important in view of the fact that it appeared at the end of the 1960s, during a very intense phase of French theoretical Marxism when it was engaged in the debate raised by the works of Louis Althusser and his young disciples.

Prior to that, the only known part of the *Grundrisse* was the 'Introduction'. This had been translated by Edgar Milhaud immediately after its first appearance in German and published in 1903 in *La revue socialiste* [*The Socialist Review*]. In 1909, Laura Lafargue, Marx's daughter, produced a new translation of it that was included as an appendix to her French rendition of *A Contribution to the Critique of Political Economy*. The first translation, based on the German 1953 edition of the *Grundrisse* and thus closer to Marx's original, was only made in 1957 and printed, as it had become customary, as an appendix to *A Contribution to the Critique of Political Economy*.

The 'Introduction' was a key text for the dispute over Marx's philosophy initiated by Althusser's *Pour Marx* [*For Marx*] and subsequently developed in the collective work *Lire le Capital* [*Reading Capital*]. The debate concerned the theory of the construction of the object of knowledge through scientific abstractions, the need to rethink materialist dialectics without identifying them with their Hegelian form, the concept of *coupure épistémologique* [epistemological break] and the critique of historicism, and centred precisely on Marx's theory of knowledge. Thus the 'Introduction' became one of the main points of reference for the whole discussion. However, amongst the participants to this debate – Maurice Godelier, Henri Lefebvre, Pierre Vilar and Lucine Sève – with the exception of the latter, nobody took into serious consideration the *Grundrisse* as a whole, which had not yet been analysed even by Althusser, who only gave attention to the 'Introduction', that in *Lire le Capital* he defined as Marx's essential epistemological and philosophical writing.

As the 'Introduction' was separated from other parts of the *Grundrisse*, so too was the fragment on 'Forms which Precede Capitalist Production'. These pages drew the attention of Godelier who, at the time, was engaged in a confrontation between Marxism and Claude Lévi-Strauss' structural anthropology. He edited a volume of Marx and Engels' selected writings *Sur les sociétés précapitalistes* [*On Precapitalist Societies*], where the section on 'Forms which Precede Capitalist Production', which he had re-translated, was given a prominent place. Godelier discussed it within his long introduction to the book, in the passages where he summarised the framework of the historical evolution of society, and questioned the articulation of social relations of production and family relations. In his opinion Marx's development of this question was not confined to 1858. On the contrary, he highly rated Marx's comments – formulated in the last years of his life – on the works of ethnologists Lewis Henry Morgan, Edward Burnett Tylor and Maksim Maksimovič Kovalevskij, because they succeeded in complicating rigid evolutionist patterns and reassessing the structural function of family relations.

At the end of the 1970s, Ernest Mandel published *La formation de la pensée économique de Karl Marx de 1843 jusqu'à la rédaction du 'Capital'. Etude génétique* [*The Formation of the Economic Thought of Karl Marx, 1843 to Capital*] where much consideration was given to the *Grundrisse*, from the reflections on the dialectics of labour time and free time, to those on the 'Asiatic mode of production' or alienation, the work was defined as 'the research where the development of *Capital* was prepared' (Mandel 1967: 77).

In 1968, the *Grundrisse* was partially re-translated and published again in the prestigious collection *Bibliothèque de la Pléiade* of Gallimard. The publisher entrusted the Marxologist Maximilien Rubel with the editing of Marx's writings independently from the influence of the French Communist Party (PCF). Four volumes were produced as a result, the second of which was dedicated to the manuscripts on the critique of political economy, *Economie II* [*Economics II*], and included the *Grundrisse* with the title *Principes d'une critique de l'économie politique. Ebauche, 1857–1858* [*Principles of a Critique of Political Economy. Draft, 1957–1858*]. Translated by Rubel and Jean Malaquais from the German edition of 1953, in this volume the *Grundrisse* did not follow the original order but was rearranged into themes chosen by Rubel. He divided the texts in three sections: 'L'utopie monétaire' ['Monetary Utopia'], 'Le capital' ['Capital'] and 'Formes précapitalistes de la production, types de propriété' ['Precapitalist Forms of Production, Kinds of Property'], to which he added the notes on 'Bastiat and Carey'. The footnotes to the text were also very valuable as they provided much philological information and emphasised Marx's intellectual debt to G.W.F. Hegel.

An unabridged and rigorously translated edition of the *Grundrisse* in French only appeared in 1980, when Éditions Sociales, the publishing house affiliated to the PCF, printed the text. This edition was based on the German version of 1953 and the first volume of the one in MEGA[2]; the translation was produced by a multidisciplinary team of Germanists coordinated by Jean-Pierre Lefebvre and published in two volumes and 2,000 copies with the title *Manuscrits de 1857–1858 (Grundrisse)* [*Manuscripts of 1857–1858 (Grundrisse)*]. This publication was part of Édition Sociales larger plan to translate the whole of Marx and Engels' works. This initiative was not accomplished however, and, following the publisher's demise due to the decline of the PCF, the project was interrupted when only 26 out of the intended 35 volumes had been printed. In the introduction to this edition, Lefebvre emphasised the unclassifiable character of the text, which he thought to be due to its status as a mixture of the economical and the philosophical, the frequent references to Hegel and his *Science of Logic*, as well as an extremely complex language (Lefebvre 1980).

In fact, the interpretations of the *Grundrisse* developed in France were of a highly varied nature. They can be broadly classed in two main trends: one regarded these writings as a work in its own right, the other saw it mainly as a stage in the development of Marx's thought, one that needed to be compared to the final effort of *Capital*.

The first interpretation, which emphasised the independent status of the *Grundrisse* and defended its importance as being equivalent to that of *Capital*, found its main exponent in the Italian scholar and political militant Antonio Negri. Invited by Louis Althusser to give a series of lectures on the *Grundrisse* at the École Normal Supérieure in 1978, the following year he published its results in France and Italy as *Marx au delà de Marx. Cahier de travail sur les Grundrisse* [*Marx Beyond Marx. Lessons on the Grundrisse*]. In this work, which rightfully belongs to the French reception of the *Grundrisse*, Negri underlines how for Marx's theory it is an absolutely decisive work in which, for instance, the conception of communism is formulated more radically than anywhere else. Far from seeing the *Grundrisse* as a testing ground for *Capital*, on the contrary, one needed to rethink the 1867 text starting from the *Grundrisse*.

The second interpretation of the *Grundrisse* as an autonomous text can be found in Jean-Luc Petit's book, *Du travail vivant au système des actions. Une discussion de Marx* [*From Living Labour to the Stock Exchange. A Discussion on Marx*]. The author mainly emphasised the importance of the issue of the opposition between living and dead labour but believed that by conceiving of a communist society as a new and indestructible totality, Marx compromised the outcome of his thoughts.

The second line of interpretation of the *Grundrisse*, the one, so to speak, of a genetic kind, was also the most popular. It considered the manuscripts of 1857–8 in relation to the rest of Marx's works and in particular to the ones preceding 1848 and *Capital*. Three different theses can be identified within it: 1 the homogeneity between the *Grundrisse* and *Capital*; 2 the transitory function of the *Grundrisse* and its theoretical inferiority in relation to *Capital*; 3 the superiority of the *Grundrisse* over *Capital*.

1   According to the first line of interpretation, the *Grundrisse* was essential to the critique of Althusser's reading of Marx, in which it was claimed that the category of alienation disappeared in Marx's later works and was replaced by the more scientific notion of exploitation. The scholar who was most engaged in opposing these thesis was Lucien Sève, the first French author to explore the *Grundrisse*. In his *Marxism et théorie de la personnalité* [*Marxism and the Theory of Human Personality*], the *Grundrisse* was seen as a clear demonstration of the continuous presence of the theory of alienation in Marx, even in his mature writings and could be considered as 'an overall objection to the anti-humanist interpretation of Marxism' (Sève 1969: 161). Marxian theory of alienation was not an abstract theory of man in itself, but rather a category of the achievement of individual and collective autonomy against all of the powers that threatened its development. The *Grundrisse* provided grounding for scientific anthropology, sketched a theory of the historical forms of individuality, and *Capital* confirmed the theses expressed therein without breaking with them at all.

Another important interpretation of the *Grundrisse* that emphasised continuity can be found in the important and sizeable work by Michel Henry entitled *Marx*. Influenced by times characterised by numerous attempts at reformulating Marx's theory in view of the philosophical currents that then predominated in France, Henry's phenomenological reading of Marx tried to restore what he believed to be Marx's original conception in opposition to the Marxism that was professed by the bureaucratic apparatuses, regarding the *Grundrisse* as an 'essential' work that perfectly suited this purpose (Henry 1979: II, 21). 'This book, which Marx wrote for himself before writing *Capital* for others' gave light to the foundational intuition that *Capital* would later arm with its science. The critique of political economy was made bare in a phenomenology of concrete existence that provided the sole principle of explication of the economic system (Henry 1979: II, 251).

2   Readings that theorised an affinity between the *Grundrisse* and *Capital* were questioned in Jacques Bidet's *Que faire du Capital?* [*What to Make of Capital?*], a work inspired by Althusser's thesis. According to Bidet, the *Grundrisse* was raw evidence of Marx's development, marking the points where he resorts to Hegelian dialectics and thus, also to their insurmountable aporiae. Bidet claimed that these induced Marx to either ratify – albeit often implicitly – or to completely eliminate from his writings the theoretical features on which the *Grundrisse* was based. Thus Bidet actually purged the work whilst crediting it for its conceptualisation of the category of surplus value in its relation to profit. But the *Grundrisse* was still an 'experimental text' and transitional too, featuring a speculative anthropology and leaving room for *Capital* precisely because of its inadequacies (Bidet 1985: 64).

3   Finally, the last orientation is presented in Henri Denis's *L''économie' de Marx. Histoire d'un échec* [*Marx's 'Economics'. The Story of a Loss*]. In the two chapters dedicated to the *Grundrisse*, the author claims that this text

avoids the aporiae concerning the transition from value to price found in *Capital* and, more generally, that it constitutes the basis of a refoundation of Marxian critique.

In addition to the interpretations expounded so far the *Grundrisse* was read and commented on by many other scholars in France; amongst them, in particular, is André Gorz, who amply used it in his 1998 book entitled *Métamorphoses du travail. Quête du sens. Critique de la raison économique* [*Critique of Economic Reason*].

To conclude, the *Grundrisse* had a rather problematic reception in France. Published at the end of the 1970s, it circulated in Dangeville's poor translation; when it reappeared in 1980, interest in Marx had waned and it was only read by a limited number of people. However, in the last few years there has been a countervailing tendency and thus some of his writings are being republished. Therefore one is led to believe and, given the importance of this text, also to hope that with such renewed interest in the philosopher from Trier the *Grundrisse* will receive the attention it deserves.

[Translated from the French by Arianna Bove]

Bibliography

Complete editions

Marx, Karl (1967, 1968) *Fondements de la critique de l'économie politique*, Paris: Éditions Anthropos.
Marx, Karl (1980) *Manuscrits de 1857–1858 («Grundrisse»)*, Paris: Éditions Sociales. Trans.: Gilbert Badia, Étienne Balibar, Jacques Bidet, Yves Duroux, Michel Espagne, Luc Favre, François-Michel Gathelier, Marie-Odile Gathelier-Lauxerois, Almuth Grésillon, Vincent Jezewski, Françoise Joly, Jean-Baptiste Joly, Elisabeth Kauffmann, Jean-Louis Lebrave, Jean-Pierre Lefebvre, Michèle Lhomme, Claude Mainfroy, François Mathieu, Jean-Philippe Mathieu, Jacques Poumet, Philippe Préaux, Régine Roques, Chantal Simonin, Michel Werner and Françoise Willmann.

Partial editions

Marx, Karl (1903) 'Introduction à une critique de l'économie politique' ['Introduction to a Critique of Political Economy'], trans. Edgar Milhaud, *La revue socialiste*, 222: 691–720.
Marx, Karl (1909) 'Introduction à une critique de l'économie politique' ['Introduction to a Critique of Political Economy'], trans. Laura Lafargue, in Karl Marx, *Contribution à la critique de l'économie politique* [*Contribution to the Critique of Political Economy*], Paris: V. Giard – E. Briere, pp. 305–52.
Marx, Karl (1957) 'L'Introduction de 1857' ['The Introduction of 1857'], trans. Maurice Husson and Gilbert Badia, Paris: Éditions Sociales, pp. 147–75.

Marx, Karl (1968) *Œuvres. Economie II*, in Maximilien Rubel (ed.), Paris: Éditions Gallimard, pp. 171–359.

Marx, Karl (1970) 'Formes qui précédent la production capitaliste' ['Forms which Precede Capitalist Production'], in Maurice Godelier (ed.), *Sur les sociétés précapitalistes*, Paris: Éditions Sociales, pp. 180–226.

Critical literature on the Grundrisse

Althusser, Louis, Balibar, Étienne and Establet, Roger, Macherey, Pierre and Rancière, Jacques (1965) *Lire le Capital*, 2 vols, Paris: Maspéro.

Bidet, Jacques (1985) *Que faire du Capital?*, Paris: Presses Universitaires de France.

Denis, Henri (1980) *L'«Économie» de Marx. Histoire d'un échec*, Paris: Presses Universitaires de France.

Godelier, Maurice (1970) 'Préface' ['Preface'], in Maurice Godelier (ed.), *Sur les sociétés précapitalistes*, Paris: Éditions Sociales, pp. 13–142.

Gorz, André (1988) *Métamorphoses du travail*, Paris: Galilée.

Henry, Michel (1979) *Marx I. Une philosophie de la réalité, II. Une philosophie de l'économie* [Marx I. A Philosophy of Reality, II. A Philosophy of Economics] Paris: Gallimard.

Lefebvre, Jean-Pierre (1980) 'Introduction' ['Introduction'], in Karl Marx, *Manuscrits de 1857–1858 («Grundrisse»)*, Paris: Éditions Sociales, vol. 1, pp. VII–XIX.

Mandel, Ernest (1967) *La formation de la pensée économique de Karl Marx de 1843 jusqu'à la rédaction du 'Capital'. Etude génétique*, Paris: Maspéro.

Negri, Antonio (1998) *Marx au-delà de Marx*, Paris: Bourgois.

Petit, Jean-Luc (1980) *Du travail vivant au système des actions. Une discussion avec Marx*, Paris: Seuil.

Sève, Lucien (1969) *Marxisme et théorie de la personnalité*, Paris: Éditions Sociales.

18 Italy

Mario Tronti

The *Grundrisse* erupted onto the Italian scene at the end of the 1970s amidst students' and workers' struggles. The first unabridged translation by Enzo Grillo, based on the German edition of 1953, was published by La Nuova Italia as *Lineamenti fondamentali della critica dell'economia politica 1857–1858* [*Outlines of the Critique of Political Economy 1857–1858*] in two separate volumes, the first in 1968 and the second in 1970. After some debate, it was decided that the text should be partitioned at the point where Marx turns from production to circulation, so that the first volume included the 1857 'Introduction', the chapter on money and the section on 'The Production Process of Capital', and volume two opened with 'The Circulation Process of Capital'. The book was reprinted twice, in 1978 and 1997, and enjoyed astonishing success.

A second translation by Giorgio Backhaus, based on the edition of 1939–41, was published in two volumes by Einaudi in 1976, as *Lineamenti fondamentali di critica dell'economia politica* [*Outlines of the Critique of Political Economy*]. It was reprinted in 1977 with additional critical apparatus, a name index, and an analytical index compiled for the Italian edition.

It should be noted that the *Grundrisse* was published not by Editori Riuniti, the house officially affiliated to the Italian Communist Party, but by two independent publishers. Editori Riuniti finally reprinted Backhaus's translation only in 1986, as volumes 29 and 30 of Marx's and Engels' *Opere* [*Works*], which were projected to reach 50 volumes in total but then stopped at 32, just enough to allow for the much-awaited *Grundrisse*.

The *Urtext*, the preparatory materials for *A Contribution to the Critique of Political Economy* first published in 1963 (Marx 1963), was absent from Grillo's translation but featured in Backhaus' translation and was later also reprinted separately (Marx 1977). Neither translation included Marx's notes on Ricardo from 1850–1.

After the Second World War Marx's oeuvre appeared in mass editions in the 'Classici del marxismo' ['Classics of Marxism'] series of the Rinascita house, later to become Editori Riuniti, which also published shorter texts and extracts by Engels, Lenin and Stalin in a smaller series called 'Piccola biblioteca marxista' ['Small Marxist Library'].

The publication of Marx's *Opere filosofiche giovanili* [*Early Philosophical*

Works] had a strong impact. These consisted of Galvano Della Volpe's translation of the 1844 *Economic and Philosophical Manuscripts* and the *Critique of Hegel's Philosophy of Right.* Whereas Della Volpe adopted the *Critique* for his anti-Hegelian reading of Marx, the *Economic and Philosophical Manuscripts* provoked a discussion on alienation that culminated in an accentuation of humanist interpretations of Marx. The cultural milieu of the time was heavily influenced by the national historicist and idealist legacy of Marxism that ran from Francesco De Sanctis and Antonio Labriola through to Benedetto Croce and Antonio Gramsci.

The publication of the *Grundrisse* in Italy involved a break with this cultural milieu. It unveiled the laboratory of ideas, research and analyses that resulted in the first volume of *Capital* and the drafts of subsequent volumes, thus revealing a Marx deeply engaged in the critique of political economy. The Italian translation of *Theories of Surplus Value*, which appeared in 1961, followed Marx's original sketch-like draft (that is, as it had existed before Engels included parts of it in the posthumous second and third volumes of *Capital*). Interestingly, the editor of the Italian edition, Giorgio Giorgetti, used a section of the preface to describe the other manuscript, the *Grundrisse*; this was the first significant sign of its reception in Italy. Giorgetti claimed that, in order to understand the development of Marx's research from 1860–1 onwards, it was absolutely necessary to regard the 1857–8 manuscripts as a 'primary source' (Giorgetti 1961: 49).

Thus, in the early 1960s the *Grundrisse* began to be addressed as a book in its own right, almost a 'new' work by Marx. Two fragments, 'Forms which Precede Capitalist Production' and the 1857 'Introduction', had already appeared in the mid-1950s: the former, for instance, was first translated by Girolamo Brunetti in 1954, and reprinted in 1967 with Eric Hobsbawm's introduction to the 1964 English edition; and in 1979 the same excerpt received an original interpretation in Andrea Carandini's *L'anatomia della scimmia* [*The Anatomy of the Ape*].

The 1857 'Introduction' followed a course of its own, even more widely read and commented on than the famous 1859 'Preface' to *A Contribution to a Critique of Political Economy.* Unlike that 'Preface', a relatively clear and simple text strewn with the formulations of classical historical materialism, the 1857 'Introduction' is difficult, sketchy and not intended for publication. However, the school of thought led by Galvano Della Volpe and carried on by Lucio Colletti adopted it as the main text on Marxian historical–logical method. The 1857 'Introduction' concentrates on abstract determinations, C–M–C (commodity–money–commodity) and M–C–M corresponding to concrete–abstract–concrete and abstract–concrete–abstract respectively, and on history interpreted from the highest logical point of view: it is man who holds the key to understanding the ape, Marx says; as it is capitalism that provides the explanation of previous societies, and the highest forms of capitalism that explain the less developed. Colletti was the most vocal interpreter of the 'Introduction' and also the first to translate it, in 1954. Indeed, the second part of his book, *Il marxismo e Hegel* [*Marxism and Hegel*], is marked by a continuous engagement with it. The theoretical crux of Colletti's argument is based on his account of the relationship between Kant, Hegel and Marx, and his section on 'The Method of Political Economy' takes up Marx's critique of Hegel's critique of Kant. Colletti maintains that 'natural' development is the real process, whereas 'conceptual' development is the logical process; real and logical presuppositions, *causa essendi* and *causa cognoscendi*, induction and deduction, are two processes that involve and entail each other. From Hegel, Marx derived the conception of a unity of logical and real processes, a logical unity of thought and being that comes to take the place of their real difference; whereas from Kant he drew the notion of real existence as a 'surplus' in relation to all that is contained in the concept.

Here Colletti returns to and probes Della Volpe's idea of logic as historical science only to find a 'total and absolute homogeneity' between the pages of the 1857 'Introduction' and the young Marx's *Critique of Hegel's Philosophy of Right*:

> In both texts, his critique hinges on exactly the same issue: that Hegel reduces the real process to a merely logical one; that he turns the Idea into the subject or foundation of reality. Then, just as empirical reality becomes for Hegel the phenomenon or 'appearance' of the Idea, so the process through which reality becomes *known* necessarily has to become the process of its *creation*.
>
> (Colletti 1969: 275)

The logical universal, that is the predicate, is turned into subject, whilst the concrete particular, that is the real subject, becomes 'predicate of its own predicate' (Colletti 1969: 283).

This framework of reference and interpretation was later applied by Mario Rossi to the history of philosophy, by Giulio Pietranera to economic theory, and, more independently, by Mario dal Pra in his research on dialectics. It met with great opposition from the historicist school of Italian Marxism, of which Nicola Badaloni was a representative. From a structuralist standpoint, Cesare Luporini, who made numerous references to the 'Introduction' in his *Dialettica e materialismo* [*Dialectics and Materialism*], also levelled many criticisms against this reading. He thought he had uncovered a serious 'speculative' error in Della Volpe's interpretation, which, in transposing the critique of Hegelian dialectics to the realm of political economy, had made Marx's critique of speculative philosophy equipollent with his critique of political economy, 'as if it were the same kind of *critique*'. According to Luporini, it was the critique of Hegelian dialectics that enabled Marx to apply the 'correct method of dialectical development' (Luporini 1974: 259) to his critique of political economy, as analysis of the bourgeois mode of production.

As a complete and classical work of Marxism, the *Grundrisse* was introduced to the Italian theoretical scene by Operaismo [Workerism]. Operaismo was a political and intellectual experience of the early 1960s which, using Marx's *Capital*, sought to interpret and change the advancing Taylorist–Fordist stage of industrial capital. This necessitated great innovations in the Marxist tradition, and it was the *Grundrisse*, more than *Capital*, that seemed to offer theoretical weapons of sufficient analytical, stylistic and polemical novelty. The style of the *Grundrisse* – rich in insights and suggestions, in ways of posing problems without solutions or analyses without explicit conclusions – had a boundless polemical vigour and freedom of writing that was greatly appreciated by the new heretical Marxism of the 1960s. It brought a fresh injection of theory into the heavy orthodoxy of those years. In 1964, on the initiative of Raniero Panzieri and in a translation by Renato Solmi, the fourth issue of the journal *Quaderni Rossi* [*Red Notebooks*] published the 'Fragment on Machines' (Marx 1973: 690–706). In these passages Marx discusses the means of labour, which, once subsumed by the process of production of capital, undergo a series of metamorphoses, the last of which is the machine, or, rather:

> an *automatic system of machinery* ... set in motion by an automaton, a moving power that moves itself; this automaton consisting of numerous mechanical and intellectual organs, so that the workers themselves are cast merely as its conscious linkages.
>
> (Marx 1973: 692)

The monthly journal *Classe operaia* [*Working Class*] published further short extracts from Grillo's translation of the *Grundrisse* in the course of 1964. Of particular note were a short passage in the March issue on the exchange between capital and labour (Marx 1973: 274–5) and a longer excerpt in July on workers' savings (Marx 1973: 284). At the time, the sections referring to the future of capitalist development, with their various predictions and anticipations, were by far the most popular. The *Grundrisse* was considered to be more advanced than *Capital*. Given that Marx came to be regarded as a proponent of breakdown theory of crisis [*Zusammenbruchstheorie*] and a catastrophic view of capitalism, the *Grundrisse* seemed the ground most suited to a reinterpretation of his work. For it suggested that capitalism, facing but itself fuelling the contemporary cycle of workers' struggles, was in turn pushed by the workers towards further development.

Not surprisingly, out of the experience of Operaismo came Antonio Negri, author of the most specialist monograph on the *Grundrisse* to have appeared in Italy, *Marx oltre Marx. Quaderno di lavoro sui Grundrisse* [*Marx beyond Marx. Lessons on the Grundrisse*], which was published by Feltrinelli in 1979 and reprinted by Manifestolibri in 1998. Negri's book is a collection of material used in nine seminars he held at the École Normale Supérieure in 1978 by invitation of Louis Althusser. Negri was in moderate disagreement with Vitali Vygodski and highly critical of Roman Rosdolsky. He did not accept that the *Grundrisse* should be understood as a propaedeutic to *Capital*. Indeed, he maintained that the two texts ran partly counter to one another: whereas *Capital* signalled a reduction of critique to political economy and an annihilation of subjectivity in the objectivity of the laws of development, in the *Grundrisse* theoretical analysis was itself constitutive of revolutionary practice, in as much as it addressed the subjective analysis of class antagonism. The latter ultimately made of Marxism:

> a science of crisis and subversion.... Reversing and paraphrasing Hobsbawm, we should say that the *Grundrisse* is for Marx a kind of collective theoretical shorthand: it is this ferocious obstinacy of theory for and within practice. The method of the *Grundrisse* constitutes the antagonism.
>
> (Negri 1998: 36)

Negri's theses, influenced by the heated background of the 1970s in Italy, counterpose the *Grundrisse* and *Capital* in a forced manner. Negri recognizes this too in the 'Introduction' to the second edition of *Marx oltre Marx*, where he more soberly defines the *Grundrisse* as 'an extraordinary theoretical anticipation of mature capitalist society ... a fundamental reading for anyone who wishes to engage with postfordism and postmodernism' (Negri 1998: 36).

In fact, the concept of the *Grundrisse* that has enjoyed most popularity amongst Italian intellectuals is that of the *general intellect*. Marx summarized it thus:

> Nature builds no machines, no locomotives, railways, electric telegraphs, self-acting mules etc. These are products of human industry; natural material transformed into organs of the human will over nature, or of human participation in nature. They are *organs of the human brain, created by the human hand;* the power of knowledge, objectified. The development of fixed capital indicates to what degree general social knowledge has become a *direct force of production*, and to what degree, hence, the conditions of the process of social life itself have come under the control of the general intellect and been transformed in accordance with it. To what degree the powers of social production have been produced, not only in the form of knowledge, but also as immediate organs of social practice, of the real life process.
>
> (Marx 1973: 706)

In the 1970s and 1980s, Italian post-*operaismo* made large use of this concept and paved the way for analyses of immaterial labour, cognitive capitalism and the structure of abstract domination that leads, through knowledge, to biopolitical command over social praxis and real life.

In conclusion, the Italian reception of the *Grundrisse* had a rather peculiar character. Though almost completely absent from academic milieux, it had great resonance in political and theoretical debates and a decisively critical and innovative impact on the Marxist tradition. We might say that in Italy, after the *Grundrisse*, Marx would never be the same again.

[Translated from the Italian by Arianna Bove]

Bibliography

Complete editions

Marx, Karl (1968, 1970) *Lineamenti fondamentali della critica dell'economia politica 1857–1858*, Florence: La Nuova Italia.

Marx, Karl (1976) *Lineamenti fondamentali di critica dell'economia politica. Grundrisse*, Turin: Einaudi; reprinted in Marx Engels *Opere*, vols XXIX and XXX (1986), Rome: Editori Riuniti.

Partial editions

Marx, Karl (1954) *Forme economiche precapitalistiche* [*Precapitalist Economic Formations*], 2nd edn with a Preface by E. Hobsbawm (1967), Rome: Edizioni Rinascita.

Marx, Karl (1957) 'Introduzione' ['Introduction'], in Karl Marx, *Per la critica dell'-economia politica*, Lucio Colletti (ed.), trans. Emma Cantimori Mezzamonti, Rome: Edizioni Rinascita, pp. 171–99.

Marx, Karl (1964a) 'Frammento sulle macchine' ['Fragment on Machines'], trans. Renato Solmi, *Quaderni Rossi*, 4: 289–300.

Marx, Karl (1964b) 'Lo scambio tra capitale e lavoro' ['Exchange between Capital and Labour'], *Classe operaia*, 3: 13.

Marx, Karl (1964c) 'Il risparmio dell'operaio' ['The Worker's Savings'], *Classe operaia*, 7: 16–17.

Critical literature on the Grundrisse

Badaloni, Nicola (1972) *Per il comunismo. Questioni di teoria* [For Communism. Questions of Theory], Turin: Einaudi.

Carandini, Andrea (1979) *L'anatomia della scimmia: la formazione economica della società prima del capitale; con un commento alle "Forme che precedono la produzione capitalistica" dei Grundrisse di Marx* [*Anatomy of the Ape: The Economic Formation of Society before Capital; with a Commentary on 'The Forms Which Precede Capitalist Production'*], Turin: Einaudi.

Colletti, Lucio (1969) *Il Marxismo e Hegel*, Rome-Bari: Laterza.

Dal Pra, Mario (1965) *La dialettica in Marx* [*Dialectics in Marx*], Rome: Laterza.

Della Volpe, Galvano (1956) *Rousseau e Marx* [*Rousseau and Marx*]. Rome: Edizioni Rinascita, pp. 127–41.

Giorgetti, Giorgio (1961) 'Prefazione' ['Preface'] to Karl Marx, *Teorie sul plusvalore* [Theories of Surplus Value], vol. I, Rome: Editori Riuniti, pp. 7–100.

Luporini, Cesare (1974) *Dialettica e materialismo* [*Dialectics and Revolution*], Rome: Editori Riuniti.

Negri, Antonio (1979) *Marx oltre Marx. Quaderno di lavoro sui Grundrisse*, Milan: Feltrinelli; 2nd edn (1998) Rome: Manifestolibri.

Pietranera, Giulio (1956) 'La struttura logica del *Capitale*' ['The Logical Structure of Capital'], *Società*, 3/4: 421–40 and 649–87.

Rossi, Mario (1974) *Cultura e rivoluzione* [*Culture and Revolution*], Rome: Editori Riuniti.

Other references

Marx, Karl (1963) 'Urtext' ['Original Text'], in *Scritti inediti di economia politica* [*Unpublished Writings on Political Economy*], Rome: Editori Riuniti.

Marx, Karl (1973) *Grundrisse: Foundations of the Critique of Political Economy (Rough Draft)*, Harmondsworth: Penguin.

Marx, Karl (1977) *Urtext. Grundrisse: frammento del testo originario di Per la critica dell'economia politica* [*Original Text. Grundrisse: Fragment of the Original Text of Contribution to the Critique of Political Economy*], Savona: International.

19 Cuba, Argentina, Spain and Mexico

Pedro Ribas and Rafael Pla León

Several publishers in the Spanish-speaking world have editions of the *Grundrisse* to their name, but in comparison with other of Marx's writings it has not stimulated much commentary there. It also began to circulate rather late in both Latin America and Spain, where it was illegal to publish Marxist literature until the end of the Franco dictatorship in 1975.

The translation of the *Grundrisse* came at a time when Marxism was recovering the ground lost with Franco's victory in the civil war of 1936–9. A boom in publications on Marx and Marxism coincided with the restoration of democracy, in a context marked by the rejection of Stalinist dogmatism and orthodoxy by parties of the Left. The 1857–8 manuscripts reinforced this new turn by revealing a Marx who not only criticized capitalism but also opened new and hitherto unexplored philosophical paths. The *Grundrisse* was such a novelty that no fewer than five translations were published between 1970 and 1985.

Before the unabridged editions, two fragments had already became known in Spanish. In 1962, under the title 'Preliminar a una crítica de la economía política' ['Preliminaries to the Critique of Political Economy'], the 'Introduction' was published in Cuba as an appendix to an edition of *A Contribution to the Critique of Political Economy*. In 1966, 'Forms which Precede Capitalist Production' was translated from English and published in Argentina under the title *Formaciones Económicas Precapitalistas* [*Pre-capitalist Economic Formations*]. Many Spanish translations of this excerpt were made from English, some even presenting Marx and Eric Hobsbawm as joint authors. Both sections were reprinted with the same titles by numerous different publishers.

However, a full appreciation of the meaning and importance of the *Grundrisse* was achieved only with the publication of the whole text. The first translation, by Mario Díaz Godoy, appeared in Cuba in 1970–1, but it was based on the French version of 1967–8 and reproduced the mistakes made by Roger Dangeville; it was printed in two volumes as *Fundamentos de la crítica de la economía política (Esbozo de 1857–1858)* [*Foundations of the Critique of Political Economy. Drafts of 1857–1858*]. The number of copies – 15,000 – was impressive considering the nature of the text, but the purpose of this edition was to support the teaching of Marxism in Cuban universities rather than to cater for the erudite in the field. The translation did not become known outside the country, and for the reasons already given it was also the least precise of all five Spanish versions.

Between 1971 and 1976 the publishing house Siglo XXI released the three volumes of *Elementos fundamentales de la crítica de la economía política* [*Fundamental Elements of the Critique of Political Economy*], translated by Pedro Scarón from the 1953 German edition of the *Grundrisse*. This version took into account amendments made in the Russian edition of 1968–9. In their 'Preface' the editors (José Aricó, Miguel Murmis and Scarón) pointed out that the work was scarcely known before 1960, and that the translation had posed certain difficulties. There have since been 18 editions of this version, the latest dated 2002, which demonstrate beyond all doubt that it is the best-known and most popular Spanish translation.

In 1972 the third translation of the *Grundrisse* was released in Spain with the title *Los fundamentos de la crítica de la economía política* [*Foundations of the Critique of Political Economy*], by the publisher Alberto Corazón. This edition did not feature the 'Introduction' and had little resonance because the Franco regime had not yet fallen.

On the other hand, Martin Nicolaus's article for the British journal *New Left Review*, 'The Unknown Marx', which was translated in 1968 in Cuba and in 1972 in Spain, greatly helped to raise the profile of the *Grundrisse* among Spanish-speaking readers and students. Also in 1972, the Spanish journal *Teorema* [*Theorem*] published an article by Francesco Agües that examined the differences between the *Grundrisse* and the *The Economic and Philosophical Manuscripts*. This first sign of a reception of the *Grundrisse* in Spain was followed by a volume entitled *Alienación e ideología. Metodología y dialéctica en los Grundrisse* [*Alienation and Ideology. Methodology and Dialectics in the Grundrisse*], the outcome of cooperation among a group of authors (E. Alvarez Vázquez, Herminia Bevia, Miguel Bilbatúa, Valeriano Bozal, Antonio Carmona, José Linaza, J. Martinez Reverte, Ludolfo Paramio and Laura Pozón) who sought to respond to Althusser's interpretation of Marx with interventions from various disciplines ranging from politics to ethics and law (Vv. Aa. 1973). Two articles by Gustavo Bueno in the journal *Sistema* [*System*] subsequently used a Hegelian approach to Marx to oppose Althusser's epistemological position, while at the same time the first studies on the *Grundrisse* in Mexico included an essay by Gabriel Vargas Lozano for the journal *Dialéctica*.

In 1977 the *Grundrisse* came out in a new version, the fourth. This translation by Javier Pérez Royo, based on the first German edition of 1939–41, was included in volume 21 and 22 of Marx and Engels' complete works – a project interrupted when only 12 of the planned 68 volumes had been actually printed.

In the following year, the translation of another foreign author spurred further interest in the *Grundrisse*; this time it was Roman Rosdolsky's *Génesis y estructura de El capital de Marx. Estudios sobre los* Grundrisse [*Genesis and Structure of Marx's Capital. Studies of the Grundrisse*], the subtitle having been added to the Spanish edition. Further commentaries appeared in Spain too. In 1981 an article by Luis Nuñez Ladeveze in *Cuadernos de Realidades Sociales*

[*Notebooks of Social Realities*] investigated the treatment of the division of labour in the *Grundrisse*, and in 1983 the journal *Mientras Tanto* [*In the Meantime*], edited by Manuel Sacristán Luzón, published Aureliano Arteta's 'Marx, la alienación del tiempo en su forma social capitalista' ['Marx, Alienation of Time in its Social Capitalist Form'], where the author shows how the *Grundrisse* theorizes the capitalist appropriation of human time.

The fifth and last unabridged translation of the *Grundrisse*, by the most important translator of Marx into Spanish, Wenceslao Roces, appeared in Mexico in 1985, with the famous Fondo de Cultura Econümica publishing house. Printed in 3,000 copies, this version became volumes six and seven of Marx's and Engels' *Selected Works*. In the same year, also in Mexico, Enrique Dussel's *La producción teórica de Marx. Un comentario a los Grundrisse* [*Marx's Theoretical Production. A Commentary on the Grundrisse*] outlined a particular interpretation of Marx's text and linked it to the author's philosophical principles and the Latin American liberation movement. This was the first important in-depth study of the *Grundrisse* in Spanish, as well as one of the few monographs exclusively devoted to it in the international field.

We may say that in Spain the *Grundrisse* was read mainly as a counterweight to the Althusserian School, rather than as an opening to new theoretical paths, whereas in Latin America it was used to frame a new debate on the philosophy of liberation and related questions. All in all, though, the text certainly deserves to be further investigated.

Bibliography

Complete editions

Marx, Karl (1970, 1971) *Fundamentos de la crítica de la economía política (Esbozo de 1857–1858). En anexo 1850–1859*, 2 vols, Havana: Ciencias Sociales.

Marx, Karl (1971, 1972, 1976) *Elementos fundamentales de la crítica de la economía política*, Buenos Aires: Siglo XXI.

Marx, Karl (1972) *Los fundamentos de la crítica de la economía política*, 2 vols, trans. Agustín García Tirado, Madrid: Alberto Corazón.

Marx, Karl (1977) *Líneas fundamentales de la crítica de la economía política (Grundrisse)*. Barcelona, Buenos Aires and Mexico City: Crítica.

Marx, Karl (1985) *Grundrisse 1857–1858*, Mexico City: Fondo de Cultura Económica.

Partial translations

Marx, Karl (1962) 'Preliminar a una crítica de la economía política', in Karl Marx, *Crítica de la Economía Política*, Havana: Editorial Orbe, pp. 152–69.

Marx, Karl (1966) *Formaciones económicas precapitalistas*, trans. Ariel Bignami, Buenos Aires: Editorial Platina.

Critical literature on the Grundrisse

Agües, Francesc (1972) 'Acerca de los *Grundrisse*' ['On the *Grundrisse*'], *Teorema*, 7: 81–96.

Areicó, José, Murmis, Miguel and Scarón, Pedro (1971) 'Presentación' ['Presentation'], in Karl Marx, *Elementos fundamentales de la crítica de la economía política*, vol. 1, Buenos Aires: Siglo XXI, pp. xii–xvi.

Arteta, Aurelio (1983) 'Marx, la alienación del tiempo en su forma social capitalista' ['Marx, the Alienation of Time in Its Capitalist Social Form'], *Mientras Tanto*, 16–17: 157–74.

Bueno, Gustavo (1973) 'Sobre el significado de los *Grundrisse* en la interpretación del marxismo'] *Sistema*, 2: 15–39.

Bueno, Gustavo (1974) 'Los *Grundrisse* de Marx y el espíritu objetivo de Hegel' ['Marx's *Grundrisse* and Hegel's Objective Spirit'], *Sistema*, 4: 35–46.

Dussel, Enrique (1985) *La producción teórica de Marx. Un comentario a los Grundrisse* ['Marx's Theoretical Production. A Commentary on the *Grundrisse*'], Mexico City: Siglo XXI.

Ladeveze, Luis Núñez (1981) 'La división del trabajo en los *Grundrisse*' ['The Division of Time in the *Grundrisse*'], *Cuadernos de Realidades Sociales*, 18–19: 15–44.

Lozano, Gabriel Vargas (1976) 'La introducción a la *Crítica de la economía política* de 1857' ['Introduction to the 1857 *Critique of Political Economy*'], *Dialéctica* [*Dialectic*], 1: 29–52.

Nicolaus, Martin (1968) 'El Marx desconocido' ['The Unknown Marx'], *Pensamiento Crítico* [*Critical Thought*], 18–19: 185–213.

Nicolaus, Martín (1972) *El Marx desconocido. Proletariado y clase media en Marx; coreografía hegeliana y la dialéctica capitalista* [*The Unknown Marx. Proletariat and Middle Class in Marx: Hegelian Choreography and Capitalist Dialectic*], Barcelona: Anagrama Editorial.

Rosdolsky, Roman (1978) *Génesis y estructura de* El capital *de Marx (Estudios sobre los Grundrisse)* [*Genesis and Structure of Marx's Capital. Studies on the Grundrisse*], México: Siglo XXI.

Vv. Aa. (1973) *Alienación e ideología. Metodología y dialéctica en los Grundrisse* [*Alienation and Ideology. Methodology and Dialectics in the Grundrisse*], Madrid: Alberto Corazón.

20 Czechoslovakia

Stanislav Hubík

In Czechoslovakia, the *Grundrisse* was published later than many of Marx's other writings. After seizing power in 1948, the Communist Party of Czechoslovakia, believing Marx and Engels' works to be highly important, soon instructed their publication. They appeared in 39 volumes, between 1956 and 1974, in Czech language, with the title *Marx Engels Spisy* [*Works*], whilst they were printed in Slovakian as single editions and selected writings. Like the German *Marx Engels Werke* [*Works*] on which the translations were based, the Czech *Spisy* omitted two of Marx's essential works: the *Economic and Philosophical Manuscripts of 1844*, and the *Grundrisse*. The former were published in 1961 in Czech in a separate edition but never got translated into Slovakian, whereas the latter was translated in both languages. The first translation of the *Grundrisse*, in Czech language – *Rukopisy „Grundrisse" (Ekonomické rukopisy z let 1857–1859)* [*Grundrisse Manuscripts. Economic Manuscripts of 1857–1859*] – was carried out by Mojmír Hrbek and Rút Hrbková from the 1953 German edition, amended with the 1968–9 Russian edition, and published by Svoboda of Prague in three volumes, respectively in 1971, 1974 and 1977 with a print run of 4,000 copies each. The first volume included an introduction by Radovan Richta, 'Marxova cesta revoluční kritiky' ['Marx's Mode of Revolutionary Critique'], and a preface by Bohumila Žežulková; the third volume featured the table of contents of the *Grundrisse* as conceived by Marx, and the preparatory materials to *A Contribution to the Critique of Political Economy (Urtext)*. The Slovakian translation followed shortly afterwards with the title *Základy kritiky politickej ekonómie: Rukopisy Grundrisse (Hrubý koncept: Ekonomické rukopisy z rokov 1857–1859)* [*Elements of Critique of Political Economy: Manuscripts Grundrisse (Rough Draft: Economical Manuscripts of 1857–1859)*]. Based on the 1953 German edition, this was done by Teodor Münz and printed in 5,000 copies and two volumes respectively in 1974 and 1975 by the publishing house Pravda of Bratislava. The Slovakian edition included both the introduction and the preface of the Czech version but omitted the contents of the third volume.

From the outset of its circulation the *Grundrisse* performed a very important function in the Czechoslovakian theoretical debate. In a context dominated by the schematic interpretation of Marx provided by Marxism–Leninism and the rigid contrapositions of orthodox Marxism and revisionism, the *Grundrisse*, together with the *Economic and Philosophical Manuscripts of 1844*, supplied the theoretical tools necessary to countervail the doctrinarism of Soviet Marxism, which was hegemonic at the time. The *Economic and Philosophical Manuscripts of 1844* were a symbolic text not only because they offered critical arguments against State ideology, but also because they acted as a bridge between Marx's ideas and non-Marxist philosophical notions.

The *Grundrisse* performed an analogous function, despite taking much longer to become known. It was first employed by scholars who read the German original. In particular two books used the *Grundrisse*, and they enjoyed international recognition and were translated in several languages. In 1962, Jindřich Zelený referred to the 1857–8 manuscripts in his book *O logické struktuře Marxova Kapitálu* [*The Logic of Marx's Capital*], in order to better clarify Marx's research methodology; the following year, Karel Kosík published *Dialektika konkrétního: studie o problematice člověka a světa* [*Dialectics of the Concrete: A Study on Problems of Man and World*], where some of the concepts of the *Grundrisse* were used to effect a synthesis between Marx's and Martin Heidegger's notions of man, labour and alienation.

Despite these two works, the *Grundrisse* was not really noticed until the mid-1970s, when, having been translated, it became the privileged theoretical point of reference for all the opponents of the official formulations of the concepts of labour and alienation, and providing the theoretical tools for the development of new interpretations of the capitalist mode of production and historical materialism. For this reason, party hierarchies never saw it favourably and their hostility was also reflected in the number of copies issued. In fact, in Czech language, *Capital* was printed in 50,000 copies and *Spicy* in between 15,000 and 20,000 copies, whilst the *Economic and Philosophical Manuscripts of 1844* and the *Grundrisse* had a print run of merely 4,000 copies.

Moreover, theorists of the Czechoslovakian Marxist apparatus used these two works considerably less than *Capital, The German Ideology* and much-circulated party manuals. The only exceptions were the 'Introduction', published in Czech in 1953 and subsequently inserted in compendia of canonical Marxism, and 'Forms which precede capitalist production', translated in Czech in 1967, i.e. before the first full edition of the *Grundrisse*.

The attitude towards Marx profoundly changed after the Velvet Revolution. The adoration that surrounded him in Czechoslovakia before 1990 was followed by the silence in the newly born Czech and Slovakian Republics, where none of the main journals of philosophy and the social sciences has published a single article on Marx in the past 15 years. However, outside the academic environment, there seems to be a timid thaw towards him and he is read again, rather than following dogmatic Marxist interpretations, as a precious aid to the economic and social analysis of contemporary capitalism. If this were the case, the *Grundrisse* would still prove to be a useful text.

Bibliography

Complete editions

Marx, Karl (1971, 1974, 1977) *Rukopisy 'Grundrisse' (Ekonomické rukopisy z let 1857–1859)*, Prague: Svoboda.
Marx, Karl (1974, 1975) *Základy kritiky politickej ekonómie: Rukopisy Grundrisse (Hrubý koncept: Ekonomické rukopisy z rokov 1857–1859)*, Bratislava: Pravda.

Partial editions

Marx, Karl (1953) 'Úvod ke kritice politické ekonomie' ['Introduction to the Critique of Political Economy'], in Marx, Karl *Ke kritice politické ekonomie* [*A Contribution to the Critique of Political Economy*], Prague: Státní nakladatelství politické literatury, pp. 155–80.
Marx, Karl (1953) 'Formy předcházející kapitalistickou výrobu' ['Forms which Precede Capitalist Production'], in Pečírka, Jan and Pešek, Jiří (eds) *Rané formy civilizace* [*Early Forms of Civilization*] Prague: Svoboda, pp. 37–83.

Critical literature on the Grundrisse

Kosík, Karel (1963) *Dialektika konkrétního: studie o problematice člověka a světa*, Prague: Academia.
Richta, Radovan (1971) *Marxova cesta revoluční kritiky*, in Marx, Karl *Rukopisy 'Grundrisse' (Ekonomické rukopisy z let 1857–1859)*, vol. 1 Prague: Svoboda, pp. 7–25.
Zelený, Jindřich (1962) *O logické struktuře Marxova Kapitálu*. Prague: ČSAV.
Žežulková, Bohumila (1971) *Redakční předmluva k českému vydání* [*Editorial introduction to the Czech edition*], in Marx, Karl *Rukopisy 'Grundrisse' (Ekonomické rukopisy z let 1857–1859)*, vol. 1 Prague: Svoboda, pp. 27–34.

21 Hungary

Ferenc L. Lendvai

Although the publication of Marx' and Engels' works enjoyed a long tradition in Hungary, it was not until 1972 that the complete *Grundrisse* was published with the title *A politikai gazdaságtan bírálatának alapvonalai* [*Foundations of the Critique of Political Economy*]. First the Social Democratic Party of Hungary, and later the Communist Party of Hungary, made every possible effort to deliver Marx and Engels' works to the widest possible audience. After 1945, the publishing house 'Szikra' (from the Leninist 'Iskra') issued the works in a quick and steady succession and released several editions of Marx and Engels' writings in large quantities. The complete Hungarian translation of *Capital* was published around the same time. From the text of the *Grundrisse*, however, only two excerpts were translated as part of the series 'Small Library of Marxism–Leninism'. The first, in 1951, was the 'Introduction' of 1857, the second, in 1953, was 'Forms which Precede Capitalist Production'.

The series *Karl Marx és Friedrich Engels Müvei* [*Karl Marx and Friedrich Engels's Works*], the Hungarian translation of the MEW, started being published in 1957. The publication went ahead regardless of the popular insurrection, that had briefly swept away the totalitarian dictatorship only a year earlier in 1956. It was printed without the name of the publisher, and only the place and date of publication were indicated. The translator's name was omitted too, as the translation was a so-called 'collective work'. The publisher was in fact Kossuth and the translator Zoltán Lissauer. Similarly to the MEW, with the exception of the 'Introduction' of 1857 published in volume 13, the *Grundrisse* were initially excluded from this series and only later incorporated in over 2,000 copies in a two-volume supplement 46/I–II of 1972. They were also published independently as one book.

The reception of the *Grundrisse* in Hungary took place over two distinct periods. First it was received by those who could study the German edition; second, by those who had access to it through the Hungarian translation. György Lukács' main works certainly belong to the first stage of the reception of the *Grundrisse*, and he is undoubtedly the best known Hungarian philosopher with an international reputation. Lukács developed his aesthetic theory between the 1930s and the 1950s. In his fight against dogmatism, Lukács relied on Marx's original texts, including the *Grundrisse*. For instance, he used Marx's ideas on the uneven development of material production relative to artistic development, as expounded in the 'Introduction': an undeveloped society could create more valuable products of paramount artistic value, such as Homer's epics, than a more advanced and modern one (Lukács 1949). To this Lukács added that the literary products of a less developed bourgeois society, namely critical realism, could have higher artistic value than those of a socialist society, which allegedly was at a higher stage of development, i.e. socialist realism. The later Lukács of *Zur Ontologie des gesellschaftlichen Seins* [*The Ontology of Social Being*] relies on the ideas of the *Grundrisse*, especially the 'Introduction', when analysing the social character of being: that is, never a 'pure' being, but being formed by the activity of man in the process of work and social production.

In the 1960s Ferenc Tökei's analyses of the *Grundrisse* had a significant impact on the international scene; his ideas were inspired by an analysis of 'Forms which Precede Capitalist Production'. At the time, Marxist philosophy was still dominated by a schematic dogmatism which claimed that the historical stages of social development were primitive communism, slave society, feudalism, capitalism, and socialism–communism. For Tökei, who was originally a Sinologist, Marx's concept of the so-called Asiatic form of possession and mode of production was a real revelation. On the basis of these he developed his theory (Tökei 1965), and further elaborated a notion of philosophy of history into a comprehensive theory (Tökei 1968). According to him, the determinant factor or a mode of production is the pattern of the mode of possession, the 'ground form'; pre-capitalist forms of possession and production constitute a progressive series from Asiatic, to Antique, to German–feudal.

Tökei's views generated animated discussions. The assyriologist Géza Komoróczy argued that Tökei's abstract patterns could not be found in the history of Mesopotamia, the term *Grundform* could only mean 'basic form', and that Marx had integrated the parallel basic forms into 'progressive' periods of economic social formations [*ökonomische Gesellschaftsformation*] only in his 'Preface' to *A Contribution to the Critique of Political Economy*, whereas Ferenc L. Lendvai rebutted that social totality must be explained starting from the form of possession, the term *Grundform* could be interpreted as 'ground form' and the progressive forms had already been mentioned in *The German Ideology* as patriarchal relations, slavery, guilds and classes (Komoróczy 1975; Lendvai 1976).

During the 1970s and 1980s, the *Grundrisse* started to influence social philosophy. In relation to Tökei's theory in particular, Attila Ágh published several papers and his *A termelö ember világa* [*The World of Productive Man*] of 1979 presents an interesting analysis of Marx's concept of the system of production. In Hungary, after 1956, 'official' Marxism was not as dogmatic as in the rest of Eastern Europe, so it was possible to introduce the ideas of the *Grundrisse* and for them to become common currency. In fact, on the occasion of the centenary anniversary of Marx's death in 1983, excellent studies were published by the Institute for Philosophy of the Hungarian Academy of Sciences, with the title *Az élö Marx* [*The Living Marx*] (Hársing and Kelemen 1983), and many of them were inspired by the *Grundrisse*, and the 'Introduction' in particular. Moreover, in 1985 the Ministry of Culture published a brochure by Imre P. Szabó for the teaching of Marxism–Leninism on the theory of needs, which was based on the analyses present in the *Grundrisse*.

A special mention in relation to the circulation of the *Grundrisse*, not only in Hungarian, goes to Lukács' followers, members of the so-called 'Budapest School'. Amongst them, of particular relevance is the work of György Márkus who, in 1966, further developed the ideas of the 'Introduction' and the 'Forms', especially within the realm of history and historical necessity (Márkus 1966). Ágnes Heller's work is internationally renowned too, most notably his *Theory of Need in Marx*, published in 1974 and translated in many languages, and a long essay published in 1982 in the Hungarian journal *Híd*. Both were largely influenced by the *Grundrisse*. Finally, let us not forget István Mészáros, who certainly found great inspiration in the *Grundrisse* for his work *Beyond Capital*.

Bibliography

Complete edition

Marx, Karl (1972) *A politikai gazdaságtan bírálatának alapvonalai*, in *Karl Marx és Friedrich Engels Müvei*, vols 46/1 and 46/2, [Kossuth]: Budapest.

Partial editions

Marx, Karl (1951) *Bevezetés („A politikai gazdaságtan bírálatához")* [*Introduction to the 'Critique of Political Economy'*], trans. [Emil Devecseri], Budapest: Szikra.
Marx, Karl (1953) *A tökés termelés elötti tulajdonformák* [*Pre-capitalistic Forms of Property*], Budapest: Szikra.
Marx, Karl (1965) *Bevezetés („A politikai gazdaságtan bírálatához")* [*Introduction to the 'Critique of Political Economy'*], in *Karl Marx és Friedrich Engels Müvei*, vol. 13, Budapest: [n.p.], pp. 149–76.

Critical literature on the Grundrisse

Ágh, Attila (1979) *A termelö ember világa*, [Budapest]: Kossuth.
Hársing, László and Kelemen, János (eds) (1983) *Az élö Marx. Tanulmányok Marx társadalomelméleti és metodológiai koncepciójáról* [*The Living Marx. Studies on the Concept of Marx in Theory of Society and in Methodology*], [Budapest]: Kossuth.
Heller, Ágnes (1974) *La teoria dei bisogni in Marx* [Italian trans. of Hungarian manuscript], Milano: Feltrinelli.
Heller, Ágnes (1982) 'A szükségletek jelentösége és jelentése Marx gondolatrendszerében' ['Significance and Meaning of the Needs in the Thought of Marx'], *Híd*, 1: 86–100, 2: 239–60, 3: 360–5, 4: 505–22, 5: 659–75, 6: 772–84.
Komoróczy, Géza (1975) 'A földtulajdon az ókori Mezopotámiában és az ún. ázsiai termelési mód elmélete' ['Ground Possession in Ancient Mesopotamia and the Theory of the so called Asiatic Mode of Production'], *MTA II. Osztály Közleményei*: 129–44.
Lendvai, Ferenc L. (1976) 'Történetfilozófiáról és történettudományról – Mezopotámia

ürügyén' ['On Philosophy and Science of History – under Pretext of Mesopotamia'], *MTA II. Osztály Közleményei*: 331–45.

Lukács, György (1949) *Marx és Engels irodalomelmélete. Három tanulmány* [*The Literary Theory of Marx and Engels. Three Essays*], Budapest: Szikra.

Lukács, György (1971) *Zur Ontologie des gesellschaftlichen Seins*, Neuwied–Berlin: Luchterhand.

Márkus, György (1966) *Marxizmus és 'antropológia'. Az emberi lényeg fogalma Marx filozófiájában* [*Marxism and 'Anthropology'. The Concept of the Human Being in the Philosophy of Marx*], Budapest: Akadémiai.

Mészáros, István (1995) *Beyond Capital*, New York: Monthly Review Press.

Szabó, Imre P. (1985): *Marx szükséglet-elméletéröl* [*On the Theory of the Needs by Marx*] Budapest: Mûvelõdési Minisztérium.

Tõkei, Ferenc (1965) *Az „ázsiai termelési mód" kérdéséhez* [*On the Question of 'the Asiatic Mode of Production'*], [Budapest]: Kossuth.

Tõkei, Ferenc (1968) *A társadalmi formák elméletéhez* [*On the Theory of the Forms of Society*], [Budapest]: Kossuth.

22 Romania

Gheorghe Stoica

In Romania the *Grundrisse* was published in two volumes between 1972 and 1974. Based on the German edition of 1953, and inclusive of the amendments in the Russian edition of 1968–9, it was printed without mention of the translators, as was common at the time, by Editure Politica of Bucarest with the title *Bazele criticii economiei politice* [*The Grounds of the Critique of Political Economy*].

The circulation of the *Grundrisse* was very limited and the interest it aroused rather exiguous; in fact, no philosophical and political journal of note paid particular attention to its publication.

At the end of the second world war, Marx and Engels' works, alongside Lenin's, enjoyed a wide dissemination in Romania, but during the 1970s Nicolae Ceauşescu became the head of government and new political phase, characterized by conflict with the Soviet Union, began; this had its effect on the dissemination of Marx's books as they were gradually substituted by those of the dictator in charge. The Stalinist dogmatism asserted after 1945 was followed by a period of great cultural isolation: the nationalist–communist era, when much of the propagandistic effort of the Romanian Communist Party was employed in building the cult of personality of its leader, and a Romanian myth that reclaimed an alleged continuity between Ancient Rome and Romania. To understand the climate of those years suffice it to mention that every cultural work, even the mere compilation of a bibliography, had to adhere strictly to party directives, that demanded that Ceauşescu's works, printed, depending on the text, in the range of 200,000 to 500,000 copies, were mentioned before Marx's, Engels' and Lenin's.

In this context the translation of the *Grundrisse* was a mere formality, evidence of an allegiance to Moscow and a demonstration that despite divergences Romania remained anchored to the Soviet bloc. The manuscripts of 1857–8 were used for teaching and mentioned at specialists' conferences by some intellectuals, especially the ones who were dissatisfied with the ideological orientation of the government. Nonetheless, with the exception of the 'Introduction', already translated in 1954 and circulated in university departments of philosophy and economics, its theoretical impact was absolutely negligible. Given that the total number of Romanian scholars who carried out in-depth analyses of Marxism is unlikely to exceed 50 people, the same would apply to the whole production of the philosopher from Trier.

After 1989 Marx literally disappeared from Romania. Marxism is held responsible of every negative event in the political and cultural debate of the nation, and with the exception of the *Manifesto of the Communist Party*, none of his writings were reprinted for the past 20 years. Paradoxically, however, the oblivion of the Ceauşescu era and the expiation of neo-liberalism share a surprising nonsense: in neither is Marx's oeuvre read.

Bibliography

Complete edition

Marx, Karl (1972, 1974) *Bazele criticii economice politice*, Bucharest: Editura Politica.

Partial edition

Marx, Karl (1954) 'Introducere' ['Introduction'], in Karl Marx, *Contributii la critica economiei politice*, Bucharest: Editura de stat pentru literatura politica, pp. 205–36.

23 USA, Britain, Australia and Canada

Christopher J. Arthur

Interest in Marx's *Grundrisse* was a long time coming in the English-speaking world. The debate about the 'young' (1844) and 'old' (1867) Marx in the 1950s and 1960s was carried on in ignorance of it. The publication in Moscow of the full German text in 1939–41 had gone unnoticed (the British Library has two copies, and the Library of Congress one, of volume one, the main text of 1939, only). Moreover, its re-publication in 1953 did not occasion any interest in translating it for the English-speaking world.

When Eric Hobsbawm edited and introduced *Pre-capitalist Economic Formations* in 1964, he expressed surprise at its neglect; but his own attempt to remedy this through presenting the *Pre-capitalist Formations* fell flat, probably because he situated the extract translated in the context of further elucidation of the problem of 'periods' raised by the 1859 *Preface*. This gave no clue to the range of the full text. Incidentally, Keith Tribe (1974: 209) claims that Hobsbawm goes beyond a presentation of the text, constructing a theory of transition where none is present.

The 1857 'Introduction' has had a somewhat separate publishing history. It was available in English since the 1904 translation by N.I. Stone from Kautsky's *Die Neue Zeit* original publication. The poor translation does not explain why it was not studied; probably it was taken to be an abandoned draft of the *Preface* to the 1859 *A Contribution to the Critique of Political Economy*. As late as 1968 David Horowitz referred to this 'generally neglected introduction' in justifying his republication of it (in Marx 1968); however in doing so he neglected to provide part four; only the first three parts are given.

It took the student radicalisation of the late 1960s to awaken interest in Marx's *Grundrisse*. In the *annus mirabilis*, 1968, Martin Nicolaus, a young American scholar, published an article on it in the British journal *New Left Review*, titled, appropriately, 'The Unknown Marx'. This so impressed New Left circles that it was awarded the Isaac Deutscher Memorial Prize for 1969. Doubtless this article stimulated the *New Left Review* to commission a full translation of the *Grundrisse* from Nicolaus (see below). According to Nicolaus the *Grundrisse* differed from Marx's earlier work in going beyond the movement of circulation to the economics of production; here the puzzle of surplus value is solved by the distinction between labour and labour-power. Nicolaus made large claims for the text; he held it is the only complete account of Marx's theory, whereas *Capital* is 'painfully unfinished'. In particular, *Capital* provided no theory of breakdown, whereas the *Grundrisse* did so (Nicolaus 1968: 55–7).

The 1970s was the decade in which the *Grundrisse* became the centre of attention.

The second translation of the 'Introduction', translated from MEW by S.W. Ryazanskaya, appeared in 1970, again as a supplement to *A Contribution to the Critique of Political Economy.*

Moreover David McLellan, perhaps the leading British Marx scholar at the time, was enthusiastic about this text. The book *Marx's Grundrisse* he put out in 1971 consisted of extracts from it, translated from the 1953 German edition, together with a short introduction. G.A. Cohen (1972) in his review of the book complained about the misleading title: it is neither a commentary (as the title suggests) nor a full translation; indeed it translates only 84 more German pages than were already available in English. In his own Introduction McLellan says it is the 'centrepiece' of Marx's work, the 'most fundamental' he ever wrote (McLellan 1971: 3). Like Nicolaus he held that, by contrast, *Capital* is 'dramatically incomplete' (McLellan 1971: 9). However, there is something a little curious about these claims, because he says it is the 'digressions that give the *Grundrisse* its primary importance' (McLellan 1971: 8). These include such topics as 'the individual and society', 'the nature of labour', 'the influence of automation', 'the abolition of the division of labour, 'alienation', and so on. Cohen, in his review, claimed that McLellan overestimated the importance of the *Grundrisse*, and especially the place of 'alienation' within it. His own view was that the *Grundrisse* is a mixed text. 'The young and old Marx are different, but they are phases of one intellectual life, and the *Grundrisse* bridges them. But a bridge does not fill a gulf. It links its opposite sides' (Cohen 1972: 373).

The first full translation (by Martin Nicolaus) appeared in 1973, 20 years after the 1953 German edition. The title was *Grundrisse*, and the subtitle: *Foundations of the Critique of Political Economy (Rough Draft).* After the 'Introduction' and the main text was added 'Bastiat and Carey'. What was of great importance was that the publishing house was Penguin, the leading mass publisher of paperback editions of both classics and new works. Somehow *New Left Review* had persuaded Penguin to launch a 'Pelican Marx Library' with their collaboration. The very first in this series was the *Grundrisse*. New translations of the three volumes of *Capital*, and four collections of shorter pieces, followed. It has been continuously available since then (in 1993 reissued as a 'Penguin Classic') so those interested have always had ready access to it.

While Nicolaus deserved congratulations for his pioneering work, his translation was not without defects. Most importantly, it was noticed almost immediately that his translation of *Verwertung* as 'realisation' was wrong. The rendering 'valorisation' is now general usage (despite its being somewhat 'technical'), having appeared in the 1976 Penguin translation of *Capital*. The reason Nicolaus's choice was so bad is that Marx used the term 'realisation' in relation to circulation, whereas the process of valorisation is rooted in production. Nicolaus translated the tricky term *Aufhebung* as 'suspension' (Nicolaus 1973: 32). This is an unusual choice. However, he offered textual support for it.

Nicolaus provided a substantial 'Foreword' of his own, which covered somewhat different ground than his article of 1968, with the more extravagant claims muted. He accounted for the division of the manuscript between a chapter on money and one on capital in that 'money' signifies an entire system of social relationships based on certain laws and 'capital' is a system of social relationships based on altogether opposite laws (Nicolaus 1973: 14). With respect to Marx's bold perspective on total automation Nicolaus was concerned to dispel any illusion this could be accomplished within capitalism (Nicolaus 1973: 51–2). Nicolaus dealt extensively with Marx's relation to Hegel, and with the section on 'method' in the 1857 'Introduction', especially on the question of the proper beginning: he held that, when Marx settled on 'the commodity' at the end of the *Grundrisse*, he determined to start with something 'concrete' so this means the considerations in the 'Introduction' pertaining to a movement from abstract to concrete were cast aside. Nicolaus was influenced at many points by Roman Rosdolsky's commentary of 1968 *The Making of Marx's 'Capital'* even where he did not directly cite it. This was true, for example, when he wrote of *Capital*: 'The *inner* structure is *identical* in the main lines to the *Grundrisse*, except that in the *Grundrisse* the structure lies on the surface, like a scaffolding, while in *Capital* it is built *in*; and this inner structure is nothing other than the materialist dialectic method' (Nicolaus 1973: 60).

Naturally such a large and difficult text would take time to absorb. Even so, the immediate reaction by the leading Marxist economist of the day, Maurice Dobb, was disappointingly non-committal when reviewing it in *Marxism Today* (Dobb 1973). However, Nicolaus's Foreword occasioned some vigorous responses, for example: Moishe Postone and Helmut Reinicke in the American journal *Telos* (1974) argued that his understanding of Hegel was 'shallow', and that this naturally vitiated his attempt to place Marx in relation to Hegel; Erwin Marquit in *Science and Society* (1977) argued against Nicolaus that taking the commodity as the starting point is consistent with the methodological considerations of Marx's 1857 'Introduction'.

Through the 1970s in most British university towns self-organised 'reading groups' sprang up to study the *Grundrisse*. A study group on it that met in New York during 1974 was the original context out of which came Carol Gould's book on *Marx's Social Ontology* (1978). She argued that the *Grundrisse* was the one work that presented Marx's basic ideas in a complete way, and from which his ontological concepts (about society, labour, freedom and justice) emerged most clearly.

The reception of the *Grundrisse* was to some extent conditioned by the context of its appearance, which differed in the USA and the UK. In the USA, Frankfurt School 'Critical Theory' was prominent, not least because of the towering presence of Herbert Marcuse at the University of California. So the 'Hegelianism' of the *Grundrisse* was congenial to American students, such as Gould. But in England at that time Althusserianism had established a bridgehead among young scholars. Of course, the *Grundrisse* threw a bomb into the Althusserian periodisation of Marx's work. In *For Marx* Althusser did not even mention it, and in *Reading Capital* references were confined to its Introduction. Just before Nicolaus's full text appeared, a member of the school, Ben Brewster, translated from the 1953 German text, and introduced, the fragment 'On Machines' (Marx 1973: 690–706). An early draft of this was circulated at the University of Leicester in 1966. It appeared in the new British journal *Economy and Society* (Marx 1972). His Introduction concluded that 'the *Grundrisse* have no advantage over *Capital* itself, either in the *extent* of their coverage, or in the *intensity* of their examination' (Brewster 1972: 239). Two subsequent interventions in the same journal were substantial and interesting (Tribe 1974; Mepham 1978).

In 'Remarks on the Theoretical Significance of Marx's *Grundrisse*', Keith Tribe defended the Althusserian periodisation of Marx's development which establishes an epistemological break with the young Marx. Far from seeing the *Grundrisse* as a draft of *Capital*, he attempted to show it was an incoherent transitional work. Tribe claimed the concept of 'relations of production' is missing; hence Marx is still muddled on *what* is exchanged in the wage contract (Tribe 1974: 189–90). He also pointed to the role of the conceptual couple fixed/circulating capital 'whose site in the theoretical structure of the *Grundrisse* seems to be that of constant/variable capital in *Capital*' (Tribe 1974: 182). This in turn seriously distorted categories such as accumulation and reproduction. In this respect, Tribe credited Grossmann with discovering the importance of Marx's study of Quesnay's reproduction schemes in the 1860s *after* the *Grundrisse* (Tribe 1974: 192–3).

An important event in the reception of the *Grundrisse* was the translation in 1977 of Rosdolsky's pioneering work *The Making of Marx's 'Capital'*. This rapidly established itself as authoritative. However, it provoked a substantial review article in *Economy and Society* by John Mepham ('The *Grundrisse*: Method or Metaphysics?' 1978). Mepham took the two big things in Rosdolsky to be the distinction between 'capital in general' and 'many capitals' made in the *Grundrisse*, and the claim that the method of *Capital* was implicitly Hegelian, as the *Grundrisse* showed more clearly. With respect to the first, while he accepted it, he complained that 'when explaining the distinction when it is first invoked (p. 46) he [Rosdolsky] confuses it with a quite different distinction, namely that between aggregate capital and individual capital' (Mepham 1978: 432–3). In 'Capital in General and Marx's *Capital*', Chris Arthur found five different definitions of 'capital in general' in the *Grundrisse* manuscript (Arthur 2002). However, Mepham's main objection was to Rosdolsky's Hegelianism. He argued that Rosdolsky was mistaken in assuming that the *Grundrisse* and *Capital* are identical in their method; he further argued it is a mistake to assume that *Capital* is a unified discourse such that there is a unique answer to the question of whether or not it is Hegelian (Mepham 1978: 435). In contrast, Mepham argued that in the *Grundrisse* (but sometimes even in *Capital*) there are incompatible discourses where such key derivations as that to money from value, and to capital from money, are concerned. He distinguished the 'philosophical' from the 'scientific' proofs in such cases. In general Mepham read Marx's development as a struggle to release his discourse from Hegelianism, something far from accomplished in the *Grundrisse* (Mepham 1978: 436).

Stuart Hall, the influential founder of 'cultural studies', made a close study of the 1857 'Introduction' in 1974; against Althusser, he insisted that Marx's epistemology remained in contact with the real historical object and with social practice. In reprinting his paper in 2003, the editors of *Cultural Studies* claimed that it was not merely of 'archaeological' interest but remained pertinent to the field today.

Yet another translation of the 1857 'Introduction', from the German edition of 1953, was produced by Terrell Carver in his *Karl Marx: Texts on Method* (Marx 1975). He provided very substantial notes and commentary on the text. Just as McLellan saw language 'that might have come straight out of Hegel's *Logic*' (McLellan 1971: 13), Carver stressed that the philosophical sophistication of the 'Introduction' showed Marx's familiarity with Hegel, even though it was written *before* Freiligrath offered him Bakunin's old copy of Hegel's *Logic* in October (Carver 1975: 43). Recently Mark Meaney made the stronger claim that the categories of the *Grundrisse* develop in parallel to those of Hegel's *Logic* (Meaney 2002).

As may be seen from the dates, neither Nicolaus, nor the partial translations, were based on the MEGA[2] edition of the text (1976–81). However, when the second full translation, *Economic Manuscripts of 1857–58 (First Version of 'Capital')*, appeared in the Marx–Engels *Collected Works* (in two hardback volumes, volume 28 in 1986, and volume 29 in 1987; 35,000 copies of each were printed), the German source was the MEGA[2]. Volume 28, translated by Ernst Wangermann, contains 'Bastiat and Carey', the 'Introduction', and the first instalment of the main text, titled 'Outlines of the Critique of Political Economy (Rough Draft of 1857–58)'. Volume 29, translated by Victor Schnittke, contains the second instalment of the main text; among additional material is the *Urtext* to *A Contribution to the Critique of Political Economy* of 1859 (the only English translation of it). The English *Collected Works* in 50 volumes begun in 1975 is now complete; the first volume was printed in the USSR, the last in the USA; such are the peregrinations of world history.

The translation in *Collected Works* appears to be generally good; but note that in *Collected Works* 29, on pages 209–10, several times *vergegenständlichte* is incorrectly rendered 'reified' when it should be 'objectified'. Then there is the vexed question of the correct rendering of *bürgerliche Gesellschaft*, where two alternatives exist: 'civil society' or 'bourgeois society' must be chosen according to context. This is important for the 1857 'Introduction'. To begin with let us note a strange fact: in the index to *Collected Works* 28 the term 'civil society' has three entries. However, on the first two pages cited the term does not appear (Marx 1986: 17–18)! What does appear is the term '"bourgeois society"', in what are known colloquially as 'scare quotes' indicating the term is somewhat problematical. Marx was discussing the views of Smith, Ricardo and their eighteenth-century predecessors about a 'society of free competition' (Marx 1986: 17). They referred to this as 'civil society', not 'bourgeois society', of course, because they presented it ideologically as the creation of 'free' and 'equal' individuals having rights to their persons and possessions. Marx's scare quotes indicated that with *bürgerliche Gesellschaft* he followed the standard German translation of the English term 'civil society'. So *Collected Works* made the wrong choice on these pages.

Both editions of the full text are still in print. Although many scholars habitually use the Nicolaus translation, it has been superseded by the newer translation in the *Collected Works*. The reasons for this judgement are:

1   The 1953 German text used by Nicolaus has been superseded by that in the new MEGA² used for the *Collected Works*. All the advances in scholarship that make the later source superior to the earlier *ipso facto* apply to their translations.

2   Nicolaus mistranslated the central term *Verwertung*. *Collected Works* correctly rendered this 'valorisation'. Unless it can be shown that the *Collected Works* translation is definitely inferior in other respects this consideration is decisive.

3   The Nicolaus edition has no index. The *Collected Works* edition has full notes and large indexes.

Naturally, beside the US and UK reception mentioned above, our text has been discussed in other parts of the English-speaking world. The Australian scholar, Allen Oakley argued, in relation to Marx's changing plans, that he never settled on the scope of his critical theory: *Marx's Critique of Political Economy: Intellectual Sources and Evolution Volume I 1844 to 1860* (1984). Two scholars based in Canada have published monographs. Adalbert Lallier's *The Economics of Marx's* Grundrisse is an annotated summary of the text with special reference to Marx's views concerning international trade and finance (Lallier 1989). Thomas Kemple's *Reading Marx Writing: Melodrama, the Market, and the 'Grundrisse'* is a freewheeling meditation on selected 'foundational' passages from the text which reveal the literary imagination of Marx and of fiction writers he admired (Kemple 1995).

Few have mastered the labyrinth that is the main text of Marx's *Grundrisse*; more research is required before it is finally mapped. The 1857 'Introduction', in contrast, is now well-known to Anglophone scholars: for a century Engels' attribution of a 'logical-historical method' to Marx held the field; but no one now writes on methodological questions without reference to Marx's own reflections in this text. In particular, the ascent 'from the abstract to the concrete' (Marx 1973: 101) has become something of a cliché.

On the heels of the English *Grundrisse* followed an English translation of the famous 'Draft Chapter 6 of *Capital* on the Results of the Direct Production Process', appended to the 1976 Penguin *Capital*. More recently Marx's 1861–3 manuscripts came to our attention (MECW, vols 30–34, 1988–94). But it can be said that the translation of Marx's *Grundrisse* uniquely changed our understanding of Marx's development.

Bibliography

Complete editions

Marx, Karl (1973) *Grundrisse: Foundations of the Critique of Political Economy (Rough Draft)*, Harmondsworth: Penguin; New York: Vintage Books.
Marx, Karl (1986 and 1987) *Economic Manuscripts of 1857–58 (First Version of* Capital), in Karl Marx and Friedrich Engels, *Collected Works*, vol. 28, trans. Ernst Wangermann, vol. 29 trans. Victor Schnittke, London: Lawrence & Wishart; New York: International Publishers.

Partial editions

Marx, Karl (1904) 'Introduction to the Critique of Political Economy', Appendix to Karl Marx, *A Contribution to the Critique of Political Economy*, Chicago: Charles H. Kerr & Co., pp. 265–312.
Marx, Karl (1964) *Pre-capitalist Economic Formations*, trans. Jack Cohen, Eric J. Hobsbawm (ed.), London: Lawrence & Wishart; New York: International Publishers (1965), pp. 67–120.
Marx, Karl (1968) 'Introduction to the Critique of Political Economy', in David Horowitz (ed.), *Mark and Modern Economics*, London: MacGibbon & Kee; New York: Monthly Review Press, pp. 21–48.
Marx, Karl (1970) 'Introduction to the Critique of Political Economy', in Karl Marx, *A Contribution to the Critique of Political Economy*, Moscow: Progress Publishers, pp. 188–217.
Marx, Karl (1971) *Marx's Grundrisse*, David McLellan (ed.), London: Macmillan; New York: Harper and Row.
Marx, Karl (1972) 'Notes on Machines', *Economy and Society*, vol. 1, no. 3: 244–54.
Marx, Karl (1975) 'Marx's *Introduction* (1857) to the *Grundrisse*', in Terrell Carver (ed.), *Karl Marx: Texts on Method*, Oxford: Basil Blackwell, pp. 46–87.

Critical literature on the Grundrisse

Arthur, Christopher J. (2002) 'Capital in General and Marx's *Capital*', in Martha Campbell and Geert Reuten (eds), *The Culmination of Capital*, Basingstoke: Palgrave, pp. 42–64.
Brewster, Ben (1972) 'Introduction to Marx's "Notes on Machines"', *Economy and Society*, vol. 1, no. 3: 235–43.
Carver, Terrell (1975) 'A Commentary on Marx's *Introduction* (1857) to the *Grundrisse*', in Terrell Carver (ed.), *Karl Marx: Texts on Method*, Oxford: Basil Blackwell, pp. 88–158.
Cohen, G.A. (1972) 'Thoughts on the Grundrisse', *Marxism Today*, vol. 16, no. 12: 372–4.
Dobb, Maurice (1973) '*Grundrisse*', *Marxism Today*, vol. 17, no. 10: 303–6.
Gould, Carol C. (1978) *Marx's Social Ontology: Individuality and Community in Marx's Theory of Social Reality*, Cambridge, Mass.: The MIT Press.

Hall, Stuart (1974) 'Marx's Notes on Method: A "Reading" of the "1857 Introduction"', *Working Papers in Cultural Studies*, 6: 132–70; reprinted in *Cultural Studies* (2003) vol. 17, no. 2: 113–49.

Kemple, Thomas M. (1995) *Reading Marx Writing: Melodrama, the Market, and the "Grundrisse"*, Stanford: Stanford University Press.

Lallier, Adalbert G. (1989) *The Economics of Marx's 'Grundrisse'*, Basingstoke: Macmillan; New York: St. Martin's Press.

McLellan, David (1971) 'Introduction', in Karl Marx, *Marx's Grundisse*, London: Macmillan; New York: Harper and Row.

Marquit, Erwin (1977–8) 'Nicolaus and Marx's Method of Scientific Theory in the *Grundrisse*', *Science & Society*, vol. XLI, no. 4: 465–76.

Meaney, Mark E. (2002) *Capital as Organic Unity: The Role of Hegel's* Science of Logic *in Marx's* Grundrisse, Dordrecht, Boston and London: Kluwer.

Mepham, John (1978) '*The Grundrisse*: Method or Metaphysics', *Economy and Society*, vol. 7, no. 4: 430–44.

Nicolaus, Martin (1968) 'The Unknown Marx', *New Left Review*, 48: 41–61.

Nicolaus, Martin (1973) 'Foreword' to Karl Marx *Grundrisse: Foundations of the Critique of Political Economy (Rough Draft)* Harmondsworth: Penguin; New York: Vintage Books, pp. 7–63.

Oakley, Allen (1984) *Marx's Critique of Political Economy: Intellectual Sources and Evolution Volume I 1844 to 1860*, London: Routledge; Boston: Kegan Paul.

Piccone, Paul (1975) 'Reading the Grundrisse: Beyond "Orthodox" Marxism', *Theory and Society*, vol. 2, no. 1: 235–55.

Postone, Moishe and Reinicke, Helmut (1974–5) 'On Nicolaus "Introduction" to the *Grundrisse*', *Telos*, 22: 130–48.

Rosdolsky, Roman (1977) *The Making of Marx's 'Capital'*, London: Pluto Press.

Sixel, Friedrich W. (1995) *Understanding Marx*, Lanham: University Press of America.

Tribe, Keith (1974) 'Remarks on the Theoretical Significance of Marx's *Grundrisse*', *Economy and Society*, vol. 3, no. 2: 180–210.

24 Denmark

Birger Linde

For many years Denmark was poor in Marx translations. In 1952 the Communist Party of Denmark published a translation of selected writings by Marx and Engels in two volumes, edited by the Marx–Engels–Lenin Institute in Moscow (Marx and Engels 1952): the political writings of Marx and Engels were given a priority, whereas Marx's critique of political economy was almost neglected. Ten years later, the stock of Danish texts was supplemented by a small volume containing writings of the young Marx (Marx 1962).

The times were changing in the 1970s, and the publication of the *Grundrisse* was a turning point. Essential parts of the manuscript were translated and edited in 1970 by the young Marxist Kjeld Schmidt (Marx 1970). In his introduction, the editor describes the essential message of the *Grundrisse* in this way: 'In their everyday conscious activity individuals are facing a foreign power, which they produce themselves: it is the social relation of individuals appearing as an independent social power' (Schmidt 1970: 9). This is Marx's concept of alienation, of capital as a subject transforming human beings into objects, and the editor emphasizes that there is a clear thread linking the *Grundrisse* back to the *Economic and Philosophical Manuscripts of 1844*, as well as forward to *Capital*. The texts from the *Grundrisse* are carefully selected to show that Marx is deeply concerned with the relation between the alienating power of capital and the necessary liberation of mankind.

At the same time, student protests in Denmark were escalating, a new political left was formed, and students were looking for a theoretical reorientation of social science and economics. Enthusiasm for reading Marx spread in a powerful wave at Danish universities. In this process, the *Grundrisse* translation by Schmidt was very helpful. It was printed and sold out in 2,000 copies, which is a lot for a small book market.

Soon *Capital* was translated too. A fully integrated translation of the three volumes of Marx's *opus magnum* appeared in the following few years (Marx 1970, 1971, 1972). However, the editor and one of the main translators belonged to the 'old left', to the tradition of historical and dialectical materialism, and this soon aroused criticism from 'new left' Marxists.

The question is highlighted in a small pamphlet published by Modtryk and Kurasje. Here the 'old left' editors of *Capital* and the *Grundrisse* are accused of 'treating Hegel as a dead dog' (Brinch *et al.* 1974: 8). A whole range of bad translations of concepts and formulations are criticized, but the main charge seems to be 'a systematic de-Hegelisation' of Marx and a 'confusion of concepts' (Brinch *et al.* 1974: 6). Several examples demonstrate that the criticism is well-founded. The Hegelian concepts of essence, phenomenon, appearance (*Wesen–Schein–Erscheinung*) are systematically concealed or eradicated in the translation, although Marx obviously uses these forms of thought (*Denkformen*) very actively.

A fully integrated translation of the *Grundrisse* was soon going to appear. This incident brought the theoretical contrast between old and new left thinking to an open clash. The publisher Rhodos (who had published the *Grundrisse* in 1970 and *Capital* in 1970–2) authorized Witt-Hansen to edit the *Grundrisse* translation. Young Marxists in Århus found that the very dialectical and Hegelian inspired thoughts of Marx in the *Grundrisse* would be betrayed, and seized the initiative to publish a competing translation of the *Grundrisse* by the 'new left' publishers Modtryk and Kurasje.

A few years later there were two fully integrated translations of the *Grundrisse* in a country as small as Denmark: the 'old left edition' in six volumes translated by Johannes Witt Hansen with the title *Grundrids til kritik af den politiske økonomi* [*Outlines to the Critique of Political Economy*], and the 'new left edition' in four volumes translated by Mihail Larsen and Hans-Jørgen Schanz with the title *Grundrids til Kritikken af den Politiske Økonomi* [*Outlines of the Critique of Political Economy*]. Both versions were translated from the German version of 1953.

The introduction to the edition by Witt-Hansen is brief (Witt-Hansen 1974: 5–17). It highlights the historical setting in which the manuscript was worked out (the crisis of 1857), and the *Grundrisse* is emphatically presented as the first full-size draft of *Capital*. No account of the principles and the difficulties of translation are included.

The introduction to the competing edition by Larsen and Schanz is quite lengthy (59 pages). It contains a discussion of the placement of the *Grundrisse* in Marx's theoretical development, as well as a presentation of the guidelines directing the translation. The introduction clearly reveals that the editors were closely related to the German school of 'Capital logicians'. Unfortunately, the reader does not get a clear-cut justification for the necessity of an alternative translation. Denmark is the only country in the world to be bestowed with two full translations of this important manuscript that reflect a new versus old left confrontation, but in the long run this wealth of translations did not prove to be a blessing. Neither of the two full translations received the same publicity and success as the 1970 selected *Grundrisse* edition by Schmidt. One reason may be the competition itself: it probably raised confusion among students and left wing people, making it a matter for Marx experts to decide what the dispute really was about, which edition one should read, and which camp to support.

Another possible explanation is the time of publication. When the ambitious, competing undertakings were finished (in 1977 and 1978) the strong wave of interest in Marxism and the self-confidence of the youth protest was already receding a little. This is confirmed by the fact that, apart from the three introductions to the three translations, few Danish books or papers specifically relate to the *Grundrisse*. Several Danish Marxists have used the *Grundrisse* as a resource for discussing Marx's analysis of capital and capitalism in general (one example is Schanz 1973).

A close reading of the *Grundrisse* in Danish is only found in two books. The first is *Kapitalens Bevidsthedsformer* [*Forms of Consciousness of Capital*] of Anders Lundkvist published in 1972, and the second, many years later, is Birger Linde's *De Store Kriser* [*The Great Crises*], with a special section devoted to the interpretation of the *Grundrisse* (Linde 2004: 50–79).

Bibliography

Complete editions

Marx, Karl (1974, 1975, 1976, 1977, 1978) *Grundrids til kritik af den politiske økonomi*, Johannes Witt-Hansen (ed.), 6 vols, Copenhagen: Rhodos.
Marx, Karl (1974, 1975, 1976, 1977) *Grundrids til Kritikken af den Politiske Økonomi*, Mihail Larsen and Hans-Jørgen Schanz (eds), 4 vols, Århus: Modtryk; Copenhagen: Kurasje.

Partial edition

Marx, Karl (1970) *Kritik af den Politiske Økonomi, Grundrids* [*Critique of Political Economy, Grundrisse*], Kjeld Schmidt (ed.), Copenhagen: Rhodos.

Critical literature on the Grundrisse

Brinch, Jens, Finnemann, Niels Ole, Hansson, Finn and Kjær, Thyge (1974) *I anledning af Grundridsudgivelsen* [*Concerning the Edition of Grundri*sse], Århus: Modtryk; Copenhagen: Kurasje.
Larsen, Mihail and Schanz, Hans-Jørgen (1974) 'Oversætternes forord' ['Translators Foreword'], in Karl Marx, *Grundrids til Kritikken af den Politiske Økonomi*, vol. 1, Århus: Modtryk; Copenhagen: Kurasje, pp. i–lix.
Linde, Birger (2004) *De Store Kriser I. Kriseteori og kriser I 1800-tallet – inspirationen fra Marx* [*The Great Crises, Vol I. Crisis Theory and Crises in the 19th Century – The Inspiration from Mar*x], Roskilde: International Development Studies, Roskilde University.
Lundkvist, Anders (1972) *Kapitalens Bevidsthedsformer*, Grenå: GMT.
Schanz, Hans-Jørgen (1973) *Til Rekonstruktionen af kritikken af den politiske økonomis omfangslogiske status* [*Reconstruction of the Logical Status of the Critique of Political Economy*], Århus: Modtryk.
Schmidt, Kjeld (1970) 'Indledning, Fremmedgørelse og frigørelse' ['Introduction, Alienation and Emancipation'], in Karl Marx, *Kritik af den Politiske Økonomi, Grundrids*, Copenhagen: Rhodos, pp. 7–20.
Witt-Hansen (1974) 'Om "Grundrids"' ['Concerning "Grundrisse"'], in Karl Marx, *Grundrids til kritik af den politiske økonomi*, vol. 1, Copenhagen: Rhodos, pp. 5–17.

Other references

Marx, Karl (1962) *Økonomi og Filosofi. Ungdomsskrifter* [*Economy and Philosophy. Early Writings*], Copenhagen: Gyldendal.

Marx, Karl (1970, 1971, 1972) *Kapitalen bog 1–3* [*Capital vols 1–3*], Copenhagen: Rhodos.

Marx, Karl and Engels, Friedrich (1952) *Udvalgte skrifter i to bind* [*Selected Writings in Two Volumes*], Copenhagen: Forlaget Tiden.

25 Yugoslavia

Lino Veljak

The *Grundrisse* has been an important text in Yugoslavia. Its wide circulation was certainly helped by the specificity of Yugoslavian Marxism, which was always different from the soviet style Marxism–Leninism of many so-called 'socialist states'. A certain amount of freedom of philosophical and scientific research, however limited and repressed on occasions, contributed to shape a non-dogmatic Marxism that found its main expression in the journal *Praxis* and the summer school of philosophy and sociology of Korčula (1964–74). Since then, the theories of the scholars who participated in these experiences have revolved around the Marxian concepts of alienation, reification and socialist humanism that would later find many correspondences on the pages of the *Grundrisse*.

In fact, the history of the *Grundrisse* in Yugolavia had already started. In 1949, the prominent communist leader who would later become the President of the Yugoslavian Parliament, Moša Pijade, translator of *Capital* in the Serbian/Serbo-Croatian language, edited the first translation of the 1857 'Introduction'. Based on the German version of 1939–41, this was printed in 1949 with the title *Kritika političke ekonomije* [*Critique of Political Economy*].

A decade later, the first systematic account of the *Grundrisse* was published. This was the work of Predrag Vranicki, who, in his *Historija marksizma* [*History of Marxism*] of 1961, re-published in a two-volume improved edition in 1975, reworking some of the concepts found in the 'Introduction', pointed out that the Marxian method was founded on a dialectics of the concrete and that the latter represented the unity of the universal and the particular, whilst exposing the Hegelian illusion for which the real is the outcome of a process of abstraction.

Subsequent partial translations of the *Grundrisse* were made, based on the German edition of 1953 and published shortly after. Branko Petrović (father of the famous philosopher Gajo Petrović, who was the editor of *Praxis*) translated several sections of it between 1963 and 1965 for the Belgrade 'Institut za istraživanje radničkog pokreta' ['Research Institute of the Working Class Movement'], where the full translation of MEW, published between 1968 and 1979 in 45 volumes and entitled Marx and Engels *Dela* [*Works*], was also being compiled. His translations initially appeared as installments of 40 pages in the journal

Treči Program Radio-Beograda [*Third Programme of Belgrade Radio*], edited by Gajo Petrović, in 1969; later, in 1974, they were given a complete edition as *Temelji slobode* [*Foundations of Freedom*]. The latter included the 1857 'Introduction' in Pijade's translation, a selection of excerpts from the 'Chapter on Money' (around 40 pages), various sections from the 'Chapter on Capital' (150 pages) and the notes on 'Bastiat and Carey'.

Alongside these translations, the first commentaries on the *Grundrisse* started to appear. Its main exegete was Gajo Petrović. In his 1964 article 'Kontinuitet Marxove misli' ('The Continuity of Marxian Theory'), reprinted in 1965 as part of the book *Filozofija i marksizam* [*Philosophy and Marxism*], he regarded the *Grundrisse* as evidence of the continuity of Marx's thought and as necessary to understand the link between *The Economic and Philosophical Manuscripts of 1844* and *Capital*. According to Petrović, *Capital* repeated the main formulations found in the *Grundrisse* which, in turn, referred back to the theses of the Parisian manuscripts of 1844. However, this did not mean that the *Grundrisse* and *Capital* did not add anything to the *Economic and Philosophical Manuscripts of 1844*.

In his preface to *Temelji slobode*, which he edited and published in 1974, Petrović's views on the *Grundrisse* changed: the text was now mainly the primary reading for a correct understanding of Marx's theory and only secondarily the evidence of the continuity of his thought through its different chronological stages. Petrović also believed that the *Grundrisse* was philosophically superior to *Capital* because it contained a deeper critique of the contemporary world and its reification, and a more elaborate exposition of future communist societies. The *Grundrisse* demonstrated that the essence of Marx's thought lied in his critique of political economy: a critique that was also a revolutionary philosophy, not understood as an academic discipline but as a revolutionary theory that embodies the best of all philosophical, social and scientific traditions. Petrović's views had great appeal on students, scholars who were more to the Left and the more enlightened members of the Communist league of Yugoslavia, all of whom were amongst the supporters of a democratic socialism with a human face. On the contrary, the more conservative party factions ostracized it and as a result they completely ignored the relevance of the *Grundrisse*.

Scholars under the major influence of the Frankfurt School, in particular Žarko Puhovski and Hotimir Burger, criticized Petrović's interpretation too. They were concerned by what they considered to be an excessive emphasis on the philosophical aspects of Marx's theory and, from the late 1970s, they interpreted the *Grundrisse* as above all a useful text for the development of a critical theory of society.

The translation of the whole of the *Grundrisse* into Serbian/Serbo-Croatian language, based on the 1953 German edition, was finally published in 1979 in two volumes, respectively 19 and 20 of the Marx and Engels *Dela*, with the title *Osnovi kritike političke ekonomije* [*Foundations of the Critique of Political Economy*], and a preface by Petrović. Although these were printed in 5,000 copies, it must be said that the majority of them were destined to the libraries of the party (much of which was lost after 1990) and only a few hundred copies were distributed to bookshops and academic or public libraries.

In 1985 the *Grundrisse* was also published in Slovenian as *Kritika politične ekonomije: 1857/58* [*Critique of Political Economy: 1857/58*]. It was printed in two volumes and 1,000 copies, translated from the 1983 MEW edition, by a group of scholars coordinated by the philosopher Božidar Debenjak and followed by a historical and bibliographical postscript by Pavle Zgaga and Rado Riha.

Finally, in 1989 the partial translation of the *Grundrisse* also appeared in the Macedonian language as *Osnovi na kritikata na političkata ekonomija (Grub nafrlok): 1857–1858* [*Outline of the Critique of Political Economy, Draft: 1857–1858*] edited by Jonče Josifovski, which comprised of the same selections found in the 1974 Serbian/Serbo-Croatian edition.

In the same year the Slovenian philosopher Pavel Zgaga published his *Grundrisse: od renesanse do krize marksizma* [*Grundrisse: from the Renaissance to the Crisis of Marxism*], which marked a provisinal end to the reception of the *Grundrisse* in Yugoslavia. In this work, the author concentrates on the crisis investing Marxism and restates the importance of the *Grundrisse* and the need to keep remembering this text by Marx.

Although with the disappearance of Yugoslavia Marx was almost abandoned, in the past few years there has been a renewed interest in his thought and innovative Marxian studies have emerged, especially in Slovenia and Croatia, that also involve the *Grundrisse*. Slavoj Žižek refers to it too in a recent work (Žižek 1999), where some passages are quoted in his development of a new postmodern interpretation of Marx.

[Translated from the Italian by Arianna Bove]

Bibliography

Complete editions

Marx, Karl (1979) *Osnovi kritike političke ekonomije*, in Marx and Engels *Dela*, vols 19 and 20, Belgrade: Institut za izučavanje radničkog pokreta/Prosveta.
Marx, Karl (1985) *Kritika politične ekonomije: 1857/58*, Ljubljana: Delavska enotnost.

Partial editions

Marx, Karl (1949) *Kritika političke ekonomije*, Belgrade–Zagreb: Kultura.
Marx, Karl (1969) 'Izbor iz Grundrissa' ['Selected extracts from the *Grundrisse*'], in *Treći program Radio-Beograda*, 1: 25–63.
Marx, Karl (1974) *Temelji slobode*, Zagreb: Naprijed.
Marx, Karl (1989) *Osnovi na kritikata na političkata ekonomija (grub nafrlok): 1857–1858*, Skopje: Komunist.

Critical literature on the Grundrisse

Burger, Hotimir (1979) *Filozofija i kritika političke ekonomije* [Philosophy and Critique of Political Economy], Zagreb: August Cesarec.

Petrović, Gajo (1964) 'Kontinuitet Marxove misli', in *Marksova misao*: 86–104; reprint in Gajo Petrović (1965) *Filozofija i marksizam*, Zagreb: Naprijed, pp. 72–83.

Petrović, Gajo (1974) 'Smisao i značenje Marxovih *Grundrissa*' ['Sense and Meaning of Marx's *Grundrisse*'], in Marx, Karl (1974) *Temelji slobode*, Zagreb: Naprijed, pp. VII–XXIII.

Puhovski, Žarko (1980) *Povijest i revolucija* [*History and Revolution*], Zagreb: Centar za kulturnu djelatnost SSO.

Vranicki, Predrag (1961) *Historija marksizma*, Zagreb: Naprijed; reprinted in 2 vols (1975).

Zgaga, Pavel (1989) *Grundrisse: od renesanse do krize marksizma*, Ljubljana: Republička konferenca ZSMS/Univerzitetna konferenca ZSMS.

Žižek, Slavoj (1999) *The Ticklish Subject: The Absent Centre of Political Ontology*, London: Verso.

26 Iran

Kamran Nayeri

In the history of the translation of Marx's works into Farsi, the publication of the *Grundrisse: Mabani naghdeh eghtessade siasi* [*Grundrisse: Foundations of a Critique of Political Economy*] in two volumes, in 1985 and 1987, was a landmark event. Marx's writings have appeared in Farsi relatively late, mostly in bad translations (e.g., Marx 1974), and often amidst great difficulties due to anticommunist repression. Whether in bookstores or the underground market, Marx's writings have generally found an enthusiastic audience. Yet, there is little evidence of their direct influence on the intellectual or political life of Iran. The publication of the *Grundrisse* signalled a welcome change of some of these trends.

Socialist literature flourished after the revolutionary overthrow of the Pahlavi dictatorship in 1979. Bagher Parham, a sociologist and accomplished translator, was offered the task of editing the translation of the Martin Nicolaus English edition of the *Grundrisse* by Ahmad Tadayon. Parham compared and corrected Tadayon's translation against Roger Dangeville's French edition of 1967–8 and the 1953 German edition. The *Grundrisse* was the first of Marx's extensive works to be professionally translated into Farsi and thus set a much needed higher level of engagement.

By Iranian standards the *Grundrisse* was well received: it went through three print runs and sold around 11,000 copies. Yet, there is little evidence of a direct impact on the intellectual milieu: there were neither book reviews nor published commentaries on the occasion of its publication. Certainly the period between the bloody repression of socialist groups in 1982–3 and the 1989 summary execution of perhaps thousands of political prisoners played its role. There is no evidence of any *Grundrisse* study groups since, either in the academia or in socialist quarters, even outside Iran.

Other factors contributed to the poor impact of the *Grundrisse*. The relative backwardness of Iran impeded social and intellectual development and more efforts were directed towards economic development and industrialization rather than their radical critique. Iranian socialists have been influenced by Marxisms after Marx since the Second International, particularly by its Russian interpretations. The dismembering of the revolutionary Communist Party in 1931, and the consolidation of the Tudeh Party, founded in 1941, as a Stalinist organization, stifled socialist intellectual and political debate in the name of

Marxism–Leninism. Finally, state-run academic institutions have traditionally shown little interest in Marx.

However, there are promising signs of change. Since the publication of the *Grundrisse*, a number of significant works by Marx and Engels have appeared in good translations and seemed to attract new readerships. So far, there has been little reference to the *Grundrisse* in the works of the few Iranian intellectuals who have published high quality research on Marx.

Bibliography

Complete edition

Marx, Karl (1985, 1987) *Grundrisse: Mabani naghdeh eghtessade siasi*, trans. Bagher Parham and Ahmad Tadayon, Teheran: Entesharate Agah.

Other reference

Marx, Karl (1974) *Sarmaye*, Jelde 1 [*Capital*, vol. 1], trans. Iraj Eskandari, (n.p.): Tudeh Party.

27 Poland

Holger Politt

The unabridged edition of the *Grundrisse* in Polish was preceded by the publication of some of its parts. The first extract to be translated was the 'Introduction' of 1857, which appeared on the journal *Nowe Drogi* [*New Ways*] in 1948. In 1966 a new translation of this piece was published in volume 13 of *Dzieła Marksa–Engelsa* [*Marx and Engels' Works*].

The second piece to see the light was 'Forms which Precede Capitalist Production', published on the academic journal *Studia Ekonomiczne* [*Studies of Economics*] in 1966. Later, in 1981, many sections of the *Grundrisse* were included in a three-volume collection of Marx and Engels' writings. In the introduction to this collection the publishers expressed their intention to publish the whole of the *Grundrisse* before long (Marx 1981).

These translations induced Polish scholars to engage with the text and particularly with 'Forms which Precede Capitalist Production', which generated the main theoretical developments. In the meantime, Adam Schaff, the most prominent Marxist from Poland, having read the *Grundrisse* in the original language, had given it enthusiastic reviews. In his *Entfremdung als soziales Phänomen* [*Alienation as a Social Phenomenon*], published in German in 1977, he wrote: 'The *Grundrisse* has exceptional importance for an understanding of *Capital*'. Furthermore, he noted how the *Grundrisse* was 'surprising in the modernity, I would say prophetic nature, of its statements on social and theoretical problems which intrigue us today' (Schaff 1977: 37). His assessment contributed to the emergence of new research.

In fact, in 1984, the students' journal *Colloquia Comunia* [*Common Talk*] dedicated the whole of issues 3/4 to the *Grundrisse*. The introduction to these journals also included Eric Hobsbawm 'Introduction' to 'Forms which Precede Capitalist Production' and Martin Nicolaus' 'The Unknown Marx', and expressed the wish to stimulate the publication of a full translation.

This was finally issued for publication in 10,000 copies in 1986, and entitled *Zarys krytyki ekonomii politycznej* [*Outlines of the Critique of Political Economy*], translated by Zygmunt Jan Wyrozembski. The translation was based on the German edition of 1953 and also used the Russian translation of 1968–9, of which it retained the preface. The Polish edition also included Marx's extracts from David Ricardo's works, written in the two year period of 1850–1.

After the publication of the full translation, the journal *Colloquia Comunia* published another two essays on the *Grundrisse*. The first, written by Waclaw Mejbaum, focused on the concept of property; the second, by Ewa Borowska, analysed the Marxist theory of primitive and Germanic communities. Two monographs also made many references to this text, one by Stanisław Kozyr-Kowalski (Kozyr-Kowalski 1988), the other by Borowaska (Borowaska 1996).

Bibliography

Complete edition

Marx, Karl (1986) *Zarys krytyki ekonomii politycznej*, Warsaw: Ksiażka i wiedza.

Partial editions

Marx, Karl (1948) 'Wprowadzenie' ['Introduction'], *Nowe Drogi*, 8: 5–41.
Marx, Karl (1966a) 'Wprowadzenie' ['Introduction'], in *Dzieła* Marksa – Engelsa, vol. 13, pp. 703–34.
Marx, Karl (1966b) 'Przedkapitalistyczne formacje ekonomiczne' ['Pre-capitalist Economic Formations'], *Studia Ekonomiczne*, 15: 5–34.
Marx, Karl (1981) *Grundrisse*, in Karl Marx and Friedrich Engels, *Dzieło wybrane* [*Selected Works*], vol. 2, pp. 21–183.

Critical literature on the Grundrisse

Borowska, Ewa (1987) *Socjalizm i kapitał. Marksistowska teoria wspólnoty antycznej i germańskiej* [*Socialism and Capital. The Marxist Theory of the Ancient and Germanic Communities*], *Colloquia Comunia*, 6: 93–117.
Borowska, Ewa (1996) *Indie, Chiny, Rosja w badaniach Marksa. Przyczynek do ontologii wspólnoty* [*India, China, Russia in Marx's Research Work. Contribution to the Ontology of the Communities*], Warsaw: Wydaw.
Kozyr-Kowalski, Stanisław (1988) *Struktura gospodarcza i formacja społeczeństwa* [*Economic Structure and Formation of Society*], Warsaw: KiW.
Mejbaum, Wacław (1988) *Własność jako przedmiot teoretyczny* [*Private Property as a Theoretical Question*], *Colloquia Comunia*, 4–5: 89–109.
Schaff, Adam (1977) *Entfremdung als soziales Phänomen*, Wien: Europa Verlag.

28 Finland

Vesa Oittinen

Although the first volume of *Capital* had already been published as a series of pamphlets in 1913–18, a large amount of Finnish translations of Marx and Engels' works were published in Moscow by Progress publishers. Obviously without this 'Soviet support' it would not have been financially possible to issue the central corpus of Marx and Engels' works in a relatively minor language like Finnish. The 'Introduction' and 'Forms which Precede Capitalist Production' are included in the fourth of the six volumes of Marx and Engels' selected writings. The Finnish translation of the *Grundrisse* followed Progress publishers' new edition of Marx's *Capital* in three volumes. In 1975 Antero Tiusanen, a renowned translator of Marx, translated the 'Introduction' for the publishing house of the Finnish Communist Party, Kansankulttuuri, but a full translation was not to come for another decade, when in 1986 Progress publishers finally printed it in Moscow in two volumes, translated from the MEGA² edition of 1976–81, entitled *Vuosien 1857–58 taloudelliset käsikirjoitukset (Grundrisse)* [*The Economic Manuscripts of 1857–58, Grundrisse*] with an extensive commentary from the Russian edition. Initially Progress publishers were reluctant to publish it but thanks to Petteri Baer, the leader of the Kansankulttuuri at the time, who reassured them that the *Grundrisse* would sell, they decided to print 1,700 copies of it. This might seem an exaggerated amount for Finland nowadays, but volume three of *Capital* had already sold 9,000 copies.

The Communist Party of Finland had never been able to carry out much theoretical work, which reflected the fact that as a movement it was almost entirely proletarian and had very few followers amongst the intelligentia. The situation changed in the 1970s when international radical groups from the 1960s elicited interest in Marxist theory also amongst the students' movement and young university researchers. There were several 'Capital logicians' at the sociology department of the university of Helsinki who closely followed the Danish theoretician Schanz and the discussions taking place in West German universities (Backhaus, Reichelt, etc.). This was a period of great engagement with Marx's critique of political economy in Finland, and the *Grundrisse*, then only available in the German original, was clearly one of the central points of reference, though never independently from Marx's other works on political economy.

In the 1980s interest in Marxism began to wane and, significantly, the work of the Finnish Researchers' Union (*Tutkijaliitto*), founded in 1977 with the express goal of carrying out Marxist research, became increasingly influenced by postmodern discourse. By the time the Finnish edition of the *Grundrisse* was published in 1986, it no longer aroused much interest. Today, the traditions of the research on Marx are mainly kept up by the Finnish Marx Society.

Bibliography

Complete edition

Marx, Karl (1986) *Vuosien 1857–1858 taloudelliset käsikirjoitukset ('Grundrisse')*, Moscow: Progress Publishers.

Partial editions

Marx, Karl (1975) ''"Grundrissen" Johdanto' ['Introduction to the *Grundrisse*'], trans. Antero Tiusanen, Pori: Kansankulttuuri.
Marx, Karl (1979a) *Johdanto vuosien 1857–1858 taloustieteellisiin käsikirjoituksiin* [*Introduction to the Economic Manuscripts of 1857–1858*], in Karl Marx and Friedrich Engels, *Valitut teokset. Kuusi osaa* [*Selected Works. Six Volumes*], vol. 4, trans. Antero Tiusanen, Moscow: Progress Publishers, pp. 198–230.
Marx, Karl (1979b) *Muotoja jotka edeltävät kapitalistista tuotantoa* [*Forms Preceding the Capitalist Mode of Production*], in Karl Marx and Friedrich Engels, *Valitut teokset. Kuusi osaa* [*Selected Works. Six Volumes*], vol. 4, trans. Olli Perheentupa, Moscow: Progress Publishers, pp. 231–77.

29 Greece

John Milios

The *Grundrisse* was translated into Greek by Dionysis Divaris with the title *Basikes Grammes tis Kritikis tis Politikis Oikonomias* [*Outlines of the Critique of Political Economy*], and published in three volumes with a print run of 3,000 copies each by the independent left publisher Stochastis in 1989, 1990 and 1992. The translation followed the German edition of 1953, but the translator took into consideration the corresponding MEGA² edition of 1976–81, and consulted the French (1967–8 and 1980), English (1973) and Italian (1968–70 and 1976) translations. The first volume includes the 'Introduction' and the 'Chapter on Money'. Volume two contains the 'Chapter on Capital', and volume three presents miscellaneous material from the German edition. The Greek translation of the *Grundrisse* was received as an editorial success and praised by radical peer-reviewed journals both for the quality of the translation and the importance of the text.

The first part of the *Grundrisse* to be translated in Greece was the 'Introduction', published in 1927 before it was in many other European languages. However, after this edition, a long time passed before new extracts were printed in Greek. After a decade of great interest in Marx's works due to the growth of the political movement opposing the military junta of 1967–74, the 'radical' political conjuncture that followed its fall and the increasing ideological power of the left in the early 1980s, the *Grundrisse* was much awaited by Greek Marxists and parts of it cited and discussed in Greek papers and books long before its full translation was published.

Parts of the manuscript had been translated, from the German edition of 1953, several years before the publication of the full text, and excerpts were included in editions of Marx's selected works that aimed at presenting a compendium of some of the author's views. The first selection of some parts of the *Grundrisse* was *O Anthropos stin Ergasia kai tin Synergasia. Apo ta Grundrisse* [*Man in Labour and Cooperation. Excerpts from the Grundrisse*] although the publication date was absent, it presumably appeared in the period 1976–8. The text included the 'Introduction', the 'Forms which Precede Capitalistic Production' as well as several other excepts. Further extracts of the *Grundrisse* were translated in the 1977 collection *I Epistimi tis Koinonias* [*The Science of Society*]. Finally, in 1983, the collection *Eklogi apo tis Grundrisse* [*A Selection from the Grundrisse*] appeared.

Although hundreds of references to the *Grundrisse* can be found, mainly in Greek Marxist papers, very few works take the *Grundrisse* as their special object of analysis. Divaris analyses the role of the *Grundrisse* in the development of Marx's theory, with a focus on Roman Rosdolsky's classical interpretation, in his foreword to the Greek translation (Divaris 1989). Theodoros Stavropoulos and John Milios highlight the relevance of 'Forms which Precede Capitalist Production' to the notion of Asiatic mode of production (Stavropoulos 1979: 195; Milios 1988: 165; Milios 1997: 255). Marx's theses on the consequences of applying science to capitalist production are discussed in Christos Vallianos's critique of Radovan Richta's notion of 'scientific-technical revolution' (Vallianos 1983), and Milios's critique of the 'end of labour' debate (Milios 1996). More recently, Spyros Lapatsioras compares Marx's notion of money as a symbol of value in the *Grundrisse* with the ones he drew up in *A Contribution to the Critique of Political Economy* and *Capital* (Lapatsioras 2008).

Finally, the reception of the *Grundrisse* by different international Marxist theoretical currents has also been critically assessed. Vasilis Kalfas and Zisis Sarikas stress the impact of the 1857 'Introduction' on the thought of Geörgy Lukács, Galvano Della Volpe and Louis Althusser in particular (Kalfas and Sarikas 1979). Antonio Negri's interpretation of the *Grundrisse* in *Marx beyond Marx* was praised by Sakis Drosos (Drosos 1982) and Petros Linardos-Rulmond (Linardos-Rulmond 1983) but criticized by Elias Ioakimoglou (Ioakimoglou 1983).

Bibliography

Complete edition

Marx, Karl (1989, 1990, 1992) *Basikes Grammes tis Kritikis tis Politikis Oikonomias*, Athens: Stochastis.

Partial editions

Marx, Karl (without publication date) *O Anthropos stin Ergasia kai tin Synergasia. Apo ta Grundrisse*, trans. Sravros Kampouridis, Athens: Anagnostidis.
Marx, Karl (1927) 'Eisagogi gia mia Kritiki tis Politikis Oikonomias', in *Kritiki tis Politikis Oikonomias*, trans. by G. Doumas and P. Pouliopoulos, Athens: Neoi Stohoi: 311–65.
Marx, Karl (1983) *Eklogi apo tis Grundrisse*, trans. Yannis Hotzeas, Athens: A/synechia.
Marx, Karl and Engels, Friedrich (1977) *I Epistimi tis Koinonias*, trans. Thanasis Kalomalos, Athens: 'Aihmi'.

Critical literature on the Grundrisse

Divaris, Dionysis (1989) 'Prologos tou Metafrasti' ['Translator's Foreword'], in Karl Marx, *Basikes Grammes tis Kritikis tis Politikis Oikonomias*, vol. 1, Athens: Stochastis, pp. 11–34.

Drosos, Sakis (1982) 'Koinonia, Kratos kai Ergatiki Dynami' ['Society, State and Labour-power'], *Theseis* [*Thesis*], No. 1: 109–26.

Ioakimoglou, Elias (1983) 'Syllogikos Ergatis i Ergatis-Maza?' ['Collective Worker or Mass-Worker?'], *Theseis*, No. 3: 87–96.

Kalfas, Vasilis and Sarikas, Zisis (1979) 'Ena Sholio' ['A Note'], *O Politis*, No. 26: 6–13.

Lapatsioras, Spyros (2008) 'I Ennoia tou Chrimatos apo ta *Grundrisse* sto *Kefalaio*' ['The Notion of Money from the *Grundrisse* to *Capital*'], *Theseis*, No. 102: 71–96.

Linardos-Rulmond, Petros (1983) 'Marxismos kai Taxiki Ypokeimenikotita' ['Marxism and Class Subjectivity'], *Theseis*, No. 3: 97–108.

Milios, John (1988) *O Ellinikos Koinonikos Schimatismos. Apo ton Epektatismo stin Kapitalistiki Anaptyxi* [*The Greek Social Formation. From Expansionism to Capitalist Development*], Athens: Exandas.

Milios, John (1996) 'Poios Fovatai tin Ergasia?' ['Who is Afraid of Work?'], *Theseis*, No. 57: 57–65.

Milios, John (1997) *Tropoi Paragogis kai Marxistiki Analysi* [*Modes of Production in Marxist Analysis*], Athens: Ellinika Grammata.

Stavropoulos, Theodoros (1979) *Istoriki Analysi tou Agrotikou Zitimatos stin Ellada* [*Historical Analysis of the Agrarian Question in Greece*], Athens: Livanis.

Vallianos, Christos (1983) 'Gia tin Ennoia tis Epistimonikis–Technikis Epanastasis' ['On the Notion of Scientific–Technical Revolution'], *Theseis*, No. 3: 25–49.

30 Turkey

E. Ahmet Tonak

For a long time there were only abridged Turkish translations of the *Grundrisse*. These were either based on Marx's 'Introduction' (Marx 1970a, 1970b) or on the 'Chapter on Capital', specifically the section on 'Forms which Precede Capitalist Production' (Marx 1967). The latter selection on pre-capitalist formations was relevant to the debate on relations of production under the Ottoman Empire and Turkey, and hence to the political strategy of the left.

The most significant abridged translation is the 1979 edition, labelled a 'study edition' by its translator, Sevan Nişanyan (Marx 1979). Printed in 7,000 copies, and translated from the 1953 German edition, this edition contains roughly 30 per cent of the German original, summaries of the excluded sections, commentaries on the missing parts and the translations, and a 100-page foreword by Nişanyan. In his foreword, after presenting the fundamental categories of Marx's economic analysis, Nişanyan emphasizes the methodological and political significance of the *Grundrisse*. Although the subjective nature of this selection raises some concerns, the quality of the translation is considered much higher than any other in Turkish, especially in terms of its readability.

The *Grundrisse* was finally fully translated into Turkish with the subtitle *Ekonomi Politiğin Eleştirisinin Temelleri. Ham Taslak, 1857–1858* [*Foundations of the Critique of Political Economy. Rough Draft*] by Arif Gelen and published in two volumes by Sol Yayınları, an Ankara-based independent left publisher, in 1999 (volume one: 3,000 copies) and 2003 (volume two: 2,000 copies). Although the translation was made from the German edition of 1953, the translator also consulted the English edition of 1973 and the French edition of 1980.

The full translation of the *Grundrisse* went almost unnoticed in Turkey. Not a single serious study, essay or even book review was published in Turkish on this significant text. This may be explained by the general lack of interest in Marxism and socialist politics in Turkey since the military junta of 1980.

The most significant theoretical utilization of the *Grundrisse* in Turkish is found in *Sivil Toplum ve Ötesi: Rousseau, Hegel, Marx* [*Civil Society and Beyond: Rousseau, Hegel, Marx*] by Gülnur Savran, published in 1987. The central aim of the book is to develop a Marxian critical approach as a political and theoretical alternative to the very particular Gramscian perspective (Eurocommunism and its Third World variants) that put forward improvements in civil society as a valid strategy for building socialism at the time.

The *Grundrisse* is also used, in one way or another, in several writings on methodology. Among these, for example, is Tonak's piece on the 'plan problem' that deals with the various outlines of *Capital* developed in the *Grundrisse*.

The current scene of the left in Turkey has autonomist Marxist and anarchist tendencies. It is in this context that many autonomist Marxists' works with specific interpretations of the *Grundrisse* were translated into Turkish, including Antonio Negri's.

To conclude, it would be fair to say that the impact of the *Grundrisse* on the development of Marxist theory in Turkey has been limited. It is likely that, among various other factors, the tardiness of a full Turkish translation was an important reason for this. The publisher is currently considering a second edition of the unabridged translation, possibly in one volume, which might bring to this text the attention it deserves.

Bibliography

Complete edition

Marx, Karl (1999, 2003) *Grundrisse (Ekonomi Politiğin Eleştirisinin Temelleri. Ham Taslak, 1857–1858)*, Ankara: Sol Yayınları.

Partial editions

Marx, Karl (1967) *Kapitalizm Öncesi Ekonomi Biçimleri* [*Precapitalist Economic Formations*], trans. from the English by Mihri Belli, Ankara: Sol Yayınları.
Marx, Karl (1970a) 'Önsöz' ['Introduction'], in *Ekonomi Politiğin Eleştirilmesine Katkı* [*Contribution to the Critique of Political Economy*], trans. Orhan Suda, İstanbul: Öncü Kitabevi, pp. 189–225.
Marx, Karl (1970b) 'Önsöz' ['Introduction'], in Karl Marx, *Ekonomi Politiğin Eleştirisine Katkı* (Contribution to the Critique of Political Economy), trans. Sevim Belli, Ankara: Sol Yayınları, pp. 257–97.
Marx, Karl (1979) *Grundrisse. Ekonomi Politiğin Eleştirisi İçin Ön Çalışma* [*Grundrisse. A Preliminary Study for the Critique of Political Economy*], İstanbul: Birikim Yayıncılık.

Critical literature on the Grundrisse

Nişanyan, Sevan (1979) 'Sunuş' ['Foreword'] in Karl Marx, *Grundrisse*, İstanbul: Birikim Yayıncılık, pp. 7–112.
Savran, Gülnur (1987) *Sivil Toplum ve Ötesi: Rousseau, Hegel, Marx*, İstanbul: Belge Yayınları.
Tonak, E. Ahmet (1986) 'Kapital'in Planı ve Kapitalist Devlet Üzerine Bir Not' ['A Note on *Capital*'s Plan and the Capitalist State'], *ll. Tez*, 2: 123–8.

31　South Korea

Ho-Gyun Kim

The study of Marx in South Korea began during the Japanese colonial rule of the 1920s and was severely persecuted after the split of the country and the related civil war of 1950–3. Research on Marxism was not resumed until the mid-1980s, when students and social movements increasingly took on anti-capitalist features.

The *Grundrisse* was translated by Ho-Gyun Kim into Korean from volume 42 of Marx–Engels *Werke* [*Works*], printed in the former German Democratic Republic in 1983, and published in three volumes and 2,000 copies, with the title *Jeongchigyungjehak bipan yogang* [*Foundations of the Critique of Political Economy*], in the year 2000 by Baekeui publishers. This edition also comprises of Martin Nicolaus' preface to the English edition and a translator's foreword. These were preceded in 1988 by the publication of the 1857 'Introduction' and *A Contribution to the Critique of Political Economy* in a single volume (Marx 1988).

Due to the diminished interest in Marxism after the events of 1989, the *Grundrisse* was not the object of close study. However, some critical analyses investigated it with particular reference to the relationship between Marx and Hegel.

In his foreword to the Korean edition, Ho-Gyun Kim exposes some theoretical and economic peculiarities (Kim 2000). He questions the reasons why the nation state is the starting point of Marx's representation of a critique of political economy, despite the fact that the world market was the most developed stage of capitalist social formations in his view. Kim also reflects on the Marxian method of 'rising from the abstract to the concrete' (Marx 1973: 101) and on the dialectical concept of labour. Jong-Hwan Jeong recognises a 'persistent influence' of Hegel on Marx's economic analysis of alienation in the *Grundrisse* and regards the latter as a bridge between the *Economic and Philosophical Manuscripts of 1844* and *Capital* (Jeong 2000: 124). Hui-Seok Yang concentrates on the differences between the *Grundrisse* and *Capital* instead: he registers a change in the role of Hegelian dialectics from being a method of development in 1858 to becoming a mere mode of expression, mimicked by Marx in 1867 (Yang 2000). In both texts, money is a general equivalent; but in the *Grundrisse* it is the God of commodities created by commodities themselves, whilst in *Capital* it is created by human social activity. Finally, in a comparative research of Hegelian dialectics, Kuk-Jin Mun outlines the similarities and differences between Marx and Hegel and in contrast to the Marxist–Leninist interpretation of the theory of reflection and puts forward his own interpretation of the Marxian notions of transcendence [*Aufhebung*] and contradiction [*Widerspruch*] (Mun 2002).

Bibliography

Complete edition

Marx, Karl (2000) *Jeongchigyungjehak bipan yogang*, 3 vols, Seoul: Baekeui.

Partial edition

Marx, Karl (1988) 'Seoseol' ['Introduction'], in Karl Marx, *Jeongchigyungjehak bipa-neul wihayeo* [*A Contribution to the Critique of Political Economy*], trans. Kim Ho-Gyun, Seoul: Jungwonmunwha, pp. 201–35.

Critical literature on the Grundrisse

Jeong, Jong-Hwan (2000) 'Marx eui *yogang* e gwanhan yeongu' ['A Study on Marx's *Grundrisse*'], in Hangukcheolhakhoei [Korean Philosophy Society] (ed.), *Cheolhak yeongu* [*Studies of Philosophy*], 76: 123–41.
Kim, Ho-Gyun (2000) 'Translator's Postface' in Karl Marx, *Jeongchigyungjehak bipa-neul wihayeo*, Seoul: Baekeui, pp. 203–23.
Mun, Kuk-Jin (2002) *Hegel gwa Marx eui byeonjungbeop yeongu* [*A Study on the Dialectics of Hegel and Marx*], Seoul: Byeonjungbeop.
Yang, Hui-Seok (2000) 'Yogang gwa Jabonron eseo Hegel gwa Marx eui gwangye' ['The Relationship between Hegel and Marx in the *Grundrisse* and *Capital*'], in Institute for the social sciences of the University of Kyungsang (ed.), *Marx eui bangbeo-pron gwa gachiron* [*Marx's Method and the Theory of Value*], Seoul: Hanul Academy, pp. 41–92.

Other reference

Marx, Karl (1973) *Grundrisse: Foundations of the Critique of Political Economy (Rough Draft)*, Harmondsworth: Penguin.

32 Brazil and Portugal

José Paulo Netto

Portuguese is the last language into which the *Grundrisse* has been translated so far. Based on volume II/1.1 and II/1.2 of MEGA² in Mário Duayer's translation, it was entitled *Grundrisse. Elementos fundamentais para a crítica da economia política. 1857–1858* [*Grundrisse. Outlines of the Critique of Political Economy. 1857–1858*] and scheduled by the Brazilian publisher Contraponto for 2008. Prior to this edition the only sections of the *Grundrisse* translated into Portuguese were the 'Introduction' and 'Forms which Precede Capitalist Production'.

The former was first published in Brazil in 1946, as an appendix to *A Contribution to the Critique of Political Economy*, translated by Florestan Fernandes; the latter, in João Maia's translation, came out, always in Brazil, in 1975. However – it is important to point out – these were not based on the German original: the former was a translation of the French, the latter of the English. The 'Introduction' was later retranslated indirectly in several editions both in Brazil and in Portugal, until in 1974 José Arthur Giannotti and Edgar Malagodi produced the first Portuguese version based on the German original. Viceversa, 'Forms which Precede Capitalist Production' was not translated from German into Portuguese.

Unsurprisingly given the absence of a Portuguese translation of the whole of the *Grundrisse*, this work has hitherto enjoyed little noticeable resonance amongst scholars in Brazil and Portugal. Nonetheless, several intellectuals who were able to access the German original became its main interpreters. In Portugal commentaries only started to circulate after the Carnation Revolution of 1974, that put an end to nearly 50 years of fascist-like dictatorship. Their most prominent authors were Vasco de Magalhães-Vilhena, whose primary interest lied in the methodological aspects of the *Grundrisse*, and Vital Moreira, who, in his *O renovamento de Marx* [*The Renewal of Marx*], claimed that the manuscripts of 1857–8 were crucial to renew Marxism from within.

On the other hand, in Brazil the *Grundrisse* was first mentioned in Giannotti's *Origens da dialética do trabalho* [*Origins of the Dialectics of Labour*]. This author concentrated on the concept of sociability, which was also the main focus of his other book – *Trabalho e reflexão. Ensaios para uma dialética da sociabilidade* [*Labour and Reflection. Essays on the Dialectics of Sociability*].

Ruy Fausto – a scholar forced into exile during the military dictatorship that afflicted the country from 1964 to 1985 – adopted the *Grundrisse* in his trilogy *Marx: lógica e política* [*Marx: Logic and Politics*] to investigate the relationship between Marxism, humanism and historicism, and to better identify the rational shell of *Capital.*

It should also be noted that the *Grundrisse* was not only read in German. In Brazil as in Portugal, the French translation of 1967–8 and the English translation of 1973 helped its dissemination. In particular, Carlos Nelson Coutinho and José Chasin in Brazil, and José Machado Pais in Portugal, made use of the French version. Finally, Brazilian specialists often cited from the Spanish translation published in Argentine from 1971 to 1976 by Siglo XXI. For instance, in Jacob Gorender's *O escravismo colonial* [*The Colonial Slavery*], it became an important reference point for a lively historiographical debate that started in the 1970s, and focussed on the modes of production involved in the formation of Brazilian society.

In Brazil, following a period of decline for Marxism and its ability to influence the intellectual scene, various signs start pointing to an inversion of the trend. The academic interest in the development of the productive forces and their impact on the labour processes, the political controversies surrounding 'globalization' and, obviously, the renewed interest of social and political movements in his works, are indications that Marx is now an author of wider appeal. The recent attention granted to the *Grundrisse* is part of this phenomenon and evidenced by an increasing number of academic papers that make reference to it since the 1990s as well as by the publication, in 2001, of Roman Rosdolsky's important commentary and the translation of the whole manuscript, scheduled for 2008. These are encouraging signs that in the course of the next few years its reception and dissemination will reach unprecedented levels both in Brazil and Portugal.

Bibliography

Complete edition

Marx, Karl (2008) *Grundrisse. Elementos fundamentais para a crítica da economia política. 1857/1858*, 2 vols, Rio de Janeiro: Contraponto.

Partial editions

Marx, Karl (1946) 'Introdução à crítica da economia política' ['Introduction to the Critique of Political Economy'], in Karl Marx, *Contribuição à crítica da economia política* [*A Contribution to the Critique of Political Economy*], São Paulo: Flama, pp. 201–31.

Marx, Karl (1974) 'Introdução à crítica da economia política' ['Introduction to the Critique of Political Economy'], in the collection *Os pensadores* [*The Thinkers*], vol. 35 *Marx*, São Paulo: Abril Cultural, pp. 109–31.

Marx, Karl (1975) 'Formações econômicas pré-capitalistas' ['Pre-Capitalist Economic Formations'], Rio de Janeiro: Paz e Terra.

Critical literature on the Grundrisse

Chasin, José (1999) '*Ad hominem:* rota e prospectiva de um projeto marxista' ['*Ad hominem*: Direction and Prospects for a Marxist Project'], in José Chasin (ed.), *Ensaios Ad Hominem 1* [*Ad Hominem Essays 1*], São Paulo: Ensaio, pp. 9–81.

Coutinho, Carlos Nelson (1972) *O estruturalismo e a miséria da razão* [*Structuralism and the Poverty of Reason*], Rio de Janeiro: Paz e Terra.

De Magalhães-Vilhena, Vasco (1978) 'A teoria, força material' ['The theory, Material Force'], in E. Chitas (ed.), *Idéia e matéria. Comunicações ao Congresso Hegel/1976* [*Idea and Matter. Papers given at the Hegel Congress, 1976*], Lisbon: Horizonte, pp. 11–45.

Fausto, Ruy (1983, 1987, 2002) *Marx: lógica e política*, 3 vols, São Paulo: Brasiliense.

Giannotti, José Arthur (1966) *Origens da dialética do trabalho*, São Paulo: Difel.

Giannotti, José Arthur (1983) *Trabalho e reflexão. Ensaios para uma dialética da sociabilidade*, São Paulo: Brasiliense.

Gorender, Jacob (1978) *O escravismo colonial*, São Paulo: Ática.

Machado Pais, José (2002) *Sociologia da vida quotidiana* [*Sociology of Daily Life*], Lisbon: Imprensa de Ciências Sociais–University of Lisbon.

Moreira, Vital (1979) *O renovamento de Marx*, Coimbra: Centelha.

Other reference

Rosdolsky, Roman (2001) *Gênese e estrutura de 'O Capital' de Karl Marx* [*The Making of Marx's Capital*], Rio de Janeiro: Contraponto.

Index

The title of each work of Marx mentioned is given in italics.